Excel 2010 Business Basics and Beyond

by

Chris "Smitty" Smith

Holy Macro! Books
PO Box 82
Uniontown, OH 44684

Excel 2010 Business Basics & Beyond

Printed in USA by Hess Print Solutions

First Printing: November 2012

Author: Chris "Smitty" Smith

Layout: Tyler Nash

Indexer: Nellie J Willam

Cover Design: Shannon Mattiza, 6Ft4 Productions

Published by: Holy Macro! Books, PO Box 82, Uniontown OH 44685

Distributed by Independent Publishers Group

ISBN: 9781615470129, print, 978-1-61547-210-9 PDF, 978-1-61547-330-4 ePub, 978-1-61547-110-2 mobi

Library of Congress Control Number: 2012949096

Contents

Dedication

To my loving wife and daughter, Cyndi and Campbell – for being so patient with me while I worked on this, at the expense of spending time with you.

Acknowledgements

First and foremost I'd like to thank Bill Jelen (aka MrExcel). I've known Bill for close to ten years, and he has encouraged me to write for quite some time, but I never carried through on the threat until now. Bill also got me sparked and subsequently hooked on training, which has been a fantastic opportunity to learn and spread that knowledge around, although I certainly do fill some big shoes, literally! At a seminar in Florida where I filled in for Bill, an attendee bought drinks for my wife and me and said "You're good, but you're no Bill Jelen...I thought you'd be taller." Bill is 6' 3"+ and I'm 5' 9" – It's an easy distinction. Bill stands tall in a room in both stature and knowledge, whether it's at a seminar or in a room full of Microsoft folks talking about what they're going to build into Excel or fix next. In fact, watching Bill's interactions with people over the years is one of the reasons that I decided to go out on my own, and I am much better for it, so thank you Bill.

I will forever be indebted to my mother, Judith, who is widely published in her own field of expertise and who inspired me to delve deeper in my knowledge and experience and share it with people who can benefit.

Next, the fantastic team of folks who support the MrExcel publishing operation, his wife Mary Ellen; Keeper of the Inventory, his sister Barb Jelen; Project Manager, Tracy Syrstad; ScottieP and Tyler Nash (amazing editor). This wouldn't be anywhere without you. There are also the fantastic forum contributors, administrators and moderators at www.mrexcel.com, my interaction with many of whom over the years gave me the inspiration to finally write this.

And I absolutely can't leave out the amazing folks at Microsoft who helped me with terrific feedback and general knowledge/direction, Anneliese Wirth, Dan Battigan, Keyur Patel, Melissa Travers, et. al.

I would also like to thank Paul Gagliardi and Bill Carmen, two of the finest men, bosses and rock climbing partners I've had the honor of knowing. Thank you for giving me the opportunity to learn and explore the world of Excel in our day-to-day business operations, without that this book simply would never have been possible.

Finally, I'd like to thank Christopher Fennell and Zack Barresse, two gentlemen who I have gotten to know very well and consider very fortunate to have as friends. Your collaboration on this was absolutely invaluable and I could not have done it without you.

On the technical side, I definitely need to thank the folks at TechSmith (www.techsmith.com), who make both Camtasia and Snagit software (Snagit was used to capture the images for this book), as well as VMWare (www.vmware.com), which allows you to run multiple versions of Windows/Office on the same PC. I'm not a sales rep, but I'd highly recommend both if you're interested in doing this kind of thing.

Thank you all!

Foreword

I have never had a formal Excel (or computer) training class*. Like many people, I learned by the seat of my pants as a part of my job requirements. I got my first computer when I was attending TCU's Ranch Management Program, and discovered the "spreadsheet" via Borland's QuattroPro (pre-Windows). While I could barely make heads or tail of it, my experience on ranches with owners/operators who used paper ledgers to balance the books foretold that computers would play a big role in their future (and I was only thinking about the farming/ranching industry at the time). Unfortunately, few entrenched ranchers felt the same way (I was once told that I needed to be out fixing fence instead of "messing with" that damned computer-thingy), although now farmers and ranchers are among some of the most adept spreadsheet users out there, which I think is fantastic.

When I first entered the corporate world I started working with Lotus 1-2-3 (DOS based), and remember the day that we moved to the first version of Windows and started using the first Windows version of Excel. What a difference! My first insight into how powerful the spreadsheet could be came when someone told me about the VLOOKUP formula, which literally saved me 10 hours per week! Over the years I came to rely upon Excel for work and learned to do things with it that allowed me do the work of several people in just a few keystrokes. When VBA (Visual Basic for Applications) was introduced I started developing end-user applications and have never looked back. While I embraced everything that Excel can do (and I don't think any one person can ever take advantage of Excel's full capabilities just because it is so broad), I found that many people rarely get past the simple basics of using Excel as a glorified paper ledger. Case in point: I once redesigned a corporate expense report for a company, and once it past all of the various committees' approval it finally went to the head of Accounts Payable for her sign off. She loved it and wanted to try it out for a few days, but the next day the 10 year Excel veteran called me in a panic and stated that we couldn't distribute it because the report date was protected and she couldn't change it. I explained that it was a formula (TODAY()), and that when she opened the expense report the next day, the date would automatically update itself. She was both amazed and stunned that you could do such a thing.

Especially with the introduction of the Ribbon in Office 2007 it can easily appear that Excel is incredibly complicated and scary. While Excel is an incredibly complicated application, by no means does it need to be scary, and the aim of this book is to expose some of Excel's fundamental tools that will ultimately make you more productive. You don't need to be an application developer or computer programmer to be able to use Excel well, but you do need to be willing to explore a bit. If you're an advanced Excel user who understands its more complex functionality then this book isn't for you, but if you're a normal Excel user who wants to learn more about becoming more proficient and expose some of its hidden gems, then you'll be pleasantly surprised at how much you can pick up in just a short period of time.

* My wife, Cyndi swears that she taught me how to use Windows and Excel around 1994, when I first started in the corporate world.

Are you tired of tracking financial elements of your business manually, do you have to prepare staffing schedules by hand, or do you simply want to know how to get more information from your business data? Microsoft Excel is one of the most powerful tools any business has at its disposal. Learn how to harness your business data and put it to use for you. Topics include: preparing financial statements, how to best display your data for maximum impact with formatting tools, Data Tables, Charts & Pivot Tables, using customer information to create customized letters with Mail Merge, importing data from programs like QuickBooks, calculate the costs of doing business with financial formulas, learn where to find pre-packaged business templates, and much more. Throughout the course you'll find interesting tips & tricks to make your Excel use more efficient as well. The course will use real-world business examples in operation with all of these elements.

Lesson 1

Introduction to Excel – Simply put, Excel is the #1 spreadsheet application on the planet, so here's a fantastic opportunity to learn about what Excel is and how it can help you manage your business. Explore the fundamentals of what you can do with Excel, see first-hand what makes this powerful application tick, get used to how it works, and how to begin using it to simplify your business needs. Start to learn the ins-and-outs of Microsoft's new Ribbon user interface. Discover the key elements of intelligent spreadsheet design and the steps to take when starting a new project.

Lesson 2

Basic File Operations & Setting up Excel the way you want it – In this Lesson we'll continue discussing the Ribbon user interface and all of its elements. Now that you're starting to get familiar with Excel, you'll learn how to set up Excel so it's just right for you by uncovering Excel's multiple user interface options, including customizing certain elements that you want to see all the time. You'll also learn to modify the Quick Action Toolbar where you can place your favorite Ribbon controls.

Lesson 3

The Ribbon – In Depth – The Home Tab – In this lesson we'll fully expose all of the functionality behind the Home tab, which is the default Ribbon tab, and as such it contains all of your most used menu commands.

Lesson 4

The Ribbon – In Depth – Part II – The Rest of the Ribbon – In this lesson we'll move on to the rest of the Ribbon elements, which are much more specific in nature than the Home tab. This is where you'll uncover how to Insert charts, set up page formatting for printing and distribution, expose the hundreds of functions that are available, and much more.

Lesson 5

Entering and Manipulating Data & Basic Rules of Spreadsheet Design – In this lesson you'll learn the elements of good spreadsheet design and the phases involved.

- Planning
- Design & Build
- Populate
- Evaluate/Calculate
- Format
- Populate
- Report
- Distribute

Entering and Editing Data – First and foremost, see how to save your work and the options you have. Learn the difference between entering text and numeric values, and when you can use them together. Learn how to have Excel automatically enter data for you with lists and AutoFill.

Entering and Editing Formulas/Functions – Learn the differences between Formulas and Functions and how to enter them.

Lists and AutoFill – Learn some of the ways that you can Excel to do your work for you.

Data Validation – Learn how to control what information users can enter and how.

Inserting and Deleting Ranges, Rows & Columns and Worksheets – Once your data is in place learn how to add or subtract from it.

Lesson 6

Using Functions – Learn what functions are and discover the power they bring to your spreadsheet applications. We review the types of functions you have at your disposal by group, and discuss the most common. This is where the power of Excel will really start to shine. We'll also review different methods for entering functions and how to make them flexible and dynamic. Discover how to calculate the differences between times and dates and retrieve information from other worksheets.

Lesson 7

Formatting – Spice up your worksheets, so they're easier to read and present. Choose from pre-defined Styles, or apply your own formats. Learn to format cells for certain values (Currency, Date, Percentage, etc.), and discover how to apply custom formats for Phone Numbers, Zip Code, Social Security Numbers, and how to create your own. See how to quickly sort and filter data without having to rearrange things by hand.

Printing – Proper page setup can be challenging and there are a lot of printing options that are available. We'll discuss the most common print formats, how to add custom header and footer details, scaling (so you could stretch a worksheet to fit 11x17 paper for printing detailed information like shift schedules), collating and more.

Lesson 8

Working with Graphics – In Excel 2007 Microsoft introduced an entirely revamped set of graphics and tools called Smart Art. We'll discuss how to add them to your worksheets, and what you can do to customize them to meet your needs. You'll also see how to insert your own graphics, like company logos, as well as shapes and drawing objects.

Lesson 9

Charts – In terms of displaying data for at-a-glance snapshots of what's going on behind your numbers, charts are one of your most powerful tools. You'll learn how to quickly transform business data into informative charts (Bar, Stacked, Column, Line, Scatter, etc.) We'll also discuss resources and methods for using multiple charts to create business dashboards where you can compare multiple business elements in one spot.

Lesson 10

Excel Tables – The Excel Table feature was newly revised in Excel 2007 and gives you a way to easily take a group of data and tell Excel that it's all related. As you add more data, Excel will automatically expand the table to include the new information; Excel will also automatically update any charts that are based on the table data. It is really handy because it comes with multiple style options, allows you to quickly apply intuitive formulas, and filter and sort your data without effort. There is also a new tool that lets you quickly remove duplicate items from your data.

Sub-Totals – These allow you to quickly manipulate your data and sub-total by almost any data category that you have.

Lesson 11

Pivot Tables – These are one of the most powerful features in Excel, yet most users either aren't familiar with them or are afraid to use them. Pivot Tables give you the ability to interactively summarize your data without actually changing it, instead Excel automatically works on a copy of your data. Pivot Tables give you the ability to manipulate your data in ways that were previously only available in database applications, allowing you to switch rows and columns, apply different functions, sub-totals, etc., just by dragging and dropping visual rep-resentations of your data from one place to the next or toggling simple options. They also include a powerful charting feature.

Lesson 12

Importing Data from other sources – Sometimes nothing can be more time consuming for a small business than having to take information that exists in one digital environment (bank website, vendor QuickBooks, etc.) and having to print it out, just to re-enter it in Excel so you can use it. In this lesson we'll discuss ways to get data from the Internet, a POS or financial management system, and other various sources.

Mail Merge – For the small business owner there are few things more important than being able to efficiently utilize your data to communicate with your customers. If you've ever been frustrated by having to send marketing letters, special offers, billing, etc., then you'll love Mail Merge. In this lesson you'll learn to set up a customer list and automatically Mail Merge it with a Word document.

All sample files for the text can be found at: http://www.mrexcel.com/busbasics2010/bb2010sampledata/

Lesson 1 - What is Excel Anyway?

Microsoft Excel is a spreadsheet application, and has been in use for over 25 years (Application is the proper term for a computer Program). It is one of the most powerful tools in the Microsoft Suite of Office applications. It is estimated to be used by over 500 million people world-wide in business, private and education sectors. Whether you want to use Excel as an integral part of managing your business or just use it for small aspects, like employee scheduling, or maintaining customer lists, this class will prepare you to start using Excel on your own. In addition to the basic elements of Excel that you'll learn, you'll also walk away with tips and tricks that will make your everyday usage more efficient, and there will be lots of links that point you to more resources on the Internet. This is a step-by-step guide to Excel, so we'll walk through everything from how to set up Excel's default settings the way you want them, to how to enter your first formula and create your first chart.

What is a spreadsheet? (Spreadsheet Terminology)

If you've ever seen an accounting ledger, a spreadsheet is essentially a digital version, and Excel is the best and most feature packed spreadsheet application on the market. A spreadsheet is nothing more than a 2-dimensional digital grid of **Rows** and **Columns** that are divided by individual **Cells**, which are capable of housing data and performing calculations. Columns are ordered from left-to-right, and have **Column Headers** labeled alphabetically from A to XFD; Rows are ordered from top-to-bottom, and have **Row Headers** labeled numerically from 1 to 1,048,576. Excel 2007/2010 has over 16,000 columns and 1 million+ rows, meaning that there are over 16 billion individual cells on a single spreadsheet in which you can enter data! The **Active Cell** is the cell in which your cursor is at any given moment. The intersection of the Column & Row headers at the **Active Cell** makes up the **Cell Address**. For instance D3, refers to column D, Row 3. The **Active Workbook** is the one you are working in at the moment; you can have multiple workbooks open at any time, but you can only work in one at a time.

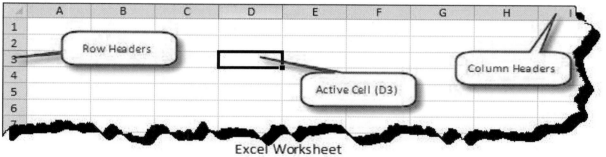

Figure 1

In Excel an individual spreadsheet page is referred to as a **Worksheet**. (Some people tend to use the term spreadsheet & worksheet interchangeably, but "spreadsheet" refers to the more broad scope of any digital spreadsheet application, and while acceptable, technically isn't accurate). A Worksheet can also be called a "Sheet". A **Workbook** is a collection of **Worksheets** (although a Workbook can contain only one Worksheet, it must contain at least one!). Think of a Workbook as a book on your desk, and Worksheets as the individual pages that are between the binding.

There are two distinct layers to any Worksheet, the first is the Worksheet layer, which holds those billions of Cells, then there's an invisible layer above the Worksheet that holds any objects that you insert (Clip Art, Graphics, Charts, etc.) When you insert an object into an Excel worksheet, it doesn't become part of the cells, but instead floats above them, and won't interfere with any values that have been inserted into them.

> The only limitation to the number of Worksheets a Workbook can hold actually isn't up to Excel, but your available system memory.

The only thing you can put into a worksheet cell is text or values, not objects. Note that in Excel 2007 Microsoft introduced some cool new in-cell features that include graphical objects, like Conditional Formatting graphics, Data Bars, and Sparklines in Excel 2010. But these are tools that have been built into the application and should not be confused with objects that reside above the worksheet layer. For instance, you can't copy an image from a website and place it in a cell, it resides above the worksheet.

Ranges – A range is a group of cells. E.G. B3:C7 would refer to the range of cells starting at cell B3, moving down and over to cell C7. Cell ranges are how you refer to areas of a worksheet in formulas.

Selection – Any range of cells you have manually selected. Selected cells will be highlighted:

In this case the range B3:C7 has been selected. Note that cell B3 is listed as the Active Cell, which indicates that's where the selection began. You can select ranges by left-clicking on a cell and dragging. You'll see keyboard shortcuts for selecting ranges later in the lesson.

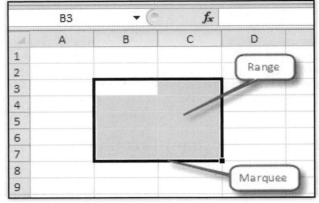

Figure 2

Marquee – The black box around the active cell or selected range. Note that the Row & Column headers are highlighted to show you where you are. If you only have one cell selected, this will still happen and they'll automatically adjust as you move around.

Dancing Ants – This is a moving Marquee that indicates you have copied a cell or range of cells:

Figure 3

Current Region – Excel knows if you are in a region of contiguous data and will consider that to be the current region. This will come in handy when we get to the navigation section, as keyboard shortcuts will be limited to the current region.

Used Range – Excel automatically recognizes the area in which you've entered data. (This can cause workbook size problems if you have a large range of data and subsequently delete all or a portion of it; just deleting the data won't erase the used range, so Excel will continue to store that in memory. To reduce the size of the Used Range you actually have to delete unused rows and columns, which will be covered later).

What can you do with Excel?

As mentioned, Excel is incredibly powerful, and it is equally diverse with regards to what one can do with it. Here are just a few examples:

- Household
  ◦ Electronic Check Register
  ◦ Household Budgeting
  ◦ Loan Calculators (home, mortgage, etc.)
  ◦ Financial Portfolio Tracker
  ◦ Manage Fantasy Sports Leagues
  ◦ Calendar
  ◦ To Do Lists
  ◦ Vehicle Maintenance Logs
  ◦ Family Tree
  ◦ Fitness & Weight Loss
  ◦ Tax Planning
  ◦ Medical Record Keeping (Blood Pressure, weight, etc.)

- ○ Wedding Planning
- School
  - ○ Academic Gradebook
  - ○ Calculate Academic Credit Status
- Business
  - ○ Invoice
  - ○ Employee Scheduling
  - ○ Inventory Management
  - ○ Expense Reports
  - ○ Calculate Product Pricing
  - ○ Commission & Compensation Planning
  - ○ Complex Financial Analysis
  - ○ Balance Sheets
  - ○ Profit/Loss Statements
  - ○ Sales Analysis
  - ○ Budget Tracking
    - ▪ Forecasting
    - ▪ Profitability
    - ▪ Breakeven analysis
  - ○ Marketing Planning
  - ○ Project Planning/Tracking
  - ○ Business Valuation
  - ○ Charts
  - ○ Create complex diagrams

DASHBOARDS

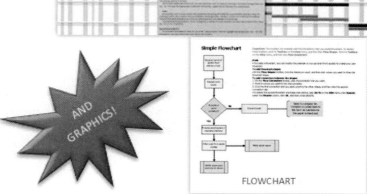

FLOWCHART

The Excel Environment – Understanding the Ribbon Interface

What is the Ribbon? The Ribbon is a collection of all of the command and menu elements that are available to you in Excel (and the other primary Office applications). If you're familiar with older versions of Office, the Ribbon has replaced the traditional menu dialogs that were originally designed in 1992.

Why the Ribbon? In 2007 Microsoft completely revamped the look of the primary Office applications when it introduced what is called the Fluent User Interface, more commonly referred to as the Ribbon. This was an attempt to introduce a more cohesive end-user environment to Office applications, and while it was reviled by most experienced Office users, it has proven to be a big hit with newer users. In addition, as Office products have evolved, so have the number of commands available to users (there are hundreds!), so Microsoft had to develop a way to easily expose all of those options graphically, instead of hiding them in more and more layers that the user had to know. In this section we'll start exploring the Ribbon and how to navigate in Workbooks and Worksheets. The next lesson goes into great detail about the Ribbon, so this is just an introduction to help you get familiar with it.

The Ribbon is a collection of **Tabs**, each of which house a group of menu commands that are all similar in nature. When you first open Excel the Home tab will be activated, and all of its related command **Groups** are located below. When you activate another tab, the commands specific to that tab will be displayed. The Ribbon consists of the following Tab groups:

- File/Office Button
- Home
- Insert
- Page Layout
- Formulas
- Data
- Review
- View
- Developer
- Add-Ins
- Acrobat (only if Adobe Acrobat is installed)

The final element of the Ribbon is the **Dialog Launcher**, which is the small button located at the bottom right-hand corner of many Tab Groups. The Dialog Launcher will expand any Tab Group that has too many controls to be efficiently displayed on the Ribbon.

Another addition in Excel 2007 is **Galleries**, which are pre-defined formats that you can quickly apply to a worksheet. Each Gallery has a drop-down option that will automatically expand the Gallery items related to that Tab Group. Galleries are very similar to Dialog Launchers in that they expose additional menu commands that won't efficiently fit on the Ribbon.

Figure 4

Ribbon Elements

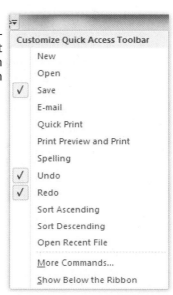

Quick Access Toolbar (QAT) – This is the section that's circled in red in the upper left-hand corner of the example above. This is a toolbar where you can put your favorite menus items to quickly access them. By default it is pre-loaded with Save, Undo & Redo. The down arrow on the right activates another menu with more selections that you can quickly add to the toolbar:

Figure 5

There is also a *More Commands* option, which is where you can further customize the QAT, which we'll discuss in the next lesson with Customizing Excel. Finally, there is a *Show Below the Ribbon* option that allows you to move the QAT closer to the worksheet. There's no need to do so, it's simply an option.

Tabs

File – The File menu is where all of your application level commands are located, like Open, Close, Save, Save As, Send, Print, Workbook Properties, and most importantly your Application Options, where you can change Excel's default behavior to suit your tastes.

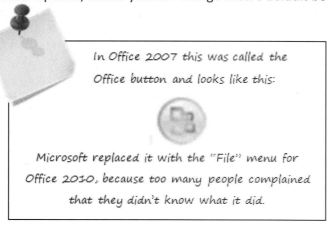

In Office 2007 this was called the Office button and looks like this:

Microsoft replaced it with the "File" menu for Office 2010, because too many people complained that they didn't know what it did.

Home – The Home tab holds the most commonly used menu items (Text Formatting, Text Alignment, Number Formatting, Cell Styles, Cell Formatting and Editing) housed in the following Groups:

- Clipboard
- Font
- Alignment
- Number
- Styles
- Cells
- Editing

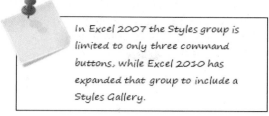

In Excel 2007 the Styles group is limited to only three command buttons, while Excel 2010 has expanded that group to include a Styles Gallery.

Insert – The Insert tab allows you to insert objects in your worksheet, like Pivot Tables, Charts, Smart Art, Clip Art, etc. It consists of the following Groups:

- Tables
- Illustrations
- Charts
- Sparklines
- Filter
- Links
- Text
- Symbols

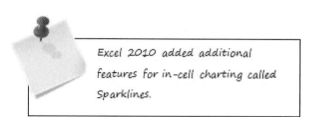

Excel 2010 added additional features for in-cell charting called Sparklines.

Page Layout – The Page Layout tab is where you can apply Themes (pre-defined styles with colors, fonts, and effects) to an entire document, Page Setup options for printing, Sheet options (hide grid-lines, Column & Row headings), as well as tools for ordering objects (alignment, grouping, rotating). Page Layout has the following Groups:

- Themes
- Page Setup
- Scale to Fit
- Sheet Options
- Arrange

Formulas – The Formulas tab is perhaps the most powerful of the Ribbon Tabs, because this is where you can unleash the true power of Excel and its calculation abilities. It groups functions into categories (AutoSum, Insert Function, Recently Used, Financial, Logical, Text, Date & Time, Lookup & Reference, Math & Trig and More Functions). It's comprised of the following groups:

- Function Library
- Defined Names
- Formula Auditing
- Calculation

Data – The Data tab is your gateway to accessing data from external sources, like databases, other Excel workbooks, text files, etc. It also holds several Data Analysis tools, like a Duplicate Removal Wizard and Outlining. It has the following groups:

- Get External Data
- Connections
- Sort & Filter
- Data Tools
- Outline
- Analysis

Review – When you're ready to publish your workbook, this is where you go. The Review tab has all of the editing tools you'll need to make sure that your work is free of grammatical and spelling errors. You can also add comments as visual aids for those receiving your workbook. The Review tab has the following groups:

- Proofing
- Language
- Comments
- Changes
- Share
- View

View – This gives you the flexibility to set all of your viewing options, like if you want to see the worksheet the way it will be printed, display grid-lines or headings, and even view multiple worksheets or workbooks side-by-side.

Developer – When you first open Excel this tab will be disabled (we'll discuss how to enable it in the next lesson when we review how to set up Excel's default options). This class isn't going to delve into programming, but it is worth introducing so that you're aware of it. Within each Office Application resides a powerful application-specific programming language called Visual Basic for Applications (VBA). It is a subset of the Visual Basic program language that many professional programmers use to write applications, and it allows you to harness the power of programming code to automate your tasks in Excel. Any repetitive task you perform in Excel (and other Office Applications) can be automated, so that the program does the work for you. A common example is automatically sending a workbook through Outlook with a press of a button. Fortunately, Microsoft has made it so that you don't have to be a computer programmer to work with VBA, because the Developer tab includes a tool called the ***Macro Recorder***. All you need to do is record a macro, do something in Excel, and when played back, your actions will be repeated exactly as you performed them.

The Developer tab consists of the following groups:

- Code
- Add-Ins
- Controls
- XML
- Modify

Add-Ins – Add-Ins are third party tools (many written by Microsoft) that allow you to access additional functionality that doesn't come native to Excel. Add-ins are generally created with VBA. As a beginner in Excel you might not have any need to use Add-Ins, but there are many add-ins that are created with certain businesses in mind. For instance there is an add-in for carpenters and home builders that can convert cell entries into inch/foot measurements. Similarly, there are enhanced Finance Add-Ins for stock market traders, Statistical Add-Ins for scientists, Metric System converters, and many more. The Add-Ins tab only has one group called Menu Commands. As you add and activate Add-Ins they will be listed in this group.

Acrobat – Adobe Acrobat, which is a powerful application by Adobe Systems for creating PDF documents, automatically installs a Ribbon Tab in Excel and other Office applications. If you don't have Acrobat then it won't appear in your version of Excel.

Additional Options

At the very bottom of the Ribbon you'll see two other dialog windows:

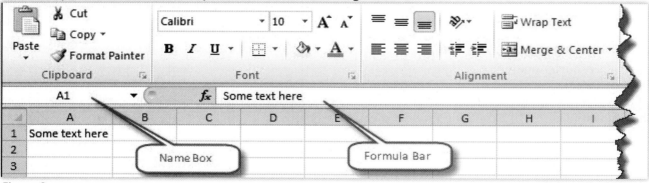

Figure 6

The leftmost box is called the ***Name Box*** and it will display the address of the cell which is active at the moment. If you happen to have an object like a chart selected, the chart name will be displayed. You can also enter a cell address here to automatically jump to it. E.G. entering "G24" would take you right to cell G24.

The box to the right of it is called the ***Formula Bar*** and it will display the value of the active cell.

On the right-hand side of the Ribbon there are several more controls, which are common to all Office applications:

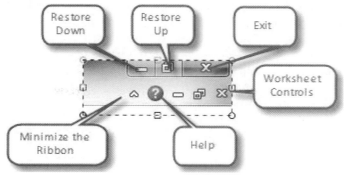

Figure 7

The top three controls are for the application itself. The small bar on the left will minimize the application (restore down), the middle will maximize it (restore up), and the Red "X" will Exit.

The lower set of controls is specific to the worksheet and will do the same thing as their application counterparts.

The button to pay the most attention to is the one on the lower left, the Caret ("^"). This will minimize the Ribbon in the event you need additional space to see more of the worksheet. Activating any Ribbon Tab group will temporarily restore that group's Ribbon controls, and will automatically re-hide when you click off of it. This is a good control with which to be familiar as many people have gotten confounded when the Ribbon "disappears", and they don't know how to restore it!

Finally the question mark will launch the Excel Help file. It can also be accessed by pressing the F1 key.

Worksheet Tabs, Status Bar & View Buttons

There is an additional set of tools at the bottom of the Excel screen:

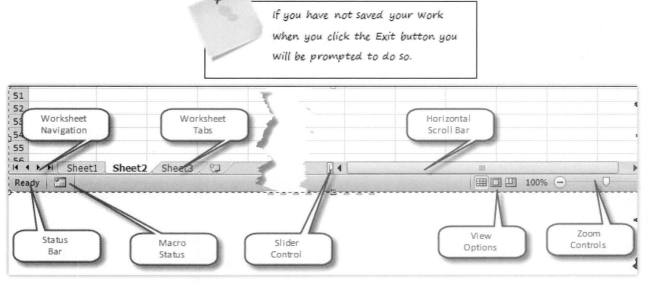

Figure 8

Worksheet Navigation – This is a series of 4 buttons. The first will scroll to the first worksheet in the workbook, the second will take you to the next sheet to the left, the next will take you to the next sheet on the right, and the last one will take you to the last sheet in the workbook. You can right click it for a snapshot list of all the worksheets in your workbook. Clicking on a worksheet name will automatically activate it:

Worksheet Tabs – This is a list of each worksheet in your workbook. Clicking on one will activate that worksheet.

Slider Control – You can drag this to the left/right to minimize or expand the horizontal scroll bar. It's useful when you have a lot of worksheets and you want to see as many as possible.

Horizontal Scroll Bar – Dragging this bar will take you to the end of your data. It goes left & right.

Vertical Scroll Bar (not shown, but it's on the right side of the worksheet window) – It's got the same functionality as the Horizontal Scroll Bar, but up and down.

Status Bar – This displays messages to you regarding Excel's state (Ready, Calculate, etc.). If you right-click it you'll be presented with a list of options you can choose to display:

It also has some neat functionality you'll discover if you select a range of numerical data.

Macro Status – You can record a new macro by clicking on this button. When you do it will change symbols to a square. Clicking it again will stop recording. Again, this isn't really relevant to this class, but you should know what it does.

View Options – There are three options here:
- Normal (default)
- Page Layout
- Page Break Preview

Zoom Controls – This is where you can increase or decrease the amount of worksheet you see. It has 4 elements:
- Zoom % - You can click on this and manually enter the % zoom

- -/+ Buttons – Clicking on either of these will incrementally resize the screen
- Zoom Slider – You can drag this left or right to incrementally resize the screen

Customize Status Bar	
✓ Cell Mode	Ready
✓ Signatures	Off
✓ Information Management Policy	Off
✓ Permissions	Off
Caps Lock	Off
Num Lock	On
✓ Scroll Lock	Off
✓ Fixed Decimal	Off
Overtype Mode	
✓ End Mode	
✓ Macro Recording	Not Recording
✓ Selection Mode	
✓ Page Number	
✓ Average	
✓ Count	
Numerical Count	
Minimum	
Maximum	
✓ Sum	
✓ Upload Status	
✓ View Shortcuts	
✓ Zoom	100%
✓ Zoom Slider	

Navigating the Excel Environment

All of the Ribbon's Tab controls are mouse activated. However they can also be activated and used from the keyboard. Pressing either of the ALT keys (left and right of the Space bar), or the forward slash key "/ " (it's the same key as the Question Mark "?"), will cause the Ribbon to appear with letters beneath each Tab group. Pressing the corresponding key will activate that tab. You'll note that when that Tab group is then activated there will be a second set of letters beneath each menu control. Pressing the corresponding letter will then activate that menu command. If you are a keyboard oriented user then you'll soon find this feature to be invaluable (The figure below is an example of 2007).

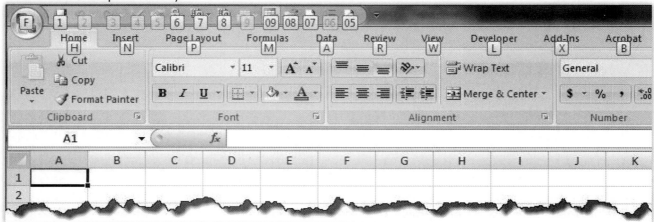

Figure 9

There are many ways to navigate within Excel, including the options listed in the previous section, and you can left-click on any cell to activate it; however these actions all require using the mouse. It's generally much more efficient to get around in Excel by using the keyboard.

Keyboard Shortcuts

Key—Key Combination¤	Action¤
→ or Tab¤	Move one cell to the right¤
← or Shift-Tab¤	Move one cell to the left¤
Up & Down Arrows¤	Move one Cell Up/Down¤
Ctrl + →¤	Jump to the right-hand side of the current region¤
Ctrl + ←¤	Jump to the left-hand side of the current region¤
Ctrl + ↓¤	Jump to the bottom of the current region¤
Ctrl + ↑¤	Jump to the top of the current region¤
Home¤	Jump to the first cell in the row (column A)¤
Ctrl + Home¤	Jump to cell A1 (Home cell)¤
Ctrl + End¤	Jump to the bottom cell containing data on the right hand side of the sheet¤
Page Down¤	Move one page down ¤
Page Up¤	Move one page up¤
Alt + Page Up¤	Move one page to the left¤
Alt + Page Down¤	Move one page to the right¤
Ctrl + Page Up¤	Jump to the next worksheet on the left¤
Ctrl + Page Down¤	Jump to the next worksheet on the right¤

Getting Help & Additional Resources

In previous versions of Office, the Helpfiles were only available directly on your PC. This was great, but unfortunately, a lot of IT/IS departments chose not to install the Helpfiles because of size concerns. When Microsoft released Office 2007, Excel and the other Office programs' internal Helpfiles were somewhat less useful than before, but Microsoft has taken great strides in making the Helpfile offerings much more robust by integrating them with online content from Microsoft. When you select the Helpfile (Question Mark above the Ribbon, or the F1 key), you'll be presented with an initial dialog like this:

Figure 10

If you are entering data and use the Tab key to move to subsequent cells, when you are done you can press Enter and you'll return one row below where you started.

If you don't want Excel to look online, or if you don't have a good Internet connection, you can choose to enable Offline help from your computer. Note that you have to have the Helpfiles installed locally on your computer in order to have this option. If you do select this option, here is the dialog you'll get:

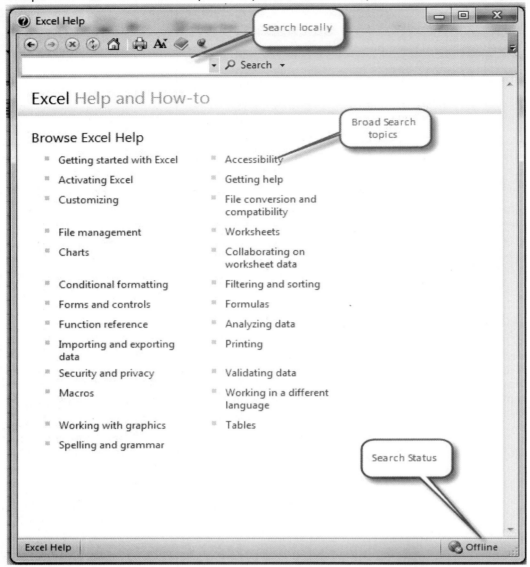

Figure 11

Search Locally - This option will return a list of all relevant articles based on the topic you enter. The difficult thing with the Helpfile is actually knowing the terminology for what you want to find. Excel has very specific function names, so sometimes if you don't know what you're looking for the Helpfile can't help you. Fortunately, Microsoft has provided some alternatives to help you narrow your search.

Broad Search Topics – Microsoft has gotten better about anticipating that users won't always know what they're looking for, so they added a broad search function, which will bring up featured discussions. Hopefully as you browse through them you'll get a better idea of the topic for which you're searching. In addition, those articles with have hyperlinks to any sub-topics mentioned therein, so you don't have to go find a reference and start a new search for that topic.

Search Status – In both online & offline search modes, the Helpfile dialog will let you know which platform you're accessing at that time.

Online Search – If you opt to have the Helpfile load online content, you'll get a dialog like the following figure:

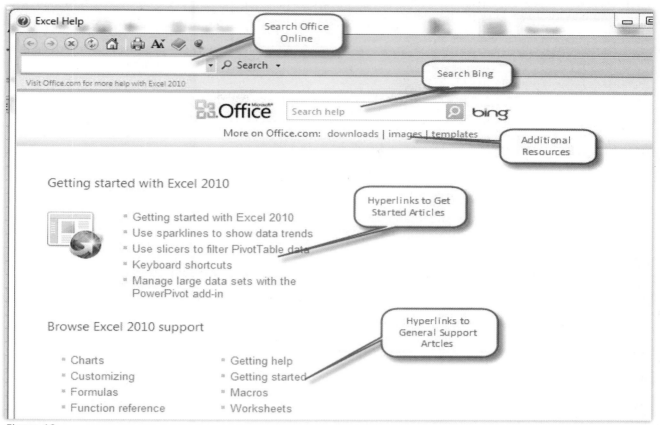

Figure 12

Search Office Online Articles – Again, the Helpfile can only be as specific as you are with your search terms.

Search with Microsoft Bing – This is a direct search through Microsoft's new search engine, Bing. While the online search method through the Helpfile will only return articles directly from Microsoft, the Bing search will return information from all relevant Internet sources. Note that Microsoft has gone to great lengths to increase the strength of their help offerings, so this will continue to be a growing resource.

Get Started Articles – Again, the Helpfile gives you some generic help topics from which to choose.

Browse Support – If you absolutely can't figure out how to find what you need then browse the list of support articles. It might take some time, but with some effort you can generally find a link that will help you get there.

Unit Summary: Getting Started

- In this lesson you learned about what a spreadsheet is, what Excel is to spreadsheets and some common spreadsheet terminology
- You were introduced to the Ribbon interface, which debuted with Microsoft Office 2007
- You saw some of the multiple ways to get around in Excel
- You learned how to get help from within Excel with its Online and Offline help resources

Review Questions

1. What is a spreadsheet?
   a. _____

2. Name the five primary components of an Excel file:
   a. _____
   b. _____
   c. _____
   d. _____
   e. _____

3. What is the Ribbon?
   a. _____

4. Name at least two of the Ribbon Tabs:
   a. _____
   b. _____

5. Name at least two Groups that belong to those Ribbon Tabs:

    a. _____

    b. _____

    c. _____

    d. _____

6. Name two ways to move between Excel Worksheets

    a. _____

    b. _____

Lesson Assignment

Your first assignment is to open a new Excel workbook and start getting familiarized with the following (there is a Notes section below for you to keep track of your observations):

- Ribbon Commands and elements
- Navigating both in a worksheet and between worksheets (the former will be easier if you add a few sets of multiple column/row sample data with at least one row & column of separation between each)
- Explore the Helpfile

Lesson 1 Notes

Lesson 2 – Basic File Operations & Setting up Excel the Way You Want It

In Lesson 1 you were introduced to several key elements about both spreadsheets and Excel in general:

- What is a spreadsheet?
- What Excel is and the role it plays in the world of spreadsheet applications.
- Some of the terminology specific to working with both spreadsheets in general and Excel itself.
- What you can do with Excel in personal, business, and academic applications.
- Understanding the Ribbon Interface
  - Developer Tab – We discussed how Microsoft gives you the ability to access the Visual Basic for Applications programming language to automate repetitive tasks, and do things that you just couldn't do otherwise (like automate e-mailing a workbook with a push of a button).
- Workbook & Worksheet navigation, including some keyboard shortcuts
- Getting help from the resources that Microsoft has made available both within and outside of Excel

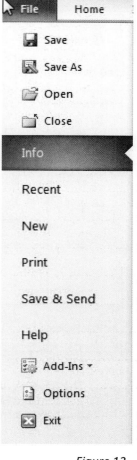

In Lesson 2 we'll dive deeper into Excel itself and teach you how to get around the Ribbon interface by exploring all of its various elements and showing you what each one does. Again, this isn't going to teach you how to use each one of their various elements, but it will serve as an introduction, so that when you start to get more comfortable with Excel you'll have the knowledge to know where to look for key elements. This lesson will primarily focus on the File tab (Office Button in Office 2007), and show you how to customize Excel to meet your personal needs each time you open it. There is a lot of detail in this lesson, as it also focuses on some of the important aspects of file/document management (which will apply to any Office application), how to save files, when and where. If you're relatively comfortable with the Office environment, then you'll breeze through a lot of it.

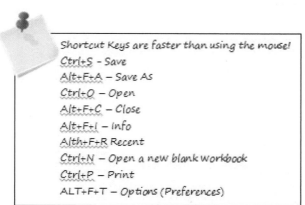

Figure 13

The File Tab

When you first open Excel, Microsoft has set your default options (preferences) to give you the most standard and user friendly options it can. If you're somewhat familiar with Excel there are certain things you might want to change, because hey, what's right for the "default" user may just not be right for you. And even if you're not all that familiar with Excel there will probably be some things you'll want to change. Fortunately, Microsoft understands this, and they let you change it. Before we discuss how to change the Default Options, we go over what each item in the File tab represents, although for the most part they're relatively straightforward:

To get started, we'll click on the File tab (in Office 2007 this would be the Office button) and you'll see the following options:

Save – This Saves the active workbook. It's fairly simple, but often forgotten until it's too late! Regularly saving your work is paramount! But make sure that if you open a workbook and make changes to it you're absolutely sure you want to keep those changes before you Save the workbook! Otherwise your previous work will be overwritten by the new, and your chances of recovery are slim! (Unless you have a backup version you can recover). Untold work around the world gets lost because of this every day (this stands true for any application)! Just remember, Save First, Save Often!

Save As – This will let you save the active workbook as something else. Let's say you make some changes to a workbook and you want to keep them, but not alter the original workbook, you would use the Save As option. When you Save As you'll be presented with an application dialog box like this:

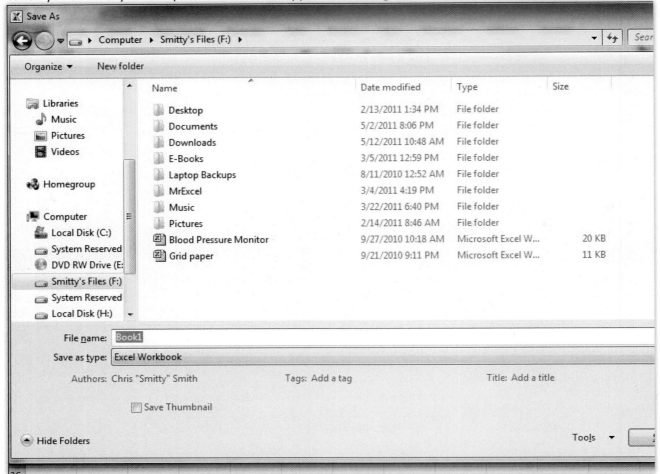

Figure 14

- The Save As dialog will take you directly to the Folder in which the active workbook was opened. Notice that the File Name is highlighted, allowing you to immediately enter a different name. If you don't do that and try to Save Excel will ask you about it:

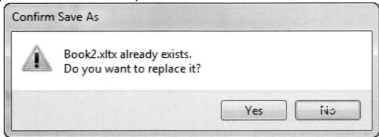

Figure 15

- If you hit Yes, you WILL save over whatever was in your workbook before you made any changes! If you don't want to do this, then just hit No and you'll still have the chance to enter a new workbook name.
- From here you can choose a different workbook name, and browse to the location of your choice. Again, one of the first things you should do when making changes to an existing workbook is perform a Save As if you want to keep the original work! Otherwise you stand a very good chance of losing it! This becomes especially important when you start working on complex models that you want to keep intact (they don't even have to be complex actually; lose an hour's worth of work and you'll be upset). To reiterate: untold hours of work get lost and have to be recreated daily around the world because of this.

- The Save As dialog gives you some additional options that can be important with regards to who you might be sharing your workbooks with later, but you first need to be aware of some naming conventions when you try to save a workbook. Microsoft has done a great job of expanding the rules for file names, but there are still some limitations (and if you break them you'll find out when you hit the Save button and you're rewarded with a wonderfully ambiguous error message):

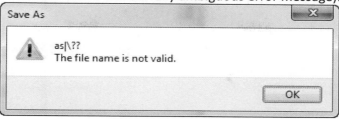

Figure 16

- Suffice it to say, you can't use the following characters in an Excel filename (or any other Windows file name for that matter): *|\?:"<>?

- Next on the list with the Save As dialog is the file type you can select. You'll see the drop-down selections directly beneath the File Name dialog. This will let you save your workbook in any manner of ways. In general the default option is fine, but you do need to know about the differences, especially if you want to share a workbook with users who have earlier versions, or if you recorded some macros and want to keep them. All software applications have what's called a file extension that's appended to the end of the file name (e.g. "MyFile.**doc**"), which identifies it, and helps separate each application from the other. Where earlier versions of Excel only had two file extensions, Excel 2007/2010 introduced some new file extensions. Microsoft also gave you a lot of new ways to save your workbook with the new versions, fortunately you shouldn't need to worry about anything but the default for now, which is an Excel Workbook (.xlsx). If at some point you do decide to start recording macros be aware that when you try to save a workbook with macros, Excel will prompt you to change the file type to a Macro-Enabled workbook. If you choose not to do so Excel will delete your macros!

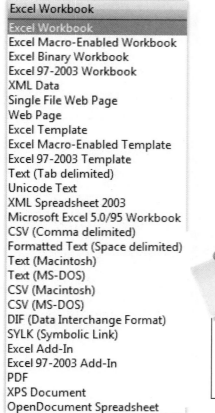

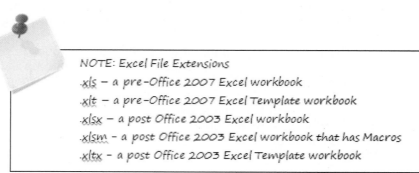

NOTE: Excel File Extensions

.xls – a pre-Office 2007 Excel workbook

.xlt – a pre-Office 2007 Excel Template workbook

.xlsx – a post Office 2003 Excel workbook

.xlsm – a post Office 2003 Excel workbook that has Macros

.xltx – a post Office 2003 Excel Template workbook

Figure 17

- You also have more options in the Save As dialog than just saving:

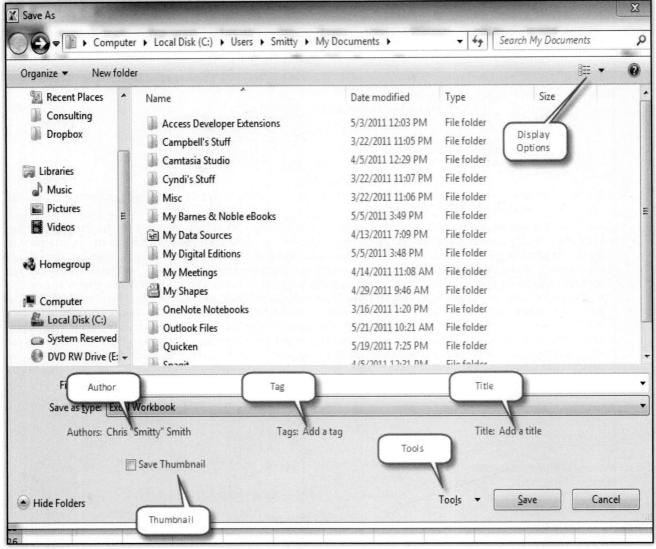

Figure 18

- **Display Options** –This is where you set the way in which you want to see documents display in your Open, Save and Search dialogs. Some people prefer icons, especially if they deal with a lot of graphic images, while others prefer just a plain list of files. Details is the view you'll see in all of the lesson examples. Detail shows the file name, Date modified, type and document size and will give you the most detail about the files you want to open or save.

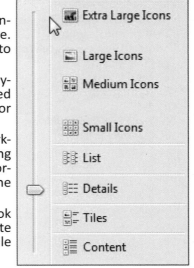

- **Author** – This is the name that you entered into Office when you installed it. But you can click on the blue text to change it right here. You can also change it in the document properties, which we'll get to shortly.
- **Tags** – This is a short description of what's in your workbook (e.g. Payroll, Schedule, etc.) This is supposed to help you speed up indexed searching when you use Windows Explorer to find files on your PC or network.
- **Title** – Very similar to Tags, this is an extended description of your workbook's function beyond the file name. Frankly, unless you're dealing with thousands of documents, or saving and sharing files on a large corporate network neither Tags nor Titles will come in very handy for the everyday Office user.
- **Thumbnail** – Clicking this will add a graphic image of your workbook that you can see when you search and open files. It's generally a waste of resources since Excel has to save that image along with other file properties.

- **Tools** – This option gives you some advanced settings that can come in handy if you need to have secure documents. There are four options here, but the one we'll discuss is General Options as the others are more broad Windows options:

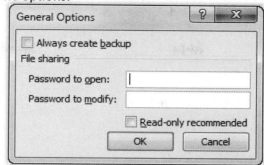

Figure 19

Always create backup – This will create a backup copy of your workbook whenever you close it. This is a good idea if you don't consistently back up files to an external source, but bear in mind that the backup copy will be created in the same folder as your workbook. Unfortunately, this means that if you lose access to the workbook's location for whatever reason (hard drive failure, folder deletion, etc.) you'll also lose the backup. Also note that a backup copy will be created as soon as you save your workbook, so if you accidentally save over a file, the backup will be a copy of what you saved over too.

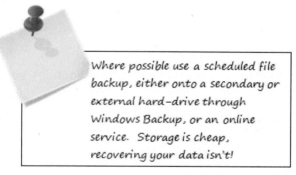

Where possible use a scheduled file backup, either onto a secondary or external hard-drive through Windows Backup, or an online service. Storage is cheap, recovering your data isn't!

- ○ **Password to open** – this is handy if you keep workbooks on a shared drive and you don't want other people to access them.
- ○ **Password to modify** – This will allow people to open your workbook, but will require them to provide a password to make changes. It's handy if you want to share your workbook, but don't want others to make changes.
- ○ **Read-only recommended** – This option can be used on its own or in conjunction with the Password options. It gives you is the ability to save your workbook as a Read-only document. This means that others can access the workbook, but any changes they make can't be saved unless they save the workbook as something else. Again, it comes in handy if you want to distribute your workbook, but don't want people changing your original.

Open – This will call the Open dialog (by default it will open to whatever location you have told Excel to save to in the application Options, which we'll cover shortly):

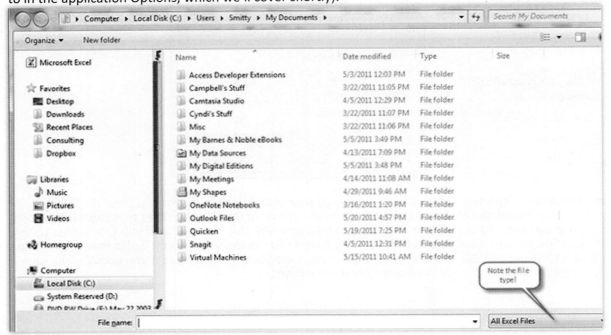

Figure 20

- Note the File Type balloon here. Similar to your Save As options, you have multiple options regarding the file types you can open, but the default is "All Excel Files", so if you're expecting to see a Text file show up here you won't unless you chose a different option from the drop-down. Additionally, the file type options listed below "All Excel Files" are the document types that Excel *can possibly* open (in general, but it's not always a given).

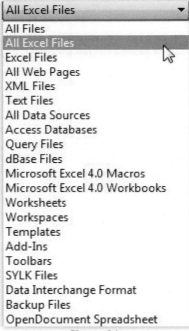

Figure 21

- If you select the All Files option and try to open an unsupported document type, like a Word document, Excel will try to do it, but you'll either get a Wizard like this:

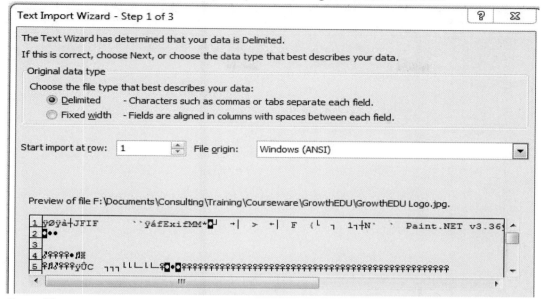

Figure 22

- Or garbage like this:

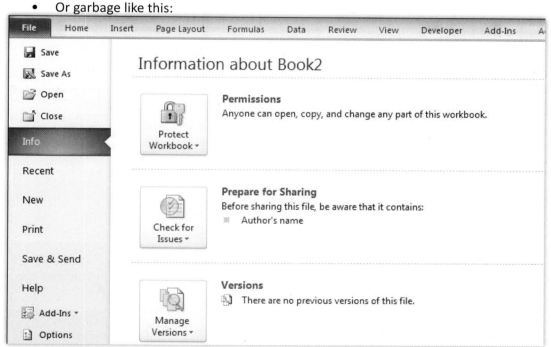

Figure 23

- That's really not Excel's fault, in fact it did the best it could to read what you wanted to open. You should know this because if you don't you'll be scratching your head for a bit until you realize you just tried to open a Word document in Excel (and it happens more than you might think!) If this does happen, just close the workbook and start over. You won't cause any damage to the file you opened (unless you try to mess with the garbage you see above and resave it as the original document, then you will have some issues, so please don't do that!)

Close - This will close the workbook. If you haven't made any changes to the workbook since you opened it then it will close without any prompts. If you have made changes to the workbook then you'll be asked if you want to save it before closing it. Sometimes you might want to open a workbook to make some quick assumptions, but close without saving them, so make sure not to confirm saving the workbook if that's the case.

> *Some functions, like those that deal with Date & Time, will cause the workbook to recalculate when it's opened, so you'll be prompted to save the workbook when you close it, even though you might not have made any physical changes to it.*

Info - This will open a new pane on the right side of the menu that displays all of the relevant workbook information:

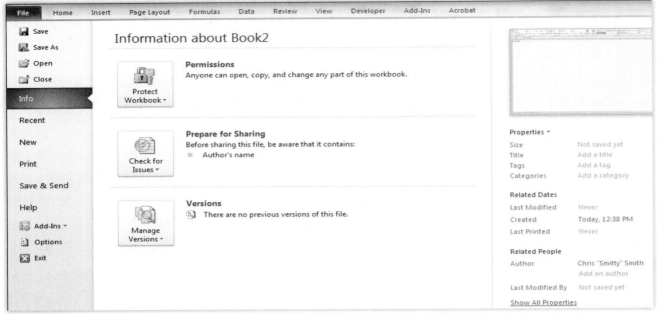

Figure 24

The information for a new workbook that hasn't been saved will be dramatically different than one that has been:

Figure 25

- **Compatibility Mode** – This dialog will be here if the workbook has been saved as an earlier version of Excel. It lets you know that some features available in Excel 2007/2010 have been deprecated in order to make the workbook compatible with earlier versions.

- **Permissions** – This dialog lets you know if the workbook has been protected. Selecting it will give you multiple options for distribution and protecting the workbook:

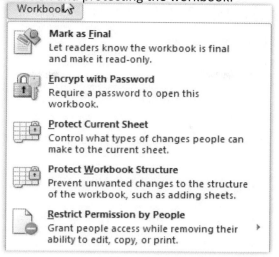

Figure 26

- **Check for Issues** – This dialog lets you evaluate the workbook for any potential problems before you share it. You'll probably rarely ever find a need to use this feature.

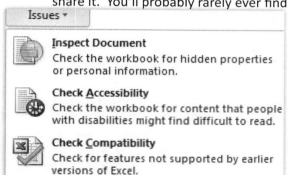

Figure 27

- **Manage Versions** – This will let you know if there are any pre-existing versions of the workbook. Again, it's not likely you'll ever use this feature.
- **Thumbnail** – This displays a thumbnail image of the active worksheet.
- **Properties** – At the bottom of the Info pane there is an option to Show All Properties or Show Fewer Properties. You can manually edit any of the editable workbook Properties simply by left-clicking on them, making your change and clicking Enter. You can't change intrinsic document properties like the Size, Modified/Created dates, etc.
- **Recent** – The Recent files list will show you a list of your most recent activity:

Figure 28

Note the little Pushpin icon, which will let you pin a file to the list so that it always appears at the top, no matter how long it's been since you last opened it. In this example the workbook at the top has been pinned in place.

New – This will launch a dialog that gives you options as to what kind of workbook you want to create. You can choose from a blank workbook, sample templates that are stored on your computer, your personal templates, or browse from Microsoft's excellent selection of templates online.

Figure 29

Ctrl+N will create a new Blank workbook.
To open the expanded New Workbook dialog use Alt+F+N

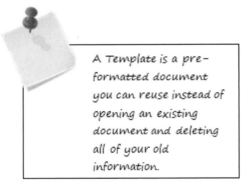

A Template is a pre-formatted document you can reuse instead of opening an existing document and deleting all of your old information.

Print – This will bring up a dual-screen dialog: your options for printing both the active worksheet and the entire workbook are on the left next to the File menu, while a preview of the active worksheet is on the right. There is a lot of detail behind this dialog, to the point that all of Lesson 7 is devoted to Printing and Page Setup, so we're not going to spend any time on it here.

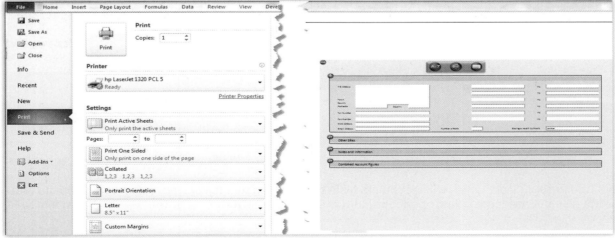

Figure 30

Save & Send – This dialog was brand new in Excel 2007 and it represents some significant advancements with regards to distributing your workbooks.

- **Send Using E-Mail** – This dialog gives you the option to send in various ways:
- **Send as an attachment** – This will use your installed e-mail client. If you have Office that's most likely going to be Outlook. This will not send through an Internet e-mail client like Gmail unless you have Outlook configured to manage your account.
- **Send a link** – This will create a link to the workbook's location in an e-mail, but the workbook needs to be saved in a shared location, like a document sharing site.
- **Send as PDF** – Excel now supports native PDF creation, so you no longer have to have a PDF writer like Adobe Acrobat installed on your computer.
- **Send as XPS** – This is a format that allows documents to be viewed online and retain its source formatting. Unless you plan on putting a lot of workbooks on the Internet, the odds of ever using this option are slim.
- **Send as Internet Fax** – This feature allows you to send a fax directly from your computer, but it does require you to have an Internet fax service. Unless you deal with a lot of documents requiring physical signatures the E-Mail option will most likely be the one you use the most.
- **Save to Web** – This is one of the best features to come along in quite some time. It allows you to save files directly to a Microsoft SkyDrive folder.

PDF is a very secure format for distributing workbooks, especially if you want to share the information, but not the formulas or structure behind your workbook

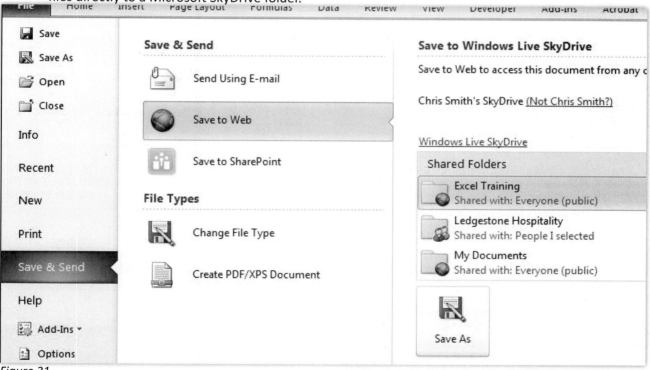

Figure 31

Microsoft's new, free SkyDrive service is an online file sharing site, which allows you to securely share files with anyone.
www.skydrive.com

Save to SharePoint – SharePoint is Microsoft's corporate collaboration server. It's used by most Fortune 1000 companies. But it's incredibly expensive, which is one of the reasons that Microsoft launched the SkyDrive service, which is a perfect alternative for small businesses.

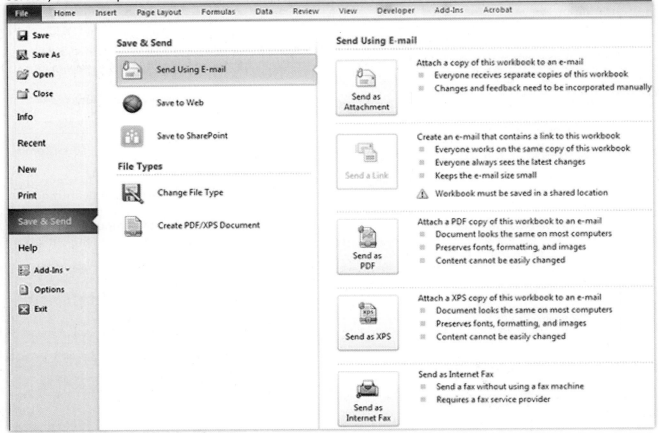

Figure 32

- **Help** – This dialog is a bit of a twist on the standard Helpfile dialog you'll find in an Excel workbook. It does give you the option to access the standard Helpfile (although it would be silly to come all the way here just to get to that!). It primarily gives you access to the tools you need if you want to check if there are updates available for Excel, find your product key, or even if you want to see how to get a hold of Microsoft for support.
- **Add-Ins** – This will list any available Add-Ins that have document preparation capabilities. In this example you'll see Adobe PDF functionality. Because this functionality is already exposed in other places, it's unlikely you'll ever this menu this unless you're in a specialized field that has an industry specific Add-In.

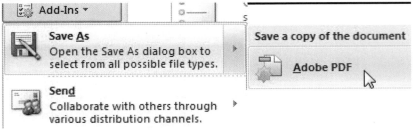

Figure 33

Changing Excel's Default Settings so They're Right for You

Options – Finally, we're getting to how you set up your defaults in Excel so that it does what you want. Some of the defaults you won't bother changing from Microsoft's factory settings, some of them you'll only change this one time, and some you'll change between workbooks depending on what you're doing. Note that changing certain options will require you to Exit and restart Excel in order for them to take effect, but Excel will let you know. The Options menu has 10 individual sections:

- **General**

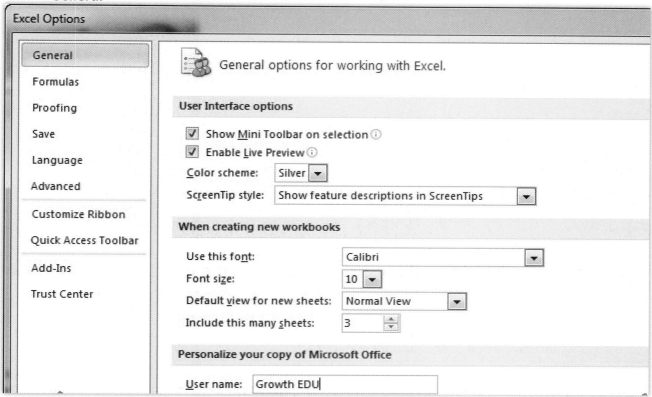

Figure 34

- ○ **Show Mini Toolbar** – This is a pretty cool feature that appears if you hover over a Ribbon control:

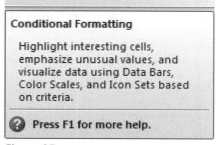

If you press the F1 key when a mini-toolbar is visible it will launch the Helpfile directly to that topic!

Figure 35

- ○ **Enable Live Preview** – This is something Microsoft has been working on for a while, and it's pretty slick. Essentially, it allows you to preview the effects of a change to an object (cell, chart, etc.), and decide if that's the change you want to make before you commit to it. Previously, you would apply a change, decide if you liked it or not, then go back and do it again until you got what you wanted. Imagine how time consuming this could be just trying to get a font right when you have a list of several hundred fonts from which you can choose? This has been such a big hit that Microsoft has a crew of people devoted to expanding it, and not just for Excel, but all of Office. Following is an example of changing the font selection for a cell. As you scroll through the list of available fonts, the text in the cell will automatically update to the font you selected (and it can go as fast as you can scroll!)

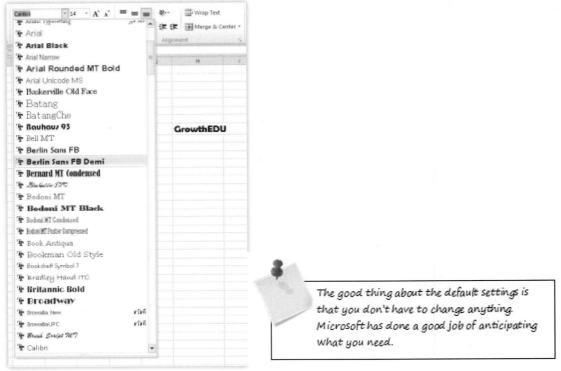

GrowthEDU

The good thing about the default settings is that you don't have to change anything. Microsoft has done a good job of anticipating what you need.

Figure 36

- ○ **Color Scheme** – The color scheme options are limited to Blue, Silver and Black. Both Blue and Silver are fairly unobtrusive, while Black is certainly noticeable.
- ○ **ScreenTip Style** – Screen Tips are small dialog boxes that appear when you hover over certain workbook elements and you have some options with how much information you want to display, or none at all.
- ○ **Default Font** – The default Font is something that's often overlooked by most finance and accounting types, who tend to stick with boring fonts like Arial or Helvetica. In Excel 2007 Microsoft changed the default to something called Calibri (which is what this course uses), and it was a substantial improvement. But some of you will want to use something different (Times New Roman is tried and true), so you can change the default font to whatever you want.
- ○ **Default Font Size** – The default font size is another element that you can change. The default is 11 point. Most people will generally never go under 10 or over 12, but you can change it until you get it to where you want.
- ○ **Default Worksheet view** - You have three options here, Normal view is the default, while the other two are primarily for Page Setup before printing, but some people prefer them to Normal view.
  - ▪ Normal View
  - ▪ Page Break Preview
  - ▪ Page Layout View
- ○ **Number of sheets in new workbooks** – The default is to open a workbook with 3 worksheets. If you do a lot of one worksheet workbooks, then you might want to cut that to 1 instead of sending out workbooks with 2 extra sheets or deleting them beforehand. The number of new worksheets you can have in new workbooks is limited purely by your sanity; most people will never need more than three on a normal basis, but if you deal with a lot of monthly scenarios you might want to set that to 12 or 13 (one for a summary worksheet). Although if this is the case, you'll probably want to consider using a template workbook, which we'll cover in Lesson V.
- ○ **User Name** – The default User Name is whatever name you entered when you installed Office, but you can change it here to be whatever you want. A lot of corporate installations simply put the company name, or a login name, so this is where you can personalize things a bit. The User Name field will accept punctuation, so you can have a proper name like "John "Doc" Halliday IV, Esq." if you want. This is one of the areas where Microsoft has gone to great lengths to allow you to personalize Excel the way you want it.

- ***Formulas (aka Functions)***

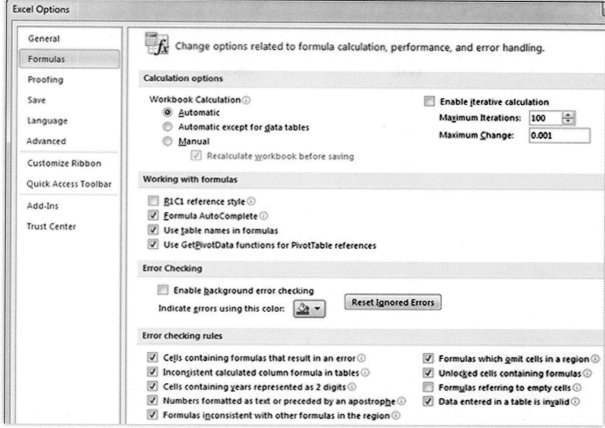

Figure 37

Note: Many of the Formula options won't yet make sense, so it's best to leave the defaults in place, but we'll still explore them.

- ○ ***Calculation Options***
  - ▪ ***Workbook Calculation*** – The primary options to consider here are Automatic and Manual. Normally a worksheet will calculate your formulas whenever you complete a formula and press Enter. You can control when a worksheet calculates by setting Calculation to Manual. This can be important if you ever build a workbook with a lot of formulas and you don't want to slow yourself down while they continuously update. The "Recalculate workbook before saving" option is another consideration, especially if you have a workbook that takes a long time to recalculate and you don't want to wait for it to do its thing while it closes. You'd think that with today's computers this wouldn't be an issue, but with Excel's expanded working area (over 1 billion cells from just over 1 million in earlier versions), it's easy to overwhelm it when you start building workbooks that have hundreds, thousands and even hundreds of thousands of formulas.
  - ▪ ***Iterative Calculation*** - This deals with certain Data Analysis tools and complex formula methodology, so it won't be a concern to you at this point.
  - ▪ ***Working with formulas***
    - - ***R1C1 Reference style*** – This will change your formula references from the A1 style, where a cell or range location uses the Column and Header address to name the address (e.g. A1:C7), to R1C1 style, which uses a much harder to read [R]1[C]1 notation (e.g. A1 vs. R1C1 (Row 1, Column 1)). This isn't something to worry about now, but it can come into play if and when you start working with Macros.
    - - ***Formula AutoComplete*** – This feature is one you should leave on! It allows Excel to finish a formula for you, and while it doesn't always get it right it does a pretty good job.
    - - ***Use Table Names in formulas*** – Again, leave this one as it is. We'll discuss Tables later in the course, but they do have their own methodology that Microsoft has designed, so unless you want to recreate what their programmers have, just leave it up to them.
    - - ***Use GetPivotData functions for Pivot table references*** – GetPivotData functions are powerful tools for referencing information from PivotTables, which we'll also be discussing. Leave this one alone as well.

○   ***Error Checking***
▪   ***Enable background error checking*** – When you have errors in formulas or inconsistencies between certain ranges, Excel will point them out for you by indicating a small green triangle in the upper right-hand corner of a cell. For now you'll probably want to leave this feature enabled, and leave all of its related default "Error checking rules" checked as well. It is a valuable learning tool. When you're comfortable with what you're doing with functions you can start disabling them. If you're not fond of green, you have the option to change the error color as you like:

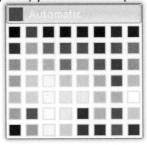

Figure 38

Proofing – This is one of the fairly minimal Option dialogs, and the only things to really discuss in detail here are Excel's AutoCorrect and Custom Dictionary options. The rest should be self-explanatory, and will largely depend on how you enter data. For instance, some people choose to enter customer details in UPPERCASE, so Excel defaults to ignore this type of entry. If Excel is set to trap this then every customer name you enter would show up as an error that Excel wants to fix.

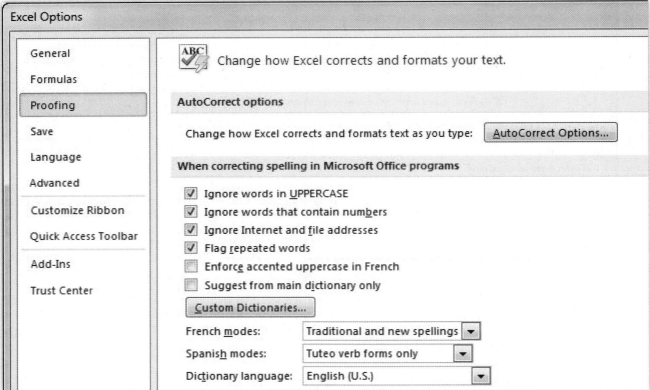

Figure 39

•   ***AutoCorrect Options*** –AutoCorrect will automatically correct your misspellings for you. While Micro-soft has done a great job of adding the most commonly misspelled words, they can't get them all, so if you find yourself consistently misspelling certain words, you can add them to the list. Just enter your commonly misspelled word in the "Replace" box, and enter the correct spelling in the "With" box. For instance you could replace "Thnaks" with "Thanks".

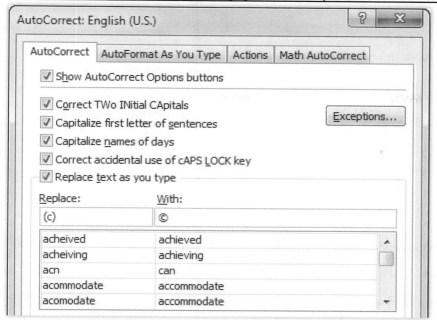

Figure 40

- ○ The ***AutoFormat As You Type, Actions*** and ***Math AutoCorrect*** options are rarely used, but feel free to explore! You might find something that pertains to your work that you want to adjust.
- ● ***Custom Dictionaries*** - If you work in a business that has specialized names for parts (like a "Fetzer" valve), and things like that, you might find yourself here quite a bit. This option gives you the ability to add your own words to the Office dictionary. You don't have to come here to add words to the dictionary though, if you run Spell Check on a sheet (Review Tab, Spelling and Grammar group) you'll have the option to add any words that Excel doesn't like just by clicking the "Add to Dictionary" button.

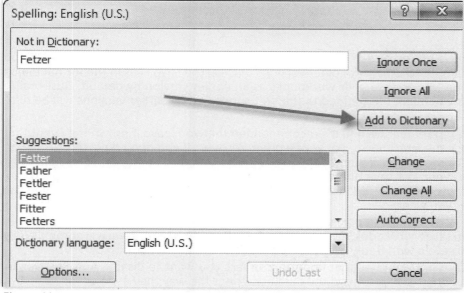

Figure 41

By now maybe you're starting to see that the folks at Microsoft have done their best to link all of these elements together, so just because a feature or option exists in one place, doesn't necessarily mean you can't access from other places. This is important as you start to get more comfortable, because you'll start discovering ways to do things that you might be more comfortable with vs. another.

- ***Save***

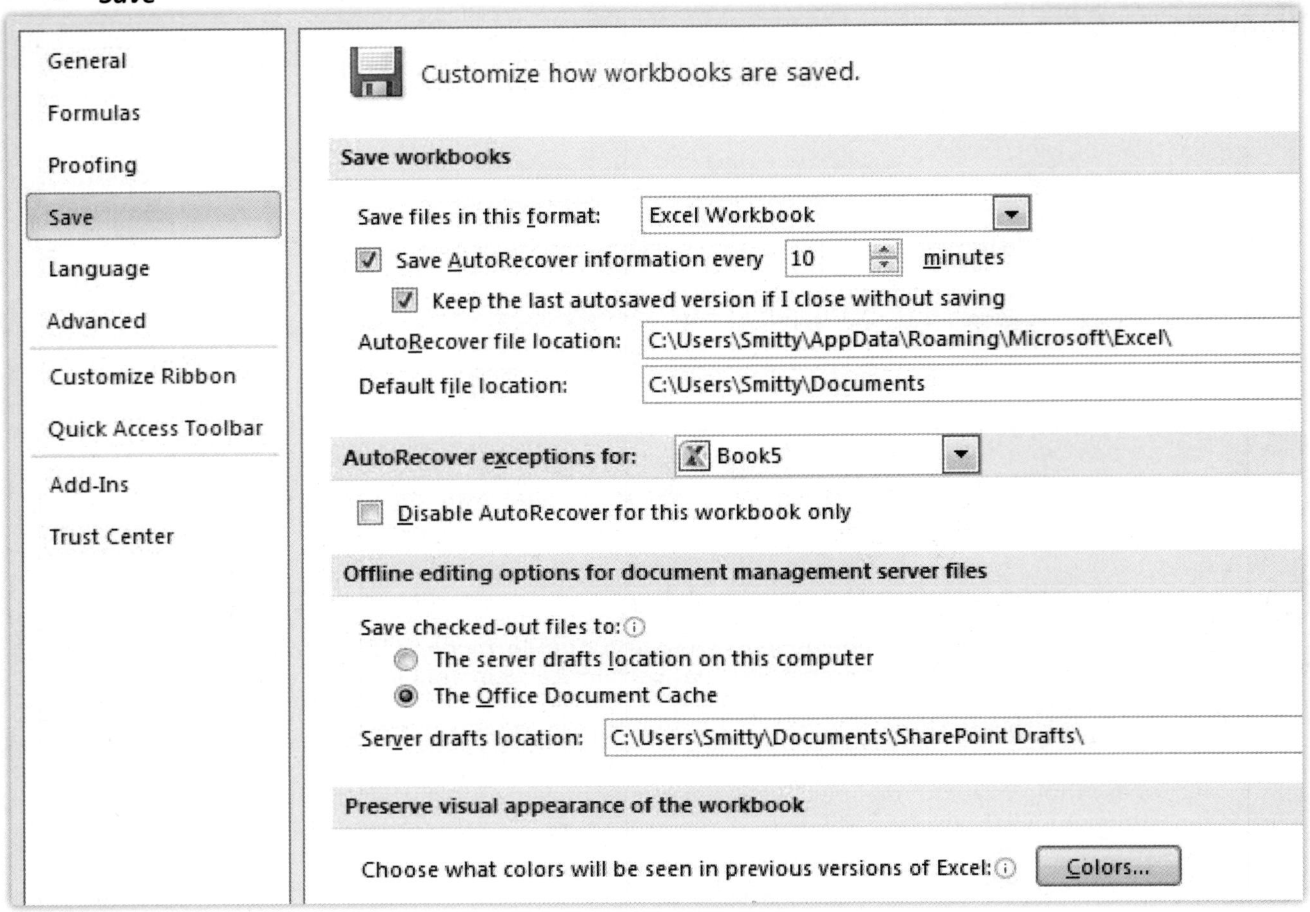

Figure 42

Your Save options are relatively straightforward and it's unlikely you'll change much of anything here. If you regularly save workbooks to distribute to users with older versions of Excel the Save Files in the format dialog might be important as it will allow you to save your workbooks as an earlier version by default. Just realize that if you do this, any elements you might have added that aren't supported by earlier versions will be deprecated.

- ○ ***AutoRecover*** is an important feature and it's recommended that you leave it on. In the event that Excel crashes it will use the latest version of your work to recover. If you don't have this turned on Excel will do its best to recover your workbook, but be aware that it's likely you will lose anything you entered between your last save and the crash. Fortunately, Excel doesn't crash very often, but it's still good to know it's there. Microsoft sets your AutoRecover location for you, but you can change it to wherever you want.

- ○ ***Default file location*** – This one is important if you don't want to have to browse to a particular location each time you save a workbook. By setting the default location here, Excel will automatically jump there when you save a workbook.

- ○ The rest of the Save settings aren't all that important unless you want to disable AutoRecover, or deal with SharePoint. Otherwise just leave the default settings the way they are.

- ○ Finally there is the ability to ***Preserve the visual appearance of the workbook***. If you're going to be saving as earlier versions of Excel that don't support as many colors as Excel 2007/2010, you can access the previous Excel color palette. Otherwise Excel will make its best effort to convert colors to be compatible with earlier versions.

- *Language*

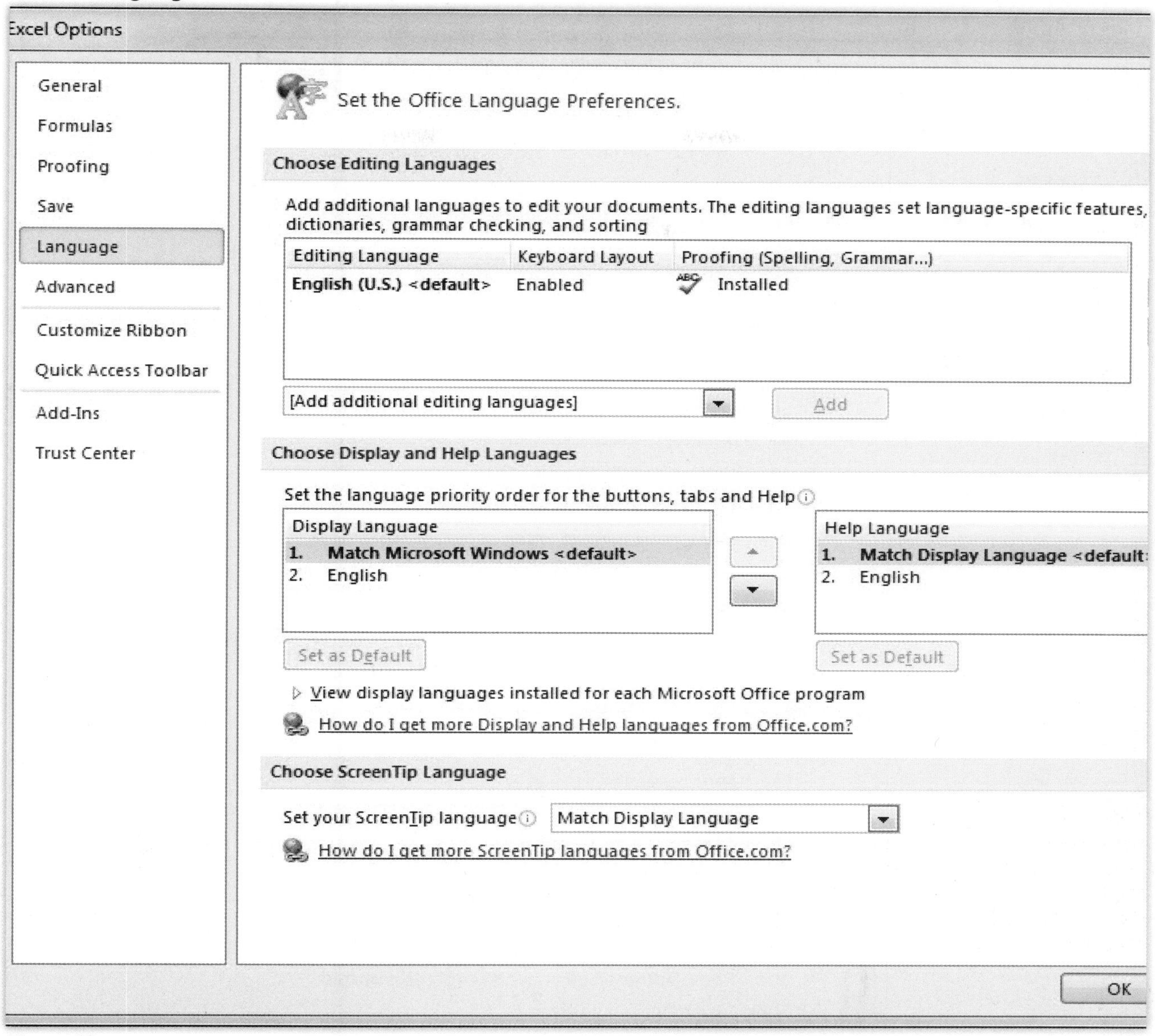

Excel Options

General
Formulas
Proofing
Save
Language
Advanced
Customize Ribbon
Quick Access Toolbar
Add-Ins
Trust Center

Set the Office Language Preferences.

Choose Editing Languages

Add additional languages to edit your documents. The editing languages set language-specific features, dictionaries, grammar checking, and sorting

Editing Language	Keyboard Layout	Proofing (Spelling, Grammar...)
English (U.S.) <default>	Enabled	Installed

[Add additional editing languages]   Add

Choose Display and Help Languages

Set the language priority order for the buttons, tabs and Help ⓘ

Display Language	Help Language
1. Match Microsoft Windows <default>	1. Match Display Language <default:
2. English	2. English

Set as Default   Set as Default

▷ View display languages installed for each Microsoft Office program

How do I get more Display and Help languages from Office.com?

Choose ScreenTip Language

Set your ScreenTip language ⓘ   Match Display Language

How do I get more ScreenTip languages from Office.com?

OK

Figure 43

- ○ If you're based in the US the odds are slim that you'll ever need to change any of these options.
- • **Advanced**

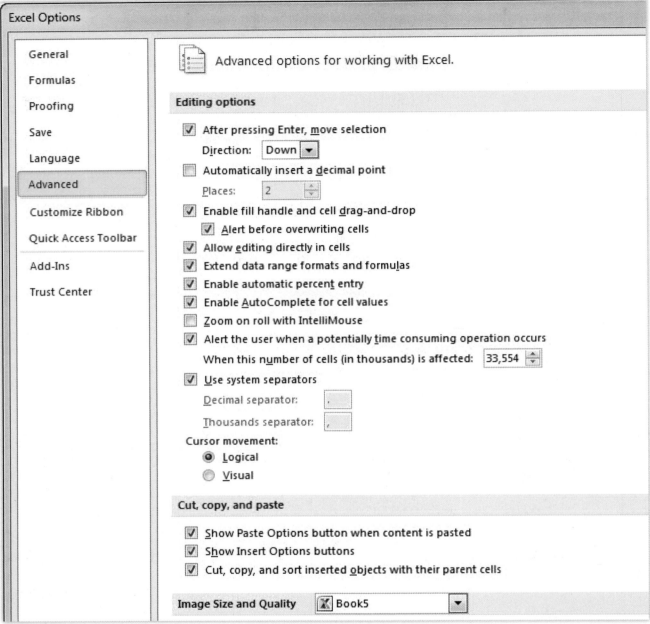

Figure 44

- • This is where you will do the bulk of your customization and consists of multiple options that will affect both worksheets and the workbook in general.
  - ○ **Editing Options** – In general you'll leave these settings as they are. These options apply to the entire workbook, and they can be changed at any time.
    - ▪ **After pressing Enter, move selection** (direction – Down, Right, Up, Left). The default is down, but in some cases you might want to change it. Specifically if you have to do a lot of data entry and are going from Left-to-Right.
    - ▪ **Automatically insert a decimal point** (how many places)
    - ▪ **Enable fill handle and cell drag-and-drop**
    - ▪ Alert before overwriting cells – If you drag the contents of one cell onto another you'll be asked if you want to do so.
    - ▪ **Allow editing directly in cells**
    - ▪ **Extend data range formats and formulas**
    - ▪ **Enable automatic percent enter**

- **Enable AutoComplete for cell values**
- **Zoom on roll with IntelliMouse**
- **Alert the user when a potentially time consuming operation occurs** (set the number of cells to evaluate for potential changes)
- **Use system separators** (decimal & thousands)
- **Cursor movement** (Logical, Visual)
- **Cut, copy and paste**
  - Show Paste Options button when content is pasted – This will give you some expanded pasting options that will appear to the right of the pasted cell.

You'll also see a shortcut key next to each Paste option. E.G. Paste (P), Paste formulas (F), etc.

Figure 45

- Try it out to see the options you have, as there are several (from right-to-left then down), just enter something in a cell, the copy & paste:
  - Paste
  - Paste formulas
  - Paste formulas and number formatting
  - Keep source formatting
  - No borders
  - Keep source column widths
  - Transpose (switch columns to rows and vice versa)
  - Paste values (numbers only, no formulas)
  - Paste values and number formatting
  - Paste values and source formatting
  - Paste formatting only
  - Paste link
  - Paste a Picture
  - Paste a Linked Picture

Keyboard shortcuts for Copying & Pasting
Ctrl+ C - Copy
Ctrl+V - Paste

- **Show Insert Options buttons** – This one will appear when you use a Ribbon command to insert rows or columns.

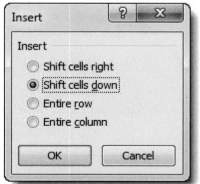

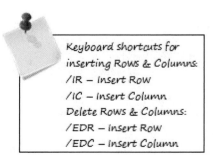

Keyboard shortcuts for inserting Rows & Columns:
/IR – Insert Row
/IC – Insert Column
Delete Rows & Columns:
/EDR – Insert Row
/EDC – Insert Column

Figure 46

- **Cut, copy and sort inserted objects with their parent cells** – This will make sure that if you resize rows and columns, then any objects (images, controls, etc.) you've added will retain their position relative to where you originally placed them. You can also change this for each object in its individual properties.

- ○ *Image Size and Quality*
  - ▪ *Discard editing data* – This deletes data Excel saves when you edit images so they can be returned to their original state if you don't like the changes.
  - ▪ *Do not compress images in file* - Checking this can result in very large image sizes (and therefore large file sizes). By default Excel will compress images so they take up less space.
  - - Set default target output to (220, 150 or 96 ppi – pixels per inch)
- ○ *Print*
  - ▪ *High quality mode for graphics*
- ○ *Chart*
  - ▪ *Show chart element names on hover* (similar to ToolTips)
  - ▪ *Show data point values on hover* (this will show you the value behind a data point on a chart)
- ○ *Display*
  - ▪ *Show this number of Recent* Documents (0-50) – This is number of recent file names that will show up in the File, Recent dialog.
  - ▪ *Ruler Units* (Default, Inches, Millimeters, Centimeters) – The default is based on your Windows Regional Settings. In the US it will be Inches.
  - ▪ *Show all windows in the Taskbar* – This will show all of your open workbooks in the Taskbar. If you uncheck this you'll need to physically move between workbooks to see them. This one is a common question when it's inadvertently turned off, because all of your workbooks seem to disappear.
  - ▪ *Show formula bar* – This one you might want to turn off if you need to distribute a workbook and don't want people easily seeing your formulas (more to come when we discuss Worksheet Protection).
  - ▪ *Show function screen tips*
  - ▪ *Disable hardware graphics acceleration*
  - ▪ *For cells with comments, show:*
    - - No comments or indicators
    - - Indicators only, and comments on hover
    - - Comments and indicators
  - ▪ *Default direction* – In the US you'll leave this as Left-to-right.
    - - Right-to-left
    - - Left-to-right (Default)
- ○ *Display options for this workbook* – There is a drop-down on the right of this option that will allow you to choose from any open workbook. The first three options can come in handy when you distribute workbooks and want to minimize what the user sees.
  - ▪ Show horizontal scroll bar
  - ▪ Show vertical scroll bar
  - ▪ Show sheet tabs
  - ▪ Group dates I the AutoFilter menus
  - ▪ For objects, show:
    - - All
    - - Nothing (hide objects)
- ○ *Display options for this worksheet* – There's a drop-down on the right of this option that will let you select from any worksheet.
  - ▪ *Show row and column headers*
  - ▪ *Show formulas in cells instead of their calculated results* (you can toggle this in a worksheet with CTRL+`).
  - ▪ *Show sheet right-to-left* – This will reverse the columns in your worksheet and put the last column on your left, column A on the right. Under normal circumstances there's no reason to do this, but it can be fun to do to unsuspecting co-workers.
  - ▪ *Show page breaks* – Many people find this to be very irritating. If you need to see Page Breaks you're better off using the Page Break view.
  - ▪ *Show a zero in cells that have zero values* – This is important for worksheets that have formulas that return 0's. Many times with a lot of information on a sheet you might not want to see a lot

of zeros from formulas that haven't populated yet. This is one option you will probably come to quite a bit.

- **Show outline symbols if an outline is applied** – Outlining is a way of compressing information into groups. The outline symbols let you expand or contract those groups, so you wouldn't want to turn this option off.
- **Show gridlines** – Gridlines are the natural dividers between cells and columns. Most times you will apply your own custom gridlines, so while it's often good to start a worksheet with this option on you may find yourself coming here to turn it off as you get your worksheet completed.
  - Gridline color – You can change the default gridline color if the default gray isn't spicy enough for you. Note that your choices are limited to the Excel 2003 color palette.

- *Formulas*
  - ◦ **Enable multi-threaded calculation** – This takes advantages of multicore processors and lets Excel calculate faster that it could before.
    - Number of calculation threads
    - Use all processes on this computer: (# of processors Windows has identified on your system)
    - Manual (spinner control to change the number)
  - ◦ **When calculating this workbook** - There is a drop-down on the right of this option that will allow you to choose from any open workbook.
    - **Update links to other workbooks**
    - **Set precisions as displayed** – This has to do with rounding and how to calculate values as displayed. Unchecking this can cause problems over time as it can affect your data and formula output with regards to multiple value rounding leading to unanticipated results.
    - **Use 1904 date system** – This is only relevant if you're using a Macintosh, which uses a different date system. Excel for windows use dates that begin on January 1, 1900. For some odd reason, Mac's start in 1904.
    - **Save external link values** – This will save values from formulas that are linked to other workbooks, as well as the formulas. It can come in handy if you send workbooks to other people who might not have the linked workbooks, so when they open your workbook, they'll see the formula results instead of errors.
  - ◦ **General**
    - **Provide feedback with sound** – When you do things like insert or delete rows or columns, the action will be accompanied by an alert sound
    - **Provide feedback with animation** - When you do things like insert or delete rows or columns, you'll see the action happen. If you turn it off, the action will still take place, it just won't be as evident until it's done. It's generally not an issue unless your graphics card has a hard time keeping up, in which case you might want to turn it off.
    - **Ignore other applications that use Dynamic Data Exchange (DDE)** – Unless you use multiple monitors this won't be an issue. If you do though and you want to see Excel on multiple monitors, unchecking this will force each new workbook to open in a new instance of Excel. From there you can drag the separate instances to your different monitors.
    - **Ask to update automatic links** – When you open a workbook that has links to another you'll be prompted if you want to update those links. If you do this a lot, this is one of those defaults that you can turn off.
    - **Show add-in user interface errors** – Unless you deal with a lot of Add-Ins, or at some point you want to create your own, you can leave this alone. By default if there is an error when an add-in tries to load there's no error message, it just doesn't load. This will let you know if there are any errors.
    - **Scale content for A4 or 8.5 x 11" paper sizes** – Excel will automatically try to fit you work to fit in an 8.5 x 11" format, which is the US standard (A4 is European).
    - Show customer submitted Office.com content – This has to do with online content you have posted through OfficeLive. It allows you to open content directly through Excel instead of browsing to a webspace.
    - **At start up open all files in** – If you have one, or several workbooks you use daily, you can set the path to them here and they will all open each time you open Excel. This isn't recommended unless you have a workbook that you have opened all day.
    - **Web Options** – This lets you set some of the options you might want to change if you plan on saving Excel workbooks as web pages, or posting documents to a website.
    - **Enable multi-threaded processing** – If you have a multi-core processor you'll probably want to leave this on. If you don't know what kind of processor you have don't worry about it.

- *Disable undo for large PivotTable refresh operations to reduce refresh time* – Leave this as the default.
- *Disable undo for PivotTables with at least this number of data source rows* (in thousands) (spinner control to adjust the default, which is 300) – Leave this as the default. Both of these PivotTable options will improve your performance if you start using them.
- *Create lists for use in Sorts and Fill sequences* – This deals with Custom Lists, and of all the General options this is one that you might actually change, especially if you have a business with some fairly repetitive information you need to enter regularly (like department names). You'll see a command button that allows you to Edit Custom Lists to the right of the option. Clicking it will bring up the following dialog, where you can add your own lists:

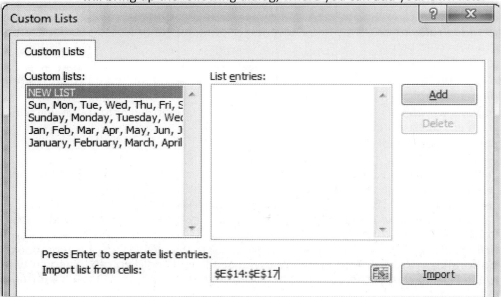

Figure 47

- Custom lists work with the AutoFill handle, which is the little icon at the bottom of an Excel cell when you activate it. If you have a defined list, you only need to enter one of the list values, then grab the fill handle and drag it down or across and Excel will complete the list entries for you for as long as you decide to go (it will repeat the list when it gets to the end of it):

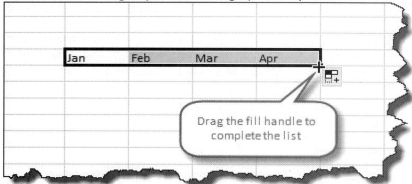

Figure 48

- ○ **Lotus compatibility**
  - Microsoft Excel menu key (set to the Forward Slash - "/" by default, which is the same shortcut launch key that Lotus 1-2-3 uses). The menu key is the same as hitting the Alt key in Excel which will bring up the shortcut keys for each Ribbon Tab and Group.
  - ○ **Lotus compatibility Settings** – By default, Excel formulas need to be entered with an = sign to start them. These settings allow you to directly enter formulas in Excel without having to preface them with an = sign. It can be handy if you're inputting a lot of formulas.

- ***Customize Ribbon***

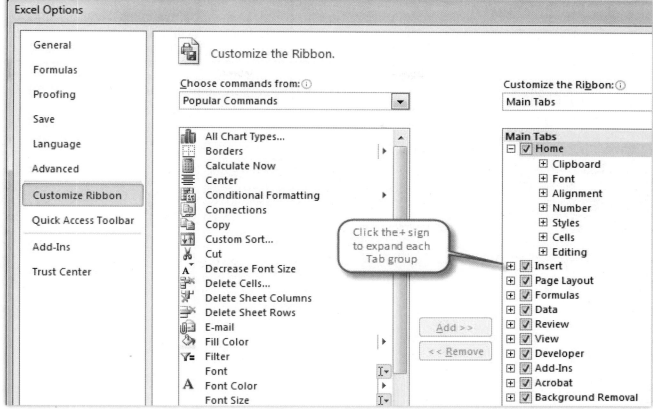

Figure 49

- This allows you to add Menu commands to the Ribbon and only display those commands that you want. This feature was not available in Excel 2007, where your only option was to customize the Quick Action Toolbar (QAT). For now the defaults should suffice, but feel free to play around with the options and see what kind of combinations you can come up with to make your experience more enjoyable. As you find yourself getting more comfortable with Excel and its Ribbon commands you may very well find yourself creating your own Ribbon tabs with just the commands you use the most. If you don't like any changes that you make then just use the Reset button toward the bottom.

- The first thing to be aware of here is the Choose Commands from option, which allows you to filter the list of available commands. If you don't see something in the current list of options, you should look here.

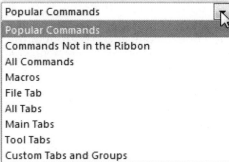

Figure 50

- The second is the Customize the Ribbon option, which will let you choose which Ribbon Tab or Group you want to customize:

Figure 51

- **Quick Access Toolbar**
    - ○ As mentioned previously, the Quick Action Toolbar (QAT) is that list of Menu commands that sits above the Ribbon, and it can hold all of your most frequently used commands. If you're a heavy mouse user then this will probably come in very handy, as it puts everything right up front for you instead of having to go through different Ribbon Tabs/Groups. If you're a keyboard user, you may never even adjust the default settings. The customize dialog for this is very similar to the Ribbon customization dialog, but it's a bit simpler. Remember, the default setting is Popular Commands, so if you can't find something in the list, just change the primary Command selection.

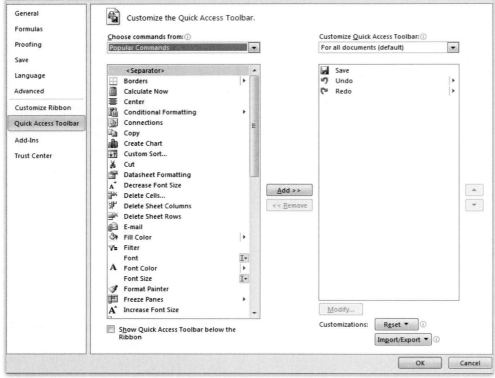

Figure 52

- **Add-Ins**
    - ○ As mentioned previously, Add-Ins are additions to what is included natively in Excel. There are Add-Ins that Microsoft creates, and then there are Add-Ins created by third parties. This will show you how to manage Add-Ins if you do find some that are useful for your particular business. This is different than either the Add-Ins Tab on the Ribbon, or the Add-Ins menu on the File Tab, in that this lets you set your Add-In options, where the others expose their functionality.
    - ○ At the top you'll see a list of active Add-Ins, and below that are inactive Add-Ins. Clicking on any of them will show a description of each one at the bottom of the dialog window.
    - ○ At the bottom there is a drop-down for Manage, which lets you select the type of Add-In you want to work with at the moment:

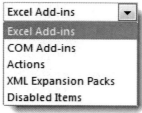

Figure 53

- Clicking the Go button will bring up a dialog that shows you the available Add-Ins. You can activate/ deactivate them by clicking the check box to the left of the Add-In's name. If you want to activate an Add-In not in the list, click the browse button and navigate to its location on your computer. Once you do it will appear in the list and you can activate it.
    - ○ **Automation** is for relatively high-end users and specialized applications. Most users will never use this feature.

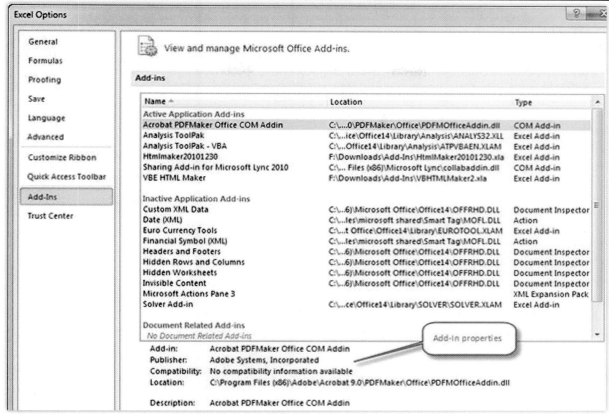

Figure 54

- **Trust Center**
  - The Trust Center primarily deals with how to tell your computer to respond to workbooks that contain VBA (Visual Basic for Applications) code, be it in the form of code you recorded, wrote, or third party Add-Ins. The links at the top of the dialog will take you to certain Microsoft explanations and offerings. What you're interested with here is the Trust Center Settings button.

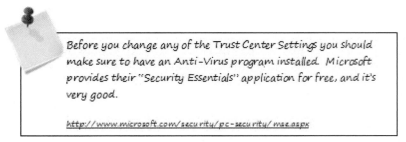

Before you change any of the Trust Center Settings you should make sure to have an Anti-Virus program installed. Microsoft provides their "Security Essentials" application for free, and it's very good.

http://www.microsoft.com/security/pc-security/mse.aspx

Figure 55

- Here you have multiple options:
  - **Trusted Publishers** – This is only relevant if you have digital certificates issued by a Microsoft third-party certificate issuer. These certificates allow certain documents to bypass security settings as they have been deemed trustworthy. As with Microsoft's SharePoint application, third-party digital

certificates are expensive and usually only used by large corporations. They general don't play a role in small business applications.

- ○ ***Trusted Locations*** – You'll want to add certain locations to this list, like your MyDocuments folder, and any other folders you access frequently, otherwise Excel will give you a message that the document didn't originate from a trusted location and do you want to Enable Content. This will get very old, very fast. You can use the Add New Location button to browse to the folder of your choice.

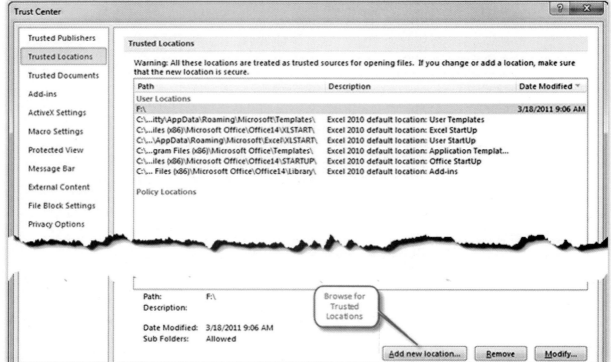

Figure 56

- ○ ***Trusted Documents*** - When you open a document from an untrusted source, such as one you've opened from an untrusted location, Excel will give you the option to permanently trust it.

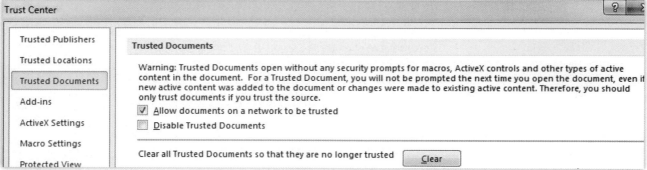

Figure 57

- ○ ***Add-Ins*** – This Add-Ins area simply gives you the option to require that Add-Ins be signed by a trusted publisher, which requires that they have a Microsoft third-party approved digital signature. If you already know who provided your Add-In and have installed it, it's unlikely you'll need to go to this length. It should however, show how serious Microsoft is about protecting you and your information.
- ○ ***ActiveX Settings*** – ActiveX controls are a type of interactive object you can add to your workbooks, like Check Boxes, Radio Buttons, etc. They are all controlled via VBA code, so here's another instance where Microsoft is trying to protect you from potentially malicious content.

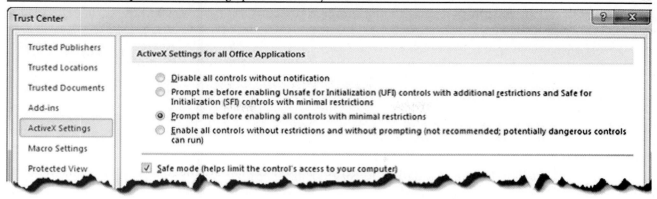

Figure 58

- ▪ Here you have several options:
  - Disable all controls without notification
  - Prompt to enable with restrictions
  - Prompt to enable with minimal restrictions (this option is generally sufficient)
  - Enable all controls without restrictions
- • **Macro Settings** – These options are designed to give you control over what VBA code can run in Excel (including your own). Generally, if you have an Anti-Virus application installed, you can opt to enable macros, but this is ONLY if you have an Anti-Virus application installed! Otherwise choose the "Disable all macros with notification" option, which will give you the opportunity to allow macros to run or not.

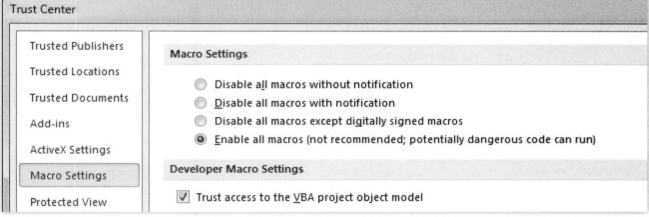

Figure 59

- • There is another setting here called "**Developer Macros Settings**" with a check box to Trust access to the VBA project object model. If you have any VBA Add-Ins installed you'll want to make sure that this is checked or your Add-Ins wont' work.
- • **Protected View** – Protected view gives you the option of allowing content from workbooks that originate from the Internet or E-Mail attachments. It's recommended that you leave these options enabled, as you never know what might be in such files. Note that if you have an Anti-Virus application installed it will scan those workbooks first as well.

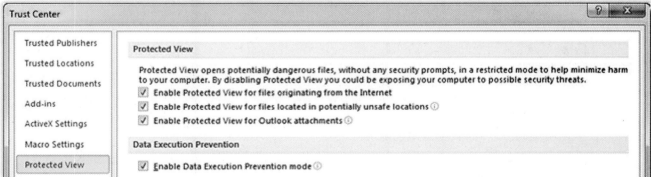

Figure 60

- **Message Bar** – The Message Bar is simply notification that Excel has blocked content. It's a good idea to leave this option enabled as well.

Figure 61

- **External Content** – These are options which you'll probably have no need to change, as the defaults should be suitable.

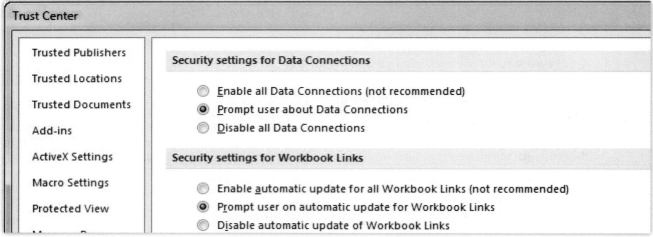

Figure 62

- **File Block Settings** – This gives you the ability to automatically flag certain workbooks types and open them in protected view. Again, the default settings should suffice, unless you find yourself opening files of a certain type frequently and want to make sure their content is disabled.

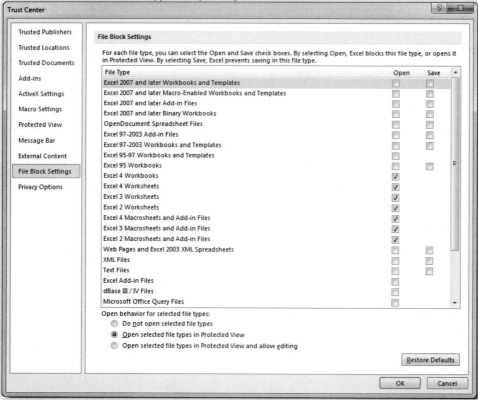

Figure 63

- **Privacy Options** – These options are largely what you want Excel to check or report back to Microsoft for you. Microsoft collects information from Excel regarding how you use it, crashes, etc., in an effort to improve the application, and they do it for all Office applications. You can opt out of any of it, but you should know that Microsoft doesn't gather any personal information about you or your data, so it all anonymous.

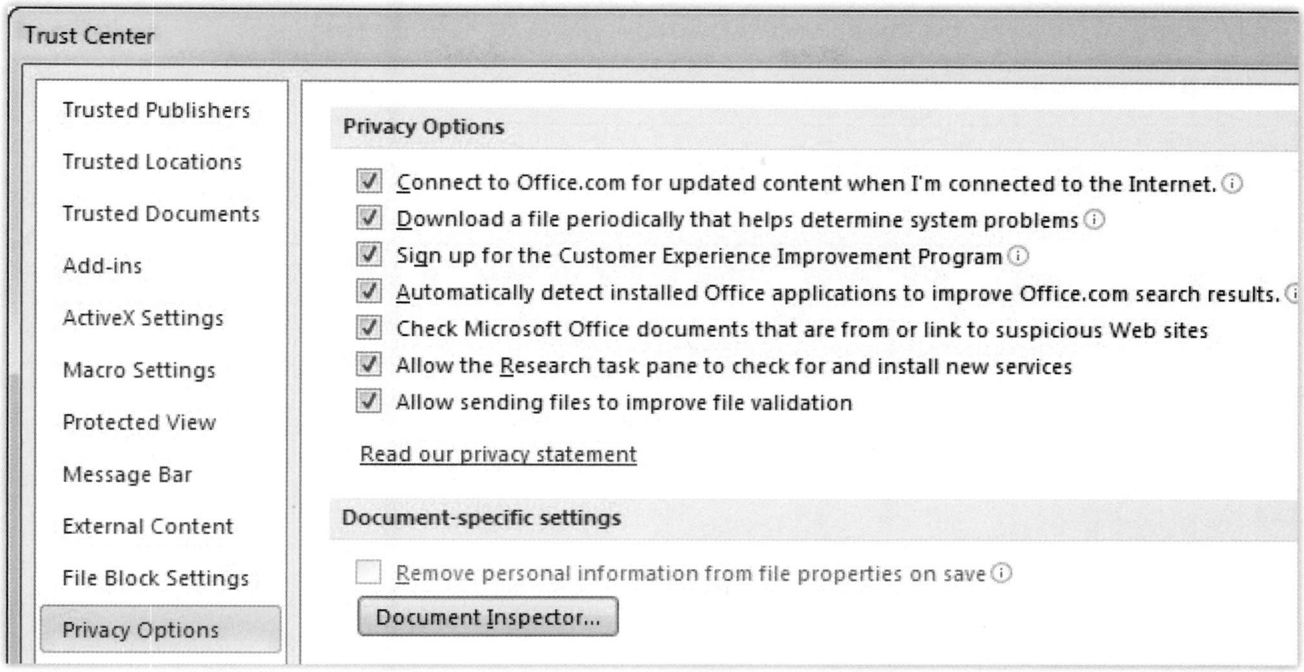

Figure 64

- The **Document Inspector** allows you to inspect a workbook for any personal information prior to distribution and allows you to remove it.
- The **Translation and Research** options allow you to set your language preferences for Translation & Research tools when you're proofing a workbook prior to distribution.

Unit Summary: Basic File Operations & Setting up Excel the way you want it

- In this lesson you learned about basic file operations, like saving and opening workbooks.
- You walked through all of Excel's options for enabling/disabling certain workbook and worksheet features, both features you can use for every instance of Excel and those you can toggle off for specific instances.

Review Questions

1. Name keyboard shortcuts for Opening, Saving/Save As, Closing and creating New workbooks (Extra credit for creating a new template with a shortcut):
   a. _____
   b. _____
   c. _____
   d. _____
   e. _____

2. Give examples of valid vs. invalid file names
   a. _____
   b. _____

3. How would you create a Read-Only workbook with a Password to open?
   a. _____

4. What would you do if you didn't want to display 0 values on a worksheet?
   a. _____

5. How do you change Excel's default Font?
   a. _____

6. What Menu Commands can you add to the Ribbon? What about the Quick Action Toolbar (QAT)?
   a. _____
   b. _____

Lesson Assignment – Lesson 2 – Basic File Operations & Setting up Excel the way you want it

Your first assignment is to open a new Excel workbook and start getting familiarized with the default options, including making adjustments to the Ribbon and Quick Action Toolbar (QAT) commands (there is a Notes section below for you to keep track of your observations):

Lesson 2 Notes

Lesson 3 – The Ribbon In-Depth – The Home Tab

In Lesson 2 you got an introductory/refresher course in basic Windows file operations, like Saving, when and where, as well as a deep dive into how to set up Excel the way you want it by walking through all of your setup options through the File/Office menus. In general you'll likely only set those options once, and never worry about them again; however there are a few you might change between workbooks and worksheets depending on what you're doing:

- Changing the direction of the cursor when you hit Enter (Down, Right, Up, Left)
- For the workbook it could be showing Comments, ScrollBars, Sheet tabs
- For worksheets you might change Displaying Zero values, Gridlines, etc.

In Lesson 3 we'll review the Ribbon's Home tab and all of its elements. The Home Tab is the default tab for the Ribbon, and as such Microsoft has lumped most of what you do the most there, so this will get the most attention of the Ribbon elements. Before we do that though , you should understand a bit of the history behind the Ribbon - The original Excel menu interface was designed in 1992, and as with all products, Excel has gone through some significant changes since then, each one giving users more capabilities than the next. The engineers at Microsoft did a great job of keeping this product the number #1 spreadsheet application in the world for a long time, but then a new generation of engineers came on board and had some great new ideas based on their experiences with computers. Just as computer games have evolved since the days of the Commodore and Atari, the Ribbon is nothing less than an evolutionary step in the Excel product life cycle, and it's something that had to happen if Excel was to remain the most used application on the market. Oddly enough, Bill Gates was against the Ribbon, fearing that its introduction would alienate a large group of experienced users who had grown comfortable enough to memorize all of Excel's keystrokes, and more importantly, knew where everything was. But he was outvoted and development on the Ribbon for Office applications really took off. Was Bill Gates right? To a certain degree, but most experienced users have now adopted the Ribbon; those who haven't have been left behind because their customers have moved on. Probably the most important element of the Ribbon is that it puts everything right out in the open for you in a great graphical display, which earlier versions lacked. For newer generations of users who are as comfortable with a mouse as they are a keyboard, the Ribbon is a natural step, and Microsoft has done a great job of it. There have been some hiccups along the way, which is why you'll find certain things in the Excel (and Office 2010 Ribbon) that weren't available in 2007, like customizing the Ribbon, but that's just another evolutionary step (and Microsoft continues to do a good job of listening to their customers with regards to making the whole thing more user friendly).

- To get an idea of the difference between a Ribbon and non-Ribbon version of Excel, here's a screen shot of Excel 2003, which was the last version of Excel without the Ribbon:

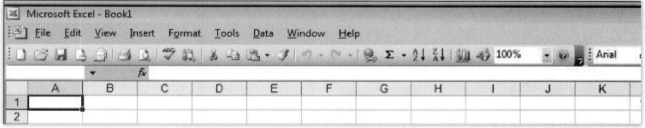

Figure 65

- Now compare that to Excel 2010 with the Ribbon:

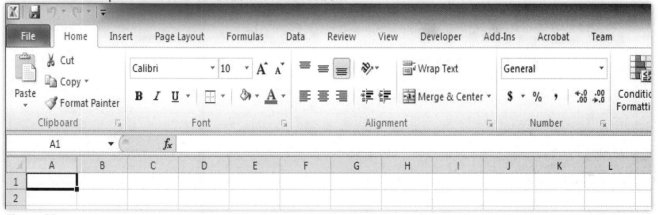

Figure 66

- It may not seem like that much, but the big difference is that the toolbars you see beneath the Excel 2003 File menus (File, Edit, View, etc.) didn't change no matter what Menu you selected (although you could add or remove Icons from the Toolbars). Instead the rest of your options were Dialog selections, like New, Open, Close, etc.

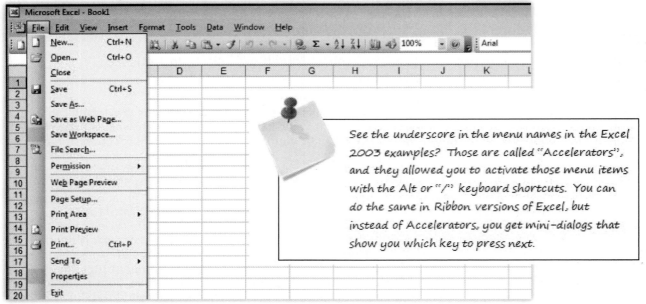

See the underscore in the menu names in the Excel 2003 examples? Those are called "Accelerators", and they allowed you to activate those menu items with the Alt or "/" keyboard shortcuts. You can do the same in Ribbon versions of Excel, but instead of Accelerators, you get mini-dialogs that show you which key to press next.

Figure 67

- With the Ribbon however, when you select a new Tab group from the Ribbon it exposes an entirely different set of graphical menu commands:

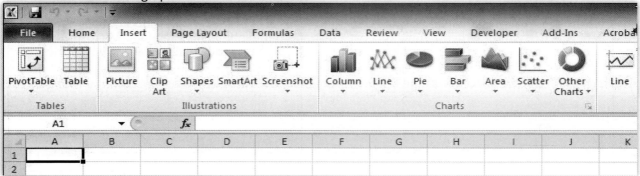

Figure 68

- This advancement in the graphical menu commands has made it a lot easier for new Excel users to get a grasp of where everything is located, while users who were comfortable with earlier versions had often worked with them for years and had just learned where things were. If you're serious about using Excel to help you with your business, then this will dramatically speed up your learning curve. .
- As we already discussed the features you'll find on the File Tab, we jump right into the Home Tab, which is the default Ribbon Tab anytime you open Excel (the following screenshot is from Excel 2010 – If you're in Excel 2007 it will be slightly different, but not drastically, you just won't see as many commands exposed):

Figure 69

- The Home Tab primarily deals with most of the things you'll do all the time when you're working in a worksheet, like formatting, inserting/deleting cells and some degree of editing. Here we'll go over each group and what it does. For this lesson you should work in Excel alongside the course material and use some of these menu commands so you can start to get comfortable with them yourself. And don't worry about messing anything up, we're not working on workbooks with any data in them yet, just sample data that you'll enter as we go along. There's no need to worry about saving any of this unless you want. So go ahead and open a new workbook, look through the Ribbon Tab items again, and when you're ready, goto the Home Tab and come back here.

Let's get started with the Home Tab!

Home Tab

This is the Ribbon Tab that's always going to be active when you open Excel. It holds the following Tab Groups that we'll go through one by one:

- *Clipboard* – This is where you control copying and pasting, and the myriad of things you can do with pasted data. Lesson 2 covered some of those with regards to showing your Pasting options on the worksheet, but this is where you get to try some of them on your own. In your blank workbook, just enter some sample data (it doesn't matter what it is).

Figure 70

As we're dealing with the Ribbon, which is largely mouse oriented, you're going to follow along with the mouse, but if you want to try some of the keyboard shortcuts you're already learned, then feel free. (Where appropriate you'll see more pointed out in StickyNotes like this along the way).

- Enter the following into any cell: =1+1 (hit enter when you're done to confirm the formula and move to the next cell)
- Now click the Copy button, select the destination range, either with the mouse or using the arrow keys to scroll to it (you can copy an entire range too, you're not limited to copying one cell at a time), and paste using the Paste button. If you just click on the Copy/Paste Icons, you will perform a simple Copy/Paste, but if you select the drop-down arrow beneath either you'll get expanded functionality (this holds true for any Ribbon Group Command that has a drop-down beneath it).

Terminology:

Edit Mode – When you're in a cell entering data then it's *really* the ActiveCell and it's in "Edit Mode". Nothing else can happen in Excel until you exit Edit mode by either confirming your entry with Tab/Enter, or hitting the ESC key, which will revert to what was in the cell originally and disregard any changes you were making.

Source/Destination Range – When you copy and paste, what you copy, whether it's a single cell or a range of cells it's called the Source range. The location where you paste the copied data is called the Destination range.

- When you paste you'll see the Paste Options dialog to the right of the cell, which was mentioned in Lesson 2), and at that point you can choose to invoke any of those operations (from left-to-right, then down – if you hover the mouse pointer over any of these commands a ToolTip will appear):

You can copy multiple non-contiguous cells*, but only if they're in the same row or column, and they will be pasted as a contiguous range (e.g. copy A1, C1, D1 & E1, now paste it to A2 and see what happens). If you copy the entire range you'll retain the gaps between the copied cells. *You can select multiple non-contiguous cells with Ctrl+Left-Click.

- *All* – Pastes formulas, cell formatting, font style, etc. This is the same as a straight Copy/Paste using either the Ribbon commands, or keyboard shortcuts.

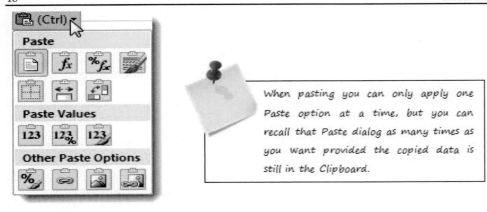

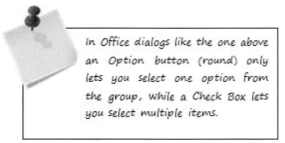

Figure 71

- **Formulas** – Will only paste the source range's formula, not any formatting
- **Values** – Will only paste the source range's Values – it will eliminate formulas.
  - ○ This trick comes in handy if you want to create a snapshot of a range and don't want any inputs to alter the formulas. It's also very good for distributing workbooks for a number of reasons: it can greatly reduce workbook size, no one can alter your data by using the formulas, and if you have complicated formulas then no one can delete them. Many workbooks have been compromised when someone sent it out only to get it back with formulas changed.
- **Formats** – Will only paste the source range's formats
- **Comments** – Will only paste the source range's Comments
- **Validation** – Will only paste any Data Validation associated with the source range (we'll discuss Data Validation in the lesson on Entering and Editing Data).
- **All using Source theme** – will paste the source range's contents and whatever theme was applied to the worksheet.
- **All Except Borders** – Will only paste the source range's contents
- **Column widths** – Will only paste the source range's column widths. This can be handy if you have column sizes that are greater/less than the default column sizes and don't want to have to manually adjust them to match the source.
- **Formulas and number formats** – Handy for pasting formatted data to unformatted cells
- **Values and number formats** – Same, but will eliminate any formulas that were in the source range
- **All merging conditional formats** – Conditional Formatting is a way of evaluating a range for certain criteria and formatting the range based on the criteria. We'll discuss Conditional Formatting later in this lesson (and in more detail in the Formatting lesson), but this option evaluates a range of cells (it won't be an option on a single cell source or if no Conditional Formatting has been applied) and will copy any conditional formats applied within the source range. Where any Conditional Formats are the same, they'll be pasted.
- What we didn't discuss on the Clipboards's Paste menu was the Paste Special dialog, which offers you some additional tools not found on the worksheet paste dialog. To get to this dialog you have to copy a range first, then use the Paste drop-down from the Clipboard group and select the Paste Special option from the bottom, and you'll get the following dialog box (you can also call the Paste Special dialog with ALT+E+S):

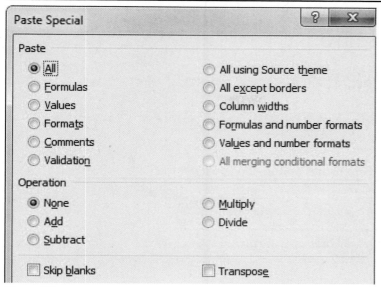

Figure 72

- Here you see a list of three groups, and if you compare this dialog to the one from the Ribbon side by side you'll see that much of the functionality is shared between the two (the Paste Special dialog above is actually from Excel 2003). While the Ribbon gives you the ability to paste a picture or a linked picture, which the Paste Special dialog doesn't, the Excel 2003 dialog gives you a few things that the other doesn't (this is one of those things that Microsoft will fix in later versions, and you'll probably see the dialog above go away or be changed to match the new look at that time):

  ○ Operation

    ▪ This is a very neat set of options that lets you copy a source value and mathematically apply that value to a range with one of the four major operators (Add, Subtract, Multiply & Divide). Let's say you have a range of product prices and you need to apply a 3% increase across the board. Enter a set of sample values in a few cells then put 1.03 in a cell outside of that range. Now select the range of prices and Paste, Paste Special, Multiply and see what happens.

Prices	Change by
$66.95	1.03
$44.59	
$88.91	
$66.01	
$64.59	
$53.31	
$42.52	

You can apply number formats with keystroke shortcuts:

Ctrl+Shift+1 – General Number format

Ctrl+Shift+4 – Currency format

Ctrl+Shift+5 – Percent format

Prices	Change by
68.96103	1.03
45.92935	
91.57606	
67.99335	
66.52403	
54.91318	
43.79691	

Figure 73

  ○ Unfortunately, as you might expect the destination receives the source range's number format. But, in this case, even though you were multiplying a percentage increase, if you didn't want to reformat the destination after pasting you could simply format the destination as currency beforehand and that format would apply.

  ○ Skip Blanks

    ▪ This is another cool feature that even a lot of seasoned Excel pros don't know about. It lets you paste a range of data that has blank cells in it onto a range of data that doesn't, and only the source range's data will be copied - any blank cells in the source range will be ignored and the destination data won't be disturbed. So let's say you have a range of cells like this:

	A	B	C	D	E	F	
1	January	PY	February	PY	March	PY	
2	$122.67	$286.31	$830.73	$743.27	$823.67	$86.88	
3							
4	Variance	($163.64)		$87.47		$736.79	
5							
6							

Figure 74

- And you realize that instead of having your monthly variances at the bottom, you want to have them where last year's figures are. You can select the variance range and copy it (this example is included in the Lesson 3 workbook):

▲	A	B	C	D	E	F
1	January	PY	February	PY	March	PY
2	$122.67	$286.31	$830.73	$743.27	$823.67	$86.88
3						
4	Variance	($163.64)		$87.47		$736.79
5						

Figure 75

- Then paste special and select the Skip Blanks option and you'll get this:

▲	A	B	C	D	E	F	G
1	January	PY	February	PY	March	PY	
2	$122.67	($163.64)	$830.73	$87.47	$823.67	$736.79	
3							(Ct
4	Variance	($163.64)		$87.47		$736.79	
5							

Figure 76

- **_Transpose_** – This is another cool feature that lets you physically flip your data's orientation. Suppose you have a series of data that runs in rows/columns left-to-right like the example above, but for a certain application it really needs to go the other way. You could come up with all kinds of complicated formulas to transpose the data, or you could use this feature. Just copy the range from the previous example (A1:F2), find an unused range somewhere you want to put it and goto Paste,Paste Special,Transpose (*Alt+E+S+V+E*) and you'll get this (and all of your formatting will be copied over to the destination too).

8		
9	January	$122.67
10	PY	$286.31
11	February	$830.73
12	PY	$743.27
13	March	$823.67
14	PY	$86.88
15		

- **_Paste Link_** – Finally, you can paste links to the range you copy. So let's say you want to have a copy of those figures in A1:F2 on another sheet, but you don't want to have to update both sets of records. The PasteLinks option will paste the source data as formulas that reference it. Anytime you change the source data, the pasted links will automatically update. Note that when you paste links you'll lose your formatting, so it's a good exercise for working with the different pasting options. While your paste range is still active, click the paste options button and select the Keep Source Formatting option. Viola!

- **_Clipboard Dialog Launcher_**
  - Next click the Clipboard Dialog Launcher in the lower right hand corner of the Clipboard Group. A new pane will immediately open on the left of the worksheet window:

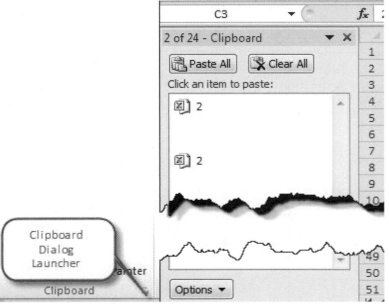

Figure 77

- The Clipboard will store the 24 most recent items you've copied, and you can come back to any of them and paste them anywhere in your workbook as long as the item(s) is in the Clipboard (even pictures, graphics, etc.). And this isn't just the Excel Clipboard, but the Windows Clipboard, so you'll see what you copy from other applications appear in this list too.

- The first options you see are Paste All and Clear All.
  - ○ Paste All will paste everything in the Clipboard
  - ○ Clear All option will delete everything in the Clipboard
- In order to paste something from the Clipboard, all you have to do is have the cursor on the cell in which you want to paste the item in question, then click on the item in the list, and select Paste or Delete from the drop-down that appears on the right (remember, if you paste an object it won't paste into the cell, but on top of it):

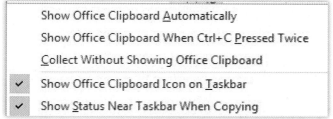

  - ○ Note: choosing Delete won't delete the item from the worksheet, just the Clipboard.
- At the bottom of the Clipboard window you have some options regarding how you can control the Clipboard's behavior:

	Show Office Clipboard Automatically
	Show Office Clipboard When Ctrl+C Pressed Twice
	Collect Without Showing Office Clipboard
✓	Show Office Clipboard Icon on Taskbar
✓	Show Status Near Taskbar When Copying

Figure 78

- ***Font***
  - ○ This is where you control the Font type/style, Size, Effects (Bold, Italicize, Underline), Font/Cell Color, and Gridlines. It's all relatively straightforward, so go ahead and apply some different formatting to a range of cells.

Figure 79

  - ○ ***Toggle Font Size*** - Of note are the two A's to the right of the Font Size box. Both are clickable; the first will increase the selected range's font size, while the second will decrease it.
  - ○ ***Borders*** - The icon that looks like an underlined grid lets you control the border pattern your range will have. Border options are pretty simple to grasp, but the Draw Borders tools aren't quite so. There aren't a whole lot of practical applications for them, but some people do find them handy, especially if you need to apply borders to several non-contiguous ranges. The Line Color/Style options are very handy if you don't like the default black gridline colors or you want a different style of line. Just note with colored gridlines that they may be hard to see on some monitors, so you're generally better off with a darker color than a light one.
    - ▪ ***More Borders*** – Here you actually have the chance to completely define your border style(s) if none of the above suit you. That option will launch the Format Cells dialog, which we'll discuss next.

The Font Group's Dialog Launcher will load an Excel 2003 dialog with the following Tab groups (when selected from the Font Dialog Launcher Font will be the active Tab):

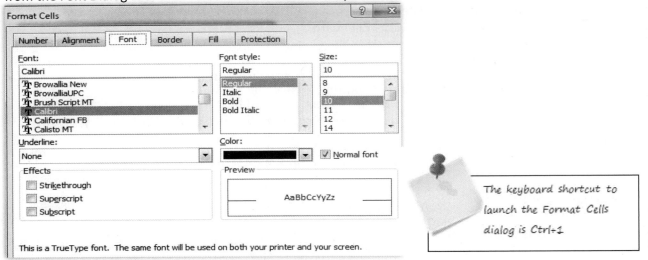

Figure 80

- **Number Format**
  - ○ **General** – The default number format is General, meaning that any numerical value you enter in a cell will appear just as you entered it.
  - ○ **Number** – A number with comma separator(s) and a variable number of decimal places you select.
  - ○ **Currency** – A number with a Currency symbol, comma separator(s) and variable number of decimal places you select. You can also change the format for negative values – ($123.45)/($123.45). You also have your choice of currency symbol.

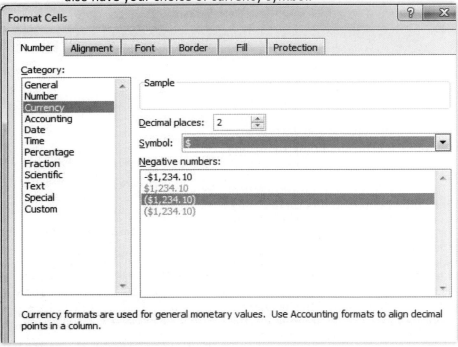

Figure 81

  - ○ **Accounting** – Same as Currency, but with no color change for negative values and the Currency symbol is automatically placed on the left side of the cell. Unless you're an accountant you'll probably find this to be a pretty strange way to display currency.
  - ○ **Date** – Allows you to apply different date formats to a range. By default, Excel will recognize any values entered in mm/dd/yy format as a date. 1/1/11 would automatically be converted to 1/1/2011. There are multiple date formats you can select:

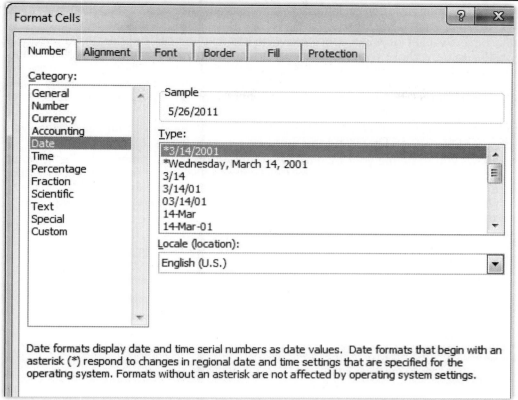

Figure 82

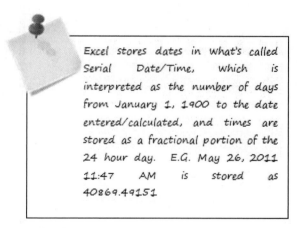

Excel stores dates in what's called Serial Date/Time, which is interpreted as the number of days from January 1, 1900 to the date entered/calculated, and times are stored as a fractional portion of the 24 hour day. E.G. May 26, 2011 11:47 AM is stored as 40869.49151

- ○ **Time** – Time entries can be formatted many ways as well, including Military 24-Hour time. The standard time display is HH:MM AM/PM.
- ○ **Percentage** – Applies a % format to a range with a variable number of decimal places. With percentage format it's generally advisable to format the range before entering the decimal values (unless they're the result of a calculation), because Excel will convert existing values. E.G. 125 would be converted to 12500% if it wasn't formatted first. But if you format the range first, then entering 125 would result in 125%.
- ○ **Fraction** – Allows you to convert values into their fractional equivalents. If you deal with fractions a lot you'll find that this format isn't the most dependable, and won't always give you the desired results.

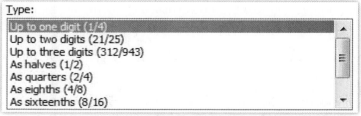

Figure 83

- ○ **Scientific** – Applies Scientific Notation to values. This is generally reserved for very large numbers. E.G. 123456789 is represented as 1.23E+08
- ○ **Text** – This will convert values into text. Once converted to text you can't perform mathematical calculations on the value without converting it back to a number. This can be useful for things like part numbers that have leading zeros, because interpreted numerically Excel will strip the leading zeros. Since you won't likely be performing mathematical calculations on part numbers it's generally not an issue. Some data imports can convert values to text and leave you puzzled as to why you can't work with them as numbers, so you should be aware of it.
- ○ **Special** – Allows you to apply Zip Code, Phone and Social Security formats to numeric values you enter. E.G. enter 2125551212 and it will automatically be represented as (212) 555-1212.
- ○ **Custom** – This allows you to define your own custom number formats if the ones available won't cut it. You can learn a lot about a number format by applying a standard format to a cell with a value it in, then select the Custom option and Excel will show you the number format that was applied (along with all the technical stuff you'll need to copy it). From there you can select one of the number formats from the Custom list, or build your own.

> *When entering numeric values that need to be formatted ($, %, Dates, Social Security #'s, Phone Numbers, etc.) you don't need to add any of the formatting characters as you type. E.G. if you format a cell as Currency with 2 decimal places, when you type 123.45 Excel will automatically display it as $123.45. Just knowing you can do that will save you a lot of time vs. trying to add those characters in by hand!*

- • **Alignment** – This controls the way your data is represented in a range.

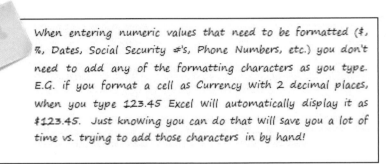

Figure 84

- ○ **Text Alignment**
  - ▪ Gives you control over Horizontal and Vertical alignment, and allows you to set an Indent if you want.
- ○ **Text Control**
  - ▪ **Wrap Text** – this allows text to continue to a new line within a cell if the text gets to the right side of the cell.
  - ▪ **Shrink to fit** – Instead of wrapping text to a new line, this will shrink the text to fit the cell. Note that it will only work for alphanumeric entries, not value entries.

- **Merge Cells** – NEVER merge cells. It can cause all kinds of problems, especially with sorting. It's here to ostensibly help you format better, but in almost any practical application it's absolutely useless. Imagine wanting to merge a report header across multiple months – most people would merge cells. An alternative is to put your header text in the first column of the report, then select the cell and all the columns in that row for the report. Then in the Alignment option goto Horizontal, Center Across Selection. Excel won't merge the cells, it just looks like it did. And it's not going to cause any problems down the road.

- **Orientation**
  - ○ This allows you to change the angle at which your data is displayed in a range. By default, Excel will display data horizontally, or at 0 degrees. You can change that up to 90 degrees up or down by dragging the control arm in the Orientation window and dragging it in either direction, or use the Spinner control at the bottom of the window (you can also enter your own value manually there).

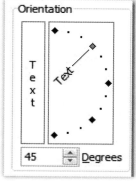

Figure 85

  - ○ Be aware that any gridlines you might have applied will follow the same angle as your text; if you're at 0 or either 90 degree intersection (Up/Down) you're fine, but if you're in between, like in the 45 degree example above you'll get some strange behavior:

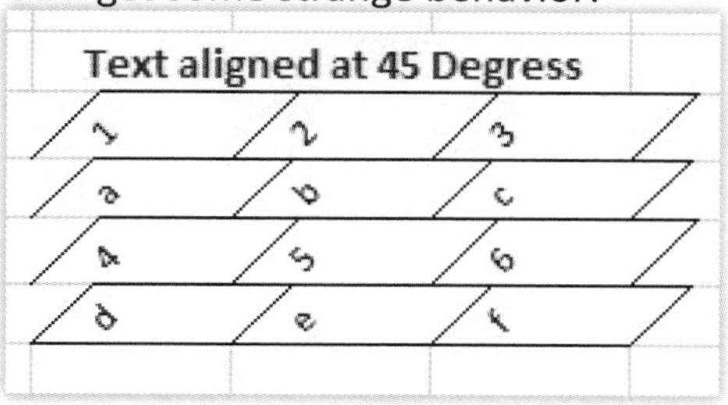

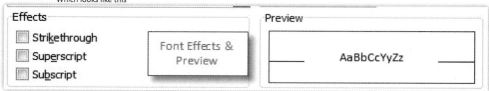

Figure 86

- **Font** – The Font tab on the Format Cells dialog is essentially an expanded version of what you can get on the Ribbon group, with the exception of being able to add the following effects to your range – There's also a live preview window so you can see what your proposed changes will look like:
  - ○ Strikethrough – ~~Which looks like this.~~
  - ○ Superscript – ^Which looks like this^
  - ○ Subscript – ₍Which looks like this₎

Effects
☐ Strikethrough
☐ Superscript
☐ Subscript

Font Effects & Preview

Preview

AaBbCcYyZz

Figure 87

- **Border** – This exposes the same functionality as the Border control on the Ribbon. Generally there's not really any reason to use this dialog, unless you've launched the Format Cells dialog by using the Ctrl+1 shortcut.

- **Fill** – The Fill tab on the other hand can be very handy because it exposes functionality that's not included in the Ribbon, namely Fill Effects and Patterns.
  - ○ **Fill Effects** – These are handy tools that allow you to apply gradient shading to a range. You can get very creative with these, and they can be great tools for formatting things like Dashboards or areas to which you want to attract special attention. Just remember that colors should be used sparingly and not too loud. Bright pink and yellow may look great to you, but probably not to someone else

(like a banker or investor). Excel 2007+ gives you the ability to access a lot more colors than before, but that doesn't mean you need to use them all. The following example shows you fill effects applied to a range of cells, then to a range that's been merged in a Dashboard type of example.

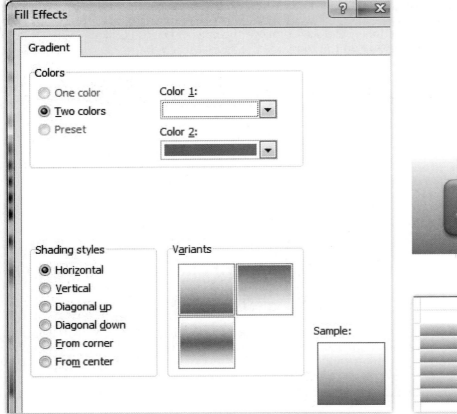

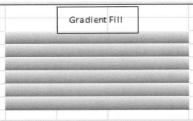

Figure 88

Here is one exception for using Merged Cells:

If you want to create a background on which you'll place objects, like buttons or smart art (like a Dashboard), you can do so in this case. But in this situation you're not using the range for data input, so if it's for display only, then Merged Cells are OK.

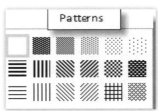

- ◦ **Patterns** – These are very simple cross-hatched and dotted designs you can apply to a range. Note that they can make it difficult to read the underlying data and some printers that can't achieve the detail necessary to render them will simply render them as black.
- • **Protection** – The ability to protect Excel worksheets is one of its coolest features. You can protect a worksheet so that no one can make any changes, or you can unprotect certain cells so that users can only enter information where you want. You can also hide formulas from view so that only their resulting values are visible. By default all cells on a worksheet are Locked. In order to allow entry, you need to select those cells, then in the Protection tab uncheck Locked (you would check Hidden if you don't want your formulas to be visible, but you're generally not going to mix the two, as you normally won't have formulas in data entry cells). After doing this, when you protect the worksheet (see the Review Tab on the Ribbon), only those cells will accept entries.

CAVEAT: Protected workbooks and worksheets are only as good as your recipients. Excel is not a secure environment, nor has it ever been marketed as one. If you need to distribute sensitive material and there's the slightest chance that someone could alter or otherwise use your data in a manner inconsistent with your expectations, then save it as a PDF. Think of Excel protection like a lock on a door; all it does is keep honest people honest. Excel security is good enough for 99.9% of the population, but just be aware that if someone wants to break your passwords and access your information they can…

When you protect a Worksheet with unlocked cells Excel introduces a natural Tab order between the unlocked cells that goes from left-to-right, then down. You can design data entry forms with this in mind to make it easier for you and users to quickly enter data without having to select or navigate to the data entry cells.

- **Alignment**
  - ◦ The Alignment Ribbon group is where you control how your text will behave in a range. This is probably as close as you'll get to trying to have Excel act like Word. Just be aware that it's limited in what it can do (just as Word is limited in the calculations it can perform - But the two programs do work brilliantly with each other as we'll discuss in the Mail Merge lesson). Note that everything you see in this Ribbon group is also contained in the Format Cells dialog we just discussed. Again, Microsoft has given you multiple ways to expose certain command elements. In many cases, using CTRL+1 to launch the Format Cells dialog is a lot faster than using the mouse to get to the Ribbon commands, but it's all personal preference.

Figure 89

  - ◦ In the following example you'll see what might be a bit surprising with the way things are lined up, but it's completely natural: Excel will align text to the left of a cell and numbers to the right of a cell.

Figure 90

  - ◦ The alignment options here on the Ribbon are almost the same as are contained in the Format Cells dialog. On the top are your Vertical Alignment options (Top, Center, Bottom) and beneath that are the Horizontal options (Left, Center, Right), but to Justify text you'll need to open the Format Cells dialog and look in the Horizontal options there.
  - ◦ Next you have the Orientation options, and beneath that are the Decrease/Increase Indent controls.
  - ◦ To the right of those is the Wrap Text option and the Merge & Center, which you should avoid at all costs (hence it being marked out!)

A lot of people are tempted to use spaces before their text as a means of indenting. Use the Indent controls instead, because they don't add unwanted spaces to your data, it just appears that way. Adding spaces can cause problems later if you ever want to work with those values, because then you need to get rid of the spaces.

- **Number**
  - Most of your numeric formatting options are here, but if you want something not in the default list, then you can either click the More Number Formats selection at the bottom or use the dialog launcher, both of which will launch the Format Cells dialog. Note that in the Number drop-down Excel will preview what your data will look like (provided it is a number, if you're attempting to format a text range then all you see is text with no formatting).

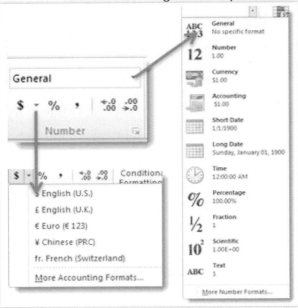

Figure 91

  - Both the Currency and Comma number format will give you two decimal places by default. If you want more or fewer decimal places you can use the decimal toggle buttons to the right. The Currency selection has an additional option that will let you change the currency symbol (Dollar, Pound, Euro, Yen & Franc). If you need more, there's a list of expanded options.

- **Styles**
  - **Styles** are where you can really put Excel to work in terms of making your work look good with minimal effort. This section will get you started with knowing where everything is, but the only way to really learn to apply the different options is with practice, so start seeing what you can do.

Figure 92

  - **Conditional Formatting** - This allows you to apply rules to cell values and graphically distinguish those cells that meet the criteria. Common uses are for dates that fall before or after a certain period or to highlight cells that are above/below a certain value. For instance you can format all cells where customer payments are over 30 days due.
    - There are five major Conditional Formatting components:
      - Highlight Cell Rules
      - Top/Bottom Rules
      - Data Bars
      - Color Scales
      - Icon Sets
    - Within those components, you have the ability to define formats based on:
      - Cell values (like High and Low ranges)
      - Only format cells that contain certain values
      - Top or Bottom ranked values
      - Values above or below average
      - Format only unique or duplicate values

- Use a formula to determine what cells to format – This is probably the most powerful because you can write your own complex rules, but by no means are any of the other choices lightweights!
- Data Bars, Color Scales and Icon Sets are all new additions to Excel with the introduction of the Ribbon and they can really help you tell a story with your data quickly. They can be especially good tools for people who aren't graphically oriented. If you look in the Lesson 3 workbook you'll see examples of them.

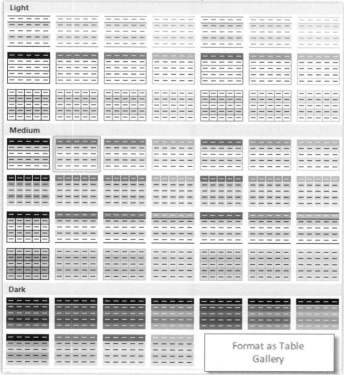

Figure 93

Format as Table – This is another cool feature that lets you quickly apply formatting to your data, provided it has as contiguous structure. Select any cell in your data area then select the table format that you want to apply from the table gallery. As soon as you select a table style you'll get a dialog asking you if it got the range right and if you have headers for your data:

Figure 94

- Make sure that if you do have headers for your table (always recommended) that you select this option or else you may get unintended consequences, like funky table formatting where your headers get lost in the shuffle.

- ○ Once you select the Gallery Style you want, then your unformatted data will look like this:

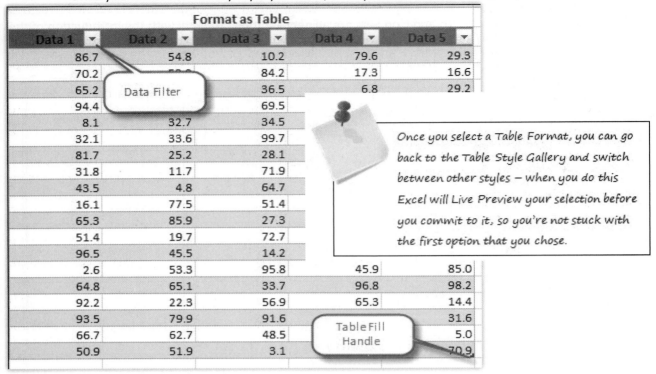

Figure 95

- ○ Note the callouts in the image that point to Data Filter drop-downs in your header row, and the Table Fill Handle. Both of these are very handy tools that can speed up your work.
- ○ Data Filter allows you to quickly filter your data table by the criteria you select. Clicking on any of the drop-downs in any header column will expose the Data Filter options:

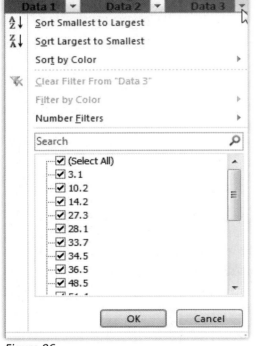
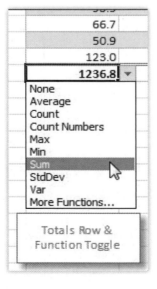

Figure 96

- ▪ Certain types of data will expose certain Filtering options, for instance a date column filter will let you filter by week, month, quarter, etc., while a numeric filter will let you select values equal to, greater than or less than a certain value, top ten values, averages, etc. Filtering is a hugely powerful tool for displaying just the snapshot data that you want to see at any given moment. And Excel doesn't alter your base data, it just hides what you don't want to see until you want to see it again.

- The Table Fill handle lets you drag the format of the table down as far as you want it. Although once you've created a data table, all you need to do to expand it is add data to the bottom. Excel will automatically add it to the table and format it for you.

- Now if you go to the bottom of the table and select any function you want from the AutoSum control from the editing toolbar, the data table will automatically add a Totals row and the function you chose will apply to the entire column. When you do that you'll see that you can quickly toggle between functions.

  ○ **Styles Gallery** – The final element of the Styles Group is the Styles Gallery. With this tool you can select a range of data, let's say a header row, or individual input cells, and quickly apply a format to give users certain visual clues as to what they should do. This can be a very useful tool for your users, but there are a lot of options here, and it's very easy to add so many to a worksheet that it's more confusing than helpful, so make sure to use them judiciously.

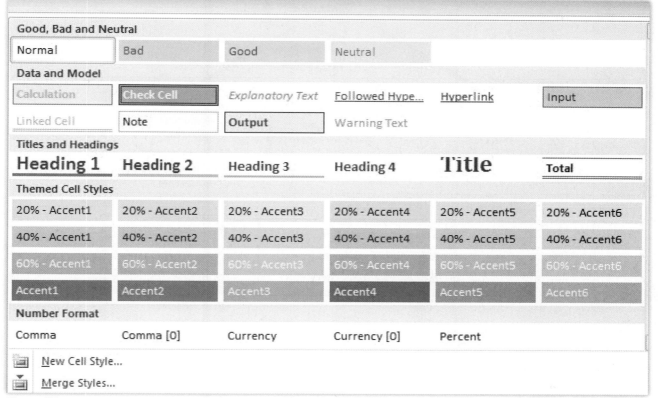

Figure 97

- **Visual Clues – Who Really Cares?**

  ○ The easier you make it for people to interact with your workbooks and worksheets, the least resistance you'll find when getting them to use them. If you make it difficult for people to give you the information you need then they'll make getting it difficult as well. You can easily overwhelm users with too many styles, but as you attempt to direct users to enter data in certain areas, it can be a very important feature to providing seamless user interaction. Balance is key, but it's up to you to determine what's right for you. Seamless user interaction also goes back to the comments on Worksheet Protection and how you can unlock certain cells for data entry and direct users to those cells/ranges. You can make that interaction easier with styles, but the folks at Microsoft understand that they can't make everyone happy, so they give you the chance to define your own way of doing things wherever possible which you'll find by clicking on the New Cell Style button. From there you can define your own style(s).

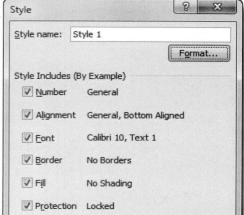

Figure 98

- **Cells** - The options on the Cells group are as simple as they come. Insert/Delete Rows & Columns and apply formatting elements like height, width. There are also some more advanced options that deal with the not just Rows & Columns, but the worksheet itself.
  - ○ **Visibility** – You can hide Rows & Columns in any worksheet. If you protect the worksheet prior to distribution, your users can't unhide those Rows & Columns. Let's say you need to send out some information from an employee table, but you don't want anyone to see certain details, like Social Security Numbers. Simply hide that column and protect the sheet. You also have the option to hide the worksheet itself, which can come in very handy if you have sensitive information on some sheets and you don't want people to see it.

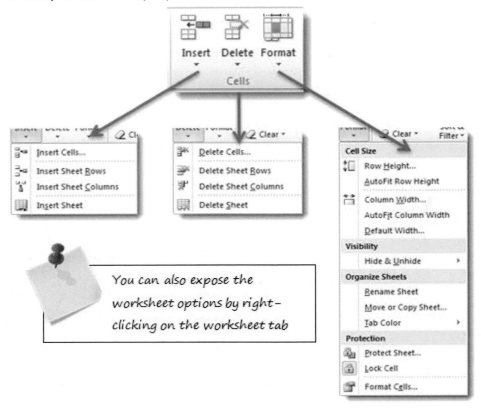

Figure 99

  - ○ **Organize Sheets**
    - ▪ **Rename Sheet** - You can rename the sheet through this control, and you can also double-click on the worksheet tab itself. Note that you can't have invalid characters (: \ / ? * [ ])in a sheet name and it can't exceed 31 characters.
    - ▪ **Move or Copy Sheet** – this is a neat feature that lets you perform some tasks that you would otherwise need to do manually.

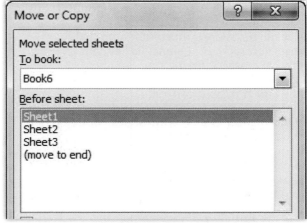

Figure 100

- In the "To book" section you can choose any open workbook, or even have Excel create a new workbook for you. From there your option is to move the sheet to another location in the current workbook or to another one. You can also create a copy of an existing worksheet. This can be particularly handy if you don't want someone to see your entire workbook and you don't want to go hide all of your worksheets. Let's say you have a workbook with all of your prices by supplier, and each supplier has its own worksheet. You can copy one supplier's worksheet to a new workbook, send it to them for updates, and then replace it when they send it back.

- ○ **Tab Color** – After years of begging for this feature, which has been a part of Lotus 1-2-3 for years, Microsoft finally gives you the ability to color your worksheet tabs. This is a great feature because it helps quickly group/identify which worksheets do what. For instance, data entry can be yellow, reports - green, sensitive data - red, summaries – blue, and so on. Again, you can go overboard with your color selections, so don't try to do too much lest you actually end up confusing your users.

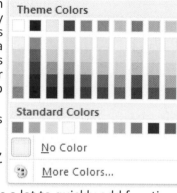

- ○ **Protection** – We discussed worksheet protection, and this just gives you another location to invoke it.

- ○ **Format Cells** – This brings up the Format Cells dialog, so this is again, just another place where Microsoft gives you access to a particular tool in multiple places.

- • **Editing-** This is the last stop on the Home Tab, and is where you'll come a lot to quickly add functions without writing them yourself, add or remove data to/in ranges with just a few clicks, Sort & Filter your data and Find and/or Replace hard to spot data.

- ○ **AutoSum** – If you're not all that comfortable with Excel's functions, then this can do a lot of work for you. All you need to do is go directly beneath a column of data to the first empty row beneath the data and click the AutoSum tool. You'll immediately be presented with a list of common functions:

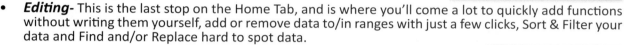

  - ▪ Sum – Returns the Sum of the values in the range
  - ▪ Average – Returns the Average of the values in the range
  - ▪ Count Numbers - Returns the Count of the values in the range
  - ▪ Max – Returns the Highest value in the range
  - ▪ Min – Returns the Lowest value in the range
  - ▪ The More Functions option will launch the Insert Function dialog, which we'll discuss in more detail in the Function lesson.

- ○ **Fill** – This is an interesting feature, and it's an extension of what you can do with the AutoFill Handle. If you're comfortable with the AutoFill handle and what it can do, there is probably only one compelling reason to use this command, and that is you can tell it to fill a number of rows or columns you choose, instead of dragging the handle all the way yourself (so if you don't want to drag down/

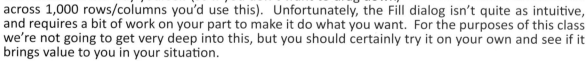

across 1,000 rows/columns you'd use this). Unfortunately, the Fill dialog isn't quite as intuitive, and requires a bit of work on your part to make it do what you want. For the purposes of this class we're not going to get very deep into this, but you should certainly try it on your own and see if it brings value to you in your situation.

- ○ As you already learned, the AutoFill command will allow you to input the beginning of a series and Excel will do its best to complete the series for you. Let's say you wanted a list of row numbers, you could type 1 & 2 in adjacent cells, select them both and then drag the AutoFill handle down and Excel would complete 1, 2, 3, 4, 5, for as long as you drag it. You can create an even numbered list by entering 2 & 4, then filling, while odd would simply be 1 & 3. You can do the same with Dates, Months, etc. Excel will try to recognize the pattern and complete it for you. This can be a huge timesaver when it comes to setting up your worksheets.

○ With the Fill command you don't enter your initial data in one cell then the increment you want in the next cell (e.g. 1 & 2), you simply enter your starting value in any cell, then select the Fill option, where you have several options:

Figure 101

○ Let's say you want to start with 1 and fill it down, but increment by 0.5 for each subsequent row. Enter 1 in A1 and reselect A1, then invoke the Fill command and select Series:

▪ The default options will be Rows (so change that to Columns to go down), and Linear, which simply adds the Step Value you input to the next entry down/across). Then in the Step value enter .05, and in Stop value enter the maximum number to which you want extend this iteration. Hit OK and you'll see something like this:

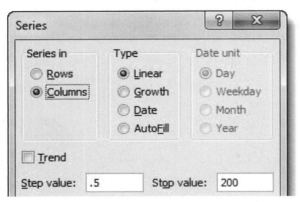

Figure 102

○ That's a lot easier than trying to do it with the AutoFill handle, especially if you're looking at hundreds even thousands of rows. And you can do the same thing across columns instead of rows.

○ Your other options are:

▪ Growth – This will build your list by multiplying each subsequent value by whatever you put in the step box.

▪ Date – This allows you to increment dates and when you select it you'll see the Date Unit options become enabled.

▪ AutoFill – This extends the same AutoFIll behavior as dragging the fill handle.

▪ Justify – This allows you to work with text without having to Merge Cells or Wrap Text. It's invaluable for maintaining data integrity if you do happen to have text strings in a document.

- If you want to use Excel as a text editor, which isn't recommended, you do have some options with arranging text the way that you need it. Let's say you have a long line of text that you've input to be at the bottom of a form, but you want it all to wrap within the confines of your form's width.

Figure 103

- You could try to select the right number of cells that the text might fit into and then Word Wrap/Merge Cells and experiment with it a bit. Or you could use the Fill, Justify command to do it for you. Just select the cell holding your text, drag it down to the end/side of your form, then select Fill, Justify:

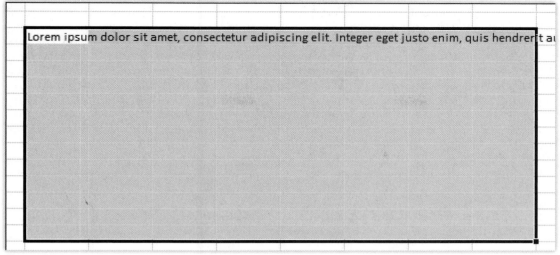

Figure 104

- And you'll end up with this:

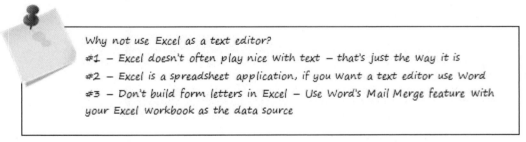

Figure 105

- Note that Excel automatically slices your text string into smaller chunks that fit the range you selected. As you look at it, yes, it has been physically separated, but don't worry, Excel can put it back the way it was too. To revert back to your original text string, just select the entire range of justified text then extend it across as many columns as it will take to put it back. From there select Fill, Justify and Excel will reverse it for you.

> Why not use Excel as a text editor?
>
> #1 – Excel doesn't often play nice with text – that's just the way it is
>
> #2 – Excel is a spreadsheet application, if you want a text editor use Word
>
> #3 – Don't build form letters in Excel – Use Word's Mail Merge feature with your Excel Workbook as the data source

○ **Sort & Filter** - Sorting is something you'll probably do quite a bit of if you have data that you want to rearrange. To quickly sort data, just put the cursor in any cell in any dataset (the key is to put the cursor in the column that you want to sort first), then select the Soft & Filter option. Excel will automatically select the sorting range for you based on where the cursor is at the time. If you want to sort by multiple criteria, then you need to select the Custom Sort option, which will launch a new dialog:

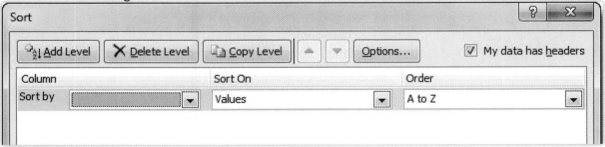

Figure 106

▪ With earlier versions of Excel you only had 3 Sort by options, now you have up to 64! Although it's not likely you'll ever need that many. There is a Sorting & Filtering worksheet in your Lesson 3 companion workbook that you can work on to see all of your sort options.

> **WARNING: One of the best ways to completely screw up your data when sorting is to have Column gaps in it. If you invoke the AutoSort command, then please make sure that any data you want to sort is in contiguous ranges and doesn't have any empty columns between vital data. E.G. if you put an empty column in between your data to give it a visual spacer (which is very common when people want to separate right justified numbers from left justified text), Excel won't recognize the range past the blank column UNLESS you have manually selected the entire range (and even then you can have problems). The result will be that the portion of your data where the cursor was when you invoked the sort will be fine. BUT, the range that was outside of the range because of that Column separation will no longer be associated with the data that was sorted! If you find yourself in this position then the first thing to do is UNDO (Ctrl+Z)! If you're too late to catch that, then close the workbook without saving it! You might lose some work, but at least your customer data won't be completely screwed up.**

- Here's an example of some customer data with an empty column (D) as a spacer:

	A	B	C	D	E	F
1	Customer Name	Customer #	Order #		Item	Ivoice Amount
2	Bob Smith	1234	456		Fetzer valve	$200.00
3	Tom Jones	35546	A123		Sprocket	$125.00
4	Larry Thompson	325	B768		Manual	$50.00
5						

Figure 107

- Here's what happens if you choose to auto sort from the Ribbon with the cursor in cell A1 and not select the entire range:

	A	B	C	D	E	F
1	Customer Name	Customer #	Order #		Item	Ivoice Amount
2	Bob Smith	1234	456		Fetzer valve	$200.00
3	Larry Thompson	325	B768		Sprocket	$125.00
4	Tom Jones	35546	A123		Manual	$50.00

Figure 108

- Uh ohh, Excel just did exactly what you told it to do, which was to sort the contiguous range. But look what happened to the items and Invoice amounts! They didn't change in relation to their rightful orders...Unfortunately, it's not uncommon at all to lose an entire data set because of something like this.

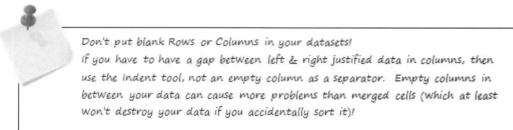

Don't put blank Rows or Columns in your datasets!
If you have to have a gap between left & right justified data in columns, then use the Indent tool, not an empty column as a separator. Empty columns in between your data can cause more problems than merged cells (which at least won't destroy your data if you accidentally sort it)!

- Now here's an example of the same dataset sorted, but with the entire range manually selected before invoking the sort:

	A	B	C	D	E	F
1	Customer Name	Customer #	Order #		Item	Ivoice Amount
2	Bob Smith	1234	456		Fetzer valve	$200.00
3	Larry Thompson	325	B768		Manual	$50.00
4	Tom Jones	35546	A123		Sprocket	$125.00
5						

Figure 109

- The rule of thumb here is to let Excel perform relatively simple sorting for you. If you need to go beyond that then you need to go through some manual steps, but fortunately, they're there for you.
- In the Sort dialog you have Add/Delete/Copy Level options, which let you add or delete criteria, and copy one level to repeat, as well as an Options selection. The most important menu item here is the "My data has headers" check box. In most cases your data will have headers (as in our previous customer example), so you'll generally want to have this selected. If you don't, then

Excel will sort your header row along with all of your data. If that happens you'll know about it immediately, because your header will disappear to some place in your data.

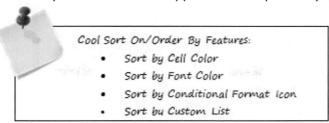

Cool Sort On/Order By Features:
- Sort by Cell Color
- Sort by Font Color
- Sort by Conditional Format Icon
- Sort by Custom List

- ○ **Find & Select** – This Ribbon group exposes a lot of functionality that can come in very handy.
  - ▪ **Find** – This does just what it sounds like, it lets you find items in a worksheet or an entire workbook (text or values), formulas and in comments. You can even tell it to find certain applied formats. Simply enter your search criteria and tell Excel how you want to search for it. When you first call the Find dialog you'll see a short version, and an expanded version that you expose by clicking the Options button:

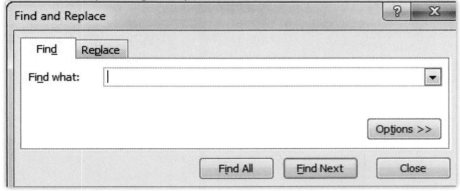

Figure 110

  - ▪ Something to note is that the simple Search doesn't always return the results you expect, so if that happens, expand the Options dialog and narrow your search criteria:

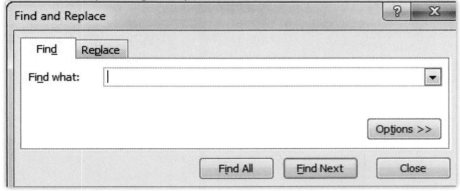

Figure 111

  - ▪ **Search Criteria**
    - Within – Sheet or entire workbook
    - Search – By Rows or By Columns
    - Look in – Formulas, Values or Comments
    - Match case – Allows you to specify an Upper or Lower case search
    - Match entire cell contents – Only use this one if you know exactly what you're looking for, like a product or employee name.
  - ▪ **Method**
  - ▪ Find All – Finds all matching instances of your search criteria
  - ▪ Find Next – Finds the first instance of your search criteria. Each successive button press will move on to the next match.

○ ***Replace*** – The Replace dialog is contained in the Find dialog and follows the same constraints as Find, but it allows you to not only find something, but replace it with something else. This is incredibly useful for making mass changes to a worksheet or workbook, and not have to do it manually. It's especially powerful for making changes to a lot of formulas too, just note that it will replace whatever you tell it to, so you can inadvertently reduce your formulas to garbage if you're not careful. Replacing "E" with "A" in this formula (=Sheet1!E1) without selecting the Match Case option will result in =ShAAt1!A1, which won't be exactly what you were after (Excel will also pop up an irritating dialog asking you to locate the workbook where "ShAAt1" is located – you'll learn this lesson when you change 500 formulas at once and get the criteria wrong). When replacing formula elements it's best to be as specific as possible. In this case you could have used Find: "!A", Replace with: "!E", which would resolve the problem. As you start getting into more functions later in the course, you'll be able to quickly identify which elements you can use in your Find/Replace criteria.

○ ***Go To*** – This gives you the option to go to a specific cell or range, and will also give you the option to select the Go To Special Option. If you need to do this it's generally much faster to just use the F5 shortcut key to invoke this dialog, or even just enter the cell address in the name box (left of the Formula bar).

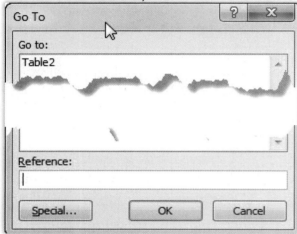

Figure 112

○ ***Go To Special*** – The Special dialog gives you a lot of features that you probably won't use at a beginner or intermediate level, but it does a lot of things of which you should be aware. Here you have the ability to select cells with all kinds of different characteristics, such as all the formulas or blank cells in a region. Think of the Special dialog as an auditing tool that lets you identify areas that you would otherwise need to find manually.

Figure 113

- ◦ *Criteria*
  - • *Comments* – Finds all cells with cell comments (Comments are entered through the Review Ribbon group cell, and are addendum you can make to cells that are independent of the cell's value – think of them like sticky notes for users).
  - • *Constants* – Any non-calculated cells, like text entries (e.g. employee names, city, state, etc.)
  - • *Formulas* – Any calculated cells
  - • *Blanks* – Any blank cells in a region. This one can be really helpful for identifying or filling in missing data.
  - • *Current Region* – Selects the current region of contiguous cells. This is helpful if you have disparate datasets on the same worksheet and need to isolate them for sorting, charting, etc. You can accomplish this with the shortcut Ctrl+* (from the 10-Key pad), or CTRL+SHIFT+* from the regular keypad.

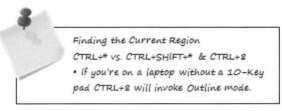

Finding the Current Region
CTRL+* vs. CTRL+SHIFT+* & CTRL+8
• If you're on a laptop without a 10-Key pad CTRL+8 will invoke Outline mode.

  - • *Current Array* – We won't cover Arrays in this course, but they're a way of getting Excel to evaluate a large range and produce multiple results. If you're interested in Arrays you'll find lots of documentation on the Internet and in the Help File, but they can be very difficult to implement, and often inefficient with regards to calculation dynamics. Suffice it to say, it's not likely that you'll ever need to get this far.
  - • *Objects* – This selects any objects you may have on a worksheet (buttons, graphics, charts, etc.)
  - • *Row Differences* – This will highlight any rows that are different from the active cell. It's essentially invoking the error checker in case you turned it off. Note that you need to select a range or entire row to be able to do this; if all you have selected is the active cell, then it won't do anything.
  - • *Column Differences* – Same as the Row differences option, but selects column differences.
  - • *Precedents* – This finds any cells that lead to the active cell via formulas (any cells that the active cell references).
  - • *Dependents* – This finds any cells that are dependent on the active cell for calculations (any cells that reference the active cell).

A little thing called BLOAT – Why is my workbook so big?
• Excel workbooks can blow up in size if you apply formats or formulas to a large range even if you don't use them. Let's say you add a formula to A1:A1046000, but only use A1:A110 – Excel views the last cell with the formula (or format) as the last cell that had data input, not what you might actually be using at the moment. The problem with this is that you can delete the formulas/formats you're not using, but Excel will still remember that you had something there and can blow up your file size as a result. The only way to get rid of unused ranges is to actually delete the unused Rows & Columns. So only add formulas/formatting to the ranges you actually need!

  - • *Last Cell* – This finds the last cell in a worksheet that contains data. This one can be very useful if you have what should be a relatively small workbook that's blown up in size.
  - • *Visible Cells Only* –Why do I need to select Visible Cells Only? Well, Data Filter is great for segmenting data that you need to distribute to individual employees or customers, but you might find that once you apply a filter to get just the data you want shown, when you copy the data to a new workbook all of the data you filtered out is shown! What happened? Excel doesn't know you don't want the entire dataset, and it doesn't want you to forget it, so it copies all of it. Using the Visible cells only option will only copy the data you filtered. Do this once or twice and you'll have one of those "Ahh-haa!" moments.
  - • *Conditional Formats* – Selects all cells that have Conditional Formatting applied. Why is this important? Not really, but if you've applied some formats and forgotten about them, this will help you find them. This generally isn't a problem, since Conditional Formatting is very visual.

- *Data Validation* – This is similar to the Conditional Format option, but Data Validation cells can be harder to find than Conditional Formats, as Data Validation options don't appear until you actually activate a cell. Both of the above can be handy tools when you're preparing a workbook for distribution and want to make sure you have the user interface is perfect.
  - *Formulas* – This will identify all formulas on a worksheet. It's useful for if you want to distribute a workbook without formulas and check if you haven't gotten rid of all of them. It also gives you some useful functionality in that you can edit the first cell (F2), then Tab between all of the selected Formulas cells in case you need to edit them.
  - *Comments* – This will find any comments you might have entered. Again, why is this important? Probably, not really, but if you have a workbook with comments to aid users with data entry and now you're at the distribution stage you might want to know where there are in case you need to get rid of them.
  - The remaining menu items in the Find & Select group (Conditional Formatting, Constants, Data Validation, Select Objects and Selection Pane) will expose the same elements as the Go To Special dialog, but give you a more direct approach than the Go To Special dialog:

Unit Summary: Lesson 3 – The Ribbon In-Depth – The Home Tab

- In this lesson you learned about the in-depth ins and outs of the Home tab on the Excel Ribbon. Since it's where you'll generally spend the most time, it's probably the most important Ribbon element to learn.
- You walked through the Home tab's elements, and also saw how there are multiple ways to expose the elements with keyboard shortcuts and Dialog Launchers.

Review Questions – Lesson 3 – The Home Tab

1. Name 4 groups on the Home tab, and what do they do?
   a. _____
   b. _____
   c. _____
   d. _____
2. On the Clipboard group, what does the Format Painter do?
   a. _____
3. If you wanted to change formatting elements on a worksheet, how many ways can you do it, both through the Ribbon and shortcuts?
   a. _____
   b. _____
   c. _____
4. Why would you want to format your data as a Table (Styles group)
   a. _____
5. Why would you want to use Styles?
   a. _____
   b. _____
6. Where do you find quick access to functions?
   a. _____
7. What would you do if you wanted to fill in a series of dates, but skip weekends?
   a. _____

Lesson Assignment – Lesson 3 - The Home Tab

This assignment is to open the Lesson 3 workbook and start getting familiarized with the following (there is a Notes section below for you to keep track of your observations):

- The Home Tab
  - General Navigation – What can you find? What can't you find?
  - Paste Operations & Fill Effects
  - Skip Blanks & Transpose
  - Text Alignment
  - Conditional Formatting & Styles
  - Sorting & Filtering
- Explore the Helpfile

Lesson 2 Notes

Lesson 4 – The Ribbon In-Depth - Part II

In the last lesson two lessons we explored two of the primary Ribbon elements, the File group lesson showed you all of the ways that you can customize the Excel environment so that it's right for you. The Home group lesson detailed all of the most commonly used Ribbon elements. In this lesson we'll explore the rest of the Ribbon elements. These elements are segmented by their overall function, like Page Layout and Formulas.

Note: all commands that show you which sequence you would follow to invoke a certain Ribbon element will still be indicated with "goto Home, Format as Table", however the main Ribbon name won't be included. It's implied that if you're in the Insert section of this lesson that the sequence would begin on the Insert tab. E.G., Table.

Insert

This group contains elements that primarily deal with objects you'll insert on in and onto the worksheet (Pivot Tables, Charts, Pictures, Smart Art, etc.).

Pivot Tables

- Pivot Tables are one of your most powerful data analysis tools, and as such they will be discussed in greater detail on their own later on in the course. They allow you to quickly get different looks at your data in a manner that would otherwise only be available through a database. Using the data you'll see in Tables example, Pivot Tables allow you to take transactional data (like customer orders) from single entries and turn them into complex and dynamic summarizations like this:

	A	B	C	D	E	F	G	H
1	Years	2009						
2								
3		Column Labels						
4		Sum of Revenue						
5	Row Labels		Jan-09	Feb-09	Mar-09	Apr-09	May-09	Jun-09	Jul-09
6	Central		$71,421	$112,143	$48,871	$88,055	$124,682	$39,872	$105,153
7	ABC		$19,045	$32,416	$15,868	$20,212	$18,290		$17,883
8	AT&T		$1,740						
9	Exxon			$13,314					
10	Ford				$4,010	$7,852			
11	General Electric		$10,445						
12	General Motors				$11,858				
13	IBM		$6,860						
14	Verizon			$11,922					
15	Wal-Mart			$7,180		$12,360	$18,290		$17,883
16	DEF			$35,066	$4,472	$47,173	$53,119	$22,004	$56,280
17	AIG							$4,060	
18	Bank of America						$7,245		
19	Boeing					$20,950			
20	Exxon					$7,233			$16,303
21	Ford			$12,282		$18,990	$16,264		$17,416
22	General Electric			$22,784	$4,472				
23	General Motors						$15,407		$13,270

Figure 114

Tables

- Tables are a feature that was introduced in Excel 2007. Originally based on what was called "Lists" in earlier versions, Tables are a great way to automatically format and extend data ranges and formulas as you add data. Most importantly, Tables allow you to work with the data in the table independent of any other data on the worksheet. Of note is that Tables introduce a new function nomenclature that refers to individual column elements in a manner that is nothing like the general worksheet functions that you'll be working with later in the course.

- Tables let you change data that looks like this:

	A	B	C	D	E	F	G	H	I
1	Region	Product	Date	Month	Customer	Quantity	Revenue	COGS	Profit
2	Central	ABC	01/09/08	Jan-08	General Motors	800	$16,416	$6,776	$9,640
3	Central	ABC	01/12/08	Jan-08	IBM	300	$6,267	$2,541	$3,726
4	Central	ABC	01/25/08	Jan-08	CitiGroup	1000	$20,770	$8,470	$12,300
5	Central	ABC	02/08/08	Feb-08	CitiGroup	100	$1,817	$847	$970
6	Central	ABC	02/09/08	Feb-08	General Motors	300	$5,157	$2,541	$2,616
7	Central	ABC	02/19/08	Feb-08	Wal-Mart	500	$10,385	$4,235	$6,150
8	Central	ABC	02/20/08	Feb-08	Exxon	600	$11,124	$5,082	$6,042
9	Central	ABC	02/27/08	Feb-08	Ford	900	$16,209	$7,623	$8,586
10	Central	ABC	03/18/08	Mar-08	Wal-Mart	800	$16,696	$6,776	$9,920
11	Central	ABC	03/22/08	Mar-08	Wal-Mart	300	$5,355	$2,541	$2,814
12	Central	ABC	03/23/08	Mar-08	Wal-Mart	200	$3,756	$1,694	$2,062

Figure 115

- Do this, in just 2 mouse clicks!

	A	B	C	D	E	F	G	H	I
1	Region ▼	Product ▼	Date ▼	Montl ▼	Customer ▼	Quant ▼	Reven ▼	CO ▼	Pro ▼
2	Central	ABC	01/09/08	Jan-08	General Motors	800	$16,416	$6,776	$9,640
3	Central	ABC	01/12/08	Jan-08	IBM	300	$6,267	$2,541	$3,726
4	Central	ABC	01/25/08	Jan-08	CitiGroup	1000	$20,770	$8,470	$12,300
5	Central	ABC	02/08/08	Feb-08	CitiGroup	100	$1,817	$847	$970
6	Central	ABC	02/09/08	Feb-08	General Motors	300	$5,157	$2,541	$2,616
7	Central	ABC	02/19/08	Feb-08	Wal-Mart	500	$10,385	$4,235	$6,150
8	Central	ABC	02/20/08	Feb-08	Exxon	600	$11,124	$5,082	$6,042
9	Central	ABC	02/27/08	Feb-08	Ford	900	$16,209	$7,623	$8,586
10	Central	ABC	03/18/08	Mar-08	Wal-Mart	800	$16,696	$6,776	$9,920
11	Central	ABC	03/22/08	Mar-08	Wal-Mart	300	$5,355	$2,541	$2,814
12	Central	ABC	03/23/08	Mar-08	Wal-Mart	200	$3,756	$1,694	$2,062
13	Central	ABC	03/27/08	Mar-08	General Motors	300	$5,358	$2,541	$2,817
14	Central	ABC	04/06/08	Apr-08	General Electric	300	$5,886	$2,541	$3,345
15	Central	ABC	04/13/08	Apr-08	CitiGroup	400	$8,016	$3,388	$4,628
16	Central	ABC	04/30/08	Apr-08	Ford	200	$3,802	$1,694	$2,108
17	Central	ABC	05/10/08	May-08	Exxon	500	$8,785	$4,235	$4,550

Figure 116

- All you do is make sure that the active cell is within the data range (it doesn't matter where), and goto, Table, then select the Table style you like from the Gallery. Excel will automatically convert your data range into a Table.

Table Styles – What if there's nothing that I like?

Out of all the options that Microsoft gives you for Table Styles you might find one close to what you like, but if it doesn't do everything you want you can customize your own!

- What's neat about Tables is that if you were to add data in row 15 in the above example, Excel would automatically extend the formatting to the new row as soon as you made an entry in column A. What you can't see is that behind the scenes, Excel has defined the entire table area as a specific range, so it knows exactly where it starts and ends. This comes into play when you add functions to the table, as Excel also automatically extends the table range. In this example if you were to goto cell J2 and invoke the AutoSum wizard you would see Excel build this function:

	G	H	I	J	K	L
1	Reven ▼	CO ▼	Pro ▼			
2	$16,416	$6,776	$9,640	=SUM(Table1[@[Quantity]:[Profit]])		
3	$6,267	$2,541	$3,726			
4	$20,770	$8,470	$12,300			
5	$1,817	$847	$970			
6	$5,157	$2,541	$2,616			
7	$10,385	$4,235	$6,150			

Figure 117

- As soon as you confirm the Wizard's solution (Enter) the table would automatically reformat itself, and extend the new Sum function to the entire column range:

F	G	H	I	J	K
Quant ▼	**Reveni ▼**	**CO ▼**	**Pro ▼**	**Colum ▼**	
800	$16,416	$6,776	$9,640	$33,632	
300	$6,267	$2,541	$3,726	$12,834	
1000	$20,770	$8,470	$12,300	$42,540	
100	$1,817	$847	$970	$3,734	
300	$5,157	$2,541	$2,616	$10,614	
500	$10,385	$4,235	$6,150	$21,270	
600	$11,124	$5,082	$6,042	$22,848	
900	$16,209	$7,623	$8,586	$33,318	
800	$16,696	$6,776	$9,920	$34,192	
300	$5,355	$2,541	$2,814	$11,010	
200	$3,756	$1,694	$2,062	$7,712	
300	$5,358	$2,541	$2,817	$11,016	
300	$5,886	$2,541	$3,345	$12,072	

Figure 118

- This is just an example of what can be done, but the function wizard can only be so smart, and in this case it included the entire numeric range in the Sum function: =SUM(Table1[@[Quantity]:[Profit]]), which is written in the Table function nomenclature. Obviously you wouldn't want the Quantity included in the sum, and you would subtract Cost of Goods Sold from Profit (=[@Revenue]-[@COGS]).

Illustrations

- This group contains all of the design objects you can place on a worksheet:
  - ○ **Pictures** – Insert a picture from a location of your choice. It has to be a picture format that Office can read, like .jpeg, .gif, .bmp, etc.
  - ○ **Clipart** – Insert an image from the Office Clipart gallery (note that this requires you to have installed the Clipart gallery when you installed Office. Otherwise you need to select the "Find more at Office. com" option at the bottom of the dialog). You also have a selection for the type of Clip Art you want to insert:

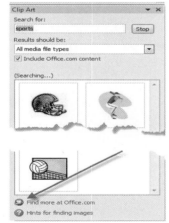

Figure 119

○ **Shapes** – You can select from a huge selection of shapes that you can resize, format (you can even add text to some of them). These are also referred to as "Drawing Objects". Select the shape you want to insert (notice that as soon as you hover your cursor over the worksheet it turns into a cross), then left-click on the worksheet wherever you want to place the shape and drag it to the vertical/horizontal size that you want (don't worry, it can be adjusted at any time), then release the button.

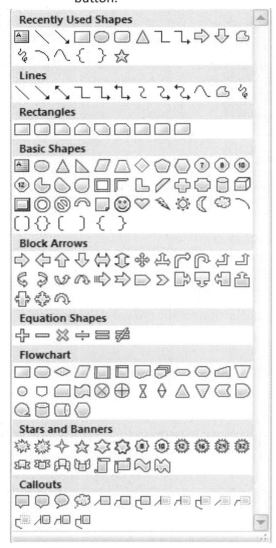

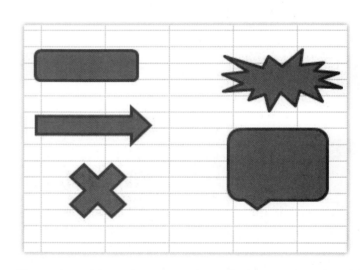

Figure 120

▪ As soon as you draw a shape you'll see the Ribbon change to show the Drawing Tools Ribbon Group:

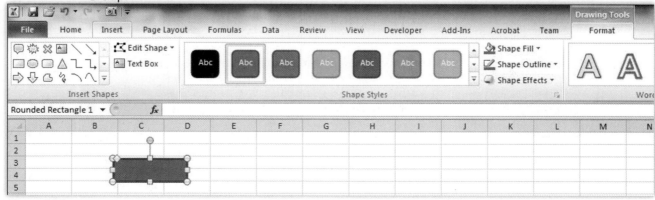

Figure 121

○ The Drawing tools group contains the following elements:

- **Insert Shapes** – This is somewhat redundant, since you just inserted a shape, and if you click off of the shape the Ribbon will revert back to the insert group, but it does contain the Edit Shape tool, which can be useful if you want to manipulate a drawn shape more than what Excel gave you.

- **Shape Styles** – This is where Microsoft's graphic artists have done an outstanding job of giving you some fantastic options. There are too many ways to customize these objects to cover here, but you're encouraged to draw some and see what kind of formats you can come up with (if you want to add text to a shape, just right-click it and select the Edit Text option):

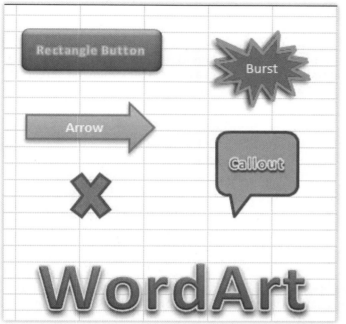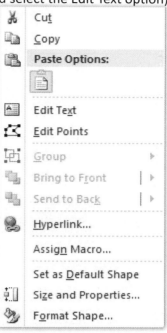

Figure 122

- **Word Art Styles** – These options only apply to text, although you can apply them to text you've embedded in a shape via the Edit Text option. There is also a Word Art command on the Ribbon, which we'll get to momentarily. Again, there are too many potential combinations to possibly cover here, so you're encouraged to work on some of your own.

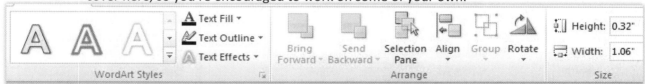

Figure 123

- **Arrange** – Arrange options are relatively straightforward:

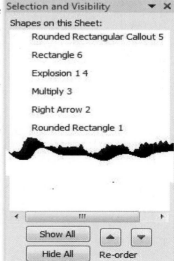

  - Bring Forward/Send Backward – If you place objects on top of each other you can use these options to determine which order they're in. For instance you might draw a callout on a chart, but Excel decides to place it beneath the chart instead of on top. With the callout selected you would just click Bring to Front from the drop-down. Forward/Back are median steps that only apply if you have three or more shapes.

  - Selection Pane – This just lists all of the shapes you have on the worksheet and allows you to order them in the list. It's not likely that you'll ever need to use this:

  - Align – This, on the other hand, you'll use frequently if you have 2 of more shapes on the worksheet. It allows you to easily position shapes in relation to each other without having to move them around manually. In the previous shape examples illustration the three shapes on the left were Aligned Center and Distributed Horizontally, which is a lot easier (not to mention faster) than trying to position them by yourself.

- Group – Once you've got your shapes where you want in relation to each other, it's a good idea to select all of them (you can use Shift + Left-Click to select multiple shapes, then select Group. This will keep the objects together.

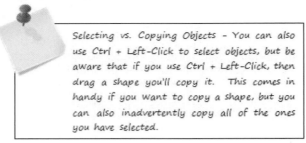

Selecting vs. Copying Objects - You can also use Ctrl + Left-Click to select objects, but be aware that if you use Ctrl + Left-Click, then drag a shape you'll copy it. This comes in handy if you want to copy a shape, but you can also inadvertently copy all of the ones you have selected.

- Size – Shows you the Height and Width of the shape. It's good reference and if you need to make sure that multiple shapes are the same size, it's often easier to adjust them all here, rather than try to get them the same size with their handles.

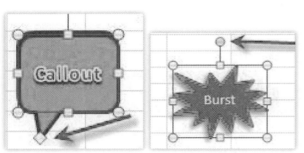

Manipulating Shapes - Shapes that have the green symbol above the shape handles can be rotated. Just hover the mouse over the green symbol until it changes into a rotation symbol and drag it to the angle you want. The Yellow symbol beneath a shape allows you drag the object's tail wherever you want.

Figure 124

- ○ **SmartArt –** This option exposes more pre-designed graphic elements that Microsoft added with Excel 2007. What you used to have to create in another application, like Adobe Illustrator or Microsoft Visio, you can now draw directly in Excel.

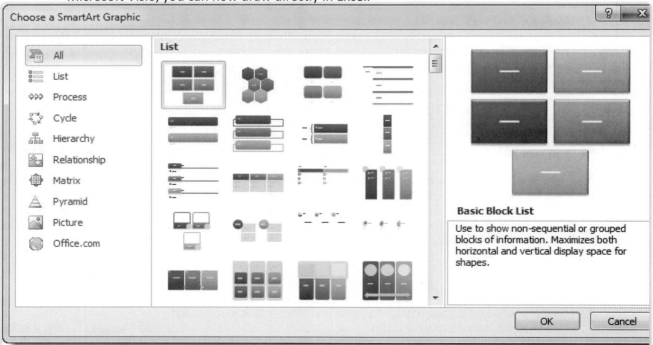

Figure 125

- Here is an example of a Basic Cycle

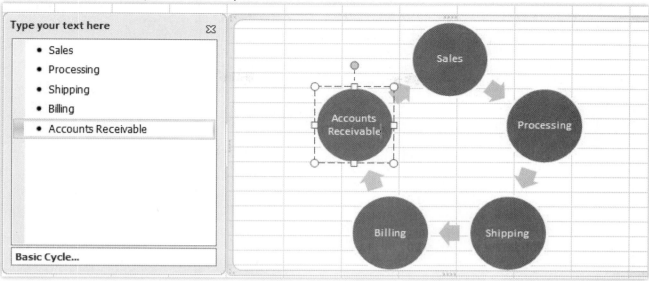

Figure 126

- When you first draw a SmartArt graphic you'll see the Text entry flyout to the left of the graphic. Once you're done entering your data and click off of the graphic, the flyout will disappear. As with other detailed properties in Excel, SmartArt will activate its own Ribbon sub-group:

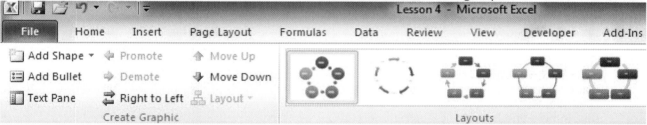

Figure 127

- You'll see that you can get pretty fancy with the Layout & Style options that you have at your fingertips. And another nice thing is that Live Preview will kick in as you hover over different Layouts and Styles, so you don't need to commit to a selection before seeing how it's going to look on your worksheet.

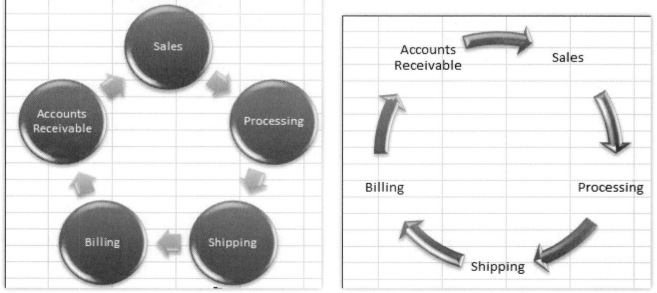

Figure 128

- ○ **Screenshot**- This allows you to insert a screenshot of any open application that has not been minimized to the Taskbar. Here is a Screenshot from this lesson. Is this all that practical in Excel? Not really, but it does come in handy in Word, especially if you're trying to document a process flow for a spreadsheet, or create a user's guide.

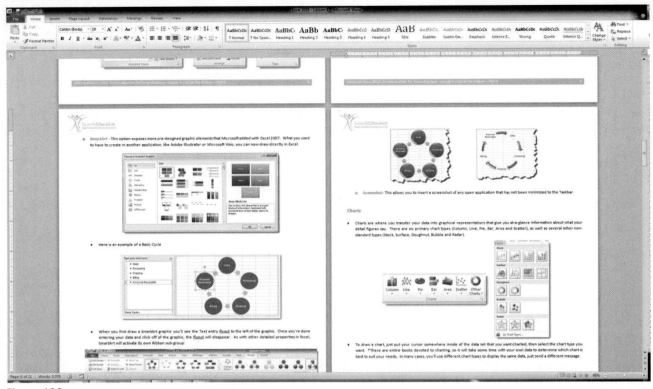

Figure 129

Charts

- Charts are where you convert your numerical data into graphical representations that give you at-a-glance information about what your detail figures say. There are six primary chart types (Column, Line, Pie, Bar, Area and Scatter), as well as several other non-standard types (Stock, Surface, Doughnut, Bubble and Radar).

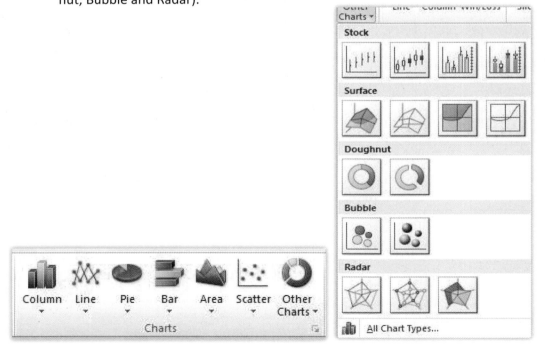

Figure 130

- To draw a chart, just put your cursor somewhere inside of the data set that you want charted, then select the chart type you want. *There are entire books devoted to charting, so it will take some time with your own data to determine which chart is best to suit your needs. In many cases, you'll use different chart types to display the same data, just send a different message.

	A	B	C	D	E	F	G	H	I
1	Region	Product	Date	Month	Customer	Quantity	Revenue	COGS	Profit
2	Central	ABC	01/09/08	Jan-08	General Motors	800	16,416	6,776	9,640
3	Central	ABC	01/12/08	Jan-08	IBM	300	6,267	2,541	3,726
4	Central	ABC	01/25/08	Jan-08	CitiGroup	1000	20,770	8,470	12,300
5	Central	ABC	02/19/08	Feb-08	Wal-Mart	500	10,385	4,235	6,150
6	Central	ABC	02/20/08	Feb-08	Exxon	600	11,124	5,082	6,042
7	Central	ABC	02/27/08	Feb-08	Ford	900	16,209	7,623	8,586
8	Central	ABC	04/06/08	Apr-08	General Electric	300	5,886	2,541	3,345

Figure 131

Chart Tips

1) If your data includes information that you don't want charted you can select just the range you want charted. Or you can select the entire data range and simply hide rows and columns you don't want charted, as hidden rows/columns won't plot on a chart.

2) To quickly create the default chart type, place the cursor in any cell in the chart data range and press ALT+F1.

- **Column Charts** – The most common are 2-D & 3-D. Sometimes a Cylinder chart is appropriate, but rarely. Cone & Pyramid shapes should never be used, because they don't always accurately represent your data. Column charts display your data in vertical columns. Column charts are especially good at displaying multiple data points for several groups, such as Revenue & Profit by company.

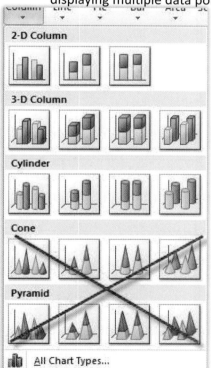

Figure 132

- **Line Charts** – Probably as common as Column charts, Line charts will display your data in a series of horizontal lines. Line charts are generally used to show data over a given period, like weeks or months.

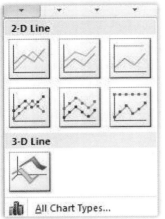
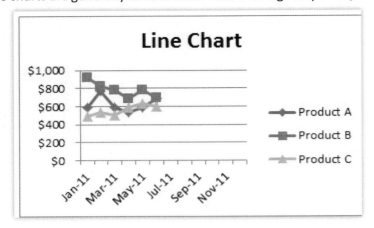

Figure 133

- **Pie Charts** – While these are also relatively common, their use isn't recommended because they can inaccurately represent data from a visual perspective, especially 3-D pie charts due to the way that they render when drawn, where the bottom/front part of the chart can look bigger than it actually is because of pixel density.

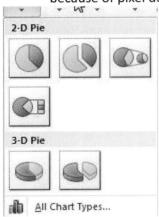
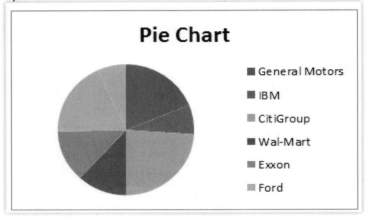

Figure 134

- **Bar Charts** – These are nothing more than column charts turned on their side.

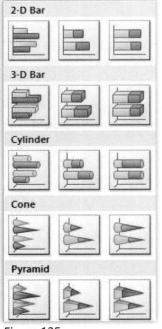
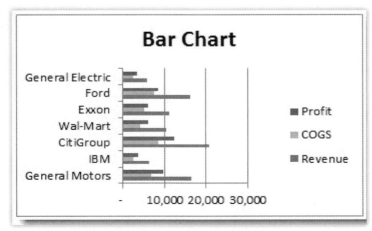

Figure 135

- **Area Charts** – These allow you to compare like data over a given timeline. They generally obscure more information than they show, and should only be used if there are enough differences between the data sets to differentiate them well.

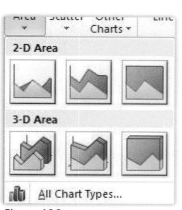

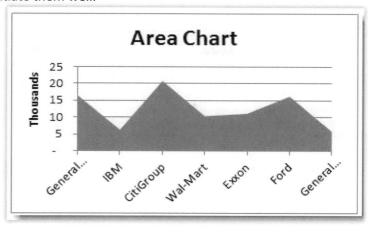

Figure 136

- **Scatter Charts** – These are good for comparing pairs of data.

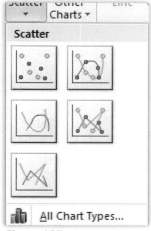

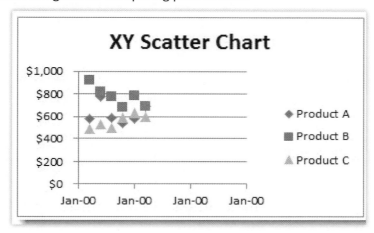

Figure 137

Sparklines

- This is a neat addition that the Microsoft Excel team has had in development for a long time, and it is a truly remarkable achievement. In essence Sparklines allow you to insert mini charts in a cell that represents the data you've selected (it doesn't have to be adjacent to the data, but it's a generally a good idea, so that you maintain a visual reference to it). Here are some Sparkline examples using the same chart data from above:

Sal	Jan-11	Feb-11	Mar-11	Apr-11	May-11	Jun-11	Line	Column	Wiin/Loss
Product A	$585	$775	$590	$537	$584	$688			
Product B	$922	$819	$776	$685	$784	$694			
Product C	$491	$532	$498	$591	$632	$598			

Figure 138

- Sparklines are great for Dashboards and summary reports, where a large chart (or a series of them) might be overwhelming.

- To insert a Sparkline, just select the data range, then the Sparkline type (you can choose from Line, Column or Win/Loss) – Note that Sparklines can only be placed in a single cell per data range, they can't span multiple rows or columns:

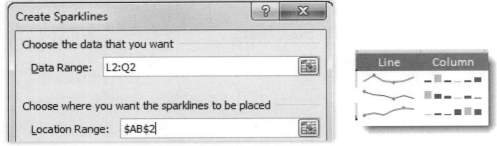

Figure 139

- As soon as you place the Sparkline on your sheet, the Sparkline Design Tools Ribbon tab will be activated.
- Here you can edit the Data points, change the Sparkline type, Show certain data points, as well as select a Style for the Sparkline. Once again, you have too many options to detail here, but feel free to experiment with the examples in the Lesson 4 workbook, or create your own. Here's an example of Sparklines with High & Low points marked.

Figure 140

Filter

- The Filter group only contains one control: Slicer. A Slicer is a control that allows you to query certain Pivot Table elements. We'll be discussing this in more detail in the Pivot Tables lesson.

Links

- This group also contains only one element: Hyperlinks. Hyperlinks allow you to insert a clickable navigation text link that will take you to a website, a different location in your workbook/worksheet, or even open another program.

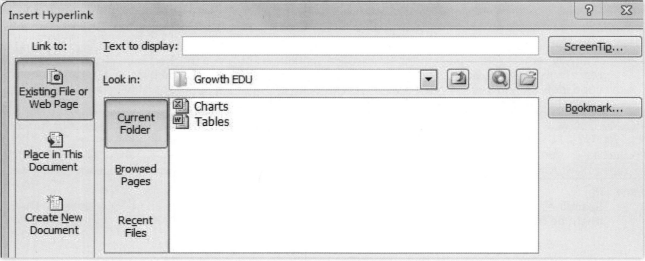

Figure 141

If by design you want to have hyperlinks in a workbook, they can be somewhat handy. For instance you can create a Table of Contents that lists all worksheets and include links to them. But they can also be irritating, especially as Excel's default nature is to insert a hyperlink for any text that includes the @ symbol in the text string. You'll notice this right away if you try to enter an e-mail address in a cell. When adding a hyperlink, you can add an input mask (see the Text to display dialog), which will allow you to add a hyperlink without what might be an otherwise confusing or long address (e.g. you can put "Link to Budget Documents" vs. http://www.somewebsite.com/documentfolder/financials/monthend/january.html).

Text

- This contains the following elements: Text Box, Header & Footer, WordArt, Signature Line and Object.
  - **Text Box** – This is a free form, floating text box that resides above the worksheet. The "sticky Notes" you see throughout this course have been created with the Word version of Text Boxes. There's generally very little use for these in Excel unless you're trying to mark a distribution document with a release note, like "DRAFT" or "CONFIDENTIAL". As with any other object, Text Boxes won't interfere with the underlying cells or their performance.

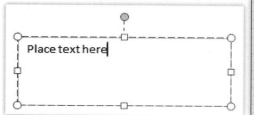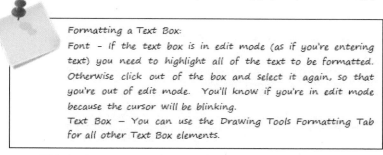

Figure 142

  - Once you click the TextBox control the cursor will turn into an inverted cross. Once you see that just left-click and drag across the sheet until you have the box the approximate size you want, then insert your text. Once you're done with that you can apply any formatting you want to it.

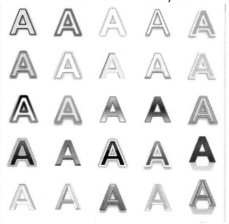

Formatting a Text Box:

Font - If the text box is in edit mode (as if you're entering text) you need to highlight all of the text to be formatted. Otherwise click out of the box and select it again, so that you're out of edit mode. You'll know if you're in edit mode because the cursor will be blinking.

Text Box – You can use the Drawing Tools Formatting Tab for all other Text Box elements.

  - **Header & Footer** – This is the same as the Header & Footer options you'll find in Page Setup, but it lets you input them directly on the worksheet, so you can see a "preview" version of what they'll look like. It can save a step or two from inputting this data through the Page Setup dialog, where you'll have to goto Page Layout, Page Setup, Header/Footer (make your additions), Print Preview to see the result. By the same token, all this does is expose the Header & Footer, but not the other Page Setup elements, so what you gain on one side, you lose on the other, because you still need to go through the Page Setup process in order to prepare your worksheet for printing. In addition, what you enter with this method is only viewable through the Page Setup view; you won't see it in Normal view.
  - **Word Art** – This was covered briefly in the Illustrations section, and gave you an example of what you can do with some of the new graphic controls Microsoft has created. WordArt can be great for introductory worksheets and on Dashboards (ample room permitting), although you won't find it widely used in financial applications. When you select the WordArt option you'll be presented with a series of styles:

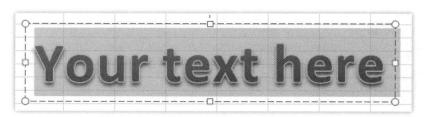

Figure 143

- Once you make your selection, Excel will automatically insert a WordArt text box for you. All you need to do is start typing your own text. As soon as the WordArt text box has been drawn you'll see the Drawing Tools Format tab appear, where you can format both the text and the text box itself.
  - ○ **_Signature Line_** – This was Microsoft's attempt at adding digital signature security to your documents, but it's very unlikely that you'll ever use this feature to its full capacity as it requires a third-party authentication service, and they're not cheap. It will however allow you to add a signature line to a document faster than if you could draw it yourself. You can dismiss the first notification:

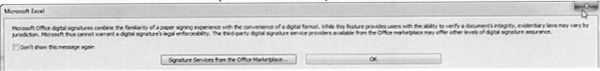

Figure 144

  - ○ Then continue to the Signature dialog and enter your relevant signature information:

Figure 145

  - ○ Object – This dialog allows you to insert an embedded object from another application, like Word. You generally won't use this in Excel, but you will often insert Excel objects into Word documents, like Monthly Reports.

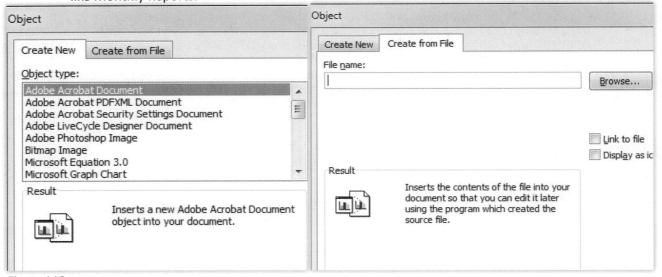

Figure 146

  - ○ The primary exception here is the Organization Chart tool, which can be a very handy tool for documenting your organizational structure.

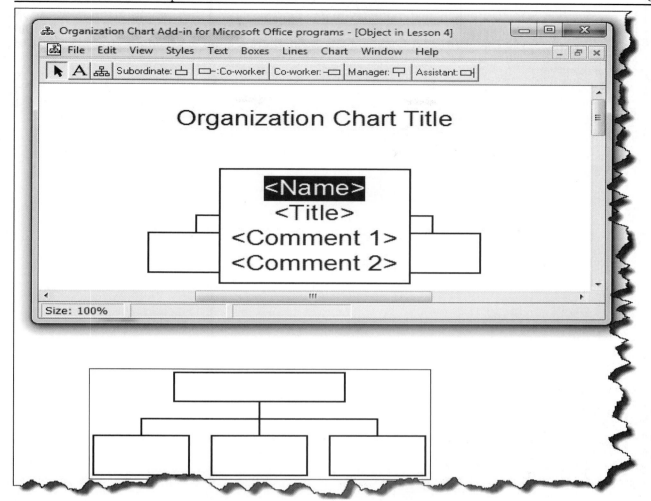

Figure 147

Symbols

- ○ ***Equation*** – If you deal with mathematics, then this is a great tool and is a far cry from the day when complicated equations really couldn't be done in Excel. When you click on the Equation command you'll see a list of detailed equation options.
  - ▪ Selecting one will place it on the sheet and activate the Equation Editing tab. Writing equations could be a topic in and of itself, but for the purposes of this course we're not going to go over it, other than to show you that it's there.

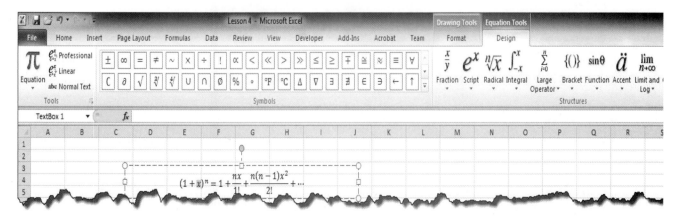

Figure 148

○   **Symbols** – You'll probably find more day-to-day functionality on the Symbols menu, which gives you different symbols for every font you have installed on your system, as well as a series of Special Characters, like Trademark ™ & Copyright ©. Again, there are too many options to possibly cover here, but feel free to explore.

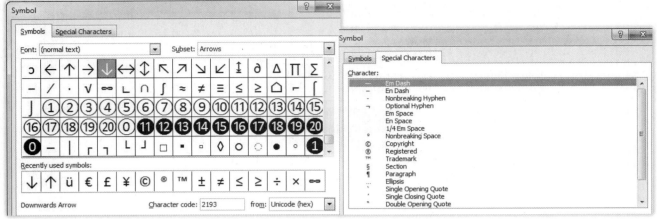

Figure 149

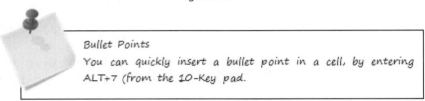

Bullet Points
You can quickly insert a bullet point in a cell, by entering ALT+7 (from the 10-Key pad.

Page Layout

This is where you can apply themes to an entire workbook, as well as preparing your worksheet for printing and distribution. The Page Layout tab consists of the following groups:

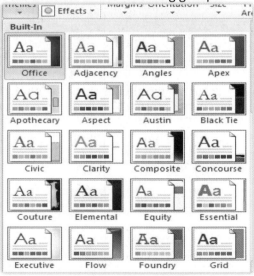

Figure 150

•   **Themes** – Themes are a series of pre-defined formats that you can apply to an entire workbook. In the Theme menu to the right you'll see that the default Theme is "Office". If you were to change it and go to format a data range as a Table you'd see the new Theme applied there. Microsoft can only give you so many themes out of the thousands of potential possibilities, but you can create your own theme, or adjust existing themes. You can change the Colors, Fonts and Effects (which deal with SmartArt), which you'll see in the next three examples.

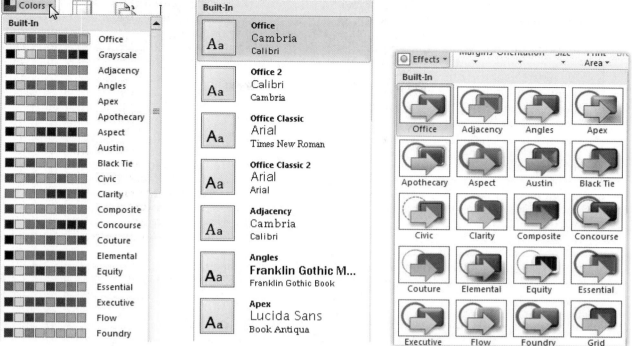

Figure 151

- *Page Setup* – This is where you set up your worksheets so that they print in the format you want. The Page Setup group consists of the following commands:
    ○ **Margins** – Displays the most common margins as well as the one you used most recently if it's not one of the defaults. The Customize Margins will bring up the Excel 2003 Page Setup dialog, the same as the dialog launcher on the Ribbon's Page Setup group.

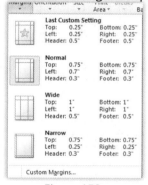

Figure 152

    ○ **Orientation** – This allows you to quickly toggle between Portrait and Landscape orientation. As you can see in the Margin selections, the example worksheet is in Portrait orientation, which is the default. Had the worksheet been in Landscape orientation, the Margin images would have reflected that.
    ○ **Size** – This lets you choose from the most common paper sizes. The default is 8.5" x 11".

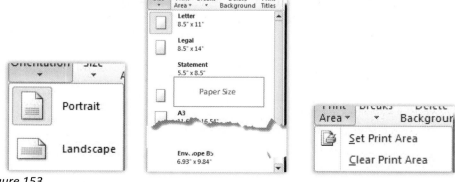

Figure 153

- ○ **Print Area** – This is something that often trips up even the most experienced users. Let's say you have a worksheet, but you only want to print part of the worksheet and not reveal certain parts of it? Excel automatically adds the entire used range into the print area, so if you try printing without checking this first you'll realize pretty quickly. The first step is to Clear the Print Area, then select the area you do want to print and select the Set Print Area option, which will then leave out what you don't want to print.
- ○ **Breaks** – This allows you to select a Row or Column and set a Page Break. Unfortunately, this isn't a very useful feature and is much easier handled in Page Break Preview, where you can just drag breaks where you want them.
- ○ **Background** – This allows you to take an image and insert it into the background of your worksheet, and is the only thing you can actually put behind the worksheet object. It's very useful if you need to add something like a company logo as a watermark, or want to have an intro page, but you need to be careful with the image you select as it can get very overwhelming and make your worksheet all but impossible to work with if you're not careful. The image also gets tiled (repeats) across the entire worksheet, so it's not a display in one spot thing, it's all or none. You also only get one image, not multiple, so if you want to layer a company logo or photo in the background and add a "DRAFT" or "COMPANY CONFIDENTIAL" label as well, you'd need to prepare that in a photo editing program (Paint.Net is a good one and it's free), then import the finished image.
  - ▪ Note the difference in the two Background examples with and without Gridlines displayed.

Figure 154

- ○ **Print Titles** – Again, this launches the Excel 2003 Page Setup dialog. Print Titles gives you the ability to fix columns and rows so that they repeat on each worksheet. We'll discuss all of these print options in the Page Setup lesson.
- ○ **Dialog Launcher** – This will call the Excel 2003 Page Setup dialog, which encompasses all of the Page Setup items you'll need. Unless you're just quickly changing a setting like Margins or Orientation, you'll probably find it easier to come to this dialog to set up your worksheet for printing.
- *Scale to Fit* – This lets you choose how much of your sheet to print and on how many pages. You can select Automatic, where Excel will choose for you (remember the part about setting the Print Area here), or you can define how many pages Wide by how many pages Tall the sheet should print. The Scale to Fit Dialog Launcher will bring up the Excel 2003 Page Setup dialog. Are you noticing a common theme here? For whatever reason, Microsoft didn't redesign the Excel 2003 dialogs, but why try to fix what already works so well?
- *Sheet Options* – This is a simple dialog that lets you toggle Gridlines and Headings (the Row & Column headers). If you're distributing a workbook that's for viewing only, you'll probably toggle these off, but if you're expecting some degree of user interaction you'll leave them on to make it easier for your users to navigate your worksheet(s).
- *Arrange* – The Page Layout tab is a somewhat illogical place for this option since it deals with objects, not so much Page Layout. But it's another case where Microsoft gives you the option to interact with different menu items in different places.

Figure 155

Formulas

This is where you can access all of Excel's native Formulas (also referred to as Functions). Formulas allow to you calculate values that you enter into cells, like =1+1, or =TODAY() which would return the date in the cell. With regards to data analysis and getting the most from your data, this is where Excel really shines. Even if all you're ever going to do is use Excel to manage lists (like customer details), you'll still find at least a few of these handy. Once you start getting used to Formulas, you'll wonder how you ever got things done without Excel. We're going to review the Formula Ribbon functionality here, but because there are so many great tools here, Formulas will also be discussed in their own lesson. The Formula tab consists of the following groups:

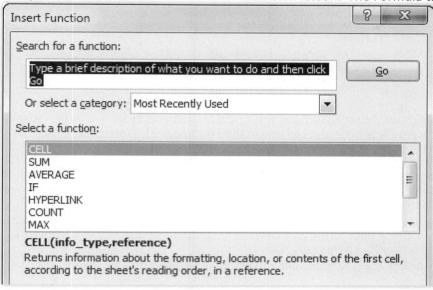

Figure 156

- **Function Library** – This group breaks down Excel formulas into the most commonly used groups.
    - **Insert Function** – This will launch the Excel 2003 Function dialog, which exposes all of the Function categories you see on the Ribbon. At the top you have the ability to search for a function if you don't know it. For instance "Look up a value" will give you a list of LOOKUP formulas. This is a useful tool, but only to the extent that you know how to define what you're looking for, otherwise it can be fairly frustrating. If you know roughly what you want to do you can narrow the list, just like you can on the Ribbon by selecting from one of the defined categories. Once you select a formula, Excel will define its syntax on the bottom, and you can also select the "Help on this function" link at the bottom, which will open the Helpfile. Once you select the formula you want, Excel will launch a Function Arguments dialog for you that details the formula:

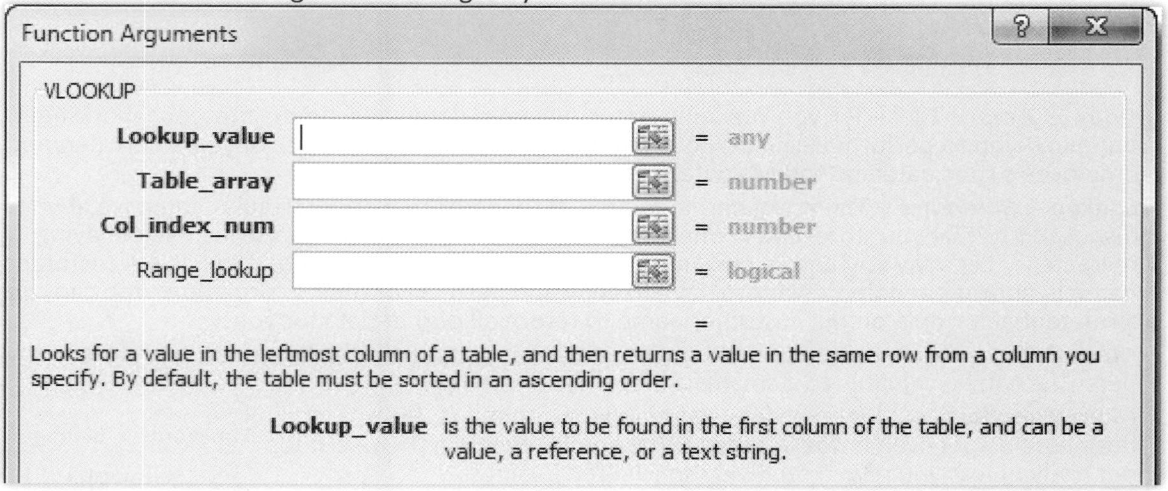

Figure 157

○ **AutoSum** – While some people strictly write their own formulas, there are many times where Excel can do it faster than if you could yourself, and when you're talking about sometimes entering literally thousands of formulas it can be really convenient to let Excel do it for you. The following example used the Sum function to Sum revenue for a particular sales person:

CELL	▼	X ✓ ƒx	=SUM(B2:M2)			

	A	B	C	D	...ber	M December	N Total
1	Salesman	January	February	March		December	Total
2	Bob	$2,936.56	$4,482.74	$7,019.22	.77	$6,345.02	=SUM(B2:M2)
3	Tom	$8,899.02	$9,147.36	$5,967.03	.70	$6,665.59	
4	Fred	$2,125.87	$1,485.90	$7,089.62	.11	$5,458.75	
5	Al	$1,651.76	$2,853.51	$5,666.59	.25	$5,078.27	
6	Mary	$9,475.19	$7,536.55	$4,177.47	.20	$9,532.36	

AutoSum Recently Finan...
▼   Used ▼   ▼
Σ **Sum**
   Average
   Count Numbers
   Max
   Min
   More Functions...

Figure 158

- With the cursor in cell N2, just select Sum from the AutoSum list and Excel will automatically apply the formula for you (you'll see it in the cell and in the Formula Bar). Note Excel it highlights the range where it thinks you want the formula but doesn't enter it, instead it wants you to verify that it got it right. If you're happy with Excel's selection, then just hit enter, then you can copy & paste the formula down to the rest of the sales people. In this case the cursor was to the right of the data, so Excel knew to go left; had you been underneath the data, Excel would have summed upwards. Will the AutoSum wizard always get it right? No, but it does a pretty good job.

- **Recently Used** – Just what it sounds like, Excel will store a list of the last 10 formulas you've used. Unless you're frequently dealing with formulas that have long names or are easy to misspell (like AMORDEGC), you probably won't use this very often.

- **Financial** – This deals with finance functions, like calculating payments on equipment at a given rate.

- **Logical** – These are used quite frequently to tell Excel to do something if a condition is met. E.G. =IF(A1=1,1,2), which simply says IF A1 = 1, then the formula should return a 1, otherwise return a 2.

- **Text** – These allow you to do things like change text case (Upper, Lower & Proper), split text apart (Parse) or join (Concatenate) text from separate cells. Lets' say you have "SMITH, JOHN" in a cell and you want to get the first & last names. You could use a few text functions to do all of that for you instead of retyping the information. There will be examples of this in the Formulas lesson.

B10	▼		ƒx	=PROPER(LEFT(A10,FIND(",",A10)-1))	

	A	B	C	D	E
9	Full Name	Last Name	First Name		
10	SMITH, JOHN	Smith	John		

Figure 159

- **Date & Time** – These let you not only enter dynamic dates and times into your worksheet, but allow you to perform calculate on them, like calculating the number of years between and employee's start date and today's date.

- **Lookup & Reference** – These are perhaps some of the most powerful formulas you have at your disposal. They let you store data in one place and retrieve it somewhere else instead of having to recreate it. Let's say you have a customer list in a worksheet, but you need to enter a customer name in another and don't want to have to copy and paste all of their information. You can use a referential formula on the customer name to return all of that data for you.

- **Math & Trig** – While these deal with mathematical equations for higher math, there are many here that can be valuable to a small business, like rounding.

- **More Functions** – This exposes non-standard functions from a daily business perspective. It doesn't mean that you'll never use them, but it's not likely unless you're in a relatively specialized business.

- **Defined Names** – Defined Names in Excel are a very powerful tool, and often overlooked. We'll discuss them in more detail in the next lesson. Essentially it allows you to give a range a name and refer to it instead of the range address. You can also apply a formula to a name, e.g. =A1*Tax, where Tax refers to a value (like =.0975), not a range. Many people feel that it makes it easier to read formulas when they use named ranges. E.G. =VLOOKUP(A1,SalesData,2,FALSE) is for many a lot easier to read than: =VLOOKUP(A1,Formulas!$A$1:$N$6,2,FALSE)

- ○ **Name Manager** – The Name Manager is where you add new names, delete old ones as well as adjusting existing names. It will launch the Excel 2003 Name Manager dialog, which like so many of them is very robust. When you open it you'll see any existing names in your workbook, and when you select one, you'll see what it refers to at the bottom of the dialog.

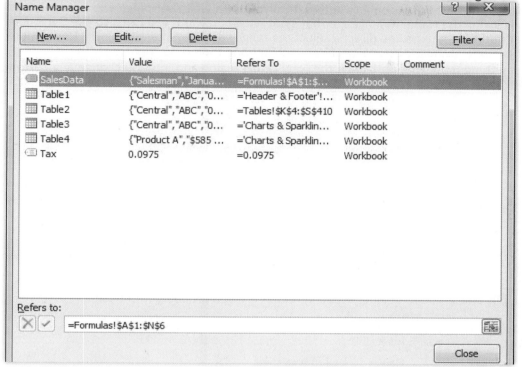

Figure 160

- ▪ Note in this case you'll see that "SalesData" refers to =Formulas!$A$1:$N$6, just as in the previous formula examples. You'll also see some Tables that have been defined. When you create a table in Excel by applying a Table Style to a range, Excel automatically names that range. Whenever you make additions to it, Excel will automatically adjust the range for you.

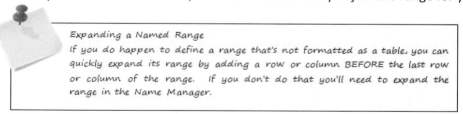

Expanding a Named Range
If you do happen to define a range that's not formatted as a table, you can quickly expand its range by adding a row or column BEFORE the last row or column of the range. If you don't do that you'll need to expand the range in the Name Manager.

- ▪ **New** – this give you the option to add a new named range or value/formula.
  - - **Name** - First you would enter a name for your range. It needs to follow some standards, like it can't have spaces in it (underscores are OK though) – You'll find the full details in the Excel Helpfile.

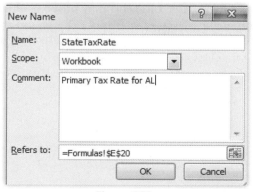

Figure 161

- **Scope** - Next define the scope of the name. Scope refers to where the name can be seen in the workbook. For the purposes of this course you'll never need to declare anything with a scope past the Workbook level.
- **Comment** - These can come in really handy when you start having a lot of names in a workbook and you want a quick reminder as to what they are, but don't worry about it if you only have a few that are obvious.
- **Refers to** - By default this is going to automatically fill with whatever range you have selected prior to invoking the Name Manager. If that's not what you want, you can also use the Range Launcher at the right to go and directly select the range you want after calling the Name Manager. This is one of those personal preference things and there's no "right" way to do it.
- *Edit* - This does nothing more than re-launch the New Name dialog and lets you change any part of what you already entered.

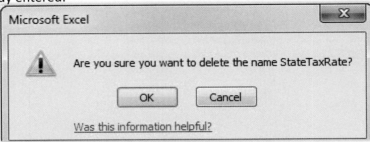
Figure 162

- *Delete* – This will Delete the Name you have selected at the time, and as with so many other things, Excel will ask if you really want to do it:
- *Filter* – This is a neat dialog in that it lets you narrow the scope of the names you want to see in the Name Manager, but unless you're dealing with a lot of names, you probably won't use it.

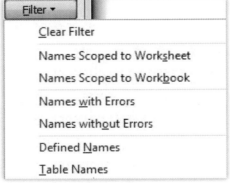
Figure 163

- *Define Name* – There are two options here:
  - Define Name - This just brings up the New Name dialog as seen in the example above.
  - Apply Names – Let's say you already wrote a few formulas then decided it might be easier to have some defined names in them. Excel won't automatically change your existing formulas to reflect the new names (it will when you start writing new formulas though), so you can use this dialog to update your named ranges in your formulas. For the purposes of this course this isn't going to be covered in depth (and it's relatively rarely used), but feel free to try it on your own. If you find yourself to be a fan of named ranges, then this may prove useful to you in the future.
  - In the following example, values were placed in A1 & B1, and the formula =A1+B1 placed below. After that, A1 & B1 were named "New" and "Old" respectively, then the Apply Names tool invoked:

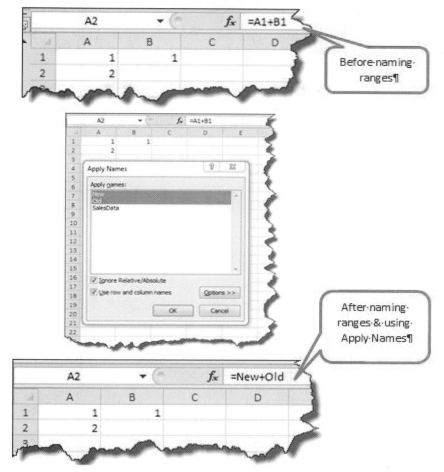

Figure 164

- **Use in Formula** – This simply allows you to select from your list of names whether you decide to start a new formula, or place a name in a formula once you're writing it. Again, this one is rarely at this level, so it's not going to be discussed in depth here.

- **Create from Selection** – Here Excel tries to read your mind, and create Named Ranges for you based on a range you select. It is not infallible, and unless your table ranges have relatively straightforward structure that you know won't go wrong, you're better off making sure by using the Name Manager and not leaving anything to chance. Hunting down an error in a Named Range is much better left avoided if at all possible.

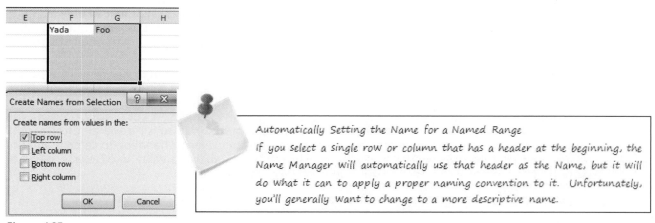

Figure 165

- **Formula Auditing** – This is a somewhat advanced feature that won't be covered in this course, but it allows you to evaluate formulas to determine if there are any cells dependent on them and vice versa, as well as watching Excel calculate a formula in steps, so you can see if some part of it isn't doing what

you expect. You'll find these methods employed in detailed models, and while very useful, the odds
that you'll use them in the beginning are slim.

- ○ **Trace Precedents** – Shows you what cells the formula depends on.
- ○ **Trace Dependents** – Shows you what cells are dependent on the formula.

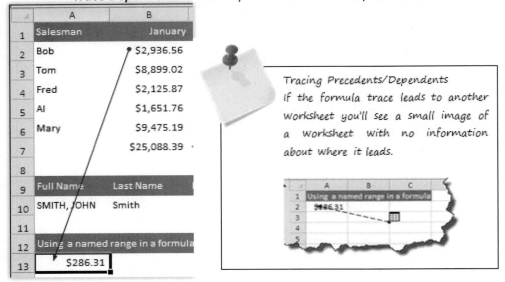

Tracing Precedents/Dependents
If the formula trace leads to another
worksheet you'll see a small image of
a worksheet with no information
about where it leads.

Figure 166

- ○ **Remove Arrows** – This resets the formula trace arrows. If you have a lot of formulas they can get overwhelming (they're literally all over the place!).

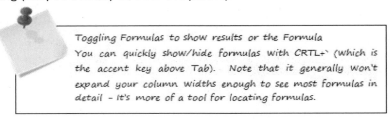

Toggling Formulas to show results or the Formula
You can quickly show/hide formulas with CRTL+` (which is
the accent key above Tab). Note that it generally won't
expand your column widths enough to see most formulas in
detail - it's more of a tool for locating formulas.

- ○ **Show Formulas** – This converts your formulas to text. It can be very handy if you want to distribute a workbook, but forgot where all the formulas are.

- ○ **Error Checking** – This is a tool for determining why certain formulas might evaluate to an error. Excel has a multitude of error messages to let you know why a formula doesn't return the results you might expect, and they're very useful (albeit somewhat scary at first). We'll be discussing Excel's Error Messages in the Formula lesson, but for now, the Error Checking option is a good consolidation tool for newer users, as it exposes 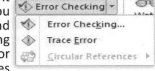 several options in one place for you. Just be warned that the Error Checking tool can only estimate why your formula evaluates to an error; it gives you a good place to start looking, but not much more. You might find yourself using Excel's Error Checking Options at first, but as you get stronger with Excel you'll find that it's often unneeded.

- ○ One reason we'll talk Excel's Formula Error Messages is because sometimes you want to suppress those errors on behalf of your users, so they don't think that your spreadsheet is "broken". Nothing will get users to scream more about that, even if the error messages are a result of them not yet entering required data. The following example shows how easy it is to get a #DIV/0 error (you can't divide by zero), and it's nothing more than =A2/B2, but B2 = 0, so it throws an error at you. But what if that 0 in B2 is dependent on user input? You can use error handling to catch it and not alarm your user like this: =IF(B2,A2/B2,0), which simply says that if a value in B2 exists, perform your function, otherwise return a 0 instead of an error message.

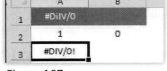

Figure 167

- ○ In the following example you'll see an error created by trying to reference a sales representative not in our list of sales reps, so it returns an #N/A error. This is one of those things where Excel will be less than useful by telling you that there's an error in your formula, but not really tell you how to fix it. Unfortunately, Excel can't read your mind even if the folks at Microsoft have done a pretty good job of trying to make it as smart as possible. Excel knows what font, size, color and even language you're using when you write a formula, but it doesn't know what you intended to do with it, so it gives you its best shot. As you get going on learning formulas you'll start to understand what causes errors and how to address them instead of having to rely on the Error Checking tool, but for now it might still be a good way to ease into things.

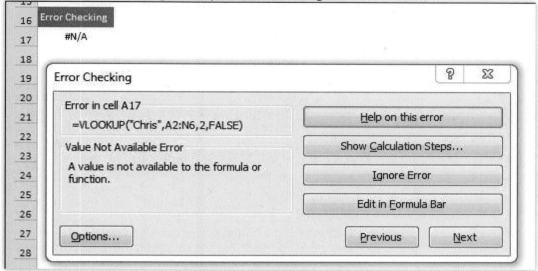

Figure 168

- ***Error Checking Options***
    - ○ ***Help on this error*** – This will launch the Office Online Helpfile and try to find you a solution. If you're not online it will resort to your PC's Helpfile (if you chose to install it). Generally these will give you an ambiguous article reference that will leave you as lost as when you started, although the Help Writers at Microsoft have really stepped up their game in getting really good help content to you, and more is to come, so this will prove to be a more valuable resource in the future.
    - ○ ***Show Calculation Steps*** – This will bring up the Evaluate Formula tool, which we'll discuss shortly
    - ○ ***Ignore Error*** – Does just that.
    - ○ ***Edit in Formula Bar*** - Does just that as well, although you could get there faster by just hitting the F2 key when the active cell houses the formula in question to activate the cell in question, or just click on the formula bar instead of taking the extra steps to invoke the Error Checker.
    - ○ ***Options*** – This will launch the Formula menu from the File, Options, Formulas dialog. It would be pretty silly to go all the way here just to invoke that, but sometimes you might find it handy.
    - ○ ***Previous/Next*** – Will look for additional errors in your worksheet, but generally if you're not disabling error messaging in formulas (which we'll discuss in the Formulas lesson) you'll know where to look, because a cell (or many cells, as is often the case) that should return a value gives you a result like #N/A or #DIV/0. Those are pretty hard to miss (they stick out like a sore thumb!)
- ***Trace Error*** – This simply draws arrows from the formula in question to any dependent cells. It's the same as using the Trace Precedents/Dependents tool. It's just a visual indication of where your cell dependencies lie.

- **Circular Reference** – A circular reference generally occurs when you try to get a cell to refer to itself. If you were to enter =A1 in cell A1 you'd get a circular reference, because a cell can't depend on itself for a value. A real-world example of this would be if you try to calculate employee bonuses based on net profit, which would be Revenue - Expenses. If you were to then try to add that bonus amount back into your Expenses you'd get an error because the bonus calculation is dependent on the difference between Revenue and Expenses, so you can't add that back in because it becomes part of the dependency, causing an error. If you do get a Circular Reference, Excel will let you know about it:

Figure 169

  ○ The Circular Reference tool simply identifies the cell(s) with those errors.

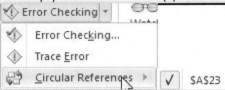

Figure 170

- **Evaluate Formula** – This is a great tool for checking your formulas if they don't give you the results that you expect. For simple formulas you probably won't need it, but for combined formulas (where you use multiple formulas together – these are sometimes referred to as Mega Formulas) it can be invaluable, as it allows you to evaluate each section of a formula without having to break the formula apart into its different elements. Many people who don't know about this tool will break a formula apart into its separate parts and test each one individually until they trace the error. With the Evaluate tool you don't need to do that, instead you let Excel do the heavy lifting for you. Here's a simple example of one of the Formulas in the Lesson 4 companion workbook: =Formulas!B2*Tax (which if you remember was defined as a named range with a value of 9.75%).

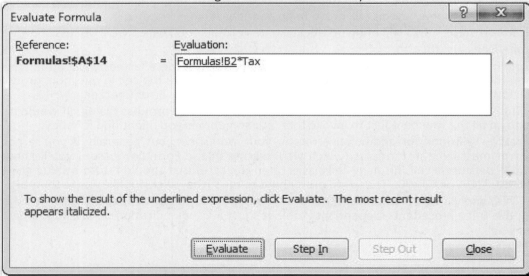

Figure 171

- You'll see the first part of the formula that will be evaluated underlined. Pressing the evaluate button will tell you what that portion of the formula evaluates to, in this case it's a static number from cell B2, so Evaluate gives you its value
- Each press of the Evaluate button will move you onto the next step in the formula. Here you'll see that it's evaluated Tax as 9.75%.
- Finally it gives you the result, now it's up to you to determine if it's right or not. This was a very simple example, but you can imagine how helpful it can be to point out what might otherwise be a very obscure error. It's also a very interesting window into how Excel calculates formulas.

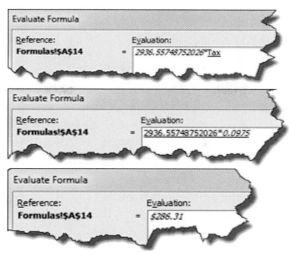

Figure 172

- **Step In** – This is just another way of showing a different level of detail.
  - ◦ **Watch Window** – This is another neat tool for testing or monitoring your formulas. Let's say you have a formula on one sheet that's dependent on the active sheet, but you don't want to have to switch between sheets to see if it's doing what it should. You can add a Watch Window to monitor it right there.

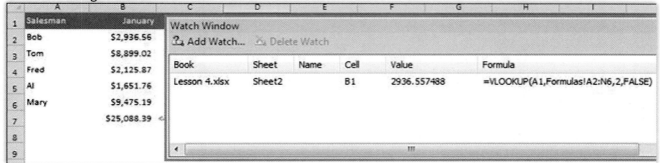

Figure 173

- ▪ In this case the formula being watched is dependent on changes in our sales table in cell B1. So changing that value will update that watched formula on the other sheet. Will you use this a great deal? Not likely, but when you do, it's an invaluable resource, just like the Evaluate tool.

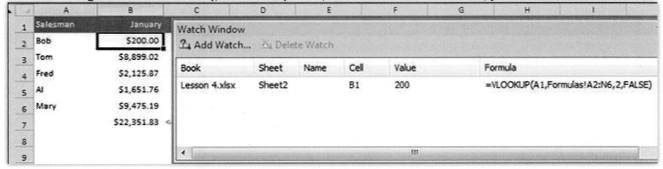

Figure 174

- **Calculation** – This is where you control how Excel calculates, whether it be Automatic or on demand (Manual). Why is this important? Let's say you have a complicated model for your business that tracks Revenue & Expenses and also calculates things like your profit. It may be dependent on a lot of data entry, but also have a lot of formulas that calculate those figures. Each time you enter data Excel will recalculate all of your formulas. If you have a lot of formulas (and with 16 billion cells on a worksheet it's not hard to imagine how many formulas you can have), each time Excel calculates can slow your data entry to a crawl, so you can turn calculation off an only recalculate when you're done.

- ○ **Calculation Options**
  - ▪ Automatic
  - ▪ Automatic Except for Data Tables
  - ▪ Manual

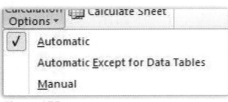

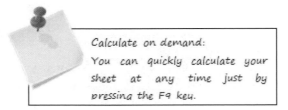
Calculate on demand:
You can quickly calculate your sheet at any time just by pressing the F9 key.

Figure 175

- ○ **Calculate Now** – Calculates the entire workbook.
- ○ **Calculate Sheet** – Calculates just the formulas on the active sheet.

Data

First, the Data tab gives you options as to what kind of external data you can pull into your Excel workbook, be it a Microsoft Access database, from the internet or even text files. You can also manage your data connections by refreshing them and even setting intervals for them. A lot of people like to use Excel to keep track of their investment portfolios, and you can have Excel update the portfolio data throughout the day, or maybe you're linked up to a company server that lets you download transactional data specific to your business. Instead of doing it manually, you can tell Excel to do it for you. We'll discuss this in depth in the Importing Data from Other Sources lesson.

Figure 176

Second, the Data tab gives you a lot of important functionality for analyzing and manipulating your data, like Sorting, Filtering and a lot of other neat tricks. We'll discuss a lot of this in the next lesson on Entering and Editing Data, so for now we're just going to cover the basics.

- • **Sort & Filter**
  - ○ **Sorting** - is relatively straightforward on this menu, you simply click on the direction you want to sort (Ascending or Descending). Just click on the A-Z or Z-A buttons to do either. Don't worry about the A-Z/Z-A label, as it will work fine with numbers too. Clicking the Sort button will launch the Excel 2003 Sort dialog, which we'll go into more detail later.

  - ○ **Filter** - is a tool you might have become familiar with if you looked at the earlier Data Table options. Again, it's something we'll discuss in more detail later. When you want to invoke Filtering the tool will automatically look for a header in your data and add drop-down to your contiguous range of data. Adding a Filter also gives you the ability to sort directly from the Filter dialog.

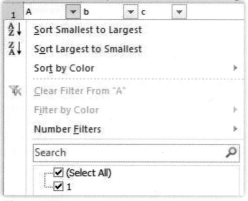

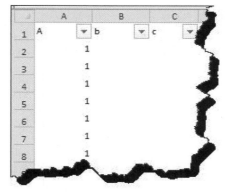

Figure 177

- ◦ **Advanced** – This is a great tool if you need to narrow down a list. Let's say you have a list of customer transactions, but you want to create a list of just the customer names, or items purchased. You can use Advanced Filter to copy the Unique Records to another place on your sheet. From there you can move it to another sheet and do what you want with it. Unfortunately, Advanced Filter will only copy your data to the same sheet, so you have to cut and paste if you want to move it somewhere else (which you generally do).

Figure 178

- **Data Tools**

This group holds several tools that let you physically manipulate your data without having to cut and paste, or otherwise do it manually.

- ◦ **Text to Columns** – This lets you quickly parse data without formulas or manual labor. Remember the formula example of breaking apart customer names ("Smith, John")? Data, Text to Columns is faster and generally a much better way to go with large data sets. It's got a good Wizard tool to help guide you, and we'll discuss it in depth in the next lesson.

- ◦ **Remove Duplicates** – This is a new tool that Microsoft released after years of begging. Previously if you wanted to remove duplicate information from you data you had to either do it manually or write code. Now you can do it in just a few steps. Simply select your data range and invoke the Remove Duplicates Wizard.

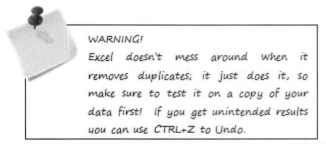

WARNING!
Excel doesn't mess around when it removes duplicates; it just does it, so make sure to test it on a copy of your data first! If you get unintended results you can use CTRL+Z to Undo.

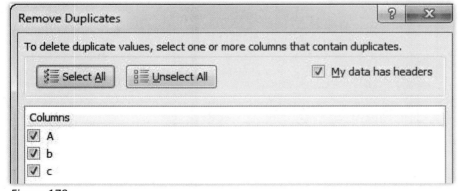

Figure 179

- ◦ **Data Validation** – This is one of your most powerful allies when it comes to defining what data your users can enter. For instance you can limit date entries to a certain range, like making sure that Time-Off requests only go from the current date forward, define a number range, like limiting an annual employee increase form to

5%. You can even use your own defined lists to select from a list of cities in which you do business to prevent misspellings, because frankly, given the opportunity, how many people are going to misspell Mississauga or Onondaga? If you have formulas depending on correct spellings then this is invaluable. Again, this is one of those tools that require some in-depth discussion, so we'll cover it in detail in the next lesson.

- **Consolidate** – This allows you to combine data from multiple ranges in a new consolidated range. For the purposes of this course we won't be discussing it, as it's not likely you'll use it this early on in the game, but if you are interested, the Helpfile documents it well.

- **What-If Analysis** – There are literally entire books devoted to these tools, so we're not going to cover them in detail here, instead we'll just quickly review them. Note that these are just the tools that are natively included with Excel's standard installation. There are additional Add-In tools that you can find both from Microsoft and other third-parties that perform a multitude of analysis tasks. If you have a relatively unique business model, then odds are you'll find that someone's written a tool to help you analyze it.

  ○ **Scenario Manager** – Allows you to define different scenarios based on certain inputs. Let's say you have a best-case scenario for your business, but you also want to be prepared for an economic downturn or catastrophic event, Scenario Manager lets you build those scenarios without having to build complicated models. You can also combine separate scenarios into a Scenario Report so you can view them side-by-side.

  ○ **Goal Seek** – This is a great tool for determining a result based on variable inputs. Let's say you need a new pizza oven and you know that it's $30,000. Your credit union will give you a rate of 7% over 60 monthly payments, resulting in a monthly payment of $594.04, but you only want to spend $500 per month. With Goal Seek you can determine that you need to find an oven in the $25,000 range. Clicking OK will accept the solution, whereas Cancel will revert to your original values.

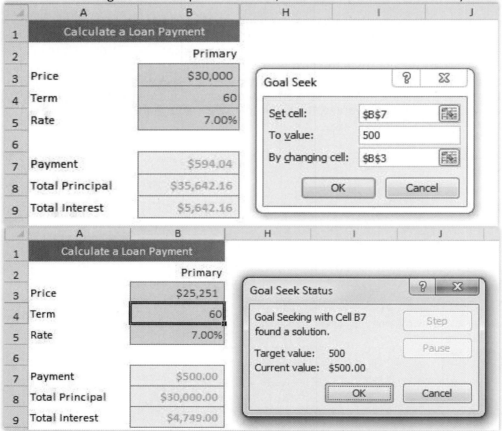

Figure 180

  ○ **Data Tables** – These are similar to Scenarios except that you can build multiple variations in one spot vs. individual scenarios that can later be consolidated. For instance you could analyze the effects of different terms on lease options for a new location. The Excel Helpfile has good documentation on both Scenarios and Data Tables should you choose to explore them further on your own.

- ### *Outline*
  - ○ **Group/Ungroup** – This lets you group rows/columns so that they can easily be hidden or displayed with the click of a button instead of having to do it manually. Simply select the range you want to group and select the Group icon. Excel will ask you if you want to group rows or columns and then apply a group for you. In order to create groups you need to have some type of range break between them, otherwise Excel will just add any additional ranges to the contiguous group. This does take some time to set up, but it can be well worth it once you do. Where would you use this? Let's say you have an employee roster that lists employee names, then days of the week. If you wanted to give each employee their own shift schedule you could group them. Once you apply a group, you'll see Excel create a number dialog (1,2) to the left of the row headings or above the column headings depending on which grouping style you selected, as well as +/- signs for each group to show you whether they're collapsed or expanded. Selecting the 1/2 will expand the entire range of groups, whereas the +/- will expand or collapse just that particular group.
  - ○ **Auto Outline** – This is a way to let Excel apply multiple groupings to rows and columns, but it's finicky at best, and should generally be avoided.
  - ○ **Subtotal** – This is a huge tool for analyzing your data quickly without having to write formulas. Just let Excel do it for you! Following is an example of some transactional data for a fictitious company that has several regional sales offices and products that they sell, and a snapshot of the Subtotal Wizard.

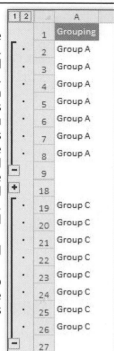

Unfortunately, you can only apply one Subtotal function at a time, so it's SUM, AVERAGE, MAX, MIN, etc. In order to use different functions you'd actually need to manipulate the subtotal formulas by hand.

	A	B	C	D	E	F	G	H	I
1					Southwest Gas General Ledger				
2									
3	Region	Product	Date	Month	Customer	Quantity	Revenue	COGS	
4	Central	ABC	01/09/08	Jan-08	General Motors	800	16,416	6,776	
5	Central	ABC	01/12/08	Jan-08	IBM	300	6,267	2,541	
6	Central	ABC	01/25/08			000	20,770	8,470	1
7	Central	ABC	02/08/08			100	1,817	847	
8	Central	ABC	02/09/08			300	5,157	2,541	
9	Central	ABC	02/19/08			500	10,385	4,235	
10	Central	ABC	02/20/08			600	11,124	5,082	
11	Central	ABC	02/27/08			900	16,209	7,623	
12	Central	ABC	03/18/08			800	16,696	6,776	
13	Central	ABC	03/22/08			300	5,355	2,541	
14	Central	ABC	03/23/08			200	3,756	1,694	
15	Central	ABC	03/27/08			300	5,358	2,541	
16	Central	ABC	04/06/08			300	5,886	2,541	
17	Central	ABC	04/13/08			400	8,016	3,388	
18	Central	ABC	04/30/08			200	3,802	1,694	
19	Central	ABC	05/10/08			500	8,785	4,235	
20	Central	ABC	05/23/08			600	11,700	5,082	
21	Central	ABC	05/31/08	May-08	General Motors	700	13,986	5,929	
22	Central	ABC	06/13/08	Jun-08	General Electric	700	12,838	5,929	
23	Central	ABC	06/25/08	Jun-08	Exxon	700	13,734	5,929	
24	Central	ABC	07/30/08	Jul-08	Wal-Mart	300	5,508	2,541	

Figure 181

- ○ With the Subtotal Wizard you can select which column you want to Subtotal (in this case we're selecting the Region, then select the Function (Formula) you want to apply, in this case we're going to use Sum. Next you can choose which columns you want to apply those formulas.   Once you click OK, Excel's going to give you instant Subtotals. Notice that it also adds grouping layers for you, similar to what we just discussed with Grouping.

		A	B	C	D	E	F	G	H	I
	1				Southwest Gas General Ledger					
	2									
	3	Region	Product	Date	Month	Customer	Quantity	Revenue	COGS	Profit
57			ABC Total				28100	538,062	238,007	300,055
99			DEF Total				24000	531,010	236,160	294,850
147			XYZ Total				25500	587,562	260,610	326,952
148		Central Total					77600	1,656,634	734,777	921,857
208			ABC Total				30300	584,251	256,641	327,610
263			DEF Total				28400	631,700	279,456	352,244
311			XYZ Total				30400	693,290	310,688	382,602
312		East Total					89100	1,909,241	846,785	1,062,456
357			ABC Total				24800	471,301	210,056	261,245
386			DEF Total				16000	349,082	157,440	191,642
421			XYZ Total				19600	458,514	200,312	258,202
422		West Total					60400	1,278,897	567,808	711,089
423		Grand Total					227100	4,844,772	2,149,370	2,695,402

Figure 182

Subtotaling Tips

• You can apply multiple subtotals by first subtotaling on your primary category (Region), then invoke the Subtotal Wizard again and select the second category, but this time uncheck the "Replace current subtotals" check box.

		A	B	C	D	E	F	G	H	I
	1				Southwest Gas General Ledger					
	2									
	3	Region	Product	Date	Month	Customer	Quantity	Revenue	COGS	Profit
145		Central Total					77600	1,656,634	734,777	921,857
306		East Total					89100	1,909,241	846,785	1,062,456
413		West Total					60400	1,278,897	567,808	711,089
414		Grand Total					227100	4,844,772	2,149,370	2,695,402

Figure 183

Review

This is where you get a workbook ready for distribution by checking spelling, adding comments and protecting workbooks and worksheets from changes.

- • **Proofing** – This is pretty straightforward.
  - ○ **Spelling** - is going to Spell Check your entire worksheet based on the Office Dictionary, including any specific words you might have added.
  - ○ **Research** - will launch an internal search pane on the right that will allow you to search for a term or word in internal content that came with Office, or the Internet, both directly from Excel.
  - ○ **Thesaurus** - will bring up Excel's internal Thesaurus tool to let you select from different terms. It also lets you use the Internet internally.

○ ***Language*** – This simply consists of a Translation tool that can translate words or entire worksheets to another language. Note that here Excel can only interpret your literal text, but it can't interpret your intentions, so use it with caution. Excel will do its best to get it right, but if you deal with translations a lot it's best to have a live person proof the document before you send it to anyone. Many a business deal has been lost in translation. Literally.

○ ***Comments*** – Comments are a twist on letting users know what's going on in your worksheet/ book. You can use Data Validation to add comments to a cell in terms of directing user input, but cell comments are simply to make note of something. You'll see a lot of Excel templates that have comments directing you how to set it up for you, and then instruct you  to delete them when you're done. They can be pretty handy, but as with colors, use them sparingly, as they can get irritating fast. Comments can be displayed constantly, or hidden from view. When they're hidden you'll see a small red triangle in the upper right-hand corner of the cell. You can just hover over the red triangle to display the comment. As soon as you move the cursor off of the cell the comment will disappear. You can also choose to selectively hide comments by selecting them, then using the Show/Hide Comment button.

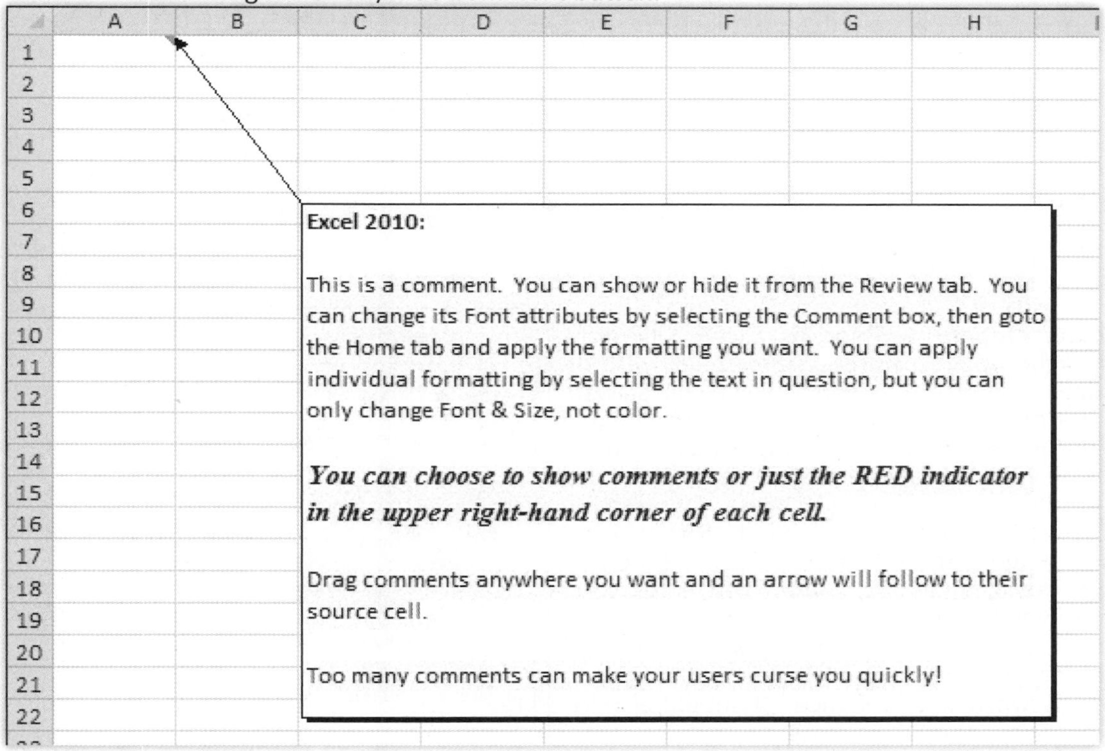

Excel 2010:

This is a comment. You can show or hide it from the Review tab. You can change its Font attributes by selecting the Comment box, then goto the Home tab and apply the formatting you want. You can apply individual formatting by selecting the text in question, but you can only change Font & Size, not color.

You can choose to show comments or just the RED indicator in the upper right-hand corner of each cell.

Drag comments anywhere you want and an arrow will follow to their source cell.

Too many comments can make your users curse you quickly!

Figure 184

▪ ***Show Ink*** – It's unlikely that you'll ever run into this unless you share your workbooks with users who use tablet PC's or stylus type input devices. Show Ink just allows you to see hand drawn annotations or notes.

● ***Changes***

○ This is where you'll do a lot of work for distributing workbooks to end users, whether you want them to only make changes to selected cells or ranges, or if you don't want the workbook to be editable at all.

Figure 185

○ ***Protect Sheet*** - By default all cells on a worksheet are Locked, so you need to unlock them prior to protecting the worksheet. First, you need to select the cells you want to allow to be editable (you can select multiple non-contiguous cells/ranges with Ctrl+Left-Click). Once selected, press Ctrl+1 to launch the Format, Cells dialog and goto the Protection tab. Uncheck the Locked check box, which will allow those cells to be editable once the worksheet is protected. The Hidden button isn't for editing, but if you want to hide the contents of cells with formulas. Why would you want to do that? Maybe you have a hidden worksheet that you don't want users to know exists, or you might reference sensitive information that you don't want people to see. If you do have some of those, then once you've unlocked your editable cells you'd go back and repeat the process, but this time check Hidden, making sure not to uncheck "Locked". One nice thing about sheet protection is that it introduces a Tab order in the unprotected cells, meaning that the Tab key will automatically move the user from one unprotected cell to the next, but it does have limits. Note that this does require some design considerations as the Tab order goes from Left to Right, then Down. If you've ever entered data into a web site form that had its Tab order out of sequence, like moving from City to Zip Code, then State, you'll be immediately familiar with this concept.

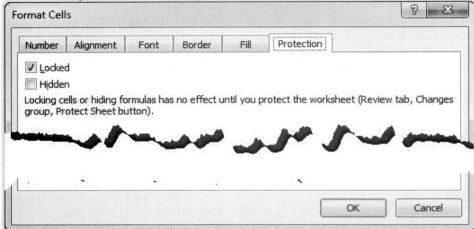

Figure 186

- ○ **Protection Options** – Prior to Excel 2003 you only had the option to protect the sheet, with or without a password. Now you have a whole slew of additional options at your disposal. For instance you can allow users to use AutoFilter or Sort data, where previously you had to write code or unprotect the sheet to allow this behavior. Unless a worksheet is specifically for you and you're protecting it to take advantage of the Tab order, then you generally want to use a password. When you enter your password you'll be prompted to enter it again. You don't need to get fancy with your password like you would with your online bank accounts though. A simple password should suffice. It should also be something easy enough to remember. If you try to change a Locked cell on a protected sheet you'll get a message telling you that the cell you're trying to change is protected.

Figure 187

- ○ **Protect Workbook** – This prevents users from making changes to the overall structure of your workbook, like adding or deleting sheets. Here again you have the option of entering a password.
- ○ **Share** – This allows you to let multiple users work on a workbook simultaneously; however it should be avoided if at all possible, because Shared workbooks can cause all kinds of problems. They also have some pretty severe limitations with regards to the native functionality they support. If you need a multi-user input tool, then you're much better off using Microsoft Access, or you can let

users collaborate on documents using Microsoft's free SkyDrive service. Note that workbooks that contain Tables can't be shared.

Figure 188

- ○ ***Protect and Share Workbook*** – This simply lets you protect a workbook before sharing it.

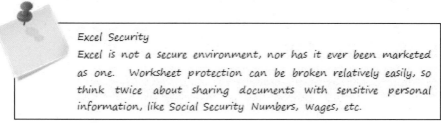

Excel Security
Excel is not a secure environment, nor has it ever been marketed as one. Worksheet protection can be broken relatively easily, so think twice about sharing documents with sensitive personal information, like Social Security Numbers, Wages, etc.

- ○ ***Allow Users to Edit Ranges*** – This is a new feature that allows you to set individual passwords and permissions to individual cells/ranges. This could be handy for something like an online timesheet application where you don't want people to be able to enter data for anyone but themselves. When you launch the dialog you'd click "New" to get started adding a range.
  - ▪ You can add a password, and anyone who knows the password could edit the range, or you can define individual user roles by proceeding to the Permissions step. If you're not familiar with setting user roles on a PC you might be better off having an IT specialist do this for you.

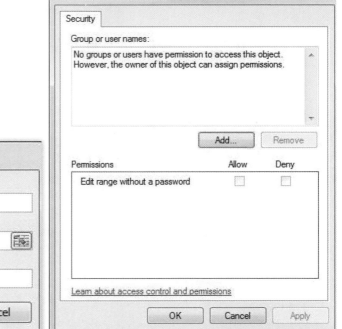

Figure 189

      ◦   Track Changes – This is a feature in Shared Workbooks that highlights changes that users make.

View

The View tab is where you control the appearance of your worksheets.

- **Workbook Views**
  - ◦ **Normal** – This is the default view for your workbooks and is most likely where you'll spend most of your time. You can also toggle Views from the Status Bar.
  - ◦ **Page Layout** – This allows you to see the worksheet as it will print, including revealing any Headers/Footers you might have. You saw an example of this view in the Header & Footer section.
  - ◦ **Page Break Preview** – This lets you see where your page breaks are, and they're displayed as dotted blue lines horizontally and vertically. The Print Area is delineated by a solid blue border and everything outside of the print area is gray.
  - ◦ **Custom Views** – This is a neat way to set up different views instead of constantly hiding rows or columns. Any existing views will be displayed in the dialog, and you can easily add new ones. In order to define a new view you first need to set up your worksheet the way that you want it, hiding rows and columns as necessary. Once you've defined the view you can unhide everything, then invoking that view will return the sheet to the view you set up. It takes some time to set up several views, but if you're in the habit of hiding rows and columns this can be a huge timesaver.

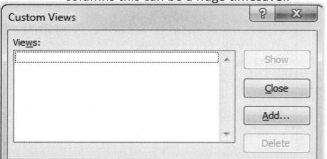
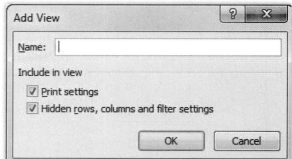

Figure 190

- ◦ **Full Screen** – This simply hides the Ribbon and Quick Action Toolbar. You can revert to normal view by pressing the ESC key.
- ◦ **Show** – This defines some of the physical elements you can have on the worksheet, like the Ruler, Gridlines, Formula Bar and Headings. In many cases you'll want to turn these off, especially with a distributed report that is for viewing only.

Figure 191

○ **Zoom** – These allow you to zoom in or out on your sheet to show more detail or less. You'll also find the Zoom controls on the Status Bar if you have them activated. Zoom will launch a dialog that has preset Zoom values, or you can enter in your own value.

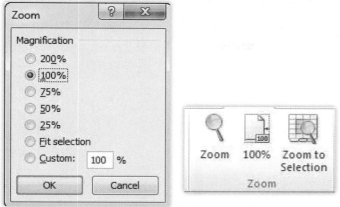

Figure 192

○ **100%** - Will return your worksheet to 100% Zoom.

○ **Zoom to Selection** – This allows you to select a range on your worksheet and quickly zoom into it. You can click on the 100% button to get back to normal.

○ **Window** – This allows you to view multiple worksheets/workbooks at once, as well as freezing rows and columns so that you can always see them regardless of where you are on a sheet.

Figure 193

○ **New Window** – Clicking this will create a copy of your workbook and an instance number will be appended to the workbook name ("Workbook1:2"). Once you've done this you can use the Arrange All selection to view the workbooks side by side.

○ **Arrange All** – This just gives you options as to how you want to compare the open workbooks, whether it's a new window or different workbooks. If you want to view different workbooks, make sure to uncheck the "Windows of active workbook" check box.

○ **Freeze Panes** – As mentioned, this lets you freeze columns and rows so that they're always visible no matter where you scroll on the worksheet. To Freeze Panes select the row below the row you want to freeze and the column to the right of the columns you want frozen, then select Freeze Panes. You can also opt to freeze just the top row and first column. This is fine if you don't have multiple detail rows and columns you want frozen in place.

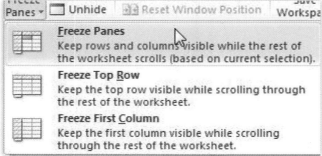

Figure 194

○   ***Split*** – This will split your worksheet into multiple panes. It can be useful for large sheets with a lot of data on them, because you can view the top of the sheet in one pane and the bottom in another.

Figure 195

○   ***Hide*** - This will hide the entire workbook.

○   ***Unhide*** – This gives you the option of unhiding any hidden workbooks.

> Hiding Worksheets - Remember, you can quickly hide worksheets by right-clicking on the Worksheet tab.

○   ***Macros*** – This course isn't going to cover Macros or VBA (Visual Basic for Applications) programming, but you can view a list of all public macros, or record a new macro from this menu. The Use Relative References is just a way to tell the Macro Recorder to change its reference style when it deals with cells and ranges.

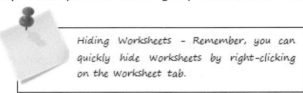

Figure 196

Unit Summary: Lesson 4 –The Ribbon In-Depth - Part II

• In this lesson you learned about the in-depth ins and outs of the Insert, Page Layout, Formulas, Data, Review and View tabs on the Excel Ribbon, while the previous lesson focused solely on the Home tab.

• You walked through the elements of each Ribbon tab, and also saw how there are multiple ways to expose the elements with keyboard shortcuts and Dialog Launchers.

Review Questions – Lesson 4 – The Ribbon In-Depth – Part II

1. Name 4 groups on the Page Layout tab, and what do they do?

a. _____

b. _____

c. _____

d. _____

2. What are four of the Formula groups?

a. _____

3. Where would you turn off Gridlines on a worksheet?

a. _____

4. What does Grouping do?

a. _____

5. Why would you want to use Comments?

a. _____

b. _____

6. Where do you find quick access to functions?

a. _____

7. How can you keep a user from changing data in a worksheet?

a. _____

Lesson Assignment – Lesson 4 - The Rest of the Ribbon

This assignment is to open the Lesson 4 workbook and start getting familiarized with the following (there is a Notes section below for you to keep track of your observations):

- *Insert Tab*
  - Start working with Shapes & SmartArt
- *Page Layout Tab*
  - Experiment with different page layout options, like Portrait vs. Landscape.
- *Formulas Tab*
  - Try working with some of the AutoSum tools in the Formulas worksheet
- *Data Tab*
  - Apply a Data Filter to some data and start exploring the different filtering options.
- *Review Tab*
  - Try Spell Checking
  - Add a few Comments and format them
  - Explore what you can do with worksheet protection and the expanded user options you can grant
- *View Tab*
  - Set up a worksheet for printing and adjust the display options, like Headings & Gridlines
  - Try the New Window feature and see how many different ways you can view worksheets & workbooks side-by-side

Lesson 4 Notes

Lesson 5 – Entering and Manipulating Data (and the basic rules of good spreadsheet design)

In the last few lessons you learned the ins-and-outs of the Excel Ribbon interface and all of the commands that the Ribbon puts at your fingertips. In this lesson we'll start exploring how to actually use them by setting up some business scenarios, entering and editing data, preparing them (a workbook) for distribution with formatting, and finally preparing it for printing.

Next to using functions to analyze your data, the actual data input is one of the most important aspects of using Excel. After all, without the data, you have nothing to analyze. In a small business scenario you might not have a large database or mainframe system to input your daily transactions, but instead rely on manual methods or some type of small business accounting software, like QuickBooks. A lot of times that information is great, but what if it doesn't adequately measure those aspects of your business that will help you manage it smarter, like customer turnover vs. retention rate, or employee sales performance? Small business accounting systems are great for telling you where you stand financially, but they don't often give you the deeper insight that can really help. While there are certainly merits to making decisions based on your gut instinct, when you have a tool like Excel right at your fingertips you should use it. The same can be said for managing household finances; why do by hand what you can have Excel do for you? Regardless of the need, it all boils down to how to you get your information from its source to Excel, and once it gets there what do you do with it.

In this lesson we're going to talk about how to enter and edit data, how to manipulate it once it's there, how to format it so it looks the way that you want, and finally prepare it for printing/distribution. In this lesson you'll work with a companion workbook that is laid out in steps to help you understand the process.

Before you just start putting your information/data into a worksheet, you need to understand some fundamental concepts behind good spreadsheet design (these concepts go beyond just Excel as well). This course is laid out in such a fashion as to reinforce those steps, but we'll go over them here and explain them in detail.

- Questions - Before you start to enter any data in a worksheet, you should ask yourself some questions, because the biggest part of the design and question phase is to determine your function and audience.
  - Is there another tool that could do this more efficiently?
  - Is this necessary? (e.g. do I really need to create a shopping list in Excel when a pen and paper will work fine?)
  - What do I want to keep track of in here?
  - What do I want to measure (both broadly and specifically)?
  - Who is my audience/user(s), will it require data input, and if so from whom?
  - What is my primary data source? Will I be pulling data from a company server or the Internet, will users manually input data, or a bit of both?
  - Will this be an analytical tool (something that you might use for business planning), is this a flashy daily sales leaderboard you want to post to pump up your team, is it something like an employee schedule or calendar that you'll just post on a wall and let people fill in by hand, or is it more of a data warehouse, like a customer list? All of those require some degree of data input, but the extent and methods are up to you.

Good planning goes a long way - there is nothing worse than expecting people to use a poorly designed spreadsheet; if you make it difficult for people to enter data, they will make it difficult for you to get it back.

If you can answer those questions to your satisfaction, then move on to Step 1.

Don't fix what ain't broken!

You don't necessarily need to resort to using Excel if there's another tool out there that does what it needs to do, especially if you already use it! Companies across the globe suffer from "report regurgitation" where someone didn't like the format that the company system (or even another department) spit out, so they have someone else re-enter the data and make it look the way they want it to look.

1. Planning
   a. This is where you conceptualize your overall design. If it's something simple that you're not going to reuse, then just go ahead and whip something together it, but if this is going to be something sustainable, like a pricing matrix for your products, then you'll be better off putting some time and effort into design before you start tapping away on the keyboard. This may sound counter-intuitive,

but most often the best spreadsheets and databases are laid out on paper before you even turn on the computer. If you can sketch out an overall idea of what you want, then it will be easier to set up something that can be flexible and grow with you. It doesn't have to be perfect, just a bit of a road map to get you going; but you certainly don't have to do it and many great spreadsheets have been built without it. However, there's nothing worse than being stuck with, or having to redesign a poorly built spreadsheet that has consumed a lot of hours building, especially when it can all be avoided up front.

b. Inalienable Design Rules

- Rows vs. Columns – Your detail data should go across, not down! This concept borrows from intelligent database design, which was probably derived from the old accounting ledgers that led to the spreadsheet in the first place. This is commonly referred to as a "flat file format". If you can just keep this single, simple precept in mind anytime you start a new spreadsheet then you'll be in pretty good shape right off the bat.

  - Following is an extreme example of data gone "bad", next to the way data should be laid out. Can you guess which one is better?

Figure 197

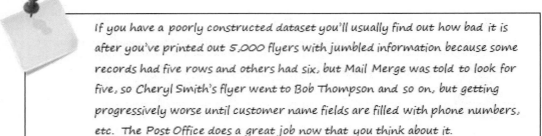

If you have a poorly constructed dataset you'll usually find out how bad it is after you've printed out 5,000 flyers with jumbled information because some records had five rows and others had six, but Mail Merge was told to look for five, so Cheryl Smith's flyer went to Bob Thompson and so on, but getting progressively worse until customer name fields are filled with phone numbers, etc. The Post Office does a great job now that you think about it.

  - If you haven't already guessed, the example on the left is the "bad" one. That data is largely unusable because there's just no way to discern one record from the next. How do you know when one record ends and another one starts? You might say that you could key on the numeric address like "123 Main Street", but what if the address doesn't lead with a number, like "Evergreen Terrace #3"? Another issue is that there's no normality, because the first two customer records don't have zip codes, but the third does. This means you can't standardize any process like Mail Merging without a large degree of failure. Another thing to think about is that even with over a million rows in Excel 2010, you might see how you could quickly run out of room by going down (exponentially), whereas you could technically* add a million+ customer records if you formatted your layout correctly (across vs. down). (*Technically – if you have a million+ customer records you need to be dealing with a database, like Access, not Excel! Just because you can store large quantities of data in Excel it should not be mistaken for a database application, which it is not. It is an analysis tool).

c. Data Separation – Wherever possible separate your data as much as possible. For instance, storing "Bob Smith" in a single cell is much less usable than having separate columns for First Name/Last Name. Both can be parsed out (split apart) with functions, or with Excel's Data, Text to Columns tool (we'll discuss both later), but it's often unwieldy at best and should be avoided if at all possible.

This becomes really important when you start dealing with middle name/initial, suffixes/prefixes, etc. To borrow a math term, the more you can break your data down into its lowest common denominators the better. Just think of all the Internet sites where you enter First Name, Last Name, Address, City, State, etc., separately. Those are all database driven, and they follow those rules for a reason.

    d.   Another thing that can chuck your data right out the window is to store it all in a single cell:

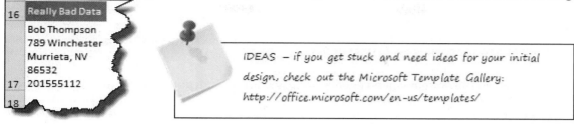

IDEAS – if you get stuck and need ideas for your initial design, check out the Microsoft Template Gallery: http://office.microsoft.com/en-us/templates/

Figure 198

- In the "Really Bad Data" example the data has been crammed into one cell, which renders it all but useless. No degree of formulas or VBA code can reliably strip that data out, so you might as well start over. Unfortunately, data like this is all too common in Excel, so this is a more than gentle hint to not let this type of data into your world.

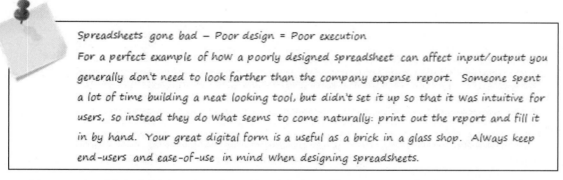

Spreadsheets gone bad – Poor design = Poor execution

For a perfect example of how a poorly designed spreadsheet can affect input/output you generally don't need to look farther than the company expense report. Someone spent a lot of time building a neat looking tool, but didn't set it up so that it was intuitive for users, so instead they do what seems to come naturally: print out the report and fill it in by hand. Your great digital form is a useful as a brick in a glass shop. Always keep end-users and ease-of-use in mind when designing spreadsheets.

- Try not to think 2-Dimensionally – Excel is just like a ream of paper in that it's a series of worksheets stacked on top of each other, but that doesn't mean that you can't develop relationships between one worksheet and another (or other workbooks for that matter). One of Excel's strongest points (thanks to its powerful functions) is the ability to store data on different worksheets and relate them via a common identifier (much like a database). For example, you can have table of employees with all of their information (Employee #, Name, Address, Wage, Hire Date, etc.) on one sheet, and then a transaction list of sales by employee number. A few simple functions will let you summarize sales by employee #, yet you can have the information remain on separate worksheets (in the case of sensitive employee or customer information, those worksheets can be hidden from your users). Grasping this can be a big hurdle for a lot of people, because it just seems so far-fetched, but it's really very easy, so keep that in mind when you're planning your workbook.

2. Design & Build

    a.   Once you've decided on a function for your spreadsheet(s) you need to focus on a design, then it's time to start building the spreadsheet. You should already have an overall concept in mind, like if this will be a balance sheet with expense categories in rows on the left and months as your column headers, or an employee schedule with employee names in rows, and days of the week as column headers. As you gain experience with building spreadsheets for different scenarios you'll find yourself reusing your favorites over and over again. The initial pain is in setting up the first few, but once you get a few under your belt you'll quickly know how to start a new one with relative ease.

    b.   The next step is to build the guts of your spreadsheet by defining the row and column headers that you want (e.g. Employee 1, 2, 3 & January, February, March, etc.). You're still very flexible at this point, so don't get too bound by the idea that you can't change your mind.

    c.   Try to keep things as simple as possible. An overly complex model can be confusing and difficult for users to understand. A spreadsheet can be very powerful thing even with a simple, time-tested design.

    d.   Try to reuse elements wherever possible. Why type in January-December for each row, when you can do it once and refer to the original values throughout the worksheet, and even the entire workbook?

3. Populate – Sample Data

    a. Once you've gotten your design down (or relatively close) it's time to start entering in some sample data. At this point there's no reason to enter in real data unless it just happens to be right there in front of you, otherwise just make up some numbers that will reasonably represent what you plan on entering later. All you're going to do here is set the stage to evaluate your functionality. You don't want to invest a lot of data entry resources at this point just in case you decide to completely change your design.

4. Evaluate/Calculate

    a. This is where you start putting Excel's true power as an analytical tool to use. Here you start developing the formulas that you'll use to summarize and evaluate your data, be it simple sums or averages, or complex ratios and relational formulas.

    b. We've got a whole lesson that will be devoted to using Excel's functions, so this won't cover much, but you should try some of the AutoSum features that we discussed earlier and see how they work in a real situation. As we get into the Function lesson, some more insight about what you can do in Excel will also help expand your design capabilities. One of the limiting factors when people design spreadsheets is that they just don't know that something is possible, so they don't think to add it. You'll instantly know when you have one of those "Ahh haa! I didn't know Excel could do that!" moments.

5. Format

    a. As much as you might be tempted to add formatting elements while you're building your spreadsheet, you should try to avoid it and wait until it's functional. Otherwise you will find yourself going back and adjusting the formatting as you adjust your sheet design. This also holds true for other applications, like Word or Power Point; saving the formatting for last will save you time in the long run. You can easily get bogged down investing time into formatting a sheet, just to throw the design away and start over, like crumpling up a piece of paper. It's a shame to have formatting time wasted like that. Fortunately, formatting is easier than ever with Excel's new styles & gallery selections, as well as themes. What used to take a lot of manual labor can now be created in just a few mouse clicks.

6. Populate – Live Data

    a. Now that your workbook/sheet is set up and doing what you want, it's time to start putting real data into the workbook. If you're entering the data yourself or pulling it from an external source you generally don't need to worry about protecting the workbook/worksheets. But if you're going to be relying on users to enter your data, then you're strongly encouraged to take advantage of Excel's protection, so they can't inadvertently overwrite your functions. As mentioned earlier, you just select the cells/ranges in which you want to allow data entry, goto Format, Cells (Ctrl+1), Protection and uncheck "Locked". Then protect the worksheet from the Review tab, selecting the particular elements that you want to allow.

7. Report

    a. Now that your workbook is set up and functioning what do you do with it? The final output should have been something you considered in the design phase when you detailed the workbook's functionality and your audience. This is where you start telling a story with your data, and all data can tell a story, it just depends on which story you want to tell and how. There is no right or wrong way to do this, it's largely a matter of preference. Some people prefer to let the numbers speak for themselves, others like to tell a story visually with Charts and other visual aids, while others want to add in end-user functionality with Pivot Tables. This is another area where you'll get some good ideas by browsing through the Microsoft Template Gallery.

8. Distribute & Collaborating

    a. The last step is distribution. Again, your audience and the data use dictates how you're going to send the information out. The first thing you do is hide any worksheets that contain sensitive personal or customer information. If you hide worksheets you'll also want to protect the Workbook, not just worksheets in order to prevent the hidden worksheets from being unhidden.

    b. If your workbook is for data entry, you'd need to take steps to protect sensitive cells or those with functions from being overwritten.

    c. If the workbook is purely for review purposes, you might want to consider creating a copy of the workbook, then on each worksheet, select all cells (Ctrl+A), Copy, Paste Special, Values. This will get rid of all your formulas, and it will also serve to shrink your workbook's size. Another option is to save as a PDF. If you don't have a PDF writer, you can find several on the Internet for free, and Office 2010 now supports creating PDF's natively (File, Save & Send). PDF's are also a good way to secure your data. If you send out an Excel workbook, even as values only, the data can still be copied, which you might not want.

d. For workbooks, and just about anything else where you need user input, in the past most people generally just e-mailed them back and forth, but the advent of online file sharing services have rendered this all but obsolete. Take a look at Microsoft's SkyDrive service, which will let you post files in a secure cloud-based environment. You can invite people to share documents with you, and set what degree of changes they can make. And Microsoft has released its new Office Web Apps, which let you work in a workbook real-time with other users with a great new feature called "Co-Authoring". If you have users spread out in different locations this is a great way to move documents back and forth without relying on e-mail and wondering which version of a workbook is the latest, who made changes to what and where. And best of all it's free, so there's no reason not to at least give it a try.

A Note on Distribution:

Excel is not a secure application, nor has it ever been marketed as one. If you have any concerns with distributing Workbooks that contain sensitive personal or customer information it is incumbent upon you to take the steps necessary to protect that information. Internally, this can simply mean hiding sensitive worksheets and protecting the Workbook. Externally, especially if a Workbook is going to multiple customers or entities, you'll probably Want to remove the information altogether, then save the Workbook as a secure PDF. Because Excel is not secure, someone who wants to view hidden information badly enough can do so with relative ease (breaking a Worksheet password takes just a few seconds for the right person). Think of Excel's protection like the locks on your house – they keep honest people honest, but if someone really wants in they can do it.

Entering and Editing Data

- Now that you've laid out your plans with regards to function and design, it's time to start developing your workbook (many people refer to this as building a model, so if you hear someone saying something like: "we calculate our pricing using a complex model", they're most likely referring to a spreadsheet). The example you'll be following in the companion workbook is a company Monthly Cash Flow statement by week. While we're only going to build one worksheet in this example, in reality you would probably have 13 worksheets, one for each month and a summary at the end (when we get to the Function lesson we'll discuss how you can quickly summarize the data from those 12 monthly worksheets).

- The first step is to determine your primary categories, in this case Cash Received, Cash Disbursed and Final Cash Position, or balance. Note that a lot of people will put their category headers in ALL CAPS as a way of making them stand out. You could also BOLD them and format the header row, it's entirely up to you.

Entering Dates - Dates can be quirky in how they're interpreted, so there are some basic rules to keep in mind when entering dates.

- You can enter just the Month & Day (mm/dd) and Excel will automatically add the current year.
- If you Want to enter a date in the previous year you actually have to enter the year as Well (e.g. mm/dd/yy).
- In either case you don't need to enter a 4-digit year for Excel to understand and convert it for you. Even if you display in mm/dd/yy format, if you look at the date in the formula bar it will read mm/dd/yyyy.
- You can separate your date components with a forward slash "/" or minus sign "-" (mm/dd/yy or mm-dd-yy). That comes down to personal preference.
- Once entered you can format a date in almost any style you Want, so you don't need to enter "January 1, 2001", just pick the format you Want in the Format Cells dialog (CTRL+1).

- Next since we know we're going to do this on a daily basis your dates will go across your columns. In this case just enter the first week of the month in column B (mm/dd), then to fill the rest of the dates you can use the formula "=B1+7", and copy that across instead of manually entering the dates, or drag the fill handle from the first cell across to the last and let AutoFill do it. (=B1+7 simply adds seven days to the original date and will repeat each time you paste it, adding seven days to the previous entry, and so on). Now that you have Rows & Columns defined, you need to break down the line items for each primary category, and then determine where you want to have sub-totals. If you don't already have expense categories for your business, you can find plenty of examples in the Microsoft Template Gallery. Fortunately, Cash Flow categories are relatively standard, so you probably won't need to make a lot of modifications to whatever list you find. In the companion workbook there are only 22 sub-items for Expenses. The nice thing about building models is that once you have the base model done, you can reuse it any time you want and not worry about having to re-enter all of that information.

Editing Data (Formulas or Text)
- Just because you've entered your category labels/titles doesn't mean that you might not have to change them at some point in the future. Fortunately, Excel makes it very easy to edit information in cells without having to re-type it!
- You can edit the cell's contents directly from the formula bar. Just put the cursor where you want it and make your changes.
- If you're on the keyboard you can use the F2 key to enter the cell directly, or double-click it if the mouse is handier.
- In both cases you can double-click on a word to select it, so you can delete it, change it, etc., and you can use the HOME/END keys to move around.
- The Shift, Ctrl & Arrows keys will also work for selecting multiple words, similar to selecting multiple cells.
- When you edit a formula Excel will show a colored border around each cell/range that the formula contains. E.G. if you edit =SUM(A1:A10), the A1:A10 will have a blue border around the range.

- Lastly is how do you want to summarize your data? Certainly you need to sub-total each primary category (Cash In, Cash Out & Final Balance), but you might also want to summarize other details, like all payroll elements (exempt vs. non-exempt wages, commissions, etc.) as separate line item sub-totals beneath the statement. In some cases if you have more than one primary revenue stream, or multiple locations, you might also want to break down your cash receipts by those elements. Now is the time to add details, because as your model progresses it becomes more of a chore to add new elements, as well as keeping track of everything you need to update those additions throughout your workbook. Think about what it might take to add a single line item to your 13 Monthly worksheets, as opposed to doing it while you're still building the first one. (Although we are going to talk about how to make the same change(s) to multiple sheets shortly). In the Cash Flow example there are several line items of operating information

Entering and Editing Formulas/Functions

What's the difference between Functions and Formulas?
- This can be confusing, and while some people use the terms interchangeably, they actually are different.
- Function – Generally this refers to the set of Excel's native Functions as found on the Formulas tab. SUM, AVERAGE, COUNT, etc. are all functions. Those standard functions have been written in code by Microsoft and will evaluate the result of the "Arguments" given to them (either manually or cell references), and return a result (also called "output"). Note that some functions, like RAND() & TODAY() don't require arguments.   As soon as a Function receives an argument it becomes a formula. You can also write your own functions in VBA.
- Formulas don't need to contain Functions though. Formulas begin as the most basic of mathematical or text operations, like =A1+A2 or ="User Name "&A1. Formulas can also contain multiple Functions and operators, like =((SUM(A1:A10)/SUM(B1:B10)) -1.

- So now you have your worksheet designed and all of the basic elements in place, but at this point it's nothing more than a shell, so you'll probably want to put some sample data in there so you can start building your formulas. Adding sample data to a model while you're building it can generally save you time vs. entering in your own information, because you can let a single repeated function do it for you, rather than manually entering a series of sample data. All you want to do is test the functionality of the formulas that analyze your data, you're not actually analyzing your own data at this point, so there's no point in representing until the model is built.

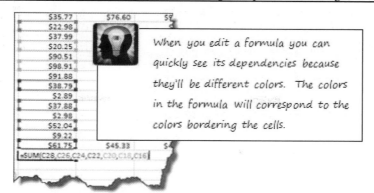

When you edit a formula you can quickly see its dependencies because they'll be different colors. The colors in the formula will correspond to the colors bordering the cells.

	A	B	C	D	E	F
1	CASH RECEIPTS	01/03/11	01/10/11	01/17/11	01/24/11	01/31/1
2	Cash Sales					
3	Collections fm CR accounts					
4	Loan/ other cash inj.					
5	TOTAL CASH RECEIPTS					
6	Total Cash Available (before cash out)					
7						
8	Purchases					
9	Salaries & Wages					
10	Payroll expenses (taxes, etc.)					
11	Outside services					
12	Supplies (office & operating)					
13	Repairs & maintenance					

Figure 199

Gridlines

When you first lay out a worksheet it's a good idea to leave gridlines on for reference. You can remove them later, when you add in your own formatting.

- A fast and efficient way to enter a lot of data is to use a function that will generate random numbers for you, so select the range that you want to fill, then in the first cell enter =RAND()*100, but don't hit **ENTER**. In this case you want to confirm the function with **CTRL+ENTER**, and you'll instantly have something like the following example. If you hadn't guessed, **CTRL+ENTER** will fill an entire range with the active cell's value, function or formula.

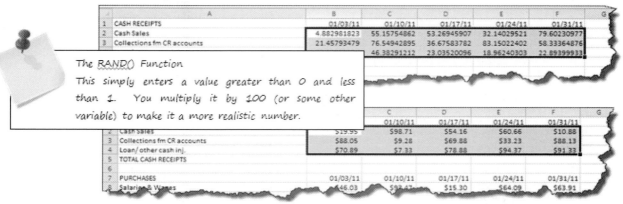

The RAND() Function

This simply enters a value greater than 0 and less than 1. You multiply it by 100 (or some other variable) to make it a more realistic number.

Figure 200

- Not very pretty is it? Before you move off of this selection, enter **CTRL+SHIFT+4**, which will instantly format that range as Currency (CTRL+SHIFT+1 = General Number format, **CTRL+SHIFT+4** = Percentage).
- Now you can select B2:F2 and copy and paste it to the other rows in the Purchases section. Remember, the shortcut for copy is **CTRL+C**, while paste is **CTRL+V**. Here's another trick for quickly entering copied data across a large range: once you've copied B2:F2, go down to the beginning of the Purchases section and in the first cell hold the SHIFT key, then arrow down to the bottom of the range. Once you

get to the bottom enter **CTRL+V** and the formulas will be pasted to the entire range. Note that you didn't need to select the entire range, just column B – Excel knows that you want to copy it across to column F.

1	CASH RECEIPTS	01/03/11	01/10/11
2	Cash Sales	$1.29	$51.31
3	Collections fm CR accounts	$93.67	$4.07
4	Loan/ other cash inj.	$10.46	$96.23
5	TOTAL CASH RECEIPTS	=SUM(B2:B4)	
6		SUM(**number1**, [number2], ...)	
7	PURCHASES	01/03/11	01/10/11

Figure 201

- By now you've probably noticed that when you paste your sample data keeps changing doesn't it? That's because the RAND function is a particular class of function called Volatile, which means that any event that takes place on the worksheet that causes calculation (like entering a value in a cell) will cause volatile functions to recalculate as well. If you want to stop that behavior you can either turn off Calculation in File, Options (you can manually recalculate at any time with F9), or, since you have your sample data in place, you can copy each range, then paste as values to remove the formulas (keyboard shortcut: **CTRL+C, ALT+E+S+V**).

- Now it's time to start summarizing some of that data, so go back to column B to the total row for Cash Receipts. Now from the Formula tab click on the AutoSum button and choose SUM. Excel will input the formula for you, but it will also give you a chance to evaluate it and see if it's gotten the range correct. If you agree with Excel's decision, then just hit **ENTER**. Then Copy & Paste cell B5 to C5:F5, by Copying and holding down the **SHIFT+RIGHT ARROW** key to select the range, then CTRL+V to paste. Note that you didn't need to move off of cell B5 in order to paste, Excel just replaces the existing function with the same thing. If the source cell and the destination range are contiguous, it's generally faster to copy the source cell and keep it as part of the destination range, than it is to move off of it. You can go ahead and repeat the AutoSum for your Expense category, then it will be time to calculate the difference (often referred to as Variance) between Cash Receipts and Expenses.

- This next exercise is a simple one, and it's not so much about learning a particular formula per se, but the steps to enter it. Go to the Cash Position row (B31) and enter "=" (this lets Excel know that you're entering a formula – if you're entering text you just start typing as you've seen). Next click on the Total Cash Receipts row (B5) and enter a minus sign (either from the primary keyboard, or the 10-Key pad). By now you'll see "=B5-" in the formula bar. Now click on the Total Cash Paid out row and hit **ENTER**. Excel will automatically return the difference between Cash In/Cash Out. You didn't need to use the mouse-click method In order to select the formula's cell references, you could have also used the keyboard navigation keys. In fact, just for practice, pick any empty cell, enter "=" and just start moving around with the arrow keys and watch the formula as you do. See what happens if you enter any operator (+, -, /, *) and move to another cell. Each subsequent action locks the previous action into the formula, so entering the minus sign in your variance formula locked B5 in the formula. And you don't always have to use mathematical operators; for instance this formula will sum cells in a non-contiguous range: =SUM(B10,C13,D20,E24,F28). To enter that function, you would type "=sum(" then click on the first cell in the range and lock it in place by entering a comma, and repeat until you have your entire range selected and hit **ENTER** to confirm it (you can actually do it really quickly if you enter the comma with your left hand, and click the cells with the mouse in your right, or vice versa if you're a lefty). Note that you don't need to capitalize the function name (Excel is blind to cases and will convert it for you), nor do you need to enter the final parenthesis to close the formula, Excel will do that for you as well.

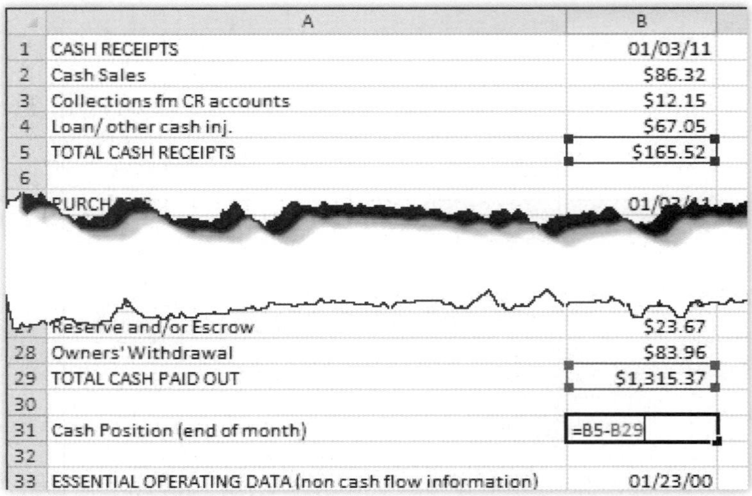

	A	B
1	CASH RECEIPTS	01/03/11
2	Cash Sales	$86.32
3	Collections fm CR accounts	$12.15
4	Loan/ other cash inj.	$67.05
5	TOTAL CASH RECEIPTS	$165.52
6		
	PURCHASES	01/03/11
27	Reserve and/or Escrow	$23.67
28	Owners' Withdrawal	$83.96
29	TOTAL CASH PAID OUT	$1,315.37
30		
31	Cash Position (end of month)	=B5-B29
32		
33	ESSENTIAL OPERATING DATA (non cash flow information)	01/23/00

Figure 202

- Now that you've entered a few formulas you need to know how to edit them if you need to make changes. If you know a formula is just plain wrong and you want to use something else it's generally just as fast to start over by simply typing right over it. As soon as you start typing, the previous values will be wiped out, although you can retrieve them by hitting ESC before confirming the new formula. If you've already confirmed it, then **CTRL+Z** will restore your original. Editing formulas is

- At this point you have your Row & Column headers defined, you've got your sample data in and checked that your vertical formulas are working, but what about horizontal totals? Right, you need to add those as well, so goto cell G1 and enter Total. Then in G2 you can invoke the AutoSum tool from the Formula bar, enter your horizontal total and copy it to the other relevant rows. Notice how the AutoSum knew to go across this time instead of up. If you don't confuse it with too much data then AutoSum will usually do a pretty good job. But you'll always want to check the blue formula border and make sure it got everything/not too much.

Copying Formulas - Absolute & Relative References

- So far you've entered some formulas, and copied/pasted them to other cells. The next concept, Absolute & Relative Referencing, is absolutely essential to know when you start working with formulas and getting them to evaluate the range/ranges that you want and expect.

- One basic precept of spreadsheet design is to make it as simple and efficient as possible. In the current Cash Flow example, the dates in C1:F1 consist of a formula that refers back to cell B1, where you would initially enter the starting date. Then B1:B7 was copied to the other date header rows. This isn't very efficient as each row of dates is dependent on the value in column B of that row, so if you wanted to change the starting date you'd need to do it in 3 places (in this example, think about how many potential changes you could make it a really big model!) We're going to change all of that and make all of the dates dependent on a single cell, B1. So go back to the Cash Flow example, cell B7, and enter =B1. Now copy that across from B7 to F7. Next copy B7 to the next date header row in B33:F33. You don't get quite the result you expected did you? You got something like this right?

| 33 | ESSENTIAL OPERATING DATA (non cash flow information) | 03/29/00 | 01/17/00 | 02/08/00 | 04/07/00 | 02/05/00 |

Figure 203

- What are those nonsensical dates you're probably asking. Before you think that Excel's broken, you should understand that Excel did exactly what it was told to do! Take a look at the formula in B33. It's =B27 right? When you copied the formula in cell C7, and moved down to B33 you moved down, or offset, 26 rows. So if the original formula in B7 was =B1, and 1 + 26 = 27, then B1 + 26 =B27. Well that's kind of stupid isn't it? Not really, because there are times you want your formulas to change like that. That's called Relative Referencing. It means that the formula is going to update relative to its position on the worksheet, not necessarily the cell to which the formula first referred. In our case we wanted to always be referring to B1 right? Yes and no; we want to refer to B1 as we copy the dates down, but what about when they're copied across? If you always referred to B1, then your Cash Flow statement would only have one date, so we really want B to change to C to change to D, and so on as it gets copied across. To do that we need to mix Relative and Absolute Referencing, which you would do with =B$1. The $ is the key to Absolute Referencing, as it fixes whatever it's attached to in place. So in this case the B will change as it's copied across, but the 1 will always remain a 1 as it's copied down. You'll see more examples of this as we get into the Functions & Formulas lesson.

- A quick way to update Absolute/Relative References is to enter Edit mode on that cell, then select the range reference you want to change and hit the F4 key. Each time you hit F4 you'll toggle between another reference state, $B1, $B$1, B$1, etc. In big formulas this can be faster than trying to add the $ by hand. Once you have the formula edited you can recopy it and this time the dates will correctly reference the master date.

- If you just want to move formulas around, you can use the Cut & Paste option (**CTRL+X**, **CTRL+V**) to move formulas from one location to the next without modifying any formulas.

Quickly Move Rows and Columns

Let's say you need to re-order a list, but Sorting won't do what you want. You can select an entire Row or Column (click the header), then hold the SHIFT key and Left-Click on the border and move the Row or Column to its new position. If the Row or Column moved includes formula dependencies, they will remain as long as you move the Row or Column within the existing formula range, not outside of it.

Lists & AutoFill

- These are two tools that often work in conjunction and can save you untold amounts of time in the course of a year (if you remember to use them). Unfortunately, these are features that are often overlooked by even seasoned users. As you may remember from the introductory lessons, Excel maintains a set of internal standard lists for Days and Months, and dates (although they are calculated vs. stored in a list). You can use those lists anywhere in your workbooks. Let's say you were building a Summary worksheet for your 12 monthly Cash Flow statements. You'd have January-December as the column headers in the summary. The logical assumption for populating those dates in the workbook would be to manually enter them, and you're partially correct, but you only need to enter one moth and let the AutoFill tool do the rest for you. In the Lists & AutoFIll worksheet example you'll see January entered in A2. Select A2 and in the lower right-hand corner, grab the Fill Handle (when you hover over it your cursor will turn into a dark cross), and drag it down. Watch the Control Tip Text as you drag it down, and you'll see each subsequent month as you drag. When you release the fill handle those months will be filled in for you. That's so much faster than continually entering months by hand. In the next example you'll see Month-Year entered, so try dragging that one down and see what happens. (If you hold down the CTRL key while dragging you'll just copy the original value, not increment it). Next look at the date, drag that down and see what it does. Before you go do anything else though, you're going to see one of the neat things that AutoFill can do with dates. Right-click on the AutoFill Options button at the bottom right-hand of the range you just filled and you'll see the following sub-menu. That's right, Excel can fill just certain incremental date elements for you. One of the most common is the ability to fill weekdays only.

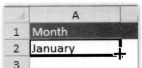

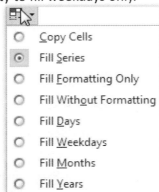

Figure 204

- Another handy tool that was discussed earlier is the ability to fill a series without having to use the AutoFill handle and drag it across or down, which is great for an extended series. For instance, let's say you were building a pricing model and you wanted to see what would happen at certain volume levels, but you don't want to enter them all in by hand. In cell E5 on the AutoFill worksheet, goto Home, Fill, Series and you'll see an expanded Fill dialog. In this case enter 250 for the Step value, and 50000 for the Stop value. When you click OK, you'll see that the 15000 entry in E5 has incremented by 250 all the way to the right until it hit 50,000.

- The List feature is one of the things that drives AutoFill, but it doesn't have to be limited to Microsoft's values, you can enter your own. Here's an all too common scenario: a company has a dedicated workbook that has a lot of relatively static company information, like Operating Units (Sales, Production, Accounting), Regions (East, West, North, South), Offices (New York, Dallas, Los Angeles), even their list of Cash Flow or General Ledger Accounts, and so on. Whenever a new workbook is created that needs one of those lists, someone opens up that other workbook, copies the list in question, returns to the new workbook and pastes it in, then goes back and closes the list workbook, or worse they copy more data. That's actually quite a few steps when you could just do it with AutoFill. The key is to build your lists into Excel, which is equally easy. On the Lists & AutoFill worksheet in the companion workbook you'll see a list of countries beginning in A20. Go ahead and select that range, then goto File, Options, Advanced, Edit Custom Lists (it's near the bottom), and you'll get the following dialog.

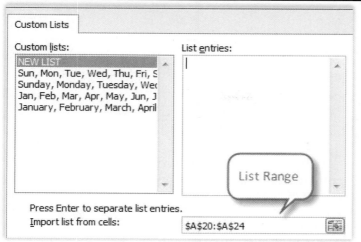

Figure 205

- Notice how Excel has already recognized your selection as the list range it's supposed to import. When you click Import you'll see your list beneath the existing Microsoft lists, and in the currently selected list box on the right.
- That's all well and good right, but what good does it do you? Well, anytime you need to populate that list in any workbook, all you need to do is enter a beginning value (it can be any value in the list), then drag the AutoFill handle down and Excel will build that list as far as you want it. It's a lot faster than copying and pasting from another workbook.

Data Validation

- This is a tool that goes hand-in-hand with lists. Data Validation allows you to use a list to limit cells to only accept values that fit parameters that you specify. This is great for ensuring that users follow your rules regarding what they can and can't enter. Some examples would be limiting an Employee Annual Wage Increase to 5%, or limiting the date range in a Time-Off Request to certain periods. Data Validation can also use your list values to give the user a drop-down list of selections that they can make, and not accept anything not in the list. This is a great tool to prevent errors, because when you provide users with a list they can select from, then they don't have to type (and possibly misspell) the input value. It can also be great for things like order forms where you might have detailed product names, and don't want users to have to re-type them for each order. Data Validation can be found on the Data tab. You can recognize a cell with Data Validation because it will display a drop-down symbol on the right-hand side of the cell when you activate the cell.

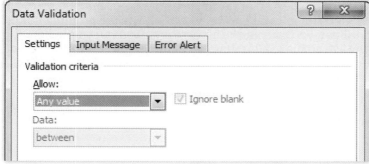

Figure 206

- First we'll look at setting up Data Validation to only accept certain values. Select any cell on a blank worksheet and invoke the Data Validation dialog. For this example we'll limit the value entered to only dates greater than today's date (using your system date), so select Date from the list of choices. As soon as you do you'll see the Validation dialog change a little bit so its Date options are exposed. In the Start date field enter =TODAY(), then OK. Now try to enter a date before today's in that cell, and you'll get a not-so-subtle error message.

Figure 207

- Fortunately, you can modify the error message to be much more palatable to your users.
- In the Data Validation dialog there were two other tabs behind the primary Settings tab (Input Message and Error Alert). The first lets you define your message while the second lets you identify which kind of errors you want to allow (if any).
- The Input Message will be seen when a user enters the Data Validation cell, while the error message will appear when an invalid entry is detected. You can disable error checking and allow user entries by unchecking the "Show error alert..." check box

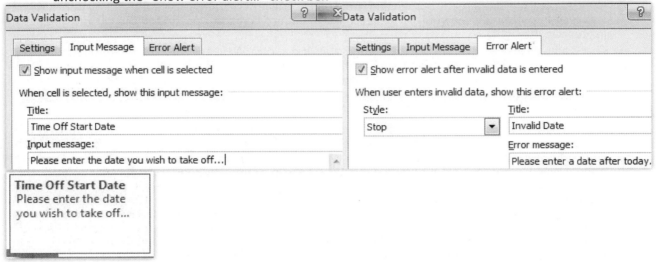

Figure 208

- Data Validation List selections don't have the same degree of flexibility as the input options, but you get to define the selection list, so you pre-determine what can be selected. For this example enter several city names in a blank area of a worksheet; you can put the list across, but as you learned earlier that's not the efficient way to maintain any list, so make sure that you enter your list from top down. The first step for setting up a Data Validation list is to call up the Validation dialog, and in the Allow box, select "List", then in the Source box you can either enter the list range or select it with the mouse. If you want to enter the list range by hand make sure to precede it with an equals sign, or the list range will be interpreted as literal text and that's what you'll see in your drop-down. If you have fairly static values you can enter them by hand: Yes,No – Male,Female – Mr.,Mrs.,Miss, etc., but you don't want to do this for lengthy lists, especially those with values that could change.

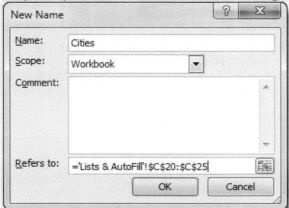

Figure 209

- Using a range reference for a Data Validation list is fine in most cases, but it requires that the list be on the same worksheet as the Data Validation. This isn't very convenient on something like an order form where several lists might be confusing to users, or worse yet, they could delete or change some of the values. You could hide those list rows/columns, but there is a trick to being able to make Data Validation seamless to your users by using a Named Range. Named Ranges are a great tool for managing end-user applications because they allow you to keep all of your list information, as well as any other details you might want hidden from the users. The first thing you want to do is insert a new blank worksheet (***ALT+I+N***). Then Cut the list you entered previously and paste it anywhere in the new worksheet (***CTRL+X, CTRL+V***) Then select the list range and goto Formulas, Define Name (***ALT+D+L***), and enter a descriptive name in the name box and click OK to add the name.

- Now you can go back to the worksheet where you want the Data Validation list to appear and invoke the Data Validation dialog again, but this time instead of entering an actual range in the Source box, you're going to enter ***=YourListName***. When you select the drop-down you'll now see the same list you did previously, but now it's out of harm's way.

- There's obviously a lot of Data Validation that we're not going to talk about here, but you should see that it certainly gives you a great many options for building end-user worksheets, as well as limiting errors.

Inserting and Deleting Ranges, Rows & Columns and Worksheets

Since a big part of building and working with spreadsheets is entering data and formulas, then naturally so is altering them, moving things around, and even deleting elements that you may have already entered. But you can't just jump into a worksheet and start adding or deleting things without first understanding what implications your actions might have on the rest of the worksheet, and possibly the entire workbook.

- ***Inserting Rows & Columns*** is fairly straightforward (***Home, Cells, Insert***, or ***ALT+I+R*** for Rows and ***ALT+I+C*** for columns), but there are a few pointers. Let's go back to the Cash Flow worksheet as an example. What if you wanted to add some more categories to either the Cash or Purchases lists? It might seem logical that you would go to the first blank cell between the ranges and enter a few rows there. Unfortunately, that's going to be the long way around. If you proceeded with entering rows below the range, then added in your new categories and values, you would then need to move and update the sub-total formulas, as they won't recognize the additions to the ranges beneath them. Instead, put your cursor anywhere inside the list range and insert your rows. Not only did you remain in the list, but the formulas automatically updated to include the new rows as well. That is convenient, and more importantly when you let Excel do it, you don't have to worry about forgetting not to do it. If that happens you now have a potential error between your actual values and what your totals show, and those errors can often be difficult to see, let alone track down. You can do the same thing with columns, just make sure that your active cell is inside the range you want to expand so that the formulas are expanded as well. If you're not worried about expanding formula ranges, then insert wherever you want provided it doesn't materially affect another range.

- ***Deleting Rows & Columns*** - (***Home, Cells, Delete***, or ***ALT-E-D-R*** for Rows and ***ALT-E-D-C*** for Columns) requires a bit more thought, because one seemingly innocuous deletion could cascade through an entire worksheet or workbook. Going back to the example of the single date entry in the Cash Flow statement, what would happen to all of those dependent cells if you deleted that value? They would all lose the values they derived from that single cell. And think about this: what you delete on one worksheet may have no affect whatsoever on that sheet, but there could be other worksheets that were dependent on it. Unfortunately, by the time you realize it, it may be too late to undo your action, so you close the workbook without saving, hoping you didn't put too much work into it beforehand. Here is an all too often repeated scenario: many detailed models rely heavily on hidden rows and columns for certain secondary and even tertiary calculations. And just assume for a moment that this is an end-user application, so formula errors have been suppressed (this is often done so that users don't get the impression that the worksheet is "broken" when they see formula errors). For whatever reason someone deletes some key information, either by deleting cell contents, or columns/rows; the remaining formulas may continue to recalculate, but without those missing components, they may well be calculating incorrectly, if at all. This can cause an organization to make all kinds of false assumptions. More than one million dollar mistake has been made as a result of an incorrect spreadsheet. Do million dollar mistakes happen all the time, no, of course not. Do mistakes of a lesser magnitude happen all the time, absolutely.

- Nothing substitutes for knowing how your worksheet is designed, but fortunately, you do have some tools that can help you make informed decisions before you delete formulas. On the Formula tab under the Formula Auditing group are the Trace Precedents/Dependents tools. If you ever have a question regarding whether or not it's safe to delete a formula, then try these tools because they'll point you to all of the places that your formula goes and where it's been (note that when a formula reference points to another worksheet, you won't be told where on the other sheet, just that it's on another sheet somewhere). Unfortunately, there is no tool to evaluate the effects of deleting rows or columns beforehand. Generally, if you have a command of your spreadsheet, then you'll have a good idea of what is safe and not safe to delete.

- *Hiding/Unhiding Rows & Columns* - This is often necessary to prevent users from seeing certain internal calculations or even creating Custom Views. Many times hiding rows & columns is a better alternative than deleting them. Simply select the row or column range (you don't need to select the entire row or column, just a single range of cells. E.G. A1:B1 to hide columns A & B; A1:A5 to hide rows 1-5). Once selected goto Home, Cells, Format, Hide & Unhide). In order to unhide you need to select the range to the immediate left and right or top and bottom of the hidden area, so that the hidden area can be included. If you run up against row 1 or column A, you would click the Select All button at the intersection of the Row & Column headers (**CTLR+A**) and then proceed with unhiding.
  - ◦ Shortcuts: **ALT+O+R+H** or **ALT+O+C+H** to hide rows & columns; **ALT+O+R+U** or **ALT+O+C+U** to unhide.

Bloat — Large File Size

Excel workbooks can sometimes blow up in size for no apparent reason, although it's usually a single culprit: the Used Range. Whenever you enter data or apply formatting to a cell, it becomes part of what Excel sees as the Used Range. Let's say you import 500,000 rows of data from a database and delete all but 10,000 records. Excel still sees that 500,000 rows have been reserved. Deleting the cell's value or removing the formatting doesn't reset the used range. The only way is to actually delete all unused rows and columns then resave the workbook.

Deleting Worksheets

- You can delete a worksheet by right-clicking on the worksheet tab and selecting delete. If the worksheet contains any data then you'll get a warning prompt. Once you delete a worksheet, there is no undo, other than closing the workbook without saving changes.

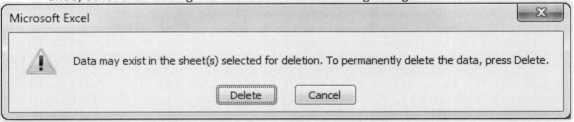

Figure 210

- Should you generally be worried about all of the aforementioned perils of deleting? No, but you should be aware of and mindful of what can happen if you delete dependent components, because there will most likely be more than one occasion that you delete something you can't get back. This is where the mantra of "Save Often, Save Early" can be a lifesaver, because it can literally determine if you can recover your data or not.

Modifying Data on Multiple Worksheets

- As we were laying out the Cash Flow worksheet, you were encouraged to make sure that it does what you want before you go and recreate it. In the Cash Flow report's case you would have recreated it 12 times; one for each subsequent month and one for the yearly summary. In most normal worksheet models you can do a relatively good job of this and be fully prepared when you start creating your copies, but there will arise the occasion where you need to make one or multiple changes to one or more worksheets. The good news is that while other people struggle making those changes to each sheet, one at a time, you're going to see how to do it all at once. This method works on the method of grouping sheets, in which you can group sheets together. And they don't need to be contiguous either (you'll see a good reason for this in a minute). Go ahead and open a new workbook (you don't need to save it as anything, it's just for an example). Once it's open add a few more worksheets to it (you can quickly add a sheet with **ALT+I+W**, or you can goto **Home, Cells, Insert, Sheet**).
- **Group All Contiguous Sheets**
  - ◦ In the new workbook select the first sheet, then hold down the SHIFT key and click on the last sheet tab. You don't have to select all of the sheets though; the SHIFT key will group the first sheet, the last sheet selected and any sheets in between. You could also right-click on the sheet tab and choose "Select all sheets", but that groups all of the sheets. Note that the tabs have all turned a

different shade; this indicates that they are now grouped, and any change that you make on the active sheet will also be made on the other selected sheets. Go ahead and apply some formatting, add some text, try anything you want, then click on any of the other sheets and see what happened.

- ○ There are certain things you can't do to grouped sheets, and once you see the list you'll realize that it's pretty reasonable, as most of the exclusions have their own sheet specific parameters, or just have too many potential combinations between sheets to be feasible:
    - Conditional Formatting
    - Format as Table
    - Anything from the Insert Ribbon other than Header & Footer and Signature lines
    - Certain Page Setup elements, like setting the Page Area (but you can by and large apply the same Page Setup properties to all sheets at once! That alone can be a huge timesaver when you're getting ready to distribute a workbook!)
    - Arranging objects
    - Formula Auditing
    - Anything from the Data tab
    - Protect Worksheets
- ○ When all of the sheets are grouped, all you need to do to ungroup is select any other sheet.
- **Group Individual (Select) Sheets**
- ○ You're not limited to grouping all of the worksheets; you can group select sheets as well. One of the most common reasons to group select sheets would be in a finance model that works on a 5-4-4 monthly basis (5 weeks, 4 weeks, 4 weeks in each month – e.g January has 5 weeks, February has 4 weeks and March has 4 weeks, then the process repeats in April, etc.) Given that structure you'll have 4 months that have 5 weeks, and 8 months that have 4 weeks. You could probably make changes to all the sheets at once for the 4-week months, since you could naturally include the 5-week months, but what about the other way around? So you can group just the 5-week months and apply the necessary changes to those without having to interfere with the 4-week months.
- ○ To group select sheets you use the CTRL key instead of the SHIFT key, and right-click on each sheet you want to select group. Then make any changes necessary. To ungroup select sheets just activate any of the non-grouped sheets. Activating a grouped sheet will not ungroup them.

Don't forget to stop grouping when you're done making your changes! More than one workbook has literally been ruined when someone forgot to ungroup and they went a while without knowing it, making their merry changes along the way (to every worksheet).

Unit Summary: Entering and Manipulating Data (and the basic rules of good spreadsheet design)

- In this lesson you learned about some of the concepts behind good spreadsheet design, beginning with the initial concept and planning phase, continuing on to design.
- You saw some of the methods of quickly populating a worksheet with repeating data like months, dates, and even sample data sets.
- You started working with some simple functions and formulas, and learned about how to copy them around a worksheet utilizing Absolute & Relative Referencing. You also learned the different ways that you can edit existing data and formulas.
- You learned about how to add your own Custom Lists and use them with AutoFill, as well as some of the user-input features of Data Validation.
- You saw how to make multiple changes to multiple worksheets at once.

Review Questions – Lesson 5 – Entering & Manipulating Data

1. How do you begin entering text in a cell
    a. _____
2. How would you enter the same text in multiple cells at once?
    a. _____
3. How do you begin entering a function/formula?
    a. _____
4. What are Absolute & Relative References? What symbol characterizes an Absolute Reference?
    a. _____

5. How would you fill a series starting at 1, ending at 10,000 in increments of 500?
    a. _____

6. What are some uses for Data Validation?
    a. _____

7. How would you make changes to sheets 1 & 3 at the same time?
    a. _____

Lesson Assignment – Lesson 5 – Entering & Manipulating Data

- Work with the Cash Flow example in the companion workbook to:
  ◦ Populate a range of sample data using RAND().
  ◦ Check out the TODAY() function.
  ◦ Use different AutoSum functions to see how they operate.
  ◦ Enter your own SUM, AVERAGE & COUNT functions.
- Work with the Lists & AutoFill worksheet to:
  ◦ Enter Months, Days and Dates in different configurations.
  ◦ Try the Fill, Series tools.
  ◦ Practice adding Custom Lists and setting up Data Validation.

Lesson 5 Notes

Lesson 6 – Using Functions & Formulas

In Lesson 5 you learned about the general rules for good spreadsheet design, regardless of whether you're working in Excel or another spreadsheet application. In that lesson you walked through the steps to designing a worksheet, beginning at the design phase, then building your base elements (row & column headers), followed by populating the worksheet with some sample data. After that you saw how to use the AutoSum Wizard to add some relatively simple formulas to the worksheet. The natural progression to that lesson is to introduce you to the more esoteric topic of Functions and Formulas. While the AutoSum Wizard can certainly do a lot for you, and you will likely come to rely on it in your day-to-day Excel activities, there is a whole world of Functions out there that the AutoSum Wizard will never touch, so we're going to devote this lesson to some of Excel's more commonly used Functions, and Formulas. We're not going to overwhelm you with obscure and industry specific functions, like those you might use in Statistical, Scientific or Engineering applications, but we will talk about some of the more advanced functions that once you learn how to use you'll wonder how you ever did without. We'll also be discussing some of the logic that goes into functions and how you evaluate certain scenarios. Some of it might smell a bit like high school Algebra, and to a certain extent it is, because you'll learn how to evaluate conditions and return different answers based on those conditions.

Remember from the last lesson that a Function in place and receiving input is a Formula, but a Formula doesn't necessarily have to contain a Function. It can be a hard concept to grasp at first, but once you start working with Functions and Formulas a bit more you'll see how they are truly complimentary. A Function is any pre-programmed function that performs some mathematical or logical task in Excel based on input or argument that you supply to it. Functions are generally intrinsic to Excel, but you can also build your own (in much the same fashion that Microsoft builds them). A formula is either a Mathematical or Text equation (=1+1, =A1+B1, ="Daily Sales "&A1, etc.), or it can be a function, or a compilation of functions (=SUM(A1:B1) or =SUM(A1:B1)/SUM(C1:D1) or even something like =SUM(A1:B1)*.0825). Essentially if you can think of a way to evaluate data then you can probably combine some type of logic in Excel to do it. In fact, if you start getting curious about more advanced functions and look for help in Excel message boards on the Internet you will be truly amazed at some of the formulas that people can create. If you can think it, someone can probably come up with a formula to do it. Why emphasize this issue? Because you will (not <u>might</u>, but <u>will</u>) become frustrated at some point or another when you're building formulas, that is just a statistical reality. In fact, it can be a fairly regular occurrence, but you shouldn't let that be a deterrent. Some people will have a much easier time grasping formulas than others, but rest assured, even the most experienced Excel users on the planet struggle with formulas from time to time, so you are certainly not alone. As soon as you let yourself know that it's OK to get frustrated, then you'll generally be much better prepared to tackle advanced formulas.

First we need to review the Functions that are on the Formula Ribbon and explain what each group does. We've briefly discussed some of this in the Ribbon lesson, but now we're going to get in depth with each one.

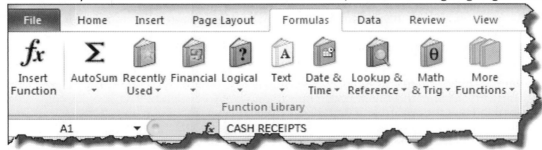

Figure 211

Insert Function

If you don't know what Function you want off the top of your head, or even what category to place it in, then you come here.

- You can enter your search term and Excel's help will do what it can to match your request with the best result. Note that the default category is "Most Recently Used", so make sure to change that to "All" before you start, otherwise you'll limit your results. On the other hand, if you know you're looking for a Function in a particular category, you may well want to narrow the list. Unfortunately, the Insert Function Wizard won't always find what you're looking for, especially if you don't know what to look for in the first place, so it is somewhat of a Catch-22 tool; you have to somewhat know what you're looking for in order to find it, but if you don't know what that is, then how do you know what to ask it to look for? Confusing isn't it? That would be one of those times you turn to the Internet and ask a question (the message board at http://www.mrexcel.com is probably the best place to look if you're stumped).

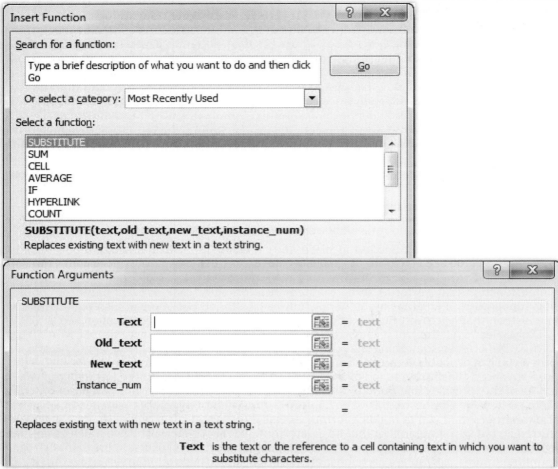

Figure 212

- If you do choose a Function from the Insert Function Wizard, then it will bring up another dialog that can help you put in the correct values or cell references, and each of the function's arguments have some help text beneath the dialog input boxes. Another benefit to this Wizard is that it will evaluate each step of the function for you so you can immediately see if you entered an argument incorrectly. If the Wizard just doesn't do enough for you to figure out how to build a function, you can always click on the "Help on this function" hyperlink to get more details.

Function Library

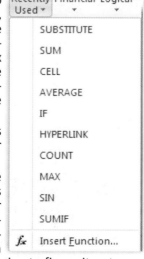

- ***AutoSum*** - As you saw in the Lesson 5 examples, AutoSum is incredibly easy to use. Just put your cursor beneath or next to the range you want to evaluate, choose your function from the wizard and let it do its thing. It's not infallible and won't evaluate data with gaps in it, but it does a pretty good job. Although your intrinsic functions are limited to S, Average, Count Number, Max & Min, you can select the More Functions option which is going to launch the Insert Function Wizard (yet another one of those things that Microsoft exposes in multiple places). You'll find examples of all the AutoSum functions in the Lesson 6 companion workbook.

- ***Recently Used*** – This is a faster way to get to your Recently Used functions than having to launch the Insert Function dialog. Just click and there's your list.

- ***Financial*** – This and the rest of the Function Library menu items function the same way; they're each going to display an alphabetical list of the functions specific to that category. Financial functions can be very powerful tools for business, because you can perform so much detailed analysis. Like determining the depreciation of a piece of equipment you are thinking about purchasing, or even determining what your monthly payment might be based on amount down, interest rate, etc. They are generally of much more use than trying to figure it out on a calculator, especially because you can reuse them. Some examples of Financial functions are:
  - ◦   FV – Future Value

- ◦ IRR – Internal Rate of Return
- ◦ NPV – Net Present Value
- ◦ SLN – Straight-Line Depreciation
- **Logical** – Logical functions allow you to evaluate certain criteria and return one result if the evaluation is true, and another if it's false (e.g. **=IF(A1="Yes",1,2)**, which simply says "if A1 = Yes, then return a 1, otherwise if A1 is anything other than "Yes", return a 2). Logical functions include:
  - ◦ **IF** – IF statements are the cornerstone of logical analysis in Excel. We will be going into these in depth.
  - ◦ **AND** – Both AND & OR allow you to add multiple criteria to IF statements. E.G. IF something is true, AND something else is false, then...Or IF something is false, OR something else is true, then...
  - ◦ **OR**
  - ◦ **NOT** – This evaluates if something is NOT equal to a condition. E.G. NOT = 1.
  - ◦ **TRUE/FALSE** – Called Boolean evaluations, these simply test if something is True or False?
  - ◦ **IFERROR** – This can be used to remove error notices from formulas that return errors. It's generally not advisable when you're first building models, because it hides all errors, but it doesn't resolve an error, so you might not know a formula isn't working. However, it is very common to use prior to distribution because users who see formula errors usually assume something is broken, and when they assume something is broken, they're less likely to use your workbook.
- **Text** – These let you work with Text in formulas. Some Text function examples are:
  - ◦ **CLEAN** – Removes not-printable characters from a reference. This often comes in handy when copying data from websites or databases.
  - ◦ **FIND** – Find a text or numeric value in a text string
  - ◦ **LEFT** – Return x characters from the Left of a string. E.G. **=LEFT("ABCDE",2)** will return "AB".
  - ◦ **RIGHT** - Return x characters from the Right of a string. E.G. **=RIGHT("ABCDE",2)** will return "DE".
  - ◦ **MID** – Returns x characters from the middle of a string given a starting point. E.G. **=MID("ABCDE",2,2)** will return "BC".
  - ◦ **TEXT** – Allows you to format numeric values when they've been concatenated with text. E.G. **="Today's date is: "&TEXT(A1,"MM/DD/YY")**. Where A1 is a valid date the formula would return "Today's date is: 01/15/11".
  - ◦ **TRIM** – Removes leading and trailing spaces from text strings. It will not remove spaces between words.
  - ◦ **UPPER** – Converts all text to Upper case. There are also LOWER & PROPER functions.
- **Date & Time** – As it might sound, these let you work with Dates & Times largely from a mathematical standpoint. E.G. determining the number of days between two dates. Some examples are:
  - ◦ **TODAY** – Returns Today's Date
  - ◦ **NOW** – Returns the Date & Time
  - ◦ **DAY** – Returns the day number of the month, from 1 -31.
  - ◦ **NETWORKDAYS** – Returns the number of standard workdays (Monday-Friday) between two dates, including system recognized Holidays.
  - ◦ **YEAR** – Returns just the year from a date reference. E.G. **=YEAR(TODAY())** would return "2011".
- **Lookup & Reference** – Lookup & Referential formulas are perhaps the most widely used outside of the data summarization functions (SUM, AVERAGE, COUNT, etc.). They let you look up values in a list and return relevant information from the list. For instance you might want to look up a customer name to get their address or phone number. Lookup & Referential functions let you do that without having to go to the source to look it up manually.
- **Math & Trig** – While some of the functions in this category are definitely reserved for those in a business that deals with Math & Trigonometry calculations, there are quite a few that you'll frequently use in the course of business:
  - ◦ **ABS** – Returns the absolute value of a number, which is the number without its sign. E.G. **=ABS(-10)** is 10.
  - ◦ **EVEN/ODD** – Rounds positive values up to the nearest Even integer, and negative numbers down. Odd does the opposite.
  - ◦ **CEILING/FLOOR** – Rounds a number up to the nearest number you specify. E.G. **=CEILING(2.6,0.25)** would be 2.75. This is good if you're pricing to the nearest x increment. FLOOR does the opposite.
  - ◦ **INT** – Rounds a number down to the nearest integer. E.G. **=INT(2.7)** is 2.
  - ◦ **RAND** – As you saw in Lesson 5, this generates a random number between 1 and 0. Remember to get meaningful numbers for testing you'll probably want to multiply RAND by a factor of 10. E.G. **=RAND()*100**.

- ◦ **ROUND** – This rounds a number to a specified number of digits. E.G. **=ROUND(1.234,2)** is 1.23
- ◦ **SUM** – Returns the Sum of a range. You're already familiar with this one from Lesson 5.
- ◦ **SUMIF** – Returns the Sum of a range given a single criterion. E.G. **=SUMIF(A1:A10,"YES",B1:B10)**, would return a sum of B1:B10 where the cells in A1:A10 = YES.
- ◦ **SUMIFS & SUMPRODUCT** – Both of these return the sum of a range based on multiple criteria. You'll find examples of both in the Lesson 6 companion workbook.
- • *More Functions* – This exposes several more categories of functions that are generally specific to a particular field, although the Information functions are used quite regularly in evaluating ranges. E.G. **=ISNUMBER(A1)** would return a True/False depending on the value ion A1. This is a very useful function, because sometimes numbers may appear to be numbers when they are actually seen as text. In cases like this your formulas won't calculate correctly, so ISNUMBER helps you track down the improperly formatted range.
- ◦ **Statistical**
- ◦ **Engineering**
- ◦ **Cube**
- ◦ **Information**
- ◦ **Compatibility**

Order of Operations

Before we start exploring some of Excel's in-depth functionality with regards to functions and formulas, you need to understand how they calculate. Excel follows a mathematical order of Operations when it calculates your functions and formulas. The Primary order of operations is as follows:

- • **Parentheses**
- • **Exponents**
- • **Multiplication/Division**
- • **Addition/Subtraction**

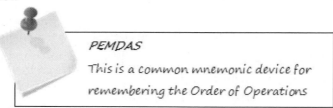

PEMDAS

This is a common mnemonic device for remembering the Order of Operations

- • Both Division/Multiplication and Addition/Subtraction carry the same weight, so if either are in the same formula, they will be carried out by whichever comes first. However, you can alter the order of any operation by adding parentheses. This is where those high school Algebra concepts will kick in.
  - ◦ The formula =2*3+4 will result in 10, because 2*3 = 6 and 6 + 4 = 10.
  - ◦ However = 2*(3+4) = 14, because 3+4 = 7, and 2*(7) = 14. In this case, since the 3+4 was in parentheses it gets calculated first.
- • Order of Operations doesn't take that long to grasp, but you need to be aware of it, because if you have an obscure calculation that doesn't generate the correct results, then a lot of other dependencies that are directly or indirectly based on that calculation can also be off. Generally, those small errors are like trying to find the proverbial needle in a haystack, so it's better to make sure you get the calculations right the first time.

Entering Functions

Entering functions is fairly straightforward. If you're beginning from the Function Wizard, then you let that do all of the work for you. Here's an example using the Depreciation example you'll find in the Financial section of the Lesson 6 workbook.

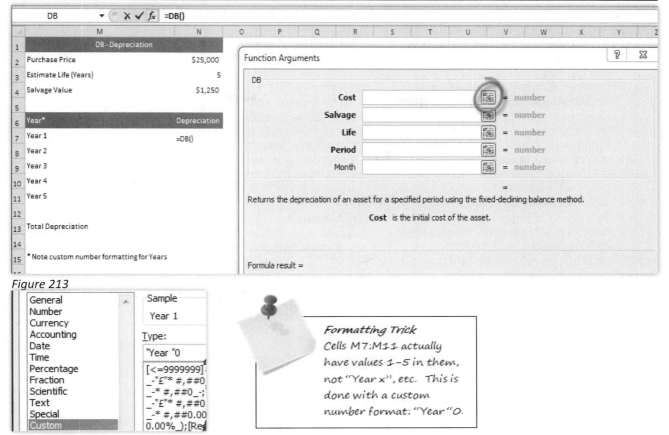

Figure 213

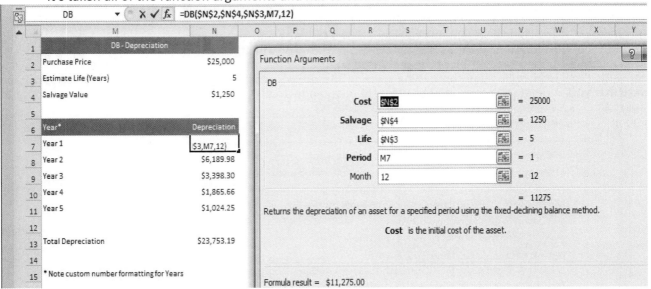

Figure 214

- As you can see, the primary cells we'll be referencing are N2:N4, and we want the depreciation cal-culations to be returned for Years 1-5, so we're going to be referencing M7:M11 for our Periods. First invoke the Formula Wizard and select the DB function. In the Cost argument, click the Range selection button (circled in red in the example), then click on cell N2. For Salvage repeat and click on N4, then for Life, click on N3. Then Period will be M7, and enter a 12 in Month (you can leave this blank if you want, as 12 is the default value for the Month argument). Notice how the Function Wizard already added Absolute References for you where they were needed. As you confirm each step, you'll see the Function Wizard evaluate it to the right of the argument. When you enter the last argument, the full function will evaluate. This is good, because you'll see if you get a valid or expected result. If you don't then you know that you have some changes to make. Next you'll see the Function Wizard after it's taken all of the function arguments and has calculated a result.

Figure 215

- If the result is what you're expecting, then go ahead and confirm the formula. Now you can copy Year 1's result down to Year 5 and you'll have your extended 5-Year depreciation results.

- As you start getting comfortable with multiple argument functions, this is probably the way that you'll want to enter them. Range only functions (like =SUM(A1:A10)) you can probably just write by hand or use the AutoSum Wizard, although it is good practice to start learning how to enter functions by hand, because it definitely has some speed advantages.

- If you're entering functions or formulas by hand then all you need to remember is to preface the function/formula with an equals (=) sign. That tells Excel that you are entering a Function/Formula. And don't forget that the Function Wizard isn't the only place that's helpful when you're entering Functions; as long as Excel recognizes the Function that you're entering it will give you a control tip text once you've entered the opening parenthesis for the Function. Each function argument will be in bold in the control tip text until you confirm it with a comma and move on to the next, at which point that argument will be bolded.

- When you're entering functions/formulas by hand and you need to select a range to feed to the function, you can navigate there with the mouse, or with the arrow keys. It's just personal preference, although you'll find times where one is more advantageous than the other and vice versa; it really depends on where the function is in relation to the range you're trying to pass to it.

- Formula views – Don't forget, you can view and edit your formulas in both the Formula bar and in the cell, and in either case you'll get those colored references that correspond between the range references in the formula and the ranges on the worksheet.

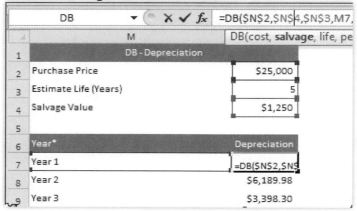

Figure 216

Excel Function/Formula Errors

As you've seen, when you properly enter a function/formula, Excel gives you a result. But what happens if you enter a function/formula incorrectly? Well, as picky as Excel is, it's going to tell you all about it, by displaying an Error message in the cell. Some error messages are fairly straightforward and can be fixed right away, while others are a bit more obtuse, and can be difficult to track down (especially if a change you made on a different worksheet causes an error and you don't see it until much later). You'll find that error management often means using Logical statements to evaluate the function and/or the error to resolve it. Errors play a big role in Excel development, as they can quickly point out problems that you need to resolve. Unfortunately, many people throw a blanket error management solution at everything, which can be misleading because it prevents Excel from telling you some thing's wrong. Before you start using error management practices, make sure that you understand errors, what causes them and how to sort out the root cause before using a shotgun approach.

IFERROR vs. ISERROR

Prior to Excel 2007, the global Error solution was *ISERROR*. Unfortunately, not only did that eliminate all errors, but it also prevented Excel from telling you when you had problems. It's also hugely inefficient as it causes Excel to calculate twice, once to evaluate the formula to see if it results in an error, and if it doesn't evaluate it again to return the formula's result. E.G. =IF(ISERROR(A1/B1),0,A1/B1)). As you'll see in the #DIV/0! Error example, there's a much more selective way to address that particular error, as there is for most errors.

IFERROR is still a shotgun approach to error management, but at least it doesn't force double calculation. E.G. =IFERROR(A1/B1,0). It's also more efficient because it eliminated the initial IF statement.

- **#DIV/0!** – You can't divide by 0 (not in Excel, or math for that matter). This is most often caused by a formula like this: =A1/B1, where B1 isn't necessarily a 0 value, it just hasn't had anything entered into it yet, so it evaluates to an error. The easiest way to fix this one is to test for the existence of the denominator; if it exists, then complete the formula, if not then return a 0 or blank value. E.G. =IF(B1,A1/B1,0) or =IF(B1,A1/B1,"")).
- **#N/A** – This means that a referential formula can't find what you told it to find. Most people will address this error with ISERROR or IFERROR. An only slightly better approach is to test directly for the NA condition, because it still requires double calculation. E.G. =IF(ISNA(FUNCTION),0,FUNCTION)).
- **#NAME?** – This means that Excel doesn't recognize the function name. Generally this is the result of a typo, like =sume(a1:a10), where "sume" should have been "sum".
- **#NULL!** – This happens when you tell a function to intersect two ranges that can't physically intersect. E.G. =(A1:C1 B1:B5) will return the value in cell B2 because that's the intersection between the two ranges. But =(A1:C1 B2:B5) will return a #NULL! Error because there is no intersection between the two ranges (row 1 can't intersect with rows 2-5).
- **#NUM!** – This happens if you try to pass a non-valid number to a function, or if you try to get Excel to calculate a number that's too big or small. =1*10^308 would cause an error, because the largest number Excel can calculate is =1*10^307.
- **#REF!** – This generally happens if you've deleted a range that a formula referred to and have severed the link. If you have this formula: =Sheet2!A1 and delete row one on Sheet2 you'll get this error: =Sheet2!#REF!.
- **#VALUE!** – This happens if you try to compare two different operands, like trying to multiply a value by text. =(A1*A2) would give you an error if one cell was numeric and one was text.

Commonly Used Business Functions

The rest of this lesson will be sharing and explaining function examples with the Lesson 6 workbook. We'll discuss where and when you might use these functions and then show you how to set up a scenario to use them, followed by actually putting them together. You'll probably spend a lot of time switching between the lesson and the companion workbook, because it's generally better to be hands on when you're learning functions and how to use them. We're going to go back through the Functions in the same order they are on the Formula Ribbon and use the top four or five from each category, as well as some beneficial formulas. Unfortunately, this is by no means an exhaustive list of all of Excel's functions, but there will be some Microsoft references in the Lesson Summary.

> **Functions & Calculations**
> Most of Excel's native functions don't require you to perform any additional calculations yourself, just enter the proper arguments and Excel will take care of the calculation for you. Function arguments that have brackets are optional. For instance the [Pv] and [Type] arguments in the Future Value function aren't required.

- **Financial** – There are plenty of functions in the Financial category that can help you manage your business, and there are many that you'll never even get close to using. While some of them are relatively complicated and do require some time to learn the ins-and-outs of the business' they target (like stocks and banking), we're going to discuss some of the Financial functions that might be the most meaningful to you in the course of normal small business operations. Fortunately, these are no less powerful tools for you than some of the functions a trading analyst might use.

  - **FV – Future Value** – Let's say you want to start an investment account. If you can get 3.2% Interest over 60 months and you put in $650/month, how much will your investment be worth at the end of 5 years? Note this is a simple example and doesn't include compounding or variable interest rates or deposit amounts.
    - =FV(Rate, Nper, Pmt,[PV],[Type])
    - Rate – Interest Rate/Number of Annual Payments
    - Nper – Number of Periods in the Investment

FV - Future Value	
Description	Data
Annual Interest Rate	3.20%
Number of Payments	60
Amount of Payment	($650)
Present Value	$0
Payment Due	1
Future Value	$42,344.99

- Pmt – Payment made each Period (this is a negative amount – think of it as the amount that comes out of your checking account to go in the IRA)
- PV - Present Value of the Investment – it can be 0, or left out.
- Type – 1 or 0 – Indicates whether the Payment is made at the Beginning or End of a Period (Optional)

○ **NPER – Number of Periods** – This will tell you how many payments you have to make over the life of an investment if you know the interest rate and payment amount. For instance if you wanted to buy a new copier and it's $5,500. If you know the Interest rate and payment periods (monthly, quarterly, etc.) then you can figure out how many payments you'll need to make before you pay it off.

NPER - Number of Periods	
Description	Data
Annual Interest Rate	3.20%
Amount of Payment	($100)
Present Value	$5,500
Future Value	$0
Payment Due	1
Number of Periods	59.38

  - =NPER(Rate, Pmt, Pv, [Fv], [Type])
  - Rate – Interest Rate/Number of Annual Payments
  - Pmt – Payment made each period
  - PV – Present Value
  - FV – Generally 0 (Optional)
  - Type – 1 or 0 – Indicates whether the Payment is made at the Beginning or End of a Period (Optional)

○ **PMT – Payment** – This will tell you what your payment is if you know the amount you want to finance and the interest rate. It's similar to the NPER function, just the other way around. In this case you know your copier is $5,500 and the interest rate the bank gave you, but you need to figure out if you can afford the monthly payments. If you compare the results from this function to the NPER function we just did you'll see that they're essentially just reverse cases of each other.

PMT - Payment	
Description	Data
Annual Interest Rate	3.20%
Number of Payments	60
Present Value	$5,500
Future Value	$0
Payment Due	1
Payment	($99.05)

  - =PMT(Rate, Nper, PV, [FV], [Type])
  - Rate - Interest Rate/Number of Annual Payments
  - Nper– Number of Periods in the Investment
  - Pv – Present Value
  - Fv – Future Value
  - Type – 1 or 0 – Indicates whether the Payment is made at the Beginning or End of a Period (Optional)

- **What-If Analysis**
  ○ We're going to take a slight detour here and show you one of Excel's Data Analysis tools, because it fits in with the calculations that we've been doing. Going back to the new copier example: you have your Interest Rate from the bank, you know what the copier costs, you know the number of months it'll take for you to pay it off, and you know the payment amount. But what if the payment's just a bit too high? In this case your copier payment is about one hundred bucks a month, but you want to know how much copier can you get for $75? So how do you do that? You break out the What-If tools. In this case we're going to use what's called Goal Seek. We'll take an existing model, the PMT model, plug in $75, and Excel's going to run through scenarios in its head until it gets to the copier that you can afford for $75/month.

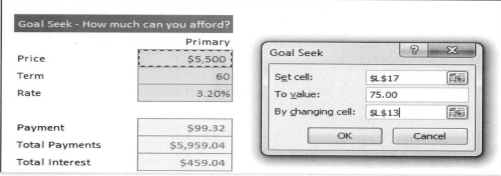

Figure 217

  ○ In this case we want Excel to change the Payment to $75, by adjusting the copier price until it gets there, so plug in the reference/value and watch what happens.

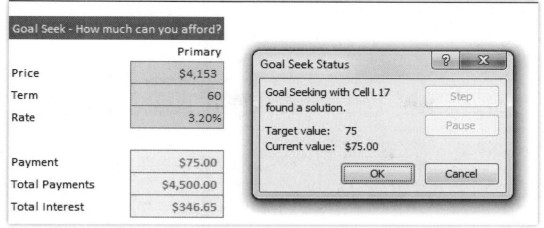

Goal Seek - How much can you afford?

	Primary
Price	$4,153
Term	60
Rate	3.20%
Payment	$75.00
Total Payments	$4,500.00
Total Interest	$346.65

Goal Seek Status

Goal Seeking with Cell L17 found a solution.

Target value: 75
Current value: $75.00

Figure 218

- ○ So now you can see that at $75/month, with those terms, you can afford a copier that costs $4,153. If you can have this information in hand before you start negotiating for that copier, then you'll be in a much stronger position. This works with buying cars too. In fact, you can figure out any purchase that has terms involved.
- ○ (Ok, we'll now return to our regularly scheduled lesson…)
- **RATE – Interest Rate per Period** – This will tell you what your Interest Rate is if you know the payments, the term of the loan and the Present Value of the loan. This can be used to find out what credit is really costing you.

RATE - Interest Rate per Period

Description	Data
Number of Payments	60
Amount of Payment	($100)
Present Value	$5,500
Future Value	$0
Payment Due	1
Interest Rate	2.999617%

  - ○ =RATE(Nper, Pmt, PV, [FV], [Type])
  - ○ Nper– Number of Periods in the Investment
  - ○ Pmt – Payment made each period
  - ○ PV – Present Value
  - ○ FV – Generally 0 (Optional)
  - ○ Type – 1 or 0 – Indicates whether the Payment is made at the Beginning or End of a Period (Optional)
- **DB – Straight Line Depreciation** – If you were to buy a piece of equipment, then you want to know how much you can depreciate it each year during its expected life cycle. This not only helps with taxes, but it also helps you figure in operating expenses for that equipment.

DB - Depreciation

Purchase Price	$25,000
Estimate Life (Years)	5
Salvage Value	$1,250

Year*	Depreciation
Year 1	$11,275.00
Year 2	$6,189.98
Year 3	$3,398.30
Year 4	$1,865.66
Year 5	$1,024.25
Total Depreciation	$23,753.19

  - ○ =DB(Cost, Salvage, Life, Period, [Month])
  - ○ Cost – the purchase price of the equipment
  - ○ Salvage – When it's time to get a new one, how much can you get if you sell this one?
  - ○ Life - How many years can you expect to use the equipment before you need to replace it?
  - ○ Period – Generally measured in years for large equipment purchases.
  - ○ Month – How many months in the first year – (Optional) – the default is 12 months if you leave it out.
- *Logical*
  - ○ **IF** – As mentioned several times, IF statements are the cornerstone to a lot of Excel logic. As you get more and more comfortable with Excel you may well find the ubiquitous IF statement being one of the functions you draw on the most. But the IF statement comes with some significant warnings that we'll get into shortly. Just as Excel has over a million rows, but using them all probably isn't a good idea, the IF statement can do a lot of things, but trying to make it do everything isn't a good idea either. We've already mentioned how earlier versions of Excel allowed you to nest up to 7 IF statements, and here's a very simple example.

=IF(A1=1,1,IF(A1=2,2,IF(A1=3,3),IF(A1=4,4),IF(A1=5,5))))

- Try reading that if it contained some truly complex comparisons!

- One of the most common uses of IF statements is to return data that matches specific criteria, or falls within a range of values. Here is a relatively common example of a nested IF statement to return letter grades based on test scores (which you'll see in the first Logical formula example in Lesson 6 workbook):

	A	B	C
1	Student	Test Score	Grade
2	Bob	89.8	B
3	Tommy	52.7	F
4	Christine	99.3	A
5	Alice	63.6	D
6	Fred	73.4	C
7	Carey	98.9	A

Figure 219

=IF(A1>=90,"A",IF(A1>=80,"B",IF(A1>=70,"C",IF(A1>=60,"D",IF(A1<60,"F")))))

- Another is calculating commission statements:

=IF(A1>25000,A1*2%,IF(A1>15000,A1*1.5%,IF(A1>5000,A1*1%,0)))

- Note that in both formulas, the criteria need to be ordered sequentially in order for the formula to calculate correctly. So in the first example A1>=90 gets evaluated first, and if that condition is true, then the formula performs the calculation associated with that condition. If the condition isn't true, then it moves onto the second, and so on. But if you get your conditions out of order, then one condition can invalidate the next and render your formula(s) useless. One of the inherent weaknesses with IF statements is that they need to be precise and ordered.

- While both of these formulas work fine, they're unwieldy and should be avoided if at all possible. Why? Primarily because the data in the formulas is static, so if the conditions driving the formula ever need to be changed, the formula needs to be manually adjusted as a result. Granted, the grades example isn't too bad, because it's not likely those grade standards will change too often, but just imagine how much work you'd have to do if you have a lot of formulas like the commission example, and you have to change the criteria? Ideally, you'll get into the habit of only using IF statements for Text comparisons like the earlier example. Yes/No/Maybe or Male/Female evaluations are very common, and the nice thing about them is that criteria aren't likely to change very often. If you find yourself with situations like this then by all means use IF statements, otherwise it's time to move up to more robust alternatives, starting with LOOKUP, which we'll get to shortly. If statements also work well for evaluating Conditional Formatting criteria, which we'll be discussing in the next lesson.

- One of the primary reasons to move away from IF statements for multiple criteria is so that you can use "table based" reference data. This gives you the ability to have your data points on a worksheet, where the values can be easily changed, as opposed to hardcoded in a formula, where changing the values can be a challenge. Many workbooks have broken because of numerous IF statements that someone didn't update. In the commission example above, what would happen if you needed to change the 2% and you had hundreds of formulas depending on that one? It wouldn't be fun, and that's a relatively small example. Imagine one with 64 conditions! And that's if you can even find the formula in the first place! Table based dependencies are much easier to change on the fly, which can mean a lot especially if you're dealing with complex models and testing multiple criteria.

○ You will find multiple examples of logical function combinations in the Lesson 6 workbook. As with so many things in Excel, the variations you can come up with are virtually limitless.

▪ **AND** - This returns TRUE if all of the arguments being evaluated are TRUE. If one or more of the evaluated arguments are FALSE, then AND returns a FALSE.

▪ **OR** – This evaluates all of the arguments and will return TRUE if any of them is TRUE. It will return FALSE ONLY if all of the arguments are false.

▪ **NOT** – This simply changes TRUE to FALSE or FALSE to TRUE. It is good if you are trying to exclude something from a comparison.

▪ **IFERROR** – As mentioned, this is strictly for error management, and remember it will suppress ALL errors, so it's generally not a good idea to use until you know that your model is functioning properly.

○ *Text – (Text functions generally go hand-in-hand, so examples will be after their explanations).*

○ **FIND** – This finds a particular value within a string and returns an integer corresponding to its position in the string starting from the left. *=FIND("*",A1).* If * was in the fifth spot in the cell, then FIND would return a 5.

○ **LEFT/RIGHT/MID** – These allow you to pull text from a string either from the Left, Middle or Right. It is used a lot in both Parsing and Concatenating names. E.G. converting "Smith, Bob" to "Bob Smith". E.G. *=LEFT(A1,5)* would return the 5 characters to the left of cell A1. If you were to change that to *=RIGHT(A1,5)* you would get the rightmost 5 characters.

○ **&** - While there is a CONCATENATE function, the Ampersand is much more robust, and is faster to use (*see TEXT for an example*).

○ **TEXT** – This allows you to reapply formatting to numeric values when you have joined them in a text string. E.G. *="Today's Date is: "&TEXT(TODAY(),"MM/DD/YY").*

▪ Concatenating Text - =PROPER(B2&", "&A2)

C2	▼	f_x	=PROPER(B2&", "&A2)	
	A	**B**	**C**	
1	First Name	Last Name	LastName, First Name	
2	TOM	JONES	Jones, Tom	
3	BOB	SMITH	Smith, Bob	
4	ALLEN	BROWN	Brown, Allen	
5	FRED	THOMPSON	Thompson, Fred	
6	KEYUR	PATEL	Patel, Keyur	
7	BILL	JELEN	Jelen, Bill	

Figure 220

▪ Parsing Text

B10	▼	f_x	=RIGHT(A10,LEN(A10)-FIND(",",A10)-1)	
	A	**B**	**C**	**D**
9	Parsing Data	Last Name	First Name	
10	Jones, Tom	Tom	Jones	
11	Smith, Bob	Bob	Smith	
12	Brown, Allen	Allen	Brown	
13	Thompson, Fred	Fred	Thompson	
14	Patel, Keyur	Keyur	Patel	
15	Jelen, Bill	Bill	Jelen	

Figure 221

- Last Name - *=RIGHT(A10,LEN(A10)-FIND(",",A10)-1)*
- First Name - *=LEFT(A10,FIND(", ",A10)-1)*

○ Using TEXT to format concatenated text & values - ="Report Date: "&TEX**T(TODAY(),"mm/dd/yy")**

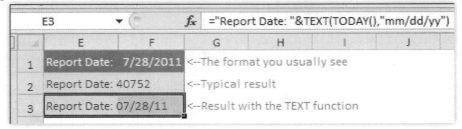

Figure 222

> **Date/Time Stamps**
> If you need to have static
> Date/Time entered on a worksheet
> you can use keyboard shortcuts:
> CTRL+; – Date
> CTRL+SHIFT+: – Time

- **Date & Time**
    - ○ **TODAY** – Simple, it gives you today's Date. It does not take any arguments and it is volatile, meaning that it will continuously update. Some people try to use Date & Time functions for static Date/Time stamps, and then wonder what happened the next day, when the date has updated.
    - ○ **NOW** – This gives you the Date and Time. It does not take any arguments and it is volatile as well.
    - ○ **YEAR** – This returns the year of the date it's referencing. E.G. *=YEAR(TODAY())*
    - ○ **WEEKDAY** – This returns the day of the week as an integer value (1-7). E.G. *=WEEKDAY(TODAY(),1)* – If it was a Wednesday the answer would be 4. Note that WEEKDAY has a Return Type argument for the starting day of the week; 1 is Sunday - Saturday, 2 is Monday - Sunday, 3 is Monday – Sunday, where Monday starts as a 0 value instead of a 1. You can convert that to a Text day with *=TEXT(WEEKDAY(TODAY(),1),"MMM")*.
    - ○ **DAYS360** – This lets you calculate the difference in days between two dates. It's great for kids who want to know how long it is until Christmas or their next birthday. E.G. *=DAYS360(TODAY(),"12/25/2011")* Note that if you manually enter the date in the function, you need to wrap it in quotes. It's generally easier to put the date in a cell and reference it directly.

> **Cell References vs. Hardcoding values in Functions**
> Try to limit the amount of physical information you put in function
> arguments. It's far more efficient to use cell references: they're out in the
> open and they're easy to change. If you have fixed values in functions, you
> have to first find the function(s) and then find the value to replace. It's
> time consuming and error prone!

-
    - ○ **EOMONTH** – This returns the last day of the month in reference to the date entered as an argument, and how many months away you specify. *=EOMONTH(TODAY(),0)* would tell you the last day of the current month. *=EOMONTH(TODAY(),6)* would give you the last day of the month six days from now. This can be handy with project planning and calculating dates, because you can let Excel figure it out for you vs. having to enter the end date manually somewhere.
- **Lookup & Referential** – These are some of the most widely used functions in Excel and once you get the hang of them you'll understand why. Lookup functions help prevent having to enter in data repeatedly. Here's a common scenario: a business has an invoice form they use for their goods and services. When it comes time to enter an order for a repeat customer, someone types in the Customer Name, then has to go look up all of their relevant information, like Address, Phone #, etc. Lookup functions do all of that for you; all you need is a unique identifier for the record you want to find. In the case of customers, it's generally a Customer ID # or Business Name. You can also return information

on sales reps, products sold, etc. Almost any information that's table based can be set up to retrieve that information via formula rather than doing it manually.

- **LOOKUP** – Remember the grades example with the long IF statement that determined what the resulting grade for a student's test score was? That is the perfect scenario to explain the LOOKUP function. LOOKUP functions essentially work like this: What do you want to look up? Where do you want to look for it? If Excel finds it, what do you want it to do with it?

    - Here's the Grades example again, but this time you'll see a table set up beneath it that shows the Number grade scale and the corresponding Letter grade. We're going to tell the LOOKUP formula to lookup the student grades in B2:B7 and compare those values with the value in the grades table and return the result.

	A	B	C
		fx	=LOOKUP(B4,$A$12:$B$16)
3	Student	Test Score	Lookup
4	Bob	89.8	B
5	Tommy	52.7	F
6	Christine	99.3	A
7	Alice	63.6	D
8	Fred	73.4	C
9	Carey	98.9	A
10			
11	Number Grade Scale	Letter Grade Scale	
12	50.0	F	
13	60.0	D	
14	70.0	C	
15	80.0	B	
16	90.0	A	

Figure 223

- - Here's the LOOKUP formula: **=LOOKUP(B4,$A$12:$B$16)**, and here's what it says:
        - Look for what? The value in B2
        - Where to look for it? The grades table A10:B14 (note that both columns were entered, because we want the LOOKUP to give us the value from the second column).
        - What to do when it's found? Return the corresponding value in the second column. Excel knows this because two columns were selected in the range and it will return the value in the rightmost column of the stated range.
    - LOOKUP is the simplest of the lookup functions, and the least robust, but it works perfectly in cases like this. LOOKUP tables must be sorted in Ascending order in order to work properly. That's why you see the grades table sorted from lowest to highest. LOOKUP will look for an exact match, and if it can't find it, it will return the largest value in the table that is Less than the lookup value. In this example, the LOOKUP found the closest possible or approximate match to the grade that was entered.
    - There is also what's called an Array version of this function and you'll see it here by example, but you should note the same cautions with using the Array method as you would when hardcoding any values in a function. In this case, as with the IF statement grade example, it's probably relatively benign though, since grades and their scales aren't likely to change anytime soon. The primary advantage to the array version is that it eliminates the lookup table.

=LOOKUP(B4, {0,60,70,80,90}, {"F","D","C","B","A"})

- - **VLOOKUP** – Short for Vertical Lookup, it looks from left-to-right. This is the most common of all the lookup functions, and probably one of the most widely used functions in Excel. If you begin using Excel with any regularity, you'll probably find this to be the case with you. VLOOKUP has a degree of flexibility that LOOKUP does not in two ways: first, it does not care which way its list is sorted, and second, you can lookup a multiple column table range and tell the VLOOKUP exactly which column you want results from.
        - Here's the Microsoft syntax for VLOOKUP:

VLOOKUP(lookup_value, table_array, col_index_num, [range_lookup])

- - - Confusing isn't it? This might be a little bit easier to understand:

=VLOOKUP(Lookup what?, Lookup where?, How many columns over should it go?, Exact or Approximate Match?)

- Following is a common example of VLOOKUP in action. There is a simple table of Account #'s and corresponding dollar figures for each month. In A8 you can enter the value you want to find in the top table, which is "456" in this case. We want to search the entire table range (A2:M4), and in January's case, we want the second column to the right, which is the ",2," part. FALSE (or 0) indicates that VLOOKUP should only return an exact match. As you might guess, when you copy the function to February you need to change the ",2," to ",3," and so on.

B8			f_x	=VLOOKUP($A8,$A$2:$M$4,2,FALSE)	
	A	B	C	D	E	F
1	Account #	January	February	March	April	May
2	123	$22	$23	$24	$25	$26
3	456	$32	$33	$34	$35	$36
4	789	$42	$43	$44	$45	$46
5						
6						
7	VLOOKUP	January	February	March	April	May
8	456	$32	$33	$34	$35	$36

Figure 224

Use COLUMN & ROW to make Lookups dynamic!

Your VLOOKUP/HLOOKUP functions don't have to rely on static row & column offsets to work. Those are a pain, because they have to be manually adjusted for each subsequent function that is copied across or down. Instead, replace the column number with COLUMN().

E.G. =VLOOKUP$A8,$A$2:$M$4,COLUMN(),FALSE)

If the columns don't match, you can adjust them with COLUMN()+1/COLUMN()-2, etc. With HLOOKUP you would use ROW() instead of COLUMN().

- **HLOOKUP** – You guessed it, this is short for Horizontal Lookup. This works the same as VLOOKUP, except it looks from top-down instead of left-to-right.

C5			f_x	=HLOOKUP($B5,$A$7:$F$16,4,FALSE)	
	A	B	C	D	E	F
1						
2						
3		Search	Profit Information			
4		Region	Gross Profit	Net Profit	Profit %	
5		Qtr3	$30,050	$19,930	22%	
6						
7		Qtr1	Qtr2	Qtr3	Qtr4	Total
8	Total sales	$50,000	$78,200	$89,500	$91,250	$308,950
9	Cost of sales	$25,000	$42,050	$59,450	$60,450	$186,950
10	Gross profit	$25,000	$36,150	$30,050	$30,800	$122,000
11						
12	Overhead	$7,500	$7,520	$5,620	$3,520	$24,160
13	Marketing	$7,000	$6,630	$4,500	$3,200	$21,330
14	Total Expenses	$14,500	$14,150	$10,120	$6,720	$45,490
15	Net profit	$10,500	$22,000	$19,930	$24,080	$76,510
16	Profit %	21.0%	28.0%	22.0%	26.0%	25.0%

Figure 225

- In the Gross Profit example the function is **=HLOOKUP($B5,$A$7:$F$16,4,FALSE),** so it's looking for the value in B4 (Qtr3), in the range A7:F16, and when it finds it, the function will offset 4 rows to the Gross Profit row. Note that the function starts at A7 instead of B7. If you were going to use the standard HLOOKUP, then B7 is where you would start, but as you've just seen it's not very dynamic is it? First you have to figure out which criteria you want to return (Gross Profit), then you have to count how many rows down the value will be given where the header row (Qtre1-Qtr4) is, in this case it's 4. But what if you have a worksheet that's hundreds of rows? You'll be there all day trying to match up all of your rows and you'll probably make a mistake. In this case you can use the MATCH function to make the HLOOKUP dynamic by finding the "Gross Profit" row for you.

=HLOOKUP($B5,$A$7:$F$16,MATCH(C4,$A$7:$A$16,0),FALSE)

- **=MATCH(C4,$A$7:$A$16,0)** finds Gross Profit on the 4th row in the range, so it feeds a 4 to the HLOOKUP. MATCH works by looking in A7:A16 for the value that's in C4. The 0 means that you want MATCH to only return an exact match. If you were to put a 1 there, MATCH would find the first approximate match.

- **INDEX/MATCH** – This is one of the most powerful function combinations you have. Have you noticed any potential shortcomings with VLOOKUP & HLOOKUP? They can only go left-to-right, or top-down. Meaning that whatever value you want to look for needs to be in the very left most, or top portion of the table range that you're going to search. In the Grades example that's fine, but what if you want to do something like search an employee table where Social Security Number is the unique identifier, and it's in the middle of the table where you need information to the left of it? The lookups can't do it. Some people will try to trick Excel by using what's called a "helper column" (and they are sometimes necessary, but in this case it's not). To use a helper column you would insert a column at the very left of your table and set a reference in that column to your unique identifier in the middle of the table. So let's say your SSN's are in column F, you would add a column in A and use =F2 to put SSN's in column A, then go about your way with VLOOKUPs (which will work fine by the way). But this approach is inefficient and error prone. What if you add more employees to the table? You have to remember to update that helper column as well. It's something that's often overlooked and leaves people scratching their heads because they can't figure out why the formula's not working, even though they know the information's there.

> **When would you use a Helper Column?**
>
> Let's say you have a customer table. Within your table are several companies who have multiple people with purchase authority, but they all buy under the same Customer ID & Name. So how do you differentiate between orders by different people at the same company? You use a helper column at the left of the lookup table to create a unique sub-id.
>
> **=CompanyName&CompanyID&PurchaserLastName**
>
> You can then use that in your Lookup where the lookup range starts with your new helper column:
>
> **=VLOOKUP(CompanyName&CompanyID&PurchaserLastName, Lookup Range, Lookup Column, 0)**

- So this is where you can combine a few functions into a dynamic formula.
    - **MATCH** - As you saw in the dynamic HLOOKUP example, MATCH looks for a value and tries to match it in the range that you specify. What's nice about MATCH is that you can have it search rows where it will return the row number of the item it finds (relative to where it's searching). Match can also work horizontally, looking for matching values in columns and returning the relevant column number (1, 2, 3, etc.). So if you can match an item in a vertical range, and then match another item in a horizontal range, you can get the intersection of those two ranges. In the HLOOKUP example, we could look for Gross Profit in A7:16 (4), then look for Qtr3 in A7:F7 (4), then look for the 4th row and 4th column in A7:F16. OK, so we've got our row and column numbers, and we know the range to use to find the intersection of the 4th row & 4th column. But how do we tell Excel to use them? This is where INDEX comes in.
    - **INDEX** – The returns a value within a given range based on the intersection of the row and column that you specify. =INDEX(Range you want to look in, Number of Rows, Number of Columns). In our case we want this:

=INDEX(A7:F16,4,4)

- But there we go with those static arguments again. Now you substitute the static value for the values that MATCH returned, and you have this:

=INDEX($A$7:$F$16,MATCH(C19,$A$7:$A$16,0),MATCH($B20,$A$7:$F$7,0))

	C20		f_x	=INDEX($A$7:$F$16,MATCH(C19,$A$7:$A$1

	A	B	C	D	E
18		INDEX/MATCH			
19		Region	Gross Profit	Net Profit	Profit %
20		Qtr3	$30,050	$19,930	22%

Figure 226

- Yes, that's a lot to absorb, but you will find these examples in the companion workbook along with a breakdown of how to get there. There is also a worksheet dedicated solely to INDEX/MATCH and how to build the final formula in pieces. When you get comfortable with INDEX/MATCH you might find yourself completely ignoring the LOOKUPs. Between VLOOKUP & HLOOKUP, the latter is the least robust, and often gets replaced with INDEX/MATCH anyway.

Build Mega-Formulas in pieces!

Sometimes you build giant formulas that are the combination of several other functions and formulas. The easiest thing to do is build each element/function separately. For instance, in the INDEX/MATCH/MATCH example, build the first MATCH, then the second MATCH, then build the INDEX function, putting in the results from the two MATCH functions. If the result is what you want, you can replace the row argument with the first MATCH function, followed by the column MATCH.

You'll find it's a lot easier to break large formulas down into manageable chunks!

- **Math & Trig**   - From a business perspective, the ability to conditionally Average, Count and Sum your data is a fantastic analytical tool, as well as a timesaver. In the past if you wanted to analyze your data by different criteria you either did it by hand or used a database application. But with this amazing functionality you have all of those tools right at your fingertips! Note that for simplicity's sake, none of the formula examples have been cluttered with Absolute References, but when you use them in real-life scenarios it's something you can't forget.
  - **SUMIF** – This is pretty much exactly what it sounds like. It lets you sum one range based on criteria in another. For instance let's say you want to sum all sales for the month where the item sold was blue. In this example we're going to Sum all values in column C where the corresponding value in column A is "Yes".

	G2		f_x	=SUMIF(A2:A17,E2,C2:C17)		

	A	B	C	D	E	F	G
1	Criteria 1	Criteria 2	Value		Sum Criteria1	Sum Criteria2	SUMIF
2	Yes	Blue	23		Yes	Blue	480
3	No	Green	88				
4	Yes	Yellow	53				

Figure 227

- SUMIF works like this: =SUMIF(The range with the Sum criteria, the Criteria, the range with the values to be summed)

=SUMIF(A2:A17,E2,C2:C17)

- Unfortunately, it reads a little bit backwards: Sum the range C2:C17, where A2:A17 equals the value in E2, in this case, "Yes".
  - **SUMIFS** – This is similar to SUMIF, except it lets you sum by multiple criteria.

	H2		f_x	=SUMIFS(C2:C17,A2:A17,E2,B2:B17,F2)		

	A	B	C	D	E	F	H
1	Criteria 1	Criteria 2	Value		Sum Criteria1	Sum Criteria2	SUMIFS
2	Yes	Blue	23		Yes	Blue	278
3	No	Green	88				
	Yes	Yellow	53				

Figure 228

=SUMIFS(C2:C17,A2:A17,E2,B2:B17,F2)

- Oddly enough, the arguments in SUMIFS aren't in the same order as they are in SUMIF: =SUMIFS(Range to Sum, 1st Range to Evaluate, 1st Criteria, 2nd Range to Evaluate, 2nd Criteria). In this case Sum C2:C17 where A2:A17 equals the value in E2 (Yes), and where B2:B17 equals the value in F2 (Blue). SUMIFS will support up to 127 different criteria pairs, but imagine trying to read that formula!

  - **SUMPRODUCT** – This can be an incredibly robust, but complicated function, and it can handle up to 255 arguments. As you'll see in the example, SUMPRODUCT here returns the same value as SUMIFS. This lesson isn't going to go into detail about how to create SUMPRODUCTS, because it is not a one-size fits all function. It is here, however, so that you know it's available. Many times analysis that seems impossible can be returned with SUMPRODUCT.

    - SUMPRODUCT breaks down the arguments that you specify, multiplies them and generates the results as the sum of those products. It's a bit easier to see if you invoke the Function Wizard and watch how Excel is evaluating the formula. In this case, SUMPRODUCT is evaluating A2:A17 where the values equal E2's value, then evaluating B2:B17 where the value equals F2, finally coming to the Sum range in C2:C17.

    - In the Function Wizard you can see that SUMPRODUCT evaluated the results of the arguments as {23;0;0;0;99;0;0;0;61;0;0;0;95;0;0;0}, which equals 278 when summed.

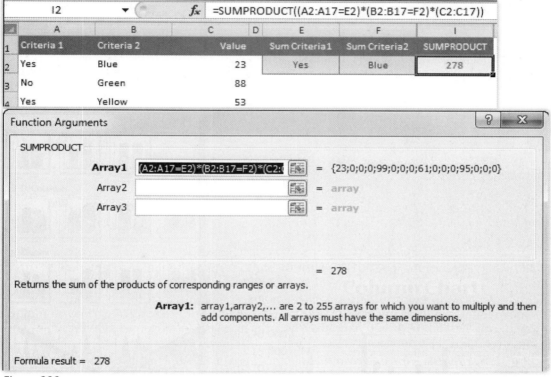

Figure 229

  - **COUNTIF** – The COUNTIF(s) & AVERAGEIF(s) are the same as SUMIF, but return a count or average of the items in a range vs. their sum. The "IF" versions will only accept a single criteria, while the "IFS" versions will accept multiple. =COUNTIF(Range to Count, Criteria to Count by).

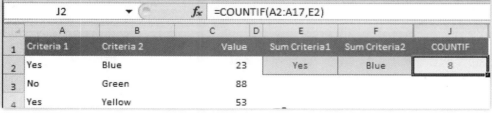

Figure 230

=COUNTIF(A2:A17,E2)

- In this case count the values in column A where the value = "Yes".

○ **COUNTIFS** – =COUNTIF(1st Range to Count, 1st Criteria, 2nd Range to Count, 2nd Criteria). COUNTIFS will only count items where both ranges meet the criteria. In this case it will only count the values that are "Yes" AND "Blue".

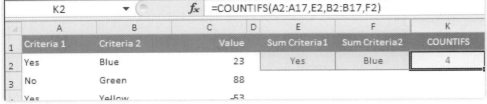

Figure 231

=COUNTIFS(A2:A17,E2,B2:B17,F2)

○ **AVERAGEIF** - =AVERAGEIF(Range with the Criteria, Criteria, Range to Average).

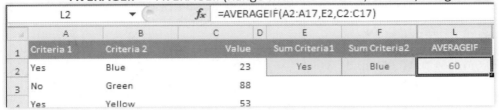

Figure 232

=AVERAGEIF(A2:A17,E2,C2:C17)

▪ In this case Average C2:C17, where the cells in A2:A17 equal E2 ("Yes").

○ **AVERAGEIFS** - =AVERAGEIFS(Range to Average, 1st Criteria Range, 1st Criteria, 2nd Criteria Range, 2nd Criteria)

	M2	▼		fx	=AVERAGEIFS(C2:C17,A2:A17,E2,B2:B17,F2)		
	A	B	C	D	E	F	M
1	Criteria 1	Criteria 2	Value		Sum Criteria1	Sum Criteria2	AVERAGEIFS
2	Yes	Blue	23		Yes	Blue	69.5
3	No	Green	88				
4	Yes	Yellow	53				

Figure 233

=AVERAGEIFS(C2:C17,A2:A17,E2,B2:B17,F2)

▪ This will Average the values in C2:C17, where the cells in A2:A17 equal the value in E2 ("Yes") AND the cells in range B2:B17 equal the value in F2 ("Blue")

○ **3D Formulas** – These are a way to perform calculations on multiple worksheets at once without cumbersome manual formulas. Imagine the first month model for a 12-Month Cash Flow summary we put together in Lesson 5? If you had all 12 Months in place and a summary worksheet, you could summarize the total like this:

=January!A1+February!A1+March!A1+April!A1+May!A1+June!A1+July!A1+August!A1+September!A1+October!A1+November!A1+December!A1

○ Which means either typing that formula by hand (not fun), or entering = in the summary sheet, click on January, then A1, add a +, then February and A1, etc. That's no fun either. This is where 3D formulas come in especially handy. You could replace that monstrosity above with this:

=SUM(January:December!A1)

○ That will sum cell A1 in January, cell A1 in December, AND cell A1 on every sheet in between those two sheets.

	B4	▼		fx	=SUM('3d Second:3D Last'!B4)			
	A	B	C	D	E	F	G	H
1							3-Year Revenue Totals	
2								
3	Region	January	February	March	April	May	June	Jul
4	North	190.0	126.0	26.1	186.9	182.2	220.2	132.
5	South	131.3	131.3	155.3	135.8	170.0	133.1	236.
6	East	214.3	107.5	215.9	261.9	175.9	156.3	134.

Figure 234

- Here is an example from the companion workbook, where there are worksheets named 3D First (the worksheet in the example), then 3D Second, 3D Third and 3D Last. So the formula in the example is summing cell B4 on 3D Second, 3D Last, and what's in between them. You'll also see an example of a 3D AVERAGE in the companion workbook.
- Excluding statistical functions, the following functions can support 3d Formula syntax:
  - AVERAGE
  - AVERAGEA
  - COUNT
  - COUNTA
  - MAX
  - MAXA
  - MIN
  - MINA
  - AND
  - OR

Unit Summary: Lesson 6 – Using Functions & Formulas

- In this lesson you learned about business centric functions in each of the Formula Ribbon's categories:
  - AutoSum
  - Recently Used
  - Financial
  - Logical
  - Text
  - Date & Time
  - Lookup & Reference
  - Math & Trig
  - More Functions
- You learned about the esoteric differences between Functions and Formulas, where Functions result in Formulas, but Formulas don't necessarily need to include Functions.
- You learned about Excel's Order of Operations and how to ensure that your formulas calculate the way that you intend.
- We went over all of Excel's Function Errors and some of the ways to deal with them, as well as the potential issues of suppressing all errors.
- Finally we walked through examples of commonly used business functions.

Review Questions

1. What functions can you find in the AutoSum Wizard
   a. _____
   b. _____
   c. _____
   d. _____
   e. _____
2. What are four of the Function Library groups?
   a. _____
   b. _____
   c. _____
   d. _____
3. What's the difference between a Function and a Formula?
   a. _____
4. How is =12+(5*2) different from =12+5*2?
   a. _____
5. What are some Functions that will be useful as you become more comfortable with Excel?
   a. _____
   b. _____
   c. _____
   d. _____

Lesson Assignment – Lesson 6 – Using Functions & Formulas

Your assignment is to open the companion workbook and review the examples there, if you haven't already. Once you've had some time to get the feel for the functions and formulas there, insert a new worksheet and start entering the functions that you identified in Question 5.

(There is a Notes section below for you to keep track of your observations):

Lesson 6 Notes

Lesson 7 – Formatting & Printing

In the last lesson you were exposed to some of Excel's most commonly used Functions and Formulas, as well as the difference between the two. We went into group in the Function Library, and you were exposed the amazing depth and powerful functionality of the intrinsic functions you have at your fingertips with Excel. We reviewed actual examples throughout the lesson so you could see different functions in action in real business scenarios. We also discussed error management, and how it can be a valuable tool in setting up your workbooks, as well as being able to hide errors from users if the need arises.

Up until now you've been primed on the evolution of a workbook, and how to take the necessary steps to bring it to the point where is fits your needs. You've:

1. Learned how to put good spreadsheet design elements into place
2. Input your primary row and column headers
3. Populated your worksheet with some sample data
4. Added some functions and formulas to test your sample data
5. Replaced sample data with live data (maybe even using referential functions like VLOOKUP or INDEX/MATCH along the way...

If you've been following along with your own example workbook, then by now you've designed the layout for the particular kind of workbook model you were creating (finance, marketing, customer management, etc.), All of your information is in your workbook, formulas have been tested, and other than some possible user input, you're good to go right? Not quite, it's not set up for distribution yet. It still needs to be formatted to make it easy for your end users to interact with, whether they're just looking at your information, or they're actually responsible for driving information back to you. A lot of financial types might tell you that what's really important is the information. Well, that's true, but presentation is how you make your information palatable to your recipients, so it's equally important. If the information is easy for them to get to and absorb, then you'll have an easier time telling your story, but if you make it hard for people to digest your information then your story loses value. Fortunately, oftentimes just some simple adjustments can make an otherwise boring workbook look great. That's what we're going to talk about in this lesson: how can you format your workbooks for the maximum impact. Once you've done that we'll discuss the various ways to print it out.

In this lesson we're going to show a few different workbook scenarios and ways to improve on them. Again, there is no one way to properly format a workbook/worksheet. It largely depends on 1) your personal style, 2) your recipient's needs and expectations and 3) any technical or corporate policy limitations. Remember though, if in doubt, you'll never go wrong with conservative formatting, whereas overdoing it can be just as difficult on users.

Themes

Themes are like the primary structure for your workbooks, and you generally only need to set them once (if you choose to do so at all). Themes govern some of the default formats in your workbooks, like the color scheme that will be applied or the primary font, etc. Hopefully by now you've had some time to work with them to see what particular theme(s) fit your style or needs, because as with so many other options that Microsoft gives you, there are just too many possible combinations to cover here. The default theme is the "Office Theme", which is relatively reserved with a standard white background and unobtrusive colors.

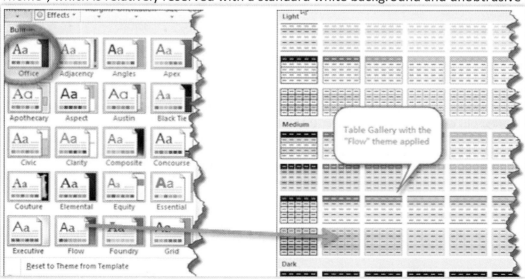

Figure 235

If you decide to change a theme and want to get an immediate idea of how it will look, goto the Home tab and expand the **Format as Table** gallery, or the **Styles** gallery. You'll see that it's assumed the colors of the Theme you selected. If it's not what you wanted, just head back to Page Setup, Themes and reset it.

Text, Cell, Row & Column Formatting

Most workbooks will have a standard font throughout with no differentiation, and that's how every workbook starts out, although many finish that way too. As mentioned previously you'll save yourself a lot of time if you build your model and get the kinks worked out of it before you start applying a lot of formatting. Otherwise you'll generally end up redoing it several times before you're done as you add/remove elements. This doesn't mean that you can't add bits of formatting here and there to make it easier to navigate the model when you're designing it. Rather, don't spend a lot of time trying hard to add in finished product formatting before you're done with the end product. Besides, when you are ready to start, formatting a workbook for distribution isn't necessarily that tough or time consuming. Even if you're not an artistic savant, you can quickly draw attention to certain key points by making them a bit larger, bolded, or even a different color. You'll generally see most of that differentiation on header rows and sub-total/totals rows. You might also find that you want to have a currency or other formatting for some of your numbers, being careful to give the user what they need. This can especially hold true with too many decimal places when 2 or 3 would probably do, or not clearly labeling what numbers have what significance. E.G. 225.99 45.67 43.98 1250.93 – How does your user know which of those numbers might be dollar amounts vs. percentages? You don't necessarily have to add number formatting to each series of numbers, but you'll find many financial models will number format at least the first row of data in each set.

Here are before and after examples of the Cash Flow summary you've worked with previously (remember that the Date and Currency formatting was applied when we added our sample data).

CASH RECEIPTS		01/03/11	01/10/11	01/17/11	01/24/11
Cash Sales		$78.26	$41.66	$87.76	$0.16
Collections fm CR accounts		$67.94	$63.35	$18.05	$16.65
Loan/ other cash inj.		$21.23	$96.19	$5.38	$56.24
TOTAL CASH RECEIPTS		$167.42	$201.20	$111.19	$73.05
PURCHASES		01/03/11	01/10/11	01/17/11	01/24/11
Salaries & Wages		$55.73	$86.65	$2.02	$10.77

Figure 236

Here's after, with less than 10 mouse-clicks.

CASH RECEIPTS	01/03/11	01/10/11	01/17/11	01/24/11	01/31/11
Cash Sales	$78.26	$41.66	$87.76	$0.16	$50.03
Collections fm CR accounts	$67.94	$63.35	$18.05	$16.65	$46.89
Loan/ other cash inj.	$21.23	$96.19	$5.38	$56.24	$61.55
TOTAL CASH RECEIPTS	$167.42	$201.20	$111.19	$73.05	$158.46
PURCHASES	01/03/11	01/10/11	01/17/11	01/24/11	01/31/11
Salaries & Wages	$55.73	$86.65	$2.02	$10.77	$69.04
Payroll expenses (taxes, etc.)	$82.33	$33.87	$59.94	$79.81	$6.49
Outside services	$29.67	$61.90	$30.91	$14.12	$33.88
Supplies (office & operating)	$18.41	$51.08	$64.02	$43.30	$90.80
Repairs & maintenance	$90.07	$3.72	$82.22	$64.60	$21.74

Figure 237

Granted, that's a very simple example, but it should give you an idea of what you can do quickly. Note in the second example the worksheet's Gridlines have been turned off, so that the applied shading and borders would be clearer. You'll find the bulk of your formatting elements back on the Home tab in the Font, Alignment & Styles tabs. Some of the companion workbook examples tried to make use of some of those styles by way of example, and using them makes formatting all the faster. And as with so many other things, you can modify Styles to suit you, so you don't have to stick with the default settings.

Quick Formatting Trick with Table styles

If you like the "format" that Table styles gives to your data, but you don't want the functionality of a table, you can quickly apply the Table format you like and then on the Table Tools tab, select Convert to Range from the Tools group. This will remove the Table behavior, but it will leave the Table's formatting intact.

Hiding Key Data - One thing you'll likely run into in your workbooks is the need to have some information not displayed. Let's say you've expanded on the Weekly Cash Flow to have a monthly rollup and you want to include a weekly average by month.

- Scenario: many organizations work on a 5-4-4 accounting schedule, which means that starting in January each month has 5 weeks, then 4, then 4, then back to 5 until the end of the year. In order to get accurate weekly averages you need to divide the total monthly revenue by the number of weeks. You could use =B8/5, =C8/4, =D8/4, etc., but that gets you into hardcoding values in formulas, which you should avoid at all costs right? Instead you can put the 5-4-4 references in an unused row (usually above your data), and reference that.

	A	B	C	D	E	F
1		5	4	4	5	4
2	CASH RECEIPTS	January	February	March	April	May
3	Cash Sales	$63.63	$7.81	$95.80	$58.51	$19.19
4	Collections fm CR accounts	$13.77	$35.02	$72.36	$60.17	$44.91
5	Loan/ other cash inj.	$17.45	$53.64	$94.42	$23.22	$0.80
6	TOTAL CASH RECEIPTS	$94.84	$96.47	$262.58	$141.90	$64.90
7						
8	Weekly Average	=B6/B$1	$24.12	$65.65	$28.38	$16.23

Figure 238

- Unfortunately, now you have some data in your worksheet that no one needs to see, so what do you do?
  - Trick #1 - The most common trick is to just hide that row. HomeCells, Format, Hide/Unhide, Hide Rows (or simply ALT+O+R+H). But what do you do if there's information on that row or column that does need to remain visible?
  - Trick #2 – You can format the cells' font the same as the cells' background. In the case of the Cash Flow example you would just format the font as white. The 5-4-4's are still there, but your users can't see them. And fortunately, what they can't see, they usually don't bother...

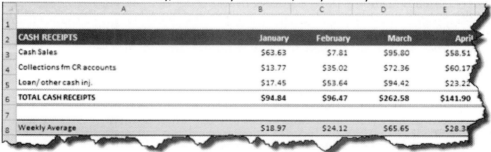

Protecting Hidden Data

Just because you use some method to hide your data, doesn't mean that it's protected from someone making inadvertent or intentional changes. Make sure that those hidden cells are locked and that you protect the Worksheet before distributing it!

Figure 239

Borders - These can be a great tool for segmenting data, but as with any other elements you need to put some thought into them. If you just format everything with borders then it's really no different than just leaving gridlines on. Ideally what you're trying to do is direct the flow of information and make it easy for your user to quickly understand what's going on. In the Cash Flow example you see that only the Total/Average rows have had borders applied, but this is a very small model. In larger models you might want to use continuous borders for all the data so that it's easier to keep everything on the right lines (a continuous border is when all four sides have a border applied). Continuous borders can also be useful when your information is going to be utilized in hard copy form, where people don't' necessarily have the convenience of highlighting a particular row/column, but need to use their fingers to follow along.

PURCHASES	January	February	March	April	
Salaries & Wages	$52.59	$68.03	$25.95	$29.19	
Payroll expenses (taxes, etc.)	$38.41	$40.45	$46.50	$72.33	
Outside services	$74.47	$91.54	$10.28	$99.78	
Supplies (office & operating)	$49.46	$19.49	$74.87	$7.68	
Repairs & maintenance	$99.35	$20.97	$46.89	$25.91	
Advertising	$94.89	$63.77	$90.66	$77.51	
Transportation	$76.15	$98.09	$45.44	$46.96	
Accounting & legal	$62.57	$54.36	$16.01	$50.24	
Rent	$30.48	$44.09	$28.75	$75.54	
Telephone	$16.68	$61.06	$49.45	$79.56	
Utilities	$16.94	$62.28	$86.42	$69.59	

Figure 240

To apply borders first select the range you want to cover, then select the Border tool from the Font group on the Home tab. The standard borders are all very easy to apply by clicking on them, although some borders do need to be applied in sequence. For instance if you were to apply a Thick Box Border to a range, then apply All Borders, you would immediately wipe out the Thick border. A general rule of thumb with borders is to apply all of your inside formatting first, then outer last.

Borders
- Bottom Border
- Top Border
- Left Border
- Right Border
- No Border
- All Borders
- Outside Borders
- Thick Box Border
- Bottom Double Border
- Thick Bottom Border
- Top and Bottom Border
- Top and Thick Bottom Border
- Top and Double Bottom Border

Draw Borders
- Draw Border
- Draw Border Grid
- Erase Border
- Line Color
- Line Style
- More Borders...

- The **More Borders** option will launch the Excel 2003 Format Cells dialog that we've already discussed previously. While the general Borders dialog has most of the settings you'll find here, the Format Cells dialog also exposes Diagonal Borders. In addition you can modify the line styles you apply, for instance the Total rows in the Cash Flow examples used a Top and Bottom Double border, which is a fairly standard financial border.

- We haven't discussed yet the Draw Border & Draw Border Grid, and Erase Border tools, which do have some advantages over other border applications methods.
  - Draw Border simply allows you to draw a border around the range of your choice instead of selecting it first. When you invoke the Draw Border tool, the first thing that will happen is your worksheet will suddenly have a case of the Chicken Pox, with bullets at the intersection of each cell. Second, your cursor turns into a pencil symbol. To draw a border, just left-click the mouse and drag to start the border, then release the button when you're done. It's a neat trick for one-off borders where it would be faster than selecting a range. Note that Draw Border only gives you an outside border, not inside.
  - Draw Border Grid on the other hand will draw all borders. Are these ground-breaking tools? Of course not, but they can speed up some tedious formatting elements.
  - Erase Border will erase all borders that you applied, whether you used the Draw Border tools or placed the borders in the traditional fashion. This can be substantially faster than selecting a range and selecting No Border.

Cell Shading - and Borders often go hand-in-hand, and it's rare you'll see a model that doesn't have a bit of both (unless you're looking at boring accounting statements of financial reports, in which case good luck to even have borders at all). Shading is equally easy to place, just select the range you want to apply the shading to then select the Shading tool (it looks like a paint bucket) from the Font group. You can select from the pre-defined Theme or Standard palette colors, or select from the entire range of colors (although this is rarely necessary, unless you just need to desperately match your company colors).

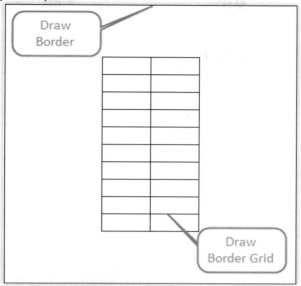

Figure 241

Fill Effects – There additional formats you can apply to cell shading, but they're not readily exposed on the Ribbon. With your range selected, launch the Format dialog (Ctrl+1), and goto the Fill tab. The two options of note here are Fill Effects, which allow you to apply gradients to your cell shading, and Patterns, which let you apply dot patterns to your cells. Note that Fill effects can end up being more distracting than it is helpful, and should be reserved for non-data ranges, like Dashboards, or an area where the pattern won't otherwise interfere with text. Some printers have an issue with rendering both properly, so you or your users might not see the output you want with certain Fill effects & Patterns applied. Generally the denser the Fill or Pattern the harder it will be to see text with it.

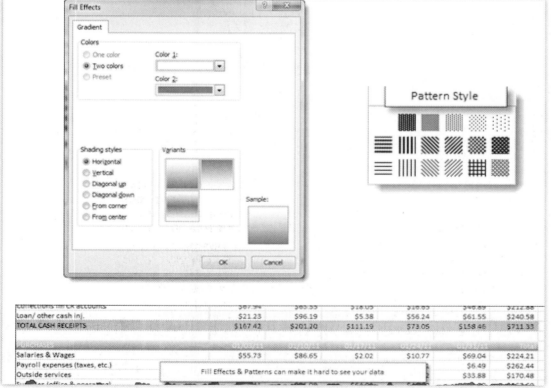

Figure 242

Styles – These are incredibly handy to use, especially in workbooks that do require user input, although you'll probably need to customize them a bit to suit your tastes. The nice thing about Styles is that you can quickly apply them to either a single cell or an entire range. If you do find yourself needing a lot of input from your users it might be well worth the time to create some customized styles of your own.

Font Types – You might also note that the Style gallery uses a mix of fonts, and it's perfectly acceptable to use the Font itself to make something stand out. Just don't use too many different fonts, because you can also overwhelm your users with so much variation that it doesn't make sense.

Font Colors – These will come into play especially if you format rows & columns with cell shading. For darker shades you'll want to format with lighter colors, and do the opposite for lighter shades. Again, your artistic creativity may not be favorable; for instance, the Blue text on Hot Pink shading in the next example probably isn't the best combination (it will also give you a headache), so keep that in mind before you send out your workbook for the first time. Another consideration is that some colors don't render too well on different monitors, so while a certain color combination may look great on your screen, it may be difficult to read on another.

CASH RECEIPTS	January	February	M
Cash Sales	$63.63	$7.81	$9!
Collections fm CR accounts	$13.77	$35.02	$7.

Figure 243

Alignment – This can play a significant role in how easy your worksheets are to interpret. One of the most common alignment faux pas is to align everything center in order to create separation between text. Instead, try to stick with the text's default alignment, which is numbers to the right, and text to the left. Here's an all too common formatting scenario with everything Centered. Unfortunately, the example doesn't do justice to the injustice that this kind of formatting does to a perfectly good report. The text alignment notwithstanding, formatting currency in the center makes it very difficult to read, especially when you get into larger values that will have issues because of where the right side of the numbers line up (or in this case don't).

CASH RECEIPTS	January	February	March	April	May
Cash Sales	$63.63	$7.81	$95.80	$58.51	$19.19
Collections fm CR accounts	$13.77	$35.02	$72.36	$60.17	$44.91
Loan/ other cash inj.	$17.45	$53.64	$94.42	$23.22	$0.80
TOTAL CASH RECEIPTS	$94.84	$96.47	$262.58	$141.90	$64.90
Weekly Average	$18.97	$24.12	$65.65	$28.38	$16.23
PURCHASES	January	February	March	April	May
Salaries & Wages	$52.59	$68.03	$25.95	$29.19	$56.47
Payroll expenses (taxes, etc.)	$38.41	$40.45	$46.50	$72.33	$3.62
Outside services	$74.47	$91.54	$10.28	$99.78	$52.99
Supplies (office & operating)	$49.46	$19.49	$74.87	$7.68	$13.47
Repairs & maintenance	$99.35	$20.97	$46.89	$25.91	$19.08

Figure 244

Indenting/Outdenting - is often overlooked, but it can be very handy in settling some of your more difficult alignment tasks. For instance, many will use leading spaces to make one row of data start a bit inside another. Unfortunately, this can make it much more difficult to use that data (text or values) down the road, because you then need to get rid of the spaces. The Indent/Outdent tools make short work of those situations. Here's an example of some of the Cash Flow report's sub-categories indented for readability.

CASH RECEIPTS	January
Cash Sales	$63.63
Collections fm CR accounts	$13.77
Loan/ other cash inj.	$17.45
TOTAL CASH RECEIPTS	$94.84

Figure 245

Alignment Tips

- Try to avoid Center alignment with Currency figures (some Dates & Percentages can be OK)
- Never use Merged Cells to try to align elements of your worksheets, use Center Across Selection instead
- Instead of using WrapText, use Home→Editing→Fill→Justify which will automatically place the text for you without physically altering the size of your cells.
- Use the Indent/Outdent tools instead of spaces or extra columns for data that butts up against other data (text and values)

Number Formatting – We discussed the available number formats in the Home Tab lesson, so we're not going to repeat it, although we will expand on Dates & Times, as well as Special formatting.

Unnecessary WORK $%&*@

Unfortunately, one of the hardest things for new users to grasp is that they don't need to enter the formatting symbols when entering numbers. I.E. In a currency formatted cell $1,234.56 can simply be entered as 1234.56. You can use the Data Validation Input Message in entry cells to let users know how to enter numbers. You'd be amazed how much time that can save some people!

- **Dates** – Excel's Standard Date format is M/D/YYYY, or 8/1/2001, but you have a myriad of choices. And if you don't find one that suits your needs you can create your own Custom formats. Changing the Date format (or any number format for that matter), is as simple as selecting your range, calling the Format Cells dialog (CTRL+1) and select the format that you want. In financial models you'll often see DD/MM/YY used because it remains a consistent length regardless of the date (e.g., 01/12/10). This can be very helpful in terms of alignment, especially if your date values are in a column. You can also format a date as a long date (Monday, January 1, 2011). As mentioned you can create any of these date or number formats in the Custom settings. For instance, the long date above could be just as easily custom formatted as: dddd, mmmm dd, yyyy. As you've seen about Dates you can also perform mathematical functions on them, so we incremented our Cash Flow example daily with a simple formula: =A1+1, where A1 holds a valid date. You can also do certain things like have a standard date but format it to show month or day only, instead of date.

1/6/2011	01/06/11
1/7/2011	01/07/11
1/8/2011	01/08/11
1/9/2011	01/09/11
1/10/2011	01/10/11
1/11/2011	01/11/11
1/12/2011	01/12/11

Inconsistent Alignment

  - Unlike currency and other numeric values like it, Dates need a valid separator between Day, Month and Year when they're entered: you can use either the forward slash "/" or hyphen "-". If you want to enter a date in the current year, just enter the day/month. I.E. 12/31. Excel automatically assumes that you're talking about the current year.
  - **Times** – Times get less play in Excel than dates unless you're dealing with things like employee schedules, time cards, etc. Unfortunately, Times can be a bit difficult to enter, and they do follow some rules.
    - Whole times (e.g. 9:00 AM) can simply be entered as "9 a" or 9 p". Note the space between the number and a/p. Entering a time without the space would be seen as an invalid time, and would result in a null calculation.
    - Fractional times must be entered in full (e.g. 9:15 AM), although you don't need to enter the "M", "9:15 a" would work, but you need to include a space between the time and AM/PM.
    - Valid times must be entered (e.g. 10:70 p is not a valid time). Fortunately most invalid times will revert to 12:00 AM and can be re-entered at any time.
    - Just as with Dates, provided they're entered properly you can use times in calculations as well. For instance you can calculate the number of hours an employee was on the job each day, including breaks, lunch, etc. You can even use Excel to perform complex Overtime calculations, although that's not a discussion for this course. You will find plenty of Excel Time resources on the Internet if you need them.
  - **Percentages** – These are fairly straightforward and the only thing you need to do is choose how many decimals places you want to display. In most cases 2-3 should suffice. Remember to apply a percentage format to a range PRIOR to entering any data or it will be multiplied by 100. There is no negative number format for Percentages, which can sometimes cause a somewhat conflicting

view if percentage values are displayed next to figures that have been formatted a particular way for negative values. E.G. the following negative currency & percentages values: *($1,234.56)* -12.5%. Fortunately, you can use Conditional Formatting for negative values, which we'll discuss shortly, when we dive into Conditional Formatting.

- ○ **Text Format** – As we've already covered, Text format will allow you to use certain value strings that you normally couldn't if formatted as numbers, such as leading 0's. In the same theme with Text formatting is the TEXT function, which we already discussed, and it can be a huge boon to you with regards to being able to mix text and referential data. All you need is your text, the & to join it with your reference, and the number format of your choice. E.G. ="Today is: "&TEXT(TODAY(),"MM/DD/YY")

- ○ **Special** – Unfortunately, this series of predefined formats doesn't get near the use they should. Invariably, if you look at worksheet with customer information, you'll see a mish-mash of formats with phone numbers and usually zip codes as well. Why? It is generally because the people who entered the data didn't know that cells could be formatted in such a way. So you might have someone enter a phone number like (760) 552-1212, and another like 760.555.1212 (you see it in websites all the time). The problem is that to do anything with that data you need to parse it out, because with the formatting characters manually entered, Excel no longer sees that as a value, but text. It's unlikely that you would perform mathematical calculations on either phone numbers or zip codes, but you would use them in mail merges. You don't want to send out a nice letter with a myriad of different number formats. If you're going to be dealing with any degree of user input, then these are the seemingly little things can eliminate so many headaches if you take care of them up front. Fortunately, you can also use Data Validation to remind people how to enter their data. Will it stop every piece of mis-entered data? Not likely, but it's going to catch most of them, and any time saved in not having to manipulate data that's already been entered it a win. Think about it this way, once data has been entered into a digital environment it should never have to be manipulated again. Sure, it can be used in calculations, and references, but no one should ever need to go back and correct a manually entered format.

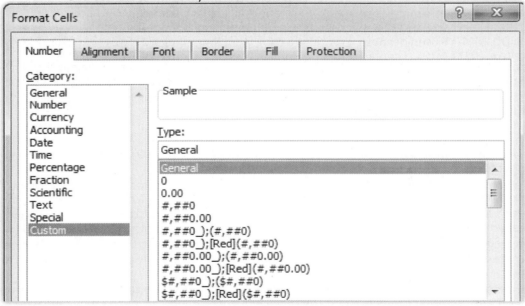

Figure 246

- ○ **Custom** – When nothing fits, come here. You can get a good idea of how to build a custom format, by changing the format of a cell, then look at it in Custom, which will display that format.

Format Painter - One of the best tools you have in your formatting arsenal is the Format Painter. This will copy the formatting applied to a cell and let you transfer that format to another cell. Even better it will let you select entire rows or columns and replicate their formatting. As a simple example we'll go back to the unformatted Cash Flow report in the Lesson 7 workbook. Select the first row of data (A1:G1) and apply the formatting that you want. The formatted example used a blue background with white text, but you can do anything you want. Once that's done select the entire row (click on the row header), then double-click the Format Painter. Now click on the total rows (7 & 33) and your formats have immediately been applied.

- • Single-clicking only enables the Format Painter for one-click.
- • Double-clicking keeps the Format Painter enables until you hit ESC.
- • When copying formats, it's generally easier to select an entire row or column, than it is a range. Excel can remember every format in the selected row or column and apply it to your destination row/

column(s). If you select a range on the other hand, you need to select a like range to apply the formatting or you'll get some unexpected results. For example, goto the formatted Cash Flow example, select A1:A10, then go back to the unformatted example and apply the formatting to A1. Oops! That's not quite what you wanted; Excel applied a repeating pattern didn't it? (FYI - unless you want that formatting to stick you should hit Ctrl+Z now).

- You can generally select a single cell and apply its format to multiple cells and ranges without issue.
- Using the Format Painter will wipe out any existing formatting in the destination range(s) to which you apply it.
- Once you start working with the Format Painter on some of your own worksheets, you'll quickly find out just how handy it can be.

Worksheet Tab Colors – This one was a long time in the making. While Lotus 1-2-3 allowed you to color worksheet tabs, it took Microsoft a while to finally relent and build that functionality into Excel. Why is this important? Most people generally don't see the worksheet tabs at the bottom of a workbook unless you point them out. This can be challenging if you're walking someone through a workbook on the phone and you say "OK, now go to the Cash Flow tab...", and they say "What?" Instead you can simply say "Just click on the Red tab at the bottom of the screen. It says Cash Flow on it." You would be amazed at how much easier it is to direct people to the worksheet tabs with just a little bit of color. You can also set up Tab groups by color. E.G. Orange could be for data input worksheets, Blue for data output sheets, Yellow for hidden sheets, etc. While this is a fantastic tool, if you're going to use it with any regularity, you should definitely come up with a consistent color convention. Otherwise you stand to confuse people if your sheet groupings are different each time. Just right-click on the sheet tab, Tab Color.

Figure 247

Conditional Formatting - This is where you can add a lot of value to your workbooks by identifying particular areas and pointing them out to your users. How do most people highlight areas of importance in documents? Right, they use highlighters, and it probably wouldn't be too much of a stretch to think that most every desk in the country has at least one in a drawer somewhere. Well, people do exactly the same thing in Excel without the slightest hesitation: they'll go into a workbook and manually highlight certain cells or ranges that have particular characteristics, like being over/under a certain value. Notwithstanding the fact that finding and marking all those areas can be like finding the proverbial needle in a haystack, you'll probably also miss some things along the way, which means that you may not accurately present your message, and it's time consuming. If one of the main points of the electronic spreadsheet is for it to save you time, this certainly isn't a good use.

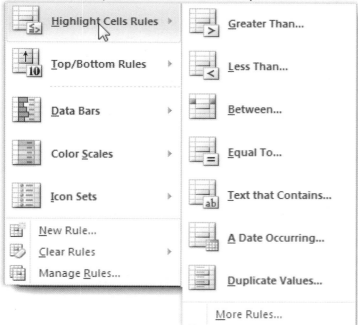

Figure 248

- Conditional Formatting allows you to define rules for cells and ranges, and then apply particular formats when it identifies cells that meet those criteria. Let's say you have an inventory tracking sheet that helps you see when you reach certain product reordering thresholds. You could look through each line item, do a little mental headcount, and say, "Oh, we're down to 5 of that, I need to reorder". Or you can set a rule in Excel to tell you when that happens by giving you a visual clue. For instance when a particular product gets to 10 pieces, the cell turns yellow, 5 it's red, and above 10 it's green. Visual clues are a lot easier than trying to manual search cells for data.

- Conditional Formatting allows up to 64 different scenarios, which is a substantial increase over the 3 conditions you had in earlier versions. But the same rules apply to Conditional Formatting as to IF statements: just because you can do something doesn't mean that you should. In this case, you'd be hard pressed to create 64 formats that are different enough from each other for your users to notice the difference between them. If the purpose of Conditional Formatting is to quickly showcase differences, then overwhelming the user with minute differences won't help. Conditional Formatting is no exception to so of Excel's many methods that has a primary Ribbon interface, as well as an underlying Excel 2003 dialog. We'll discuss the Ribbon method first, then the more traditional dialog. The Ribbon interface for Conditional Formatting is very graphically oriented, and exposes five primary Rules.

- *Highlight Cells Rules* – In terms of trapping conditions, like the inventory control example, this is probably where you'll turn first, as it is probably the most versatile. With this option you're formatting cells based on their values, and it's relatively straightforward. Each option you select will launch a secondary dialog where you'll enter your specifics. Here is the dialog for the Less Than option, and the resulting format. Note that you have some pre-defined formats, or you can choose the custom format, which will launch the Format Cells dialog. Each condition's dialog is slightly different depending on the condition. For instance Between, which will highlight all values between two values, is going to have an option for the low value, and another for the high value.

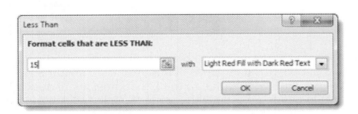

Figure 249

- There are two additional conditions you can add that previously had to be custom written with formulas in the secondary Conditional Formatting dialog.
  - A Date Occurring – Which allows you to format cells based on what a cell's date is in relation to the system date
  - Duplicate Values – Which can identify duplicate/unique values in a range.

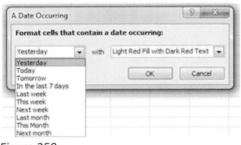
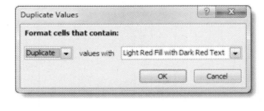

Figure 250

- *Top/Bottom Rules* – This is a very fast way to determine the rank of certain items in a list. The Ribbon options limit you to either the Top or Bottom 10/10% or Above/Below the Average value of the values list, but you can easily adjust the value range in the expanded Conditional Formatting dialog.

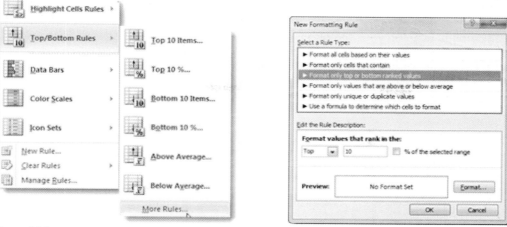

Figure 251

- **Data Bars** – These are in-cell bars that display horizontally, with the length and gradient based on each cell's value in relation to the others. They're very simple to set up, although sometimes they do need a bit of manual adjustment to have the scale properly. Otherwise certain figures seem to get too much weight and others not enough. Data bars are very easy to adjust, but if the defaults aren't enough for you, there are always the expanded options exposed by the More Rules selection.

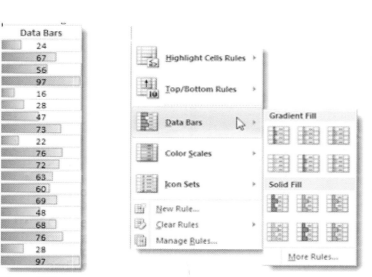

Figure 252

- **Color Scales** – These are similar to Data Bars except that instead of displaying an in-cell bar to represent the value, the entire cell is shaded, with the intensity of the shade being determined by the cell's value in relation to the others in the section. If you don't like the default color selections you can goto the More Rules dialog and add your own custom colors.

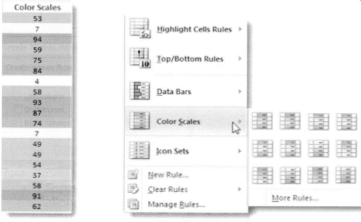

Figure 253

- **Icon Sets** - This is a way to add some graphics cells instead of the shading formats you've seen up to this point. Something to note is that the scale in which the various icons will be applied is directly related to how many objects are in your selection. If you choose the stop light pattern in the example then the breaks will be at green when the value is greater than or equal to 67, yellow when the value is less than 67, but greater than or equal to 33, and red when the value is less than 33. So three objects equates to splitting the values in thirds, 4 would be quarters as seen in the advanced selection options below, and so on. You can also change the default values to your own, although the splits aligned with the number of objects makes a lot of sense.

 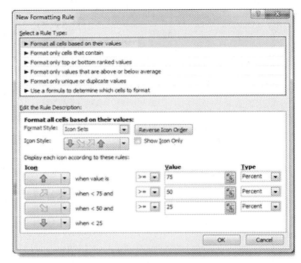

Figure 254

Secondary Conditional Formatting dialog – When you use this dialog, instead of being presented with graphical formats, instead you start with a list of 6 rules which you can apply to your data. The particular format you apply is added at the bottom of the dialog

Figure 255

- **Format all cells based on their values** – This let you make multiple decisions about what kind of values you want to format, what scale to use as the condition and format with either a 2 or 3-Color scale, Data Bars or Icon Sets. The following example has two scenarios, or Rules applied.

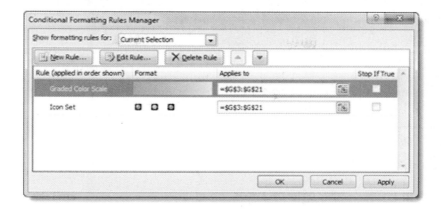

Figure 256

- **Format only cells that contain** – Here you have multiple options, although as you'll see in the example your actual formatting options are limited.
  - **Cell Values** - that fall within range parameters that you set (<, <=, =, <>, >=, >)
  - **Specific Text** - (Containing, Not Containing, Beginning With, Ending With).

Figure 257

  - **Dates Occurring** – With in a given range of options (Yesterday, Today, Tomorrow, etc.) The options are the same as from the Ribbon menu.
  - **Blanks/No Blanks** – Highlight all blank cells in a range or vice versa.
  - **Errors/No Errors** – Highlight all Errors in a range or vice versa.

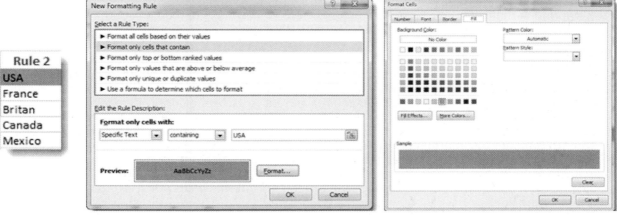

Figure 258

- **_Format only top of bottom ranked values_** – This is the same as the Ribbon Top/Bottom rules, but you have the ability to change the Top/Bottom values, where the Ribbon is limited to the Top/Bottom 10.
- **_Format only values that are above or below average_** – This is the same as the Ribbon Averages in the Top/Bottom Rules, except for the statistically oriented, you can select levels of Standard Deviation.
- **_Format only unique or duplicate values_** – This is the same as the Ribbon's Highlight Cells Rules, Duplicate Values.
- **_Use formula to determine which cells to format_** – This is the Rule that isn't exposed on the Ribbon, although a lot of its functionality has been replaced in 2010, especially with the Date formatting options. With this method you actually write the formula that Conditional Formatting needs to evaluate. Previously this was the only way to create complex evaluations, but there's little need to know it now with so many more Formatting options.

> How to Shade every other Row without Tables or Manually
>
> Select your range then goto Conditional Formatting→New Rule→Use a
>
> Formula... →Then enter the following formula: =MOD(ROW(),2)=1
>
> Then apply whatever fill you want, and every other row will be shaded,
>
> and it doesn't matter if you add or delete rows!

Preparing to Distribute your Workbook - Before you print or distribute your document you need to make sure it shows as much or as little detail as you want. We've already discussed hiding certain elements from users, by hiding rows, columns, entire worksheets, or even something as seemingly mundane as changing a font color to match a cell's background. These options all have bearing on distributing your documents electronically, or printing them. There are some additional steps you can take to manipulate the views that your users have when you distribute your documents electronically.

- **_Custom Views_** – Often times when you're creating financial statements, sales reports, even shift schedules, there are times when you don't want certain people to see information specific to others. Let's say you've got production report that shows production performance numbers by shift. You have to send it out to the shift leaders on a regular basis, but you only want each shift leader to see their own information. What do you do? Do you really want to go to the effort of creating and managing a different workbook or worksheet for each? No, because then that segments your data and makes it harder to analyze side-by-side. To you want to do a bunch of cutting and pasting, or hiding/rehiding in order to send out the information? Probably not. But you can use custom views in which you display only the information specific to each shift and name it, and repeat for each shift. Then when you're ready to send the report, you simply pull up each saved view and send that. It does require that you hide/show the relevant information one time to set it up, but that beats doing it routinely, which people do all the time.
  - ○ In this example you'll see sample financial information for a company that has different geographic divisions and facilities.

Row #	GL Category	Description	Group	Jan-11	Feb-11	Mar-11
2	1234-1	Sales - Central	Central	($288,380)	($1,156,763)	($561,461)
5	2341-1	Production - Central	Central	91,603	72,836	3,507
8	3267-1	Packaging - Central	Central	62,892	76,212	50,072
11	4987-1	Distribution - Central	Central	67,211	65,703	78,525
14	5278-1	Marketing		59,438	14,840	91,496
15	6892-1	FP&A		54,072	95,234	18,696
16	7892-1	Human Resources		71,033	27,564	54,181
17	9999-1	Total - Central	Central	(66,674)	(942,011)	(429,358)

Figure 259

  - ○ Let's say that you want to create a view for each division, Central, East and West. Start by unhiding all of your rows and columns, not including that which no one should see, so you have an unfettered view of everything. First you have to establish your baseline view, so goto the View tab, select Custom Views, then add the name for your current View. Afterwards, decide which region you're going to start with and hide the information for the other regions. In this case we'll choose Central. Once your information is hidden and the sheet looks the way that you want it, you'll repeat the Add View process. Repeat as many times as necessary to create all of your views.

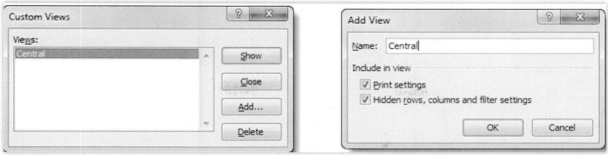

Figure 260

- ○ In the future when you want to retrieve a custom view, it's as simple as going to Views, Custom View, Select the one you want, Show.

Row #	GL Category	Description	Group	Jan-11	Feb-11	Mar-11
2	1234-1	Sales - Central	Central	($288,380)	($1,156,763)	($561,461)
5	2341-1	Production - Central	Central	91,603	72,836	3,507
8	3267-1	Packaging - Central	Central	62,892	76,212	50,072
11	4987-1	Distribution - Central	Central	67,211	65,703	78,525
14	5278-1	Marketing		59,438	14,840	91,496
15	6892-1	FP&A		54,072	95,234	18,696
16	7892-1	Human Resources		71,033	27,564	54,181
17	9999-1	Total - Central	Central	(66,674)	(942,011)	(429,358)

Figure 261

- **Auto-Filter -** This is one of the most powerful tools you can give users, especially if you're giving them a lot of data. In the previous example you were hiding information from users; with Auto-Filter you give yourself and users the ability to temporarily hide information that they don't want to see. Using the same example as Custom Views, goto Data, Filter. You'll immediately see drop-downs appear in the header row for each column. What has happened is Excel just gave you the ability to selectively hide or show data, by almost whatever criteria you want. In this case let's see we just want to see the information for the Central region. Select the "Group" dropdown, uncheck "Select All", then check "Central" and watch what happens.
  - ○ This is just a simple example, but it's a tool that shouldn't be overlooked because of its flexibility.

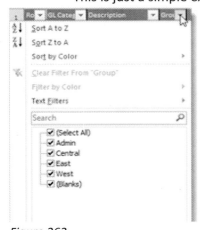

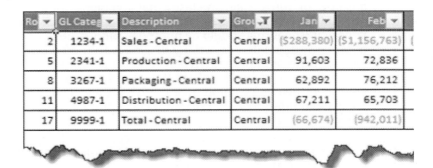

Figure 262

You'll also note that the Auto-Filter dialog also contains sorting options, as well as additional filters depending on if your data is numeric or text. You can even sort and filter by Text or Cell color!

Figure 263

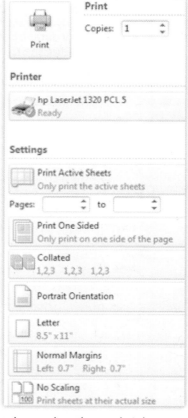

- **_Page Setup Options_** - Imagine printing a worksheet, and your printer starts going wild, spitting out pages that are mostly blank, although they might vaguely resemble some horribly disfigured image of your worksheet. Does it sound kind of hard to believe that this could happen? Unfortunately it happens all the time if you forget to go through the steps of setting your workbook up for printing. So what happened? Well, since you didn't tell Excel what to do it made some assumptions on your behalf. The first is that you want to print in Portrait orientation. The second that you want to keep the document the same size it is now, or 100% scale, and lastly that you didn't want to change any of Excel's default print options. Let's just say that you have a rather large worksheet that should be printed in Landscape orientation (most financial statements or anything dealing with months will be printed in Landscape orientation). When Excel stuck to its defaults, it automatically put page breaks where they thought they should go, so your worksheet that you wanted to print on 1 page wide by maybe 2 pages tall instead printed on 27 portrait pages. And because of the scaling not a single one of those pages is usable.

  ◦ Here's an exercise. In a blank worksheet, scroll down and across to AC250 or someplace out of the way and enter anything in a single cell, then Ctrl+Home to get back to A1. You just defined Excel's print area, or the area that it will print unless you tell it otherwise. Now Ctrl+P to bring up the print dialog. How many pages does Excel say you'll have? In this example it should be around 15, and 14 of those will be blank, while the final page will have the character that you entered. Now hit escape to get back to the worksheet and goto View, Page Break Preview. You'll see an odd grid display of your worksheet with the page numbers listed, and a gray area to the right, which is the area outside of the Print Range, so Excel's not going to print that. The blue dashed lines you see are the actual page breaks, and right now they're laid out based on what Excel thought you wanted to do even with that single character in AC250. Excel doesn't know what you're printing; all it checks for is that there is a single printable character in the defined print range. It doesn't care what or where it is, just that there's something there to print.

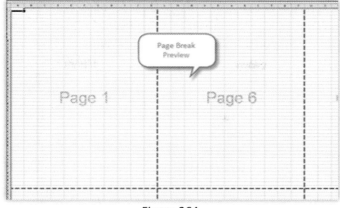

Figure 264

- ◦ Fortunately, Excel's new automatic print preview has put a halt to a great deal of errant printing, because you get a preview of what you'll print before you actually print. That doesn't mean you don't have to set up for printing though, so we're going to go through those steps now.
- ◦ Go back to the Cash Flow model and use Ctrl+P to launch the Print dialog. It's Portrait and 4 pages right? So you need to set it up for printing. You can do it right there, or from the Ribbon Page Setup menu. Since we're already here we'll set it up here first.

- • ***Print Dialog Options***
  - ◦ ***Print/# of Copies***
  - ◦ ***Printer*** selection (with a link to specific properties for the selected printer)
  - ◦ ***Settings***
1. What to print – You can choose from the active worksheet, or any grouped sheets, the entire workbook, or just an area that you might have selected.

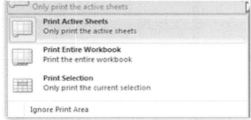

Figure 265

2. Pages – If the worksheet is more than one page, you can choose which pages you want to print, so you could choose 1-3, 2-3, 4, etc.). Strangely enough, you can tell Excel to print more than one page even if you're only set up for one, although if you try to print and the range outside of your print area is blank Excel will halt because it can't find anything to print.
3. Collated – If you're printing multiple copies of a multi-page document this can come in handy by printing each complete document one at a time. Uncollated would print each page multiple times, then proceed to the next, leaving you with a big stack of paper that needs to be shuffled by hand. Fortunately Collated is the default.
4. Orientation – Portrait or Landscape
5. Paper size – Here are all of your standard paper sizes. The default paper size is 8.5" x 11".
6. Margins – This sets how close the printable area of your worksheet will be to the sides of the page. It's generally acceptable to set left & right margins ate .25", but you need to be careful with top & bottom margins if you intend on using Page Headers & Footers, which we'll discuss momentarily.

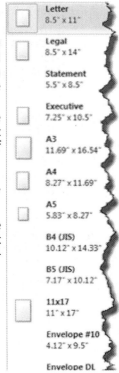

7. Scaling – This determines how much of the worksheet you want to fit on a page. Custom Scaling Options will launch the Excel 2003 Page Setup dialog, which phrases the fit options a bit differently.
    a. Fit Sheet on One Page would be Fit to 1 Page Wide x 1 Page Tall
    b. Fit All Columns on One Page would be Fit to 1 Page Wide x (blank) Page Tall
    c. Fit All Rows on One Page would be Fit to (blank) Page Wide x 1 Page Tall

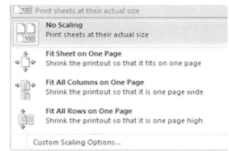

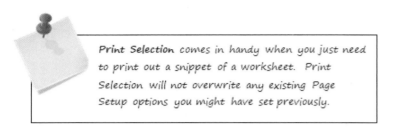

Print Selection comes in handy when you just need to print out a snippet of a worksheet. Print Selection will not overwrite any existing Page Setup options you might have set previously.

- In the case of our Cash Flow example, we want to print the worksheet on one page tall by one page wide, and Landscape orientation, so select Landscape from the Orientation selection, and Fit Sheet on One Page from the scaling dialog. You should then see the Print Preview adjust to the new settings. Once nice thing about setting up from the Print dialog is that you immediately see you the changes. This is not the same as Live Preview though, so if you don't like a change you'll need to undo it by making a different selection.

- ***Page Setup – From the Ribbon***

Figure 266

- ○ The Page Setup elements here are quite different than in the Print Preview mode, because this doesn't deal directly with printer settings, like Collating, Paper Size, or what to print. It does however; address some things that aren't exposed on the Print Preview dialog.

- ○ ***Print Area*** – This lets you override Excel's default print area and set your own. Doing this lets you exclude certain areas that you don't want to print. Many times you'll have ancillary information on a worksheet that you don't want to print, and this allows you to do that without having to hide those areas. You can also adjust the Print Area from Page Break Preview by dragging the solid blue lines in or out from their current positions.

- ○ ***Breaks*** – This is where your pages will be cut off and forced onto another page. You have the choice of Inserting/Removing Page Breaks, which can be done by selecting a row or column where you want a break and selecting the option you want. You also have the choice of Resetting page breaks, but that will not clear any breaks naturally associated with the worksheet. You can also adjust Page Breaks by dragging them from Page Break Preview, but they will still fall within the confines of the current page setup. I.E. you can't drag a page break past where it would normally fall (like trying to force two pages into one), as Excel will just put it back, but you can drag a page break inwards (like creating two pages out of one). Most times you adjust page breaks so that they follow natural breaks in your data.

- ○ ***Background*** – As you saw in the Ribbon lesson you can add a background behind your data. Just remember that people have to read past whatever you add, so make sure that it doesn't obscure your data.

- ○ ***Print Titles*** – This allows you to choose if you want to repeat Row & Column headers on each sheet. In the case of a multi-page report, like one that had dates across the top, you probably want to do this so that people know what they're looking at on later pages. Print Titles will launch the Excel

2003 Page Setup dialog. Oddly enough, even though you can launch it from the Print dialog, the option to set Titles is disabled from that way.

- **Secondary Page Setup Dialog**
  - In many ways this method of page setup is more complete than the other two, so you might just find yourself coming here first to set up printing instead of doing it in several places. The Page Setup dialog consists of 4 primary tabs, as well as some secondary options.
  - **Page** – Here you set your Orientation, Scaling, Paper size, etc.
  - **Margins** – This sets your Margins, but it also allows you to center the worksheet on the page both Horizontally and Vertically. When you select either option you'll see the gridlines in the margin example move accordingly.

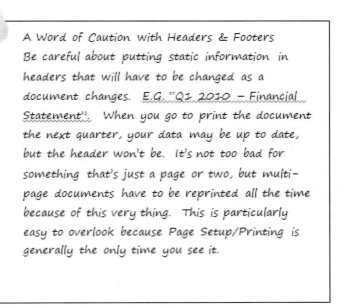

A Word of Caution with Headers & Footers
Be careful about putting static information in headers that will have to be changed as a document changes. E.G. "Q1 2010 – Financial Statement". When you go to print the document the next quarter, your data may be up to date, but the header won't be. It's not too bad for something that's just a page or two, but multi-page documents have to be reprinted all the time because of this very thing. This is particularly easy to overlook because Page Setup/Printing is generally the only time you see it.

- **Header/Footer** - This is the same as using the Header & Footer dialog from the Insert menu. It lets repeat text at the top and bottom of each worksheet. A common example is the FileName at the top, and Date/Page # at the bottom. Selecting either the Header or Footer Buttons will launch another custom dialog. The buttons, from left to right, are:

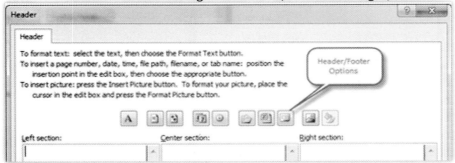

Figure 267

- **Format Text** – This is easiest done after you have added any text you want, then select it and change the format.

Figure 268

- **Insert Page Number**
- **Insert Number of Pages** - You can also use combinations of AutoText entries and your own text, like "&[Page] of "&[Pages]
- **Insert Date**
- **Insert Time**
- **Insert File Path**
- **Insert File Name**
- **Insert Sheet Name**
- **Insert Picture**
- **Format Picture**

- ○ **Sheet** – If there was any compelling reason to use this dialog over the others, then this is it. This exposes Page Setup elements that you'll only find here, like repeating Rows and Columns. You also have some other options that are worth considerations.

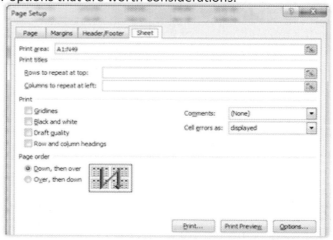

Figure 269

- **Print Area** - You can manually adjust the Print Area
- **Print Titles** – Again, you can define how many Rows or Columns you might want to repeat on each page.
- **Gridlines** – Another handy tool when first setting up a model because it helps you line up your elements on the printed page without using a ruler to keep track of everything.
- **Black & White** – If you have a color printer always check this one unless you're printing a final copy. You'll save yourself a lot of ink/toner that way.
- **Row & Column Headings** - You can toggle printing sheet titles on and off. This is handy when you're testing a document and need don't necessarily need the extra information, just the data.

- **Comments/Cell Errors** – These can be handy if you don't necessarily want to take the time to suppress anything in the worksheet itself, but don't want them to print.
- **Page Order** – This is rarely changed, unless you have a document that follows a very specific reading pattern.
- The Buttons at the bottom should be easy to figure out (Print & Print Preview will both launch the Print dialog, but Options is a little bit more complicated. The Options button is going to bring up the printer settings for your selected printer.

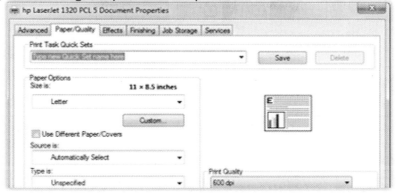

Figure 270

So there you have it for Page Setup and Printing. Most documents will be very straightforward and simple to set up with a few clicks and choices, but there will be some documents that require a little bit of extra time on your part.

Unit Summary: Getting Started

- In this lesson you:
  - Again saw how to apply and modify Themes
  - Learned about different elements of worksheet formatting, including Text, Cells, Rows & Columns
  - Saw how you can use Number Formatting to make numbers stand out
  - Saw Conditional Formatting in detail and the many options it presents
  - Setup some Custom Views, and made showing only relevant data easy for people with Auto Filter
  - Went through the various ways to set up your worksheet for printing & distribution

Review Questions – Lesson 7 – Formatting & Printing

1. Why would you format some Cells/Rows/Columns differently than other?
   a. _____

2. What are two ways you can hide key data from users?
   a. _____
   b. _____

3. What's the difference between Gridlines and Borders?
   a. _____

4. What's the standard alignment position for Text? What about numbers?
   a. _____
   b. _____

5. Why shouldn't you use spaces to indent text?
   a. _____

6. How would you add Data Bars to a range of data?
   a. _____

7. How would you highlight all cells in a range that are >= 0?
   a. _____

Lesson Assignment – Lesson 7 – Formatting & Printing

Your assignment is to:

- Test worksheet formatting in the companion workbook, and develop a style that fits you.
  - Practice using different Cell shades vs. Font colors.
  - Try aligning numbers and text differently so you can see the differences.
  - Work with Indenting/Outdenting sub categories.
- Using the Condition Formatting examples as reference, come up with your own data sets and apply the various Conditional Format to it.
- Practice setting up a worksheet to print, using Print Preview to determine if you're ready to print beforehand.

Lesson 7 Notes

Lesson 8 – Working with Graphics

In Lesson 7 you discovered the ins-and-outs of Formatting your workbooks/worksheets before you distribute them. This not only included the physical changes you can make like altering Font type, size or characteristics, but Cell shading, Styles, etc. You saw Conditional Formatting and the various Rules and Formats you can apply, from simple cell coloring, to in cell Data Bars. If you do any degree of shared work, then this is a tool you can use to make it all the easier to sell your story, and it can be mastered quickly! With regards to distributing workbooks, you saw some methods for hiding data from users, as well as creating custom views to quickly show/hide certain pre-identified ranges on a worksheet. You saw how to use the amazing AutoFilter tool, which lets users break down the mass of data available to them by fitting it into smaller groups. Finally you saw the different elements involved with setting up your worksheets so they print correctly.

In essence, Lesson 7 discussed the steps you would take to set up a standard workbook before you distributed it. Lesson 8 is going to take somewhat of a step backwards, by discussing graphical elements that you would also add to a workbook before distributing it; however, in this case we'll be discussing graphical elements that you most likely won't use in the bulk of your workbooks, but reserve for those times you really need them to make a point, have certain key data stand out, or a specific need for graphics, like a product pricing brochure. Or when developing a workbook that may be used by multiple people, you might hold back on graphics until you know the workbook functions as your users' expect. We'll discuss how to add elements like custom logos and pictures to your documents, and some of the ways you can use them. We'll explore all of the different Shape objects and how to manipulate them. And we'll also spend a good deal of time discussing Excel's SmartArt graphics, primarily because they are fantastic tools, secondly because there are quite a few of them, and they can be a bit much to absorb.

General Rules of Thumb for Graphic Use

- Don't overdo it - Too many graphics can dilute your message. Use what you need to tell the story, but not more.
- Images can be colorful and splashy, that's the whole point, but don't go overboard. Remember certain color combinations can be difficult to read on different monitors and some just plain hard to read.
- Make sure the image sends the right message – You probably don't want to use the same lighthearted ClipArt images that you dropped in your sales contest results in a corporate report.
- Be careful with image size, both how much real estate it takes up on the worksheet, but the physical size as well. Almost all digital images need to be optimized before you just clunk them down in an application. Images from digital cameras and even cell phones are usually well over 1 MB, but optimized they're usually 1/10th of that size. If you don't do this you can end up with a workbook that is so big it can't be distributed. You can also create some real issues for people (think customers) when you send someone a huge workbook that by all rights should have been relatively small. Not only do you tie up their system resources in receiving your file, you can also slow their PC to a crawl. This may seem like a relatively small issue, but it is one that is overlooked by a majority of Excel users who work with a lot of graphics in their workbooks.

Comments

While Comments aren't part of the Illustrations group, they're not necessarily used all that often either, which makes this a great place to discuss them. Think of Comments as electronic sticky notes that you can attach to individual cells. They can be set to always display or only appear when prompted. You can also turn them off completely in the Options menu. Comments are generally used as one-time notes and then deleted when the subject of them comment has been resolved. They can be notes to yourself, or notes to people with whom you're sharing your workbook.

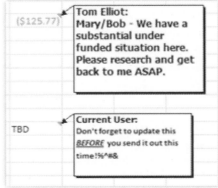

Figure 271

You'll find comments on the Review tab in the Comments section. When you want to add a comment, first make sure that the active cell is where you want the comment to be associated and then press the New Comment button. You'll immediately see a yellow comment that has an arrow leading to the active cell. At this point the Comment is the active object, so you can simply start entering your comment. Note that Excel automatically entered your Office user name for you, which you can delete; most people will know who wrote the comment. Once you're done entering your comment just hit ESC until the Comment is deactivated, meaning it no longer has the visible object border and controls around it.

Positioning - When you create a Comment, Excel does its best to add it to the right of the active cell, but multiple comments can overlap each other, or they sometimes just don't go where you like. If this happens, you can just drag the comment wherever you want. Comments are like any other tool we've discussed in that they should be used in moderation. You don't need them to point out the obvious, like "Enter Name Here". In fact, you probably shouldn't use Comments for instructions at all, instead opt for the Data Validation Input Message, which is much more discrete and less obtrusive. In the Validation example on the left the image will disappear as soon as someone starts entering information, or hits ESC. The comment isn't going anywhere unless the user deletes or hides it.

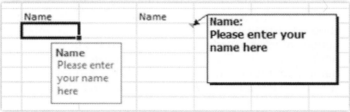

Figure 272

Object Mode vs. Edit Mode - This has to do with objects that can also receive text. In this case the object has two modes, one related just to the object, and the other to the text.

In Object Mode you can manipulate the object as a whole, sizing it or changing any of its attributes. You can change the text as a whole as well, but you can't change individual text elements, nor can you add or delete any text.

In Edit Mode you can interact with the text, delete, add selectively format, etc. You can enter edit mode by left-clicking on the object until the text section becomes active or right-click on the object and select "***Edit Text***". If you're in Edit mode you'll need to hit ESC twice to exit the object. If you're in object mode you only need to do it once. Or click on the worksheet to escape either mode.

Making Changes - Comments only have one level of Undo. Fortunately, they're relatively small so you won't have to redo too much work if you do make a mistake.

Figure 273

Formatting – From the Home tab, Font group you can format some limited font attributes, font name, and size, bold, italicize or underline, but not font color. You can also change Alignment attributes. To change font color, right-click on the comment and select "Format Comment", which gives you a much more robust set of formatting attributes. From there you can change the color of the Comment itself. Remember, if you only want to make changes to certain test, like bold a certain word, you have to have just that word selected prior to formatting, otherwise you'll format the entire comment.

Picture

This is probably one of the more common graphic tools, as people frequently add company logos to their Excel workbooks. To insert a picture, just goto Insert, Picture, then browse to your picture's location, select the picture of your choice and Insert. Depending on how your folder view options are set, you'll either see thumbnails images of the pictures, or you'll see them detailed in a list. With pictures it's generally easiest to use the Thumbnail preview, so you know which image you're choosing. However, the List or Detail views will let you know how big the image really is

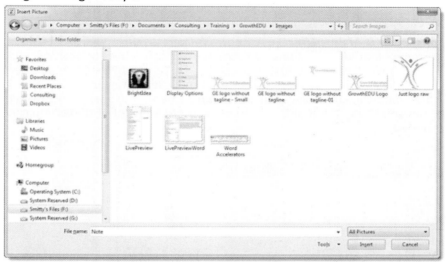

Image Size

If you have a picture image that's anything over 250Kb, you're strongly advised to compress it before moving further. Let's just say that you have a 250Kb corporate logo image, and you put that on 10 worksheets. You don't have 1 original image and 9 small copies; you have 10 x 250Kb images, which can have serious file size implications in no time at all. If you don't have a photo editing application, you can get www.paint.net for free and it's outstanding application.

Figure 274

Picture Tools

When your image first comes into Excel it will be the active object, so you'll see it selected on your worksheet. From there you can move and size it to wherever you need it. After that you have a lot of tools you can choose from to manipulate how the image interacts with your sheet. Note that the Picture Tools tab is the same in other Office applications, so if you get the hang of it here, you know it in other Office applications by default.

- ### Adjust Group

The Adjust group is where you can alter the physical attributes of your images, whether it be adjusting the color or contrast, or even adding some artistic effects.

  ○ **Remove Background** – This can be useful if you have a background that's not compatible with your image and you want to make some minor adjustments. For instance if you have logo with a white background, but your worksheet or dashboard area is dark. In this case the logo will stick out like a sore thumb unless you can remove the logo's background. Excel will do what it can to help you, but if you need better background removal you need to use an image editing application.

Figure 275

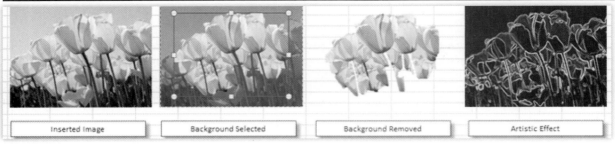

| | | | |
| Inserted Image | Background Selected | Background Removed | Artistic Effect |

Figure 276

- ○ **Corrections, Color & Artistic Effects –** As soon as you insert an image, Excel goes ahead and analyzes it to determine what kind of standard corrections it can make for you. As you can see from the Artistic Effect above, some are pretty interesting. This is one of those areas where everyone's taste will be a bit different, so when you have some time insert a few images (either your own or some of the Office samples), and make some of the adjustments you see. In practice you may never alter an image beyond sizing it, but at least you know there are a lot of things you can do with it.

Figure 277

- ○ **Compress Picture –** If you have a large image, you can certainly try this option, but you have no idea what size the resulting image is, because you don't have access to those attributes. If you do try it, just stick with the defaults and see how that works. This should be an emergency tool, not your standard. In general you should be compressing your images before you bring them into Excel (or any other application for that matter).
- ○ **Change Picture –** This simply brings up the Insert Picture dialog to the same location from whence you inserted the last image and lets you swap one for another.
- ○ **Reset Picture –** If you made any artistic changes to the image, this will reset it to the state it was in when you first inserted it.

- ### *Picture Styles Group*

Think of Picture Styles like a variety of picture frames for your picture. Sometimes images placed directly on Excel's stark white background just look a bit pitiful, so they need some depth to help them stand out. You can also create your own effects with the Border, Effect & Layout tools to the right of the Styles gallery.

Figure 278

- ### *Arrange*

These tools are primarily for dealing with multiple images that you need to organize in relation to each other.

- ○ **Bring Forward/Send Backward** – If you want to overlay certain images you can use these options to move images in front of or behind one another.
- ○ **Align** - In the previous example you saw four images of flowers that were grouped in a square configuration. If you wanted to make sure that all of those images were precisely placed in line with each other you could use the Align tools. The align tools will only be enabled if you have 2 or more objects selected, and the Distribute tools will only be enabled if you have 3 or more selected.
- ○ **Snap to Grid** – This will align an image with the worksheet's gridlines. If you move an object around when this is on, you'll see that it will automatically jump to the nearest gridline intersection, so you don't have to try to place it right on the lines with just the mouse.

ALT+Left-Click will temporarily disable the Snap To options, so you don't have to turn them off.

- ○ **Snap to Shape** – This allows you to quickly line up objects with other objects.
- ○ **Group** – Once you've aligned all of your objects you can group them, which will allow you to move the entire group at once instead of one at a time.
- ○ **Rotate** – Lets you rotate an object in standard directions, and of course if those aren't enough for you, there are more options, which will launch a new dialog (this is a truly new dialog, not one of the Excel 2003 dialogs, so you should notice a nice difference).

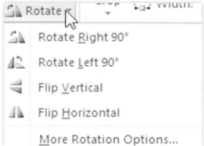

▪ You'll find all of the properties for your images in this new dialog.

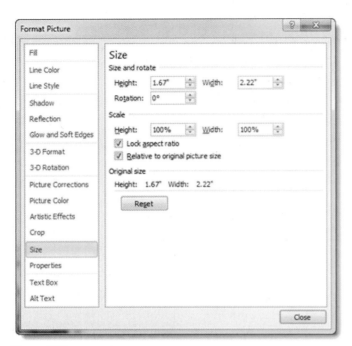

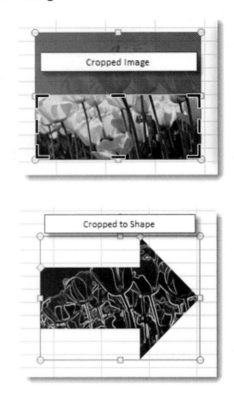

Figure 279

Size

In all likelihood you'll manipulate your images with the mouse more than anything else, and this includes adjusting the size (that's just the nature of working with objects in Windows based applications). However, there are a few tools that you might want to use from time to time, the most important is cropping.

○ ***Crop*** – This is very commonly used if you take a lot of screen shots, paste images from the Internet, or generally any time you have an image that's got more image than you need. You can simply use the cropping tool to get rid of what you don't want.

▪ **Standard Crop** - Using one of our original sample images as an example (above), roughly ½ of the image has been cropped and is still in Preview. If you were to hit ESC, the top portion would be cropped, or simply disappear. You can crop images from any direction that you see the cropping handles, which are the dark handle lines on the border of the image.

▪ **Crop to Shape** – This is a really cool tool. It lets you crop an image into the exact image of any of Excel's Shape objects. There's an example of our Artistic flowers cropped into an Arrow above. You can be very creative with this one, but by the same token you can also spend a lot of time designing creative images for a spreadsheet that might not warrant it. Or worse, come up with some artistic rendering that only you can appreciate.

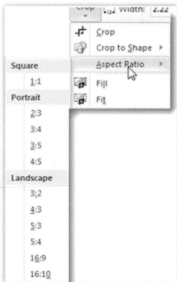

▪ **Crop to Aspect Ratio** – You can crop an image by pre-defined ratios, which can be helpful if you don't want to manually crop an image and mess with getting the size just right.

▪ **Crop to Fill & Crop to Fit** – Fill will let you reduce or enlarge an image and automatically adjust it to fit precisely within the new dimensions versus Fit, which will "Fit" the image into the new dimensions but maintain its original aspect ratio, which means it's not going to get stretched out of proportion. To use either of these, first click on the Fill type you want to use, then select the image and resize it the way that you want. Finally go back to the Crop menu and select your option, Fill or Fit and it will be applied.

▪ **Height & Width** – You can use the Spin Buttons to increase or decrease an image's size instead of dragging its handles into a new position or size. Inserted images like photographs will increase/decrease proportionately, meaning that if you adjust height, the width will automatically adjust to match the changes. When you size drawing objects this way you can adjust height & width independent of each other.

Sizing with the Image Handles

• Dragging any of an image's center handles will size the image in only that direction and will result in an out of proportion image.

• Dragging an image by any of its diagonal handles will size the image proportionately.

• CTRL+Drag will proportionately increase an image at all four corners (that's a neat trick!)

• You can use Ctrl+Drag on the center handles, but you will resize the image disproportionately in both directions.

ClipArt

Compared to what you can find on the Internet, Clip Art can be fairly boring and flat, especially what's included on your computer when Windows was installed (note that some corporate installations won't include things like ClipArt, Games, etc.) You can certainly try to find something useful though, because for whatever the reason, you will still find ClipArt images splashed across break rooms and sales offices all over the world.

To add some ClipArt enter your search term and wait for Excel to find some matches. Once you find an image you like, click on it and Excel will insert it wherever you had the cursor at the time. ClipArt images can be sized and moved like any other image, and you can change the colors, change styles, etc.

Even though there is a check box for "Include Office.com content", you will generally find a better selection by going to Office.com directly.

Figure 280

Shapes

Also called Drawing Objects, Shapes take on two specific functions. The first is primarily aesthetic, and generally serves as nothing more than an object on your worksheet. Most often you'll use shapes in this capacity to draw attention to something, like circling information in question instead of telling someone to look at AB23. The second functionality is where you can start adding automation to your workbooks by assigning macros to objects. For instance you can have a shape of an arrow assigned to a macro that will take you to the next worksheet. To give you some ideas, you'll see an example of what's called a Dashboard in the companion workbook for this lesson. A Dashboard is like a starting point for a workbook, where you lay out all of the elements right there for your users. Dashboards can be as simple as a list of instructions for filling out a form, or just a group of navigation buttons, and as complicated as buttons that can open other applications, get data from them and return them to Excel. The opportunities are literally limitless.   We're going have a short discussion on Macros at the end of the course.

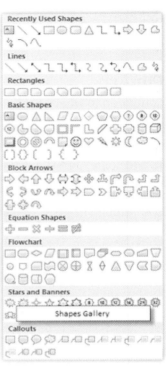

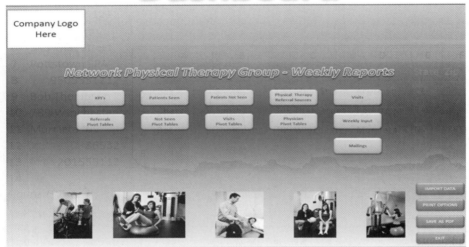

Figure 281

Shape Types - There are shapes for every occasion in the Shapes menu, and they all have the capacity to be formatted with any of the styles available on the Drawing Tools tab. Most of them can be used as Text Boxes as well, so don't think that text boxes need to be boring, for example, there's nothing stopping you from using a Burst as a text box. Considering that Excel, or any Office application, is a far cry from a professional graphics editing application, Microsoft has done a fantastic job of bringing you some remarkable graphic tools. You can create very nice additions to your worksheets in ways that only high-end graphic designers could have done just a few versions ago. There are 8 Shape categories, which should all be self-explanatory.

- ◦ Lines
- ◦ Rectangles
- ◦ Basic Shapes
- ◦ Block Arrows
- ◦ Equation Shapes
- ◦ Flowchart
- ◦ Stars and Banners
- ◦ Callouts

When drawing lines it's often best to have Snap to Grid on (from the Align menu), because it helps steady your lines

- The "buttons" you see in the Dashboard example are nothing more than Rounded Rectangles with "Intense Effect" from the Shape Styles gallery. Once they were formatted, they had macros assigned to them that do different things. You can assign macros to almost any object, certainly anything from the Shapes gallery, but pictures and images as well. You can even make your company logo do something if it's clicked.

- We already spent some time covering shapes in Lesson 4, on the Ribbon elements, so we're not going to go into detail with them again. The only reminder would be that shapes will start out as very plain and boring, so don't forget that you've got some fantastic tools to help you build appealing shapes. And as we've been saying all along, if you can increase the eye appeal of a workbook you'll increase people's attention span with it. Sometimes little things, like the buttons people press, can do a lot. Because there are so many shapes, you really just need to take some time on your own to play with one or two from each category. You'll soon see where certain objects might have a place in some of your workbooks.

SmartArt

If you recall, SmartArt is a gallery of organizational diagrams that you can fill in with your own specific details. In the past a Marketing or Art department would have been responsible for creating objects like these. Did you wonder how most of these types of corporate organizational diagrams get done? A bunch of people sit around a conference table "brainstorming". When they reach a consensus, the designated note-taker takes the scribbled ideas to Marketing, explains it all to someone who then creates it, generally not knowing or caring about the contents, just that it needs to look good. But what if you're sitting in an office trying to build some organizational diagram without a Marketing department? You turn to SmartArt, because Microsoft did a good job of identifying some very common organizational diagrams and charting models and bringing them to you in an easy to use format. However, there are several categories and different elements to discuss. Unlike Shapes, SmartArt may not necessarily be that intuitive, so it's worth discussing some scenarios and when you would use certain diagrams. We're going to go through one representative diagram in each category, detailing the steps to create, format and edit it until it's everything you could have wanted in a diagram. As we review each diagram we'll discuss a different part of the creation process, so that by the time we get to the end you'll know how to change every element of SmartArt graphics.

- As you saw in the SmartArt introduction, there are individual elements of each SmartArt graphic and they can accept text that is entered directly through a text dialog editor associated with the entire image. Generally the amount of text you enter will determine the number of objects your graphic displays. E.G. if you start with a 5-circle process chart, but only enter 4 items, then the 5th, unused item will be deleted. Some of the objects lend themselves to a good deal of descriptive text, while others should just carry key points, and can have detail follow in related documents. One of the key things to keep in mind when you're building diagrams is accurately depicting the process, structure, timeline, etc. Will the diagram make sense to others? A diagram that only holds meaning for you is great posted on your wall, but what about when you're trying to communicate thoughts or concepts to others? When you're working with graphics you want to let the graphic actually to a lot of the work for you, so that generally means being as concise as possible with the graphic text. You have plenty of room to expand on the ideas later. Right now you're trying to convey a great visual impression, so don't clutter it up!

- When you first decide on the SmartArt design you want to use, you simply click OK, and Excel will create the object on your worksheet for you. The will be placed in the center of your screen. As soon as the image is drawn, you'll see the image itself and its text dialog immediately to the left. If you click off of the image the graphic will stay in place, but the text dialog will disappear until you reselect the object. You can enter text in the text dialog, or you can enter it directly in the text boxes on the graphic itself. When you first set up your diagram it's probably better to use the text dialog, and save editing individual elements when you're done and should only need to make minor changes to one or two parts.

- Both the text dialog and the diagram itself can be moved and sized by their borders and drag handles. The text dialog defaults to a position on the left, but if you move a diagram to the far left of the worksheet, Excel will do its best to keep the text dialog close by.

All of the following examples are included in the companion workbook for Lesson 8. There will be three for each, the initial empty diagram, a diagram with just text entered, and the final diagram with formatting applied.

List – Lists are used to show blocks of information that are usually segmented into related groups. These can be anything you want: Ideas, Tasks, People, Departments, Processes and Sub-Processes, etc. Lists are a great way to add some flair to a document that might otherwise have just a boring numbered or bulleted list. Following is a basic list, followed by the same list with three text items entered and a final just a few mouse clicks later.

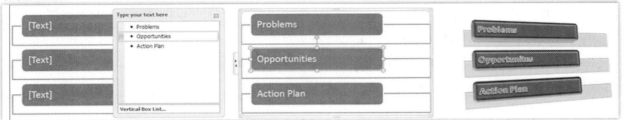

Figure 282

- Notice in the second diagram, that the text dialog is floating over the first diagram. As soon as the second diagram loses focus (meaning you click on something else) the text dialog will disappear. Also note that many diagram elements can be resized or even rotated if you want. Not that you would necessarily do this, here is the same diagram with the center text box rotated to a diagonal position.

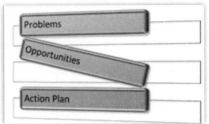

- In general, SmartArt shapes are very easy to work with, you just need to get used to them and not be afraid of experimenting a bit. As you can see, it doesn't take much time at all to change the initial design into something much less boring.

Process – These are generally designed to document some sort of flow. It can be the order in which an order goes from Marketing to Sales to Production and Fulfillment, it can be the steps to take to create something, it can be the steps to refilling the toner in the copier. Process diagrams generally detail anything that has several steps to be completed in order, like how do you get from Point A to Point B?

- **Entering Text** - Now we'll walk through some of the steps for actually entering your primary and secondary text (object permitting) with a simple 3-step process diagram.
- Start by selecting the diagram from the SmartArt dialog and let Excel place it on the sheet for you.

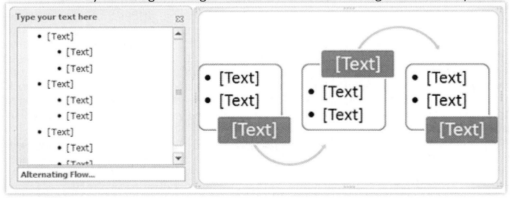

Figure 283

- Next you would start entering you diagram topics, and in this case some sub-topics as well. If you click on the very first "[Text]" in the text dialog you'll be able to enter your text. Notice that what you enter is live previewed in its corresponding text box on the diagram. To move to the next item in the list just use the down arrow key. At this point you've got your diagram filled with the important stuff, which is your content.

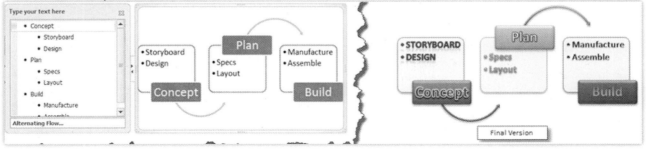

Figure 284

Cycle – These are used to represent continuing flows of actions, like a manufacturing process where a piece of raw material comes in, is run through a series of procedures and finished, immediately followed by another piece of material. Where a Process has a start and an end, a cycle is continuous until someone shuts off the power. Another example would be farming: a farmer prepares his fields, plants seeds, the seeds grow into plants which are then harvested, creating more seeds that are planted the following year.

- **Adding another Shape** – What if you get to this point and you want to add another shape, what exactly do you do? This takes us to the SmartArt toolbar, specifically the Create Graphic group. In this case you would select the Add Shape button, and depending on the type of diagram you have, you will also have some choices as to where the new shape will go.

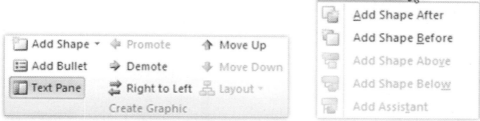

Figure 285

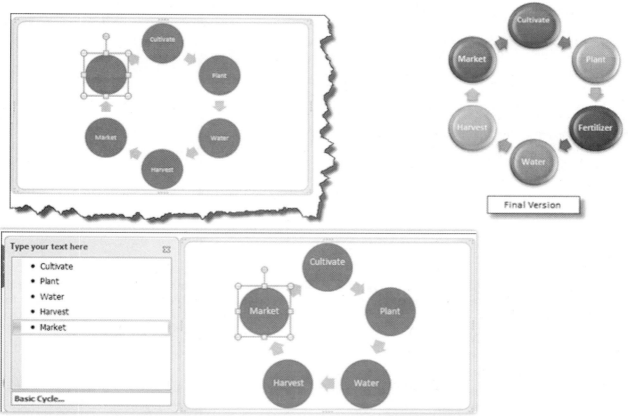

Figure 286

- Add Bullet – The shape's sub-header is called a bullet. In the previous example the bullets are the large white squares with the light blue borders.

Hierarchy – These can be used to create what are commonly called "Org Charts". They essentially define Parent/Child relationships, where there is always something or someone at the top. For instance, think of a corporation as a parent object, with multiple departments within that organization that roll up underneath it. Within those departments are managers, supervisors and staff, all with differing levels of responsibility and job functions. Within those areas of responsibility may be certain processes and procedures that need to be followed, and so on. Hierarchical diagrams often represent the top levels of an entity, slowly progressing into deeper detail with every level. There might be 20 or more Org Charts that define the structure of a single organization. A traditional org chart goes from top down, but another common theme is from side-to-side. You've probably seen something like this if you've ever looked at sports brackets, where a group starts with 16 teams, then 8 to 4 to 2, down to an eventual champion.

- **Choose Colors** – Now that you have the right number of shapes and all of your text is entered, it's time to add a color scheme, so head over to over the Change Colors menu (hidden between Layouts and SmartArt Styles) and select the color scheme that's best for you. This has Live Preview as well, so just hover over one of the combinations as watch your image change.

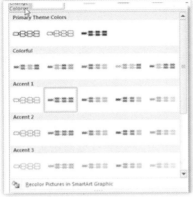 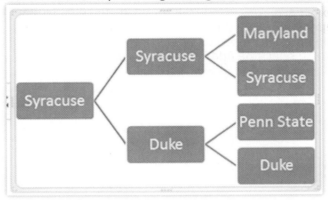

Figure 287

- **But what if these just aren't right for you?** We'll, now it's time to make individual changes. Just right-click on one of the shapes and select makes changes from the Font flyout menu, or the Format Shape menu.

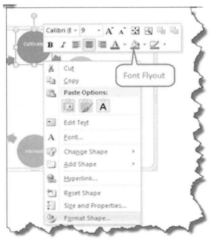

Figure 288

- Note that some shapes can be customized like this but will lose the changes if you change SmartArt Styles that don't support certain color configurations. If you click through the SmartArt Gallery for each shape you'll see which ones support multiple colors. So this particular color scale can be created, but when you try to dress it up you're a bit limited. Although you can go into the in-depth Format Shape menu and try to change the individual elements, which we'll cover toward the end of this section.

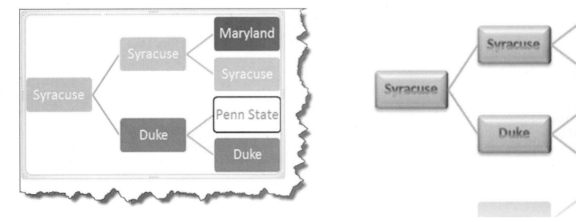

Figure 289

Relationship – These are a bit less structured than other diagrams as they generally define loose associations between objects. For instance you might have an organizational chart that details company core processes, e.g. Marketing, Sales, Production, Distribution, Finance, etc. No one department is more important than the other, because they each play a vital role in the organization (although each department will likely beg to differ). A typical example would be what's called a Venn diagram that uses a series of circles overlapping to various degrees depending on the depth of the relationship between each object (the symbol for the Olympics is a Venn diagram).

- **Change Shape** – Sometimes you might get a shape close to where you want it, but it just doesn't sit right with you, so you want to change it. On the SmartArt Tools Design tab go to the Layouts group and scroll through your selections. All of the shapes you had when you first created your shape are there. This too has Live Preview, so you'll see your changes happen on the fly.

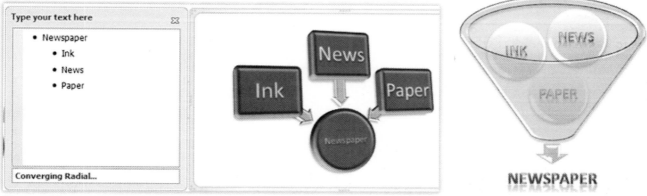

Figure 290

Matrix – This generally shows individual parts in relation to each other, or to a greater whole or concept. This is often used in brainstorming where you have disparate functions that are all related to a central theme. Matrix diagrams are generally going to be limited to 4 elements or less.

- **Word Art** – If you haven't noticed the text in SmartArt is your plain old worksheet text. Sure you can change the font type, color, or size, but those still aren't as creative as the Smart Art graphics. Fortunately, Microsoft built SmartArt right along with WordArt (which has been around for a while). When you're happy with the shape, layout, color and everything else, now you can get your font compliment it all perfectly.

Figure 291

Pyramid – Everyone's seen the USDA's Food Pyramid, which details the healthy/proper servings of food types each day. Depending on their direction, Pyramids roll up or down from greatest importance to least.

- Format Object Menu – What if, after all of these changes you still don't think your masterpiece is complete? You can dive into the Format Shape dialog and adjusting certain individual elements. Just right-click on the object in question and select Format Shape at the bottom of the menu. As you can see from the Format Shape dialog there are quite a few options that you can work on. As with many of these expanded dialogs up until now, there are far too many combinations of things you can do, so it's best to just go experiment and see what you can find.

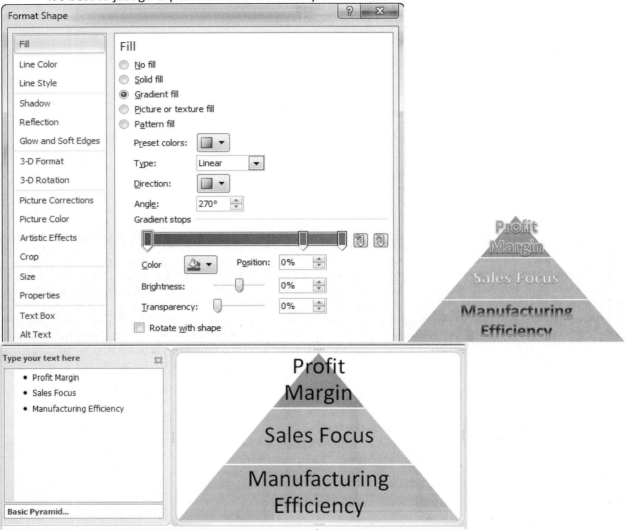

Figure 292

Picture – These are very creative diagrams in that they let you customize the objects with images as opposed to just the shape object, like a circle or square. For instance you could have pictures of individual departments, with the employee of the month in the middle. Or showcase your product line in relation to their proportion of sales. You could even create an Org Chart with pictures instead of names/positions.

- **Convert to Shape** – When you're ready to send out your workbook with your new SmartArt graphics you realize that how do you keep people from changing them? There are two ways, the first, if you still might have changes to make to the diagrams later, is to protect the worksheet, which you may have already planned anyway. That will keep the diagram as SmartArt, so when you come back you'll still be able to interact with it. If that's not something you want to do there is a trick right on the SmartArt Tools Design tab. It's the Convert to Shapes button. This will convert the diagram into a series of grouped shapes. In the following example you would still be able to change the pricing, and the text, but you can't add or remove shapes or bullets, unless you were to copy one of the existing shapes and add it manually. You lose the functionality of the SmartArt tools.

Figure 293

Office.com - This is where new designs will be placed when Microsoft periodically updates them. You can also search on Office.com for new releases.

Word Art

Something you might have been wondering through all of this work with Pictures, Shapes and SmartArt is Font attributes. If you've been following along with the companion workbook, or your own examples, you might have tried to change some of the fonts by changing the attributes from the Home tab. That's quite natural given it's where you've been shown to go up until this point. If you got a bit frustrated because the font attributes you changed didn't quite look like those in the examples, there's no reason to worry, because we're going to cover that right now. The attributes on the Home tab apply to the course of everyday functions in Word, like writing, but they're not very well suited to all but the minimalistic needs when working with Pictures, Shapes and SmartArt are they? Sure, a standard formatted font is fine for a label or a button, but if you've gone to the effort of adding some flair to your graphics you really don't want to dress them down with boring fonts. This is where WordArt comes to the rescue. WordArt has been around a while longer than SmartArt, and it's probably a good bet that Microsoft based some of the SmartArt functionality on experience gained from developing WordArt. As a result, WordArt, SmartArt and Shapes all do very well with WordArt and the elements complement each other quite nicely. Unfortunately, Pictures and ClipArt don't intrinsically support internal text, but you can add stand-alone text elements to them, much like the label text boxes you saw in some of the Picture examples.

- The easiest way to get started with WordArt is to go to Insert, Text, WordArt, Select a style and let go. You'll immediately have a text box on the page just like this one. It will behave just like any other text box, so you can resize it, rotate it, change the font size, and even change standard font attributes like Bold, Italicize, Underline, etc.

Your text here

WordArt – *(up there - this is a plain text box)*

Figure 294

- You're probably thinking "Great, a text box of my very own. Now how do I use it with shapes?" The answer is that at its simplest level, you just did. A Text Box is a shape, so even if you created it through WordArt instead of the Shapes gallery, it comes out the same. As you see above in the label, Text Boxes start with plain text, and that's what's going to come out when you first enter text for a Shape. Unlike the WordArt text box (above), which is a stand-alone entity, and is already pre-formatted in the style you choose from the gallery, you add WordArt attributes to the text box area of each graphic *after* you've created the object (provided that particular object supports text). Simply enter your text, and either select the text you want to format, or select the object itself if you want to format all it, then apply WordArt attributes to it from the WordArt group on the Drawing Tools tab. It is generally preferable to add text to your objects before applying WordArt styles, because you don't know how the text will look in relation to the object until you change it. That's one of the ways in which LivePreview is so helpful.

Figure 295

- Pictures & Clip Art – Unfortunately, neither of these support intrinsic text capabilities, so if you want to showcase them with WordArt you have to use a stand-alone text box (or some other object), format both objects the way that you want (WordArt, Picture Styles, etc.), then group them all.

- WordArt is another one of those areas that just has too many possibilities to cover here, so please take some time to work with it on your own. Adding WordArt to your graphics can make a world of difference in terms adding the final touches to everything.

Screenshot

This is rarely used in day-to-day Excel work. However, if you are tasked with creating a user's manual or some type of training material where you need to walk someone through a process, but can't be there in person, then it can be a handy tool. When you click on the Screenshot icon, you'll see a small dialog that displays images of all your open Windows.

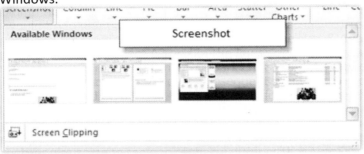

Figure 296

- Selecting any one of the images will place that full screen image back in Excel (and it will take up the entire worksheet window as you'll see in the example). The first thing you probably want to do is resize the image so that it's a bit easier to work with, so grab one of the sizing handles and resize the screenshot until you can see the whole thing. Sometimes you'll need to do it a few times, so experiment with resizing, then moving the image back toward A1, and repeat until the image is the size you want. Next, unless you actually need to show the entire screenshot, you'll use some editing tools to narrow the image down to just the specific area to which you're trying to direct the user. With the image selected, go to the Size group on the Picture Tools tab and select Crop. You'll immediately see the image's sizing handles turn into Crop handles. Start from any side and start cropping the image down around just the area that you want to keep. As you size in each direction, you'll see that the Crop tool has shaded the area that it's going to remove. Once the image area is the size that you want, all you need to do is hit ESC to finish the crop. Once the image is the final size that you want, you can start adding in some of the Shape tools, like Arrows or Callouts, to help you describe a certain process, label your image, or otherwise point out specifics to the user.

- ***Screen Clipping*** – When you were taking that first Screenshot you might have noticed a caption at the bottom of the Available Windows dialog. If you thought that whole Screenshot process might be a bit time consuming, especially if you only need to capture one specific area of a screen then you can use the Screen Clipping tool to just grab the area that you want. Just select the Screen Clipping option and your cursor will turn into a cross, which you can drag around the specific area you want to capture. Unfortunately, this is only going to work with your active screen, so unless you have multiple monitors, you'll need to go the long way around if you want to capture a shot of another application. Or if the other application happens to be an Office application, you can use the Screen Clipping tool in that application and copy the image to Excel.

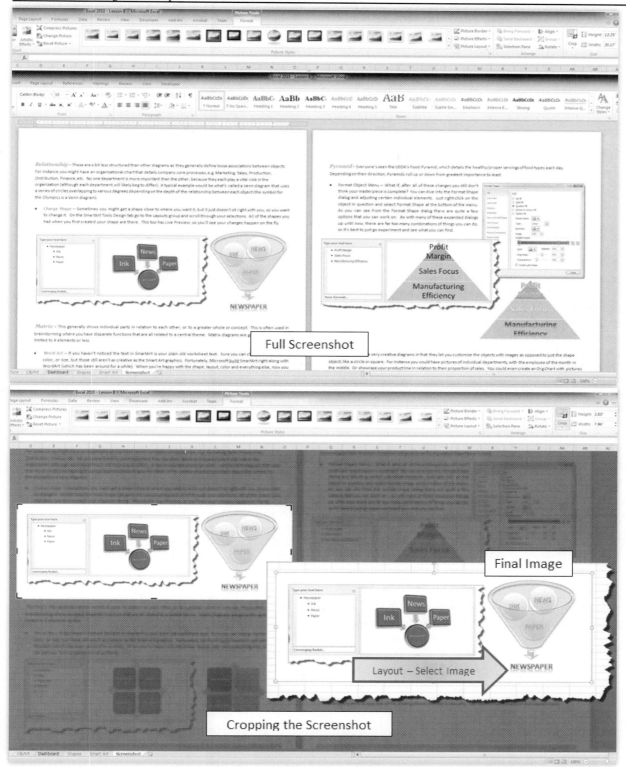

Figure 297

Camera Tool

When we reviewed Excel's Functions you saw a tool called the Watch Window, which allowed you to monitor certain cells in other worksheets for changes that occur as the result of formula calculations. The final tool to discuss in this lesson is similar, but for some reason it's one that rarely gets used, in fact Microsoft hides it from you. The Camera Tool allows you to take interactive snapshots of the current worksheet, or other worksheets. In this example there is a series of formulas on another worksheet that are all linked to cell A2 on the current worksheet. There is also a snapshot of that formula range in the second sheet, and whenever you make a change to A2 that updates the formulas on the second sheet you'll see it happen on the current sheet in real time. This is a great tool for monitoring changes on other worksheets, especially errors. It's very similar to the Watch Window, but with a live image vs. just watching changing values.

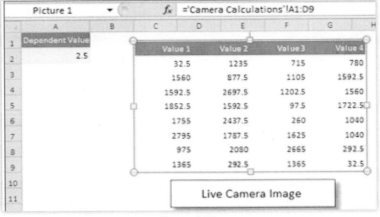

Figure 298

One of the most powerful things you can do with the Camera tool is to collect disparate ranges from different worksheets on a single sheet. Let's say you have a series of charts, all on different worksheets, but you want to display or print them on one summary sheet. Most people would recreate all of the charts on that summary worksheet (a lot of work), but now that you know better, you can simply take some snapshots of the charts and have the summary sheet done in a few minutes. And the real-time updating can also add some wow factor if you can make some of those charts dependent on information in the summary worksheet. For instance, changing a month or date that drives updates throughout the workbook, which is all reflected instantly on your summary sheet. In fact, the camera tool is a great way to build interactive summaries for presentations, because people love to see things move in real-time, especially in presentations. Another benefit is that your camera images don't need to be the same size as the source range. Let's say you have a series of monthly data worksheets, each with a summary chart that is relatively large. If the whole point of the summary is to avoid the large charts, then just take snapshots of them and create mini-charts.

So how do you use it? First, it's so well hidden, that we need to expose it from the QAT menu. Right-click on the QAT dialog launcher and select More Commands, then in "Choose commands from" select the "All Commands" option. Then in the next pane scroll down the C's and add the Camera. When you're done you'll see the Camera icon displayed on the QAT.

When you're ready, open the companion workbook and goto the "Camera Calculations" worksheet, then select range A1:D9. Once you've done that click the Camera tool, and then activate the Camera worksheet. With the left-mouse button, drag a new range border until it's the size that you want and release it. In this case, since this range is linked to cell A2 on this worksheet, go ahead and enter a different value in A2 and see what happens. The Camera tool does take some getting used to, but if you plan on summarizing data that's spread out over separate worksheets, then this will be an invaluable tool.

Unit Summary: Lesson 8 – Working with Graphics

- In this lesson you learned about the different ways you can work with ways to bring more meaning to your workbooks than just figures and text. Beginning with Comments you can leave for users, moving on towards inserting custom pictures and logos, then dealing with Shapes, SmartArt and even live action images of other worksheets.

- You saw how many options Excel gives you when dealing with pictures, including artistic effects.

- You saw some of the ways that you can spice up the graphics you use in Excel, because who says graphics need to be boring?

- You saw a Dashboard example which showed how you can create useful interfaces for your users that make it easy to get around large workbooks.

- You were exposed to the many different SmartArt types, as well as examples of where to use them. You also saw how to step past the default image that you'll get at first try and spice up your images to that they have the maximum impact on you recipients.

- You learned how you can integrate WordArt with your Shapes and SmartArt, and add WordArt elements to Pictures and ClipArt.

- You saw some of the possible uses for creating Screenshots, and being able to crop certain areas from them.

- Finally you saw how to use the Camera tool to monitor changes in other worksheets, and to consolidate multiple ranges, charts and other objects into a summary sheet, either for printing or presentation.

Review Questions – Lesson 8 – Working with Graphics

1. When using graphics it's important to keep a few things in mind:
   a. _____
   b. _____

2. Why would you use Data Validation vs. a Comment?
   a. _____

3. How do you remove the background from a picture? Why would you?
   a. _____
   b. _____

4. Name a few types of Shapes and how you might use them.
   a. _____
   b. _____

5. Which SmartArt type would be the most useful for you? In what kind of scenarios would you use it?
   a. _____
   b. _____

6. Why would you convert a SmartArt graphic to a Shape?
   a. _____

7. How do you add text to a shape or SmartArt? What about a Picture or ClipArt?
   a. _____
   b. _____

8. How would you convert that text to WordArt?
   a. _____

9. Think of a situation where the Camera tool could be helpful for you.
   a. _____

Lesson 8 – Working with Graphics Assignment

Your assignment is to review the elements that have been laid out for you in the companion workbook.

- For each Graphic type, try to create your own.
- Experiment applying different styles and formats to each
- Add Text to some Shapes and SmartArt and practice change normal text attributes (Home tab – Font group), then apply WordArt attributes to the text. Experiment with which WordArt characteristic looks best in each situation.

Lesson 8 Notes

Lesson 9 - Charts

Throughout this course we've been following the pattern of a relatively common workbook progression, from determining your needs and developing an initial layout, all the way through adding data, formulas and formatting, and preparing for distribution. The last lesson took something of a step back from the perspective of already having completed the essential elements of a workbook, then coming back to add graphical elements to make your points stand out. This lesson will continue on that theme, because Charts generally come at the very end of a workbook's development; once you have your functionality and your data in place, then it's time to start creating snapshots of it. This is exactly what charts do: they are a graphical representation of your worksheet data. Not everyone can look at a series of numbers and immediately identify a trend or pattern. Most people could probably see some of the same things given some time, but using Charts can help people come to those conclusions faster. You have a story to tell with your numbers and Charts are a fantastic way to help you tell your story better. Unfortunately, Charts are also one of the most inefficiently used tools in Excel. It's not because Charts are inherently difficult to build, in fact they're remarkably easy. The issue lies largely in that people don't know how to properly build them. Building a chart is one of the most time consuming tasks there is in Excel, and there are admittedly quite a few elements in a chart to change, let alone multiple charts. The mistake people make is building the same chart and making the same changes over and over again, not realizing that it only needs to be built once and can be reused in multiple workbooks.

In this lesson we'll be discussing the broad theory of charts, what kind of charts there are and when you might use them, followed by building one chart from each of Excel's six standard Chart categories, and showing you how to save each one of those chart types as a favorite that you can use again and again. While we do that we'll also cover some of the key tools that you can use to turn plain old boring Excel charts into something that people will think came from the Marketing department. Who says data has to be boring?

When do you use Charts?

Hypothetically, you can use a chart any time you think that a graphical representation of figures would tell a better story faster than the figures themselves, or if a chart would simply support the figures better than they could on their own. From a more practical standpoint charts do have a time and a place though. While charts can tell a great story, you should know that they merely augment the underlying data. It's not hard to overwhelm a workbook with too many charts that only display minute differences between each other, or have little or no relevance to the subject. By the same token you can also not include enough charts to get your point across. It's all a balance of what's most appropriate for the audience, and fortunately, the only judge of that is you. Just as important as the content you chart is how to place your charts both in relation to the worksheet and other charts; while certain circumstances might dictate a particular format, it's generally going to be up to you. Some people prefer to intersperse charts with data, others keep data hidden and only show charts, some people prefer charts sheets (a worksheet that Excel dedicates for single charts), and some people prefer "Dashboard" type views in which charts are clustered together with or without supporting data. Regardless of the format you choose you also need to hold yourself to providing a layout that's as user friendly as possible. If you overwhelm your audience with charts thrown all over the place then the valuable information that they can impart is lost.

Chart Design Ideas
To get a better idea of typical chart placement and design styles you should take a look at the Microsoft Template Gallery and search for "dashboard". You'll see plenty of great examples.

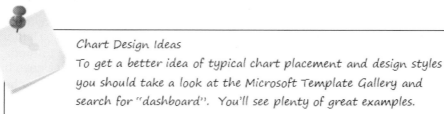

Figure 299

Charting Rules of Thumb

The most important thing to remember when working with charts is to make sure that your data structure can support them. Many times data that does not follow proper spreadsheet design conventions simply can't be charted (without a lot of work). In general your data needs to be in a Row/Column format with consistently formatted and labeled data. This means that data types can't be mixed within the same column or row (e.g. mixing currency and dates in the same recordset). Merged cells can also cause problems with charting. Note that in this example the Top Left Cell in the data range has been excluded, and isn't part of the Row or Column Headers. This empty cell indicates to Excel that you're using this data for charting and that the first row and columns should be kept separate from the data. Sound charting structure has all of these elements, as well as separation between any other data. You can have multiple contiguous chart ranges, but you should have at least one blank row/column between the different datasets, otherwise you can unintentionally chart additional ranges that you might not have intended. As you've seen throughout this course, so many things in Excel rely on having a properly designed worksheet that it's better to get it right from the start. Fortunately, once you get in the habit of building worksheets correctly, it becomes second nature.

Chart Terminology/Components

This is just a general overview of the different elements that make up a standard chart, and is by no means all inclusive.

- **Plot Area** – The only absolutely necessary component of any chart is the actual data itself. Charts do not need any of the secondary descriptive elements, like Chart Title, Legends, or Axis Labels, but it certainly helps. Especially if you have several charts where it's important to be able to quickly note differences between them.
- **Horizontal & Vertical Axes/Labels/Titles** – These are automatically added based on the information that you have in your Column Headers and data range. For the Vertical Axis, Excel will analyze your data and determine the appropriate data range to display with regards to the high and low data values. Excel will do everything it can to display Horizontal labels as true to form as possible, but many times Excel is forced to cram everything together, at which point you choose a different scale to display (we'll discuss that later). In addition to the data labels, you can also add data titles. In the following example you might use "Revenue" for the Vertical Axis Title and "Months" for the Horizontal Axis Title.
  - **X-Axis/Y-Axis** –Horizontal vs. Vertical Axes
- **Legend** – This is a summary of your Row headers. Legend entries will be colored coded to their chart equivalents. So in the following example, the East Region in the Legend is blue, corresponding to the first column of data, which is also blue.
- **Chart Title** – Self-Explanatory. If you have a title row for your data, you can link that to the Chart Title via formula so it doesn't have to be entered by hand.
- **Data Table** – These chart examples display a data table, which is just an option of including the chart data with the chart. It's not necessary by any means; it's just one of the many Chart Layout options you have available to you.

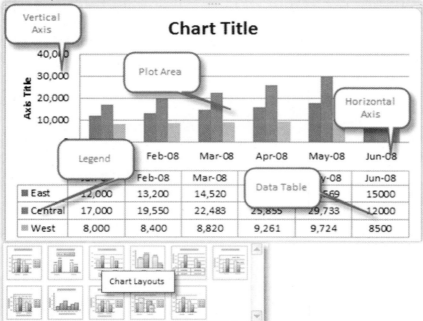

Figure 300

- This next example displays those Chart elements in relation to the data that's being charted.

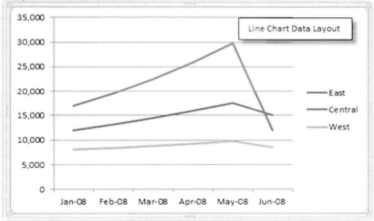

	Jan-08	Feb-08	Mar-08	Apr-08	May-08	Jun-08
East	12,000	13,200	14,520	15,972	17,569	15,000
Central	17,000	19,550	22,483	25,855	29,733	12,000
West	8,000	8,400	8,820	9,261	9,724	8,500

1 - Data Legend
2 - Date - Horizontal Axis & Axis Label
3 - Data Table
4 - Plot Area
5 - Vertical Axis Range

Chart Title

	Jan-08	Feb-08	Mar-08	Apr-08	May-08	Jun-08
East	12,000	13,200	14,520	15,972	17,569	15,000
Central	17,000	19,550	22,483	25,855	29,733	12,000
West	8,000	8,400	8,820	9,261	9,724	8,500

Figure 301

- **Columns vs. Data** – As you can see in the column chart examples the first row of data (East) is represented in the first column in each period, followed by the second and so on (a Bar chart would be similar, as it's just a Column chart laid on its side). A Line chart, on the other hand, would not reflect the data based on the header position, but the first numerical value, which in this case is the West region with $8,000, the lowest value.

Figure 302

- **Chart Area Visualizations** – Remember in the Function/Formula lesson you saw how editing a formula will cause Excel to highlight all of the Formula elements in both the Formula and referenced ranges? Charts act in a similar fashion when you select the chart's Plot Area. Provided your data is within view of the Chart, you'll see the Chart Data area highlighted in different sections. The previous chart example showed the Row Headings outlined in Green, the Column Headings in Purple, and the data in Blue. In addition, when the chart data is highlighted, you can use the drag category handles to decrease or expand the current chart area. Excel will only let you resize the chart elements in ways that it can actually chart, so don't be surprised that you can't drag in every direction.

- **Formatting** - Note how Excel carries your cell formatting over to your chart. If you were to change the date or number format in the data it would automatically reflect in the chart output. E.G. if you were to format the data range as Currency with two decimal points, the chart data and legend would display in the same format. In general, you want to keep chart data as concise as possible, limiting extraneous data like decimals unless it's absolutely necessary. Sometimes little things like that can add up and clutter a chart more than it's worth.

Getting Started with Charts

While we reviewed chart types and some of the basics when we discussed the Ribbon elements, we're going to go over them again here. However this time we're also going to get behind all of the specifics, starting with selecting the dataset, the chart type, formatting it, and the chart's final placement in relation to the worksheet and any other charts. Before you even draw a chart you should have a general idea of what you want the data to say, where the data is, and where you want the chart to be (the current worksheet, a different sheet, or a chart sheet). Once you've done that it's time to select your data; if your data is contiguous you only need to choose a single cell in the data range, provided you want to chart the entire range, otherwise you'll need to select just the range you want to chart, or the different chart elements individually. In the following example you'll see a contiguous data range that is only using a portion of the data for the chart. In this case the data range needs to be selected manually. If not, Excel will try to chart the entire range, which may or may not be too bad, depending on the outcome you expect/want.

	A	B	C	D	E	F	G	H	I
1	Region	Product	Date	Month	Customer	Quantity	Revenue	COGS	Profit
2	Central	ABC	01/09/08	Jan-08	General Motors	800	16,416	6,776	9,640
3	Central	ABC	01/12/08	Jan-08	IBM	300	6,267	2,541	3,726
4	Central	ABC	01/25/08	Jan-08	CitiGroup	1000	20,770	8,470	12,300
5	Central	ABC	02/19/08	Feb-08	Wal-Mart	500	10,385	4,235	6,150
6	Central	ABC	02/20/08	Feb-08	Exxon	600	11,124	5,082	6,042
7	Central	ABC	02/27/08	Feb-08	Ford	900	16,209	7,623	8,586
8	Central	ABC	04/06/08	Apr-08	General Electric	300	5,886	2,541	3,345

Figure 303

- Next decide on a preliminary chart type. As we've reviewed, there are six primary categories of charts, as well as some more obscure chart types that have more specific uses.

Figure 304

All of the following examples are included in Lesson 9's companion workbook.

There will be data for each, the initial unformatted chart, a formatted chart, and several other examples.

Column & Bar Charts – These display your data in vertical or horizontal columns. Both are especially good at displaying multiple data points for several groups, such as Revenue, Expense and Profit by company. Because they are almost identical, we're only going to review Column charts here, but there is a Bar chart example in the companion workbook.

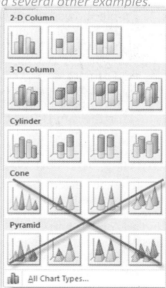

- The most common are column charts are the 2-D & 3-D style - the only difference between the two is the additional illustration to give the 3-D column a 3-Dimensional feel. 3-D charts can be difficult to use with a lot of data though, because the additional illustration area takes up needed space. Unless it's a must have design, then if possible, stick to 2-D chart types (in all styles). There should be enough additional formatting options to make up for it. With regards to the other styles, sometimes a Cylinder chart is appropriate, but rarely. And to reiterate from our earlier chart introductions, Cone & Pyramid shapes should only be used as a last resort, because they don't always accurately represent your data.

- In the following examples we'll walk through how to set up a column chart, as well as deal with a data range that is too big to plot accurately. In this case we're not going to define the data range, but allow Excel to choose it. And, as you can see, it's pretty obvious that Excel just tried to

bite off more than it could chew.   All we really wanted plotted was the Customer name and the finan-
cials associated with each. But Excel gave us the whole thing. You could easily go back and just select
that particular data, in which case the chart would turn out the way that you wanted it. Or there is
another alternative, which will work with all of your charts; however it won't necessarily fix things if
you are going to base multiple charts off of this same range.

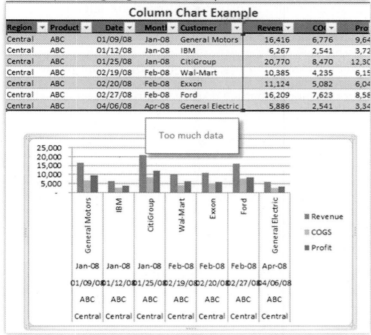

Column Chart Example							
Region	Product	Date	Month	Customer	Revenue	COGS	Profit
Central	ABC	01/09/08	Jan-08	General Motors	16,416	6,776	9,64
Central	ABC	01/12/08	Jan-08	IBM	6,267	2,541	3,72
Central	ABC	01/25/08	Jan-08	CitiGroup	20,770	8,470	12,30
Central	ABC	02/19/08	Feb-08	Wal-Mart	10,385	4,235	6,15
Central	ABC	02/20/08	Feb-08	Exxon	11,124	5,082	6,04
Central	ABC	02/27/08	Feb-08	Ford	16,209	7,623	8,58
Central	ABC	04/06/08	Apr-08	General Electric	5,886	2,541	3,34

Figure 305

- What Plots and What Doesn't?
  - Excel's default behavior is to plot only visible ranges. This means that you can hide rows and
    columns and as you do, the corresponding data in the chart will be hidden as well. Given the
    example data range you could just hide the first 4 columns and you would have the display you
    want as a result. The Hidden Range method works great if you are only going to be basing one
    chart off of a particular data range, or if you will have multiple charts that can share the same
    visible range. If you have multiple charts that are using both hidden and displayed data then you'll
    probably need to select the specific ranges for each.

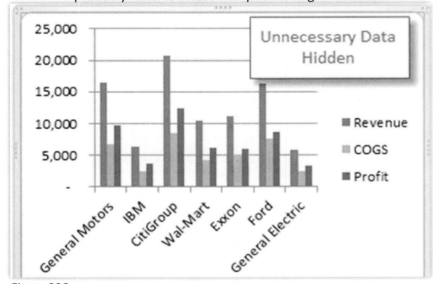

Figure 306

- **Create** - Now that you know a bit more about charts and their data, we're going to build a Column
  chart. We'll use the same data set as in the last example, but this time only selecting the data we want
  plotted (company & financial data). Next go to the Insert tab, Chart, Select the Chart type and style
  and then let Excel do its thing.

- **Inspect** – Now that Excel has created your chart, it's time to ensure that it's correct. Similar to validating a workbook for accuracy, you need to do the same with charts. While it's generally easier to spot errors in charts, because of their visual nature, it shouldn't be taken for granted. Is your data properly plotted? Are your data points properly represented for the period axis (horizontal)? What about the vertical axis distribution? Is your Legend correct? Is your chart an accurate representation of your data? Are you happy with the chart type or would it tell a story better as something different? Now is the time to address changes before you invest too much time in it. As long as the underlying data is in good shape, then most of the time your charts will come out very close to what you need.

- **Design** - If you don't like any of your major chart elements, now is the best time to change them. And this doesn't mean something is wrong at all with what you've got, you might just want to see what the chart looks like 3-D vs. 2-D, or maybe with the way your data is laid out that a Bar chart might look better than a Column chart. This is where your major formatting takes place, so whatever it might be, go ahead and change it now. All of your options are on the Chart Tools Ribbon in the Design Group.

  - ○ **Chart Type and Style** - simply look back through all of your options and choose the one you like better. Unfortunately, Chart Type isn't supported by Live Preview yet, so if you change one of the Type options, you'll need to apply it to see if it's what you want, and recall the Change Chart dialog again if it's not. It's not hard to see when a chart type might not be the right choice for your data, because it's going to look visibly awkward, as this example of our current company data displayed as a Line chart indicates. The horizontal data points indicated in the Legend aren't following a timeline, so they shouldn't be in a continuous line since one point isn't related to the next. E.G. each line (Quantity, Revenue, etc.) shows a relationship between corporations when there isn't one. IBM and CitiGroup's Revenue shares no common link, so it shouldn't be displayed that way.

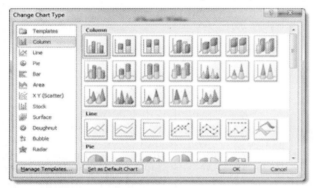
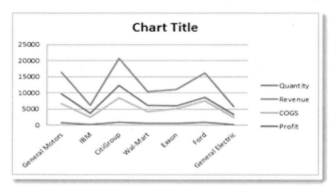

Figure 307

  - ○ **Switch the Rows/Columns** - in case the data might look better the other way around.

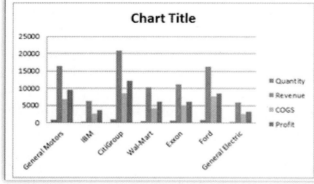
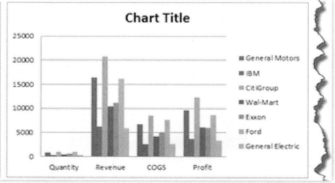

Figure 308

  - ○ **Layout** – Maybe you want to add a data table.

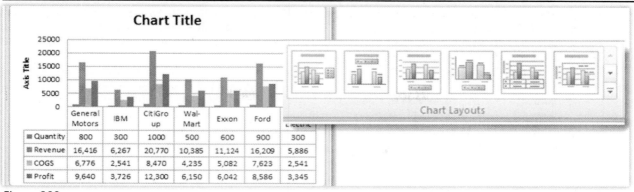

Figure 309

    ○   **Styles** – Or you didn't like the columns that Microsoft picked.

Figure 310

    ○   **Move Chart** – Maybe you decide that the chart(s) would look better on their own sheet, so you move it/them.

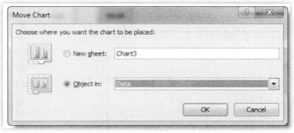

Figure 311

    ○   Here are before and after shots of the default Column chart that Excel created, and the same chart a few mouse clicks later with some formatting adjustments. It's nothing ground-breaking, but you'll quickly see how easy it is to change the default chart formats. Throughout this course we've continued to mention all of the great work that Microsoft has done in adding a plethora of graphical options to almost everything you can do in Excel (and all of Office for that matter). But by the same token you've also seen that it's impossible to please everyone, so they do their best and default to the basics, letting you create your own options if you want. Charts are no exception, so one thing we'll focus on is not only how to create a general chart theme(s) that you like, we'll also show you how to make Excel use your favorite chart themes instead of its defaults. And nothing says you have to limit yourself to one theme, in fact you can have several. You might want a very professional style for your company financials, but a more relaxed style for displaying sales performance to your team. You can do whatever you want; you just need to create the themes.

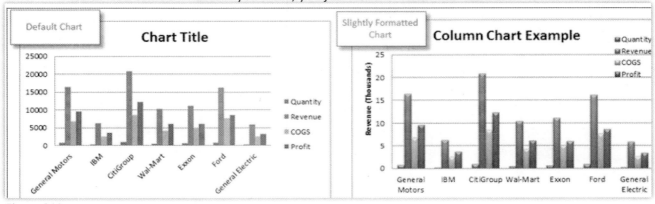

Figure 312

•   **Changing a Chart's Display Units** – Many times when you create a chart you're dealing with rather large numerical values which take up too much space on the chart. In the past the only way to change this was by creating a false data set that reduced these values, usually by dividing them by a factor of 10. Fortunately, Microsoft realized this and has created a function to automatically reduce those values by the scale you determine. Here is our Column chart example with a realistic data set involving revenues and costs in the millions of dollars. You can see how the Y-Axis labels reduce the overall size of the chart data that can be represented.

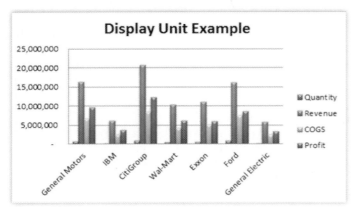

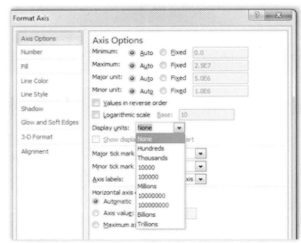

Figure 313

- ○ All you need to do to rectify this situation is right-click on the y-Axis label area and select Format Axis and then select the scale that's appropriate for your particular values. The change is dramatic, and it's significantly easier than having to alter your data to accommodate the scale change.

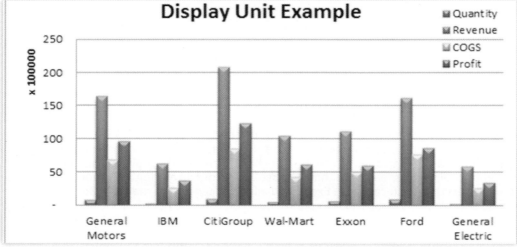

Figure 314

Line Charts – Probably as common as Column charts, Line charts will display your data in a series of horizontal lines. Line charts are generally used to show data over a given period, like weeks or months. With a line chart the Horizontal (X) Axis can only be a Category (text), like the corporations in the Column chart example, or Dates that are all evenly spaced across the axis (the chart will automatically space the date equally regardless of the data's spacing).

Figure 315

- **Create** - There is no difference in creating a Line chart (or any other chart for that matter). Select your chart range, chart type and have at it. Once you've gotten the initial chart drawn and your design elements selected, it's time to move on to the Layout phase, which is the second step in creating your charting masterpiece. You're encouraged to work with the companion examples as we go along and change them as you see fit, because just as Microsoft can't please everyone, it's quite likely that your style will be a bit different than the examples given.

- **Default Chart** - In the following example you'll see our Line chart data set, as well as what Excel thought we wanted for our chart.
  - ○ Unfortunately, Excel didn't quite get it right this time, which happens. Excel can only make its best guess as to what you want (and sometimes it's completely clueless), so be prepared to make some corrections from time to time. Fortunately, this is very easy to fix. Just goto Chart Tools, Design, Switch Row/Column, and you'll instantly have the layout you want. You can also see here how Line charts can have overlapping lines, or they can be stacked.

Sales	Jan-11	Feb-11	Mar-11	Apr-11	May-11
Product A	$585	$775	$590	$537	$584
Product B	$922	$819	$776	$685	$784
Product C	$491	$532	$498	$591	$632

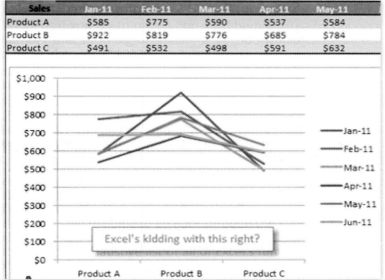

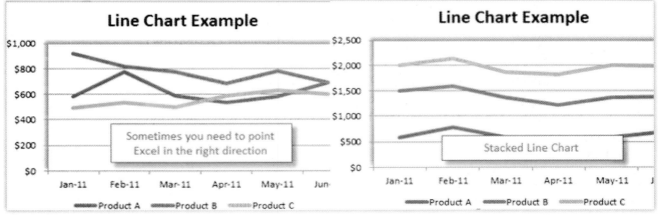

Figure 316

- **Layout** – Assuming that your chart is everything you want it to be from a data and type standpoint, then you can drag it to where you want it, keeping an eye for how large or small it will have to be when you place it. It's generally a good idea to get your chart in place and determine how big it needs to be (roughly), before you start formatting it because the chart's size can impact some features, especially Font size. If you format the chart and then shrink it, you may end up having to reformat it, although you generally won't have a problem if you start small then increase the chart size. In this section we're going to discuss the primary Layout tools and options available to you from the Chart Tools' Layout group.

○ **Current Selection** – This is just a way to scroll through all of the individual chart elements in a list as opposed to clicking on them in the actual chart. Selecting one of the elements will automatically activate it in the chart and allow you to make changes to it. This is a matter of preference and efficiency, for example, you might choose to use it if you happen to be closer to this option than the chart itself.

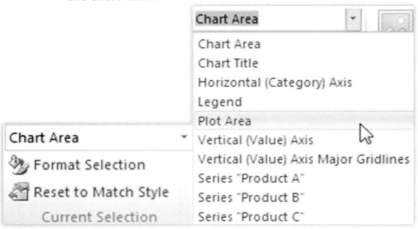

Figure 317

○ **Insert** – Excel doesn't limit you to textured fills and backgrounds, you can actually insert your own Pictures, Shapes or Text Boxes in charts, either as backgrounds or actual chart elements. From the Insert menu your options are limited to having the image as another part of the chart, as the image isn't very controllable. Unless you want to insert something that won't interfere with the chart elements, like a company logo, you'll probably use the more flexible image options found in the Format section. The commentary text boxes in some of the chart examples might give you an idea of what you can do with these options, and it's decidedly less than exciting.

○ **Labels** – Unless your chart is amazingly descriptive in its data representation you'll probably want some type of labels on it to direct users to explanations of key elements, like the chart Title or Legend. Excel gives you several pre-formatted chart layouts as you saw in the Column chart examples, and here is where you can take those selections a bit farther. Each selection has its own sub-menu of options you can choose. As you'll see you have over 25 different variables you can apply.

Figure 318

○ **Axes** – This determines how you format the X (Horizontal) and Y (Vertical) axes. You can choose to display the Axes or not, and whether or not to display gridlines in the chart area or not. And if you do decide to display gridlines, you can choose to display minor, major gridlines, or both. If you decide that the standard options aren't enough for you then you can always opt for the "More Options" dialogs, which offer an incredible amount of flexibility. Take a look at some of the changes you can make with the Major Gridlines options.

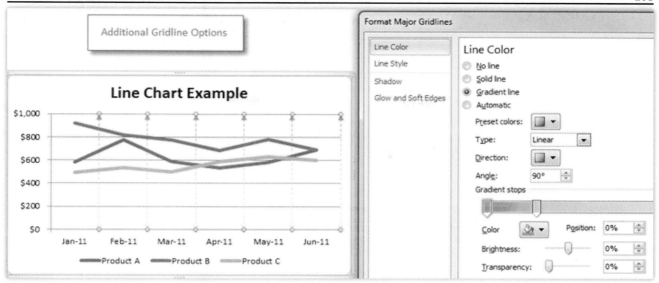

Figure 319

- ○ **Background** – The background option is full of selections, but it can get overwhelming very fast. It's important that whatever elements you add to a chart don't actually end up detracting from the chart's overall message by distracting the audience. This goes back to the conservative approach with your designs. While we all want charts to look great, there's a difference between making a purely artistic statement and actually letting your figures speak to the issue(s) that you're trying to communicate. Following are some examples of the Plot area fill that you can apply. The first is a Picture/Texture fill; the second is a Gradient fill. As you'll see there are a lot of settings for you to explore as you define your ultimate chart.

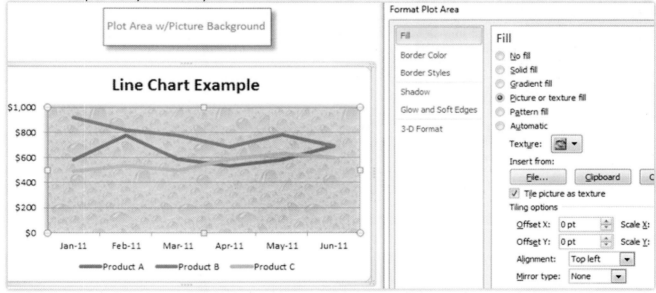

Figure 320

- **3-D Options** – If you worked at all on the Line chart example you might have noticed that the Chart Wall/Floor and 3-d Rotation options were disabled. These options will only be enabled for 3-D chart types. If you want to try those options simply change any of the example charts to 3-D types and see what you can do.

○ **Analysis** – This is where you can add additional information to your charts that Excel can calculate for you.

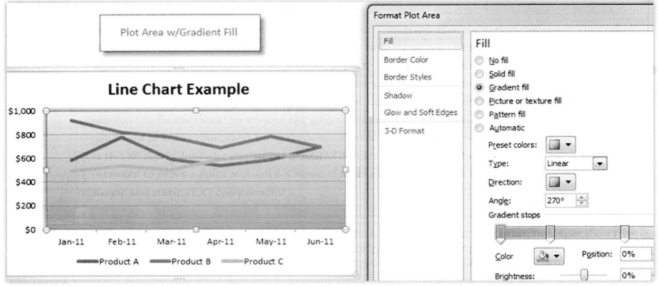

Figure 321

▪ **Trendlines** – For any chart group you select, Excel can calculate any number of Trend types (Linear, Exponential, Forecast or Moving Average). The Linear trend is the most common, but you may well find circumstances where the others prove useful as well. When you select any of the Trendline options you'll be prompted for which data set the trend should apply. In this case a Trendline shows that product A is trending downward. While a Trendline isn't going to show any level of scientific accuracy (although the calculations behind it are), because it is just a visual representation of the figures, it is a good indicator of performance, which can help you to make an informed decision.

▪ As you can probably tell by now, you have virtually limitless choices when you put together your charts, so many so that it's remarkable that so many corporate charts all look surprisingly similar. But it's simple really: most people don't realize how easy it is. Fortunately, you're learning not to be bound by those misconceptions.

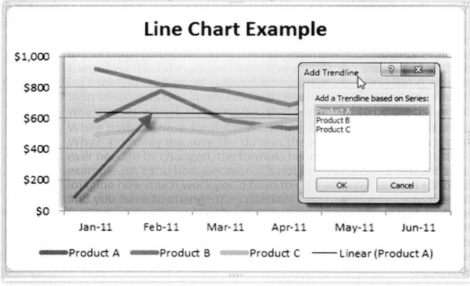

Figure 322

▪ Case in point: if you were to decide that this Trendline wasn't detailed enough, or that you wanted to add lines for additional data points, then naturally there is an expanded Trendline dialog. Following is an example with a gradient, dashed line on Product B that took all of 10 seconds to add.

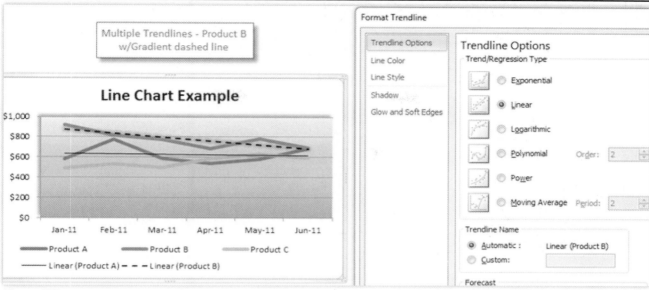

Figure 323

- **Lines** – These are relatively simple to understand. They're vertical lines that drop from either the high points of the highest data set to the floor, or the highest data set to the lowest.

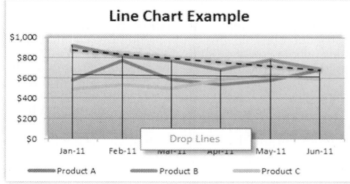

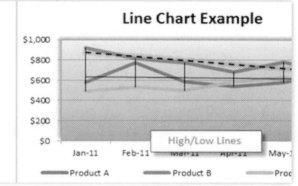

Figure 324

- **Up/Down & Error Bars** – These are just another way to indicate variances in your chart data.

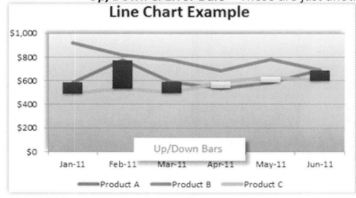

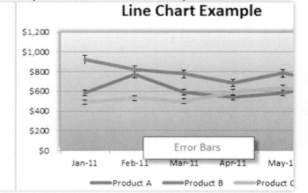

Figure 325

- **Properties** – This is nothing more than a place to give your chart a descriptive name. If you change the chart title here, you will see that change reflected in the Name box next to the Formula Bar. You don't need to change the chart title, but if you have multiple charts you might consider it just to keep track of them. By default Excel will name and number each successive chart that you add (e.g. Chart 1, Chart 2, Chart 3, etc.)

○   Here's an example of a finished Line Chart.

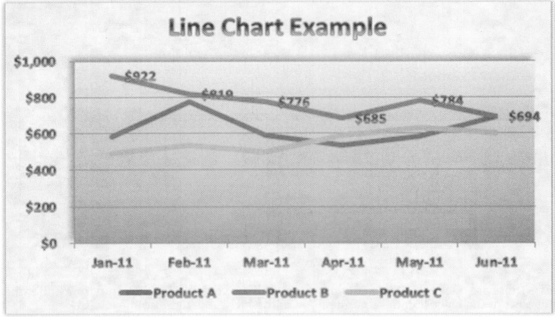

Figure 326

○   Now you've seen how to select your chart data and type and create your chart, as well as how to begin preparing your chart for its final distribution by going through the Plot, Design and Layout steps. The next step is the detail formatting, where you add Data Labels, format the Data Series, change Shape Styles, Effects, Fonts, Word Art, etc. Most of these changes are dictated by the general chart size, which is why you leave this step until you get towards the end.   None of these steps are mutually exclusive and you might not always follow them in any given order, which is fine. What matters is that you know how to quickly build and format charts the way that you want them without spending any more time on them than necessary.

•   **Pie Charts** – A Pie chart's sole purpose is to represent the share each element has of the total pie. The example below is a very basic example of a pie chart, and in this section we're going to talk about ways to add more detail to your charts with formatting elements. While Pie charts are also relatively common, their use isn't recommended because they can inaccurately represent data from a visual perspective, especially 3-D pie charts due to the way that they render when drawn, where the bottom/front part of the chart can look bigger than it actually is because of pixel density.

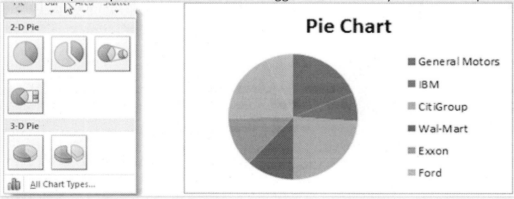

Figure 327

○   The first thing you can do with a Pie chart is expand the slices, which can be done as a group, or individual slices. To expand all of the slices, simply select the plot area (anywhere in the pie) and drag outwards in one motion. When you first select the Pie chart's plot area you'll see every intersecting point highlighted, to move individual slices, select each one and drag it out individually.

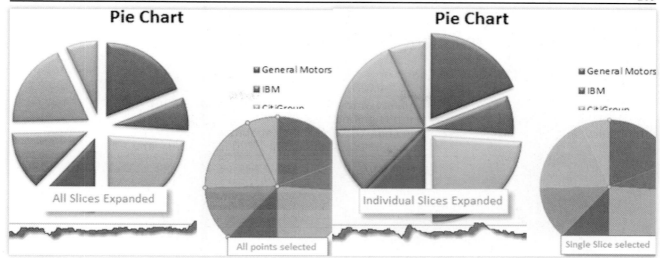

Figure 328

- ◦ **Adding Detail** - Next is adding detail to the Chart Plot Area. This generally means adding labels of some sort.

  - ▪ **Format Data Label -** With Pie charts you can add labels that represent each slice's actual values, or each slice's percentage of the whole. Just right click on the plot area to make your selection. For other chart types the Data labels represent the actual values, and you can choose to add labels to one series or multiple. You also have a lot of options with regards to formatting the labels so don't be shy about experimenting.

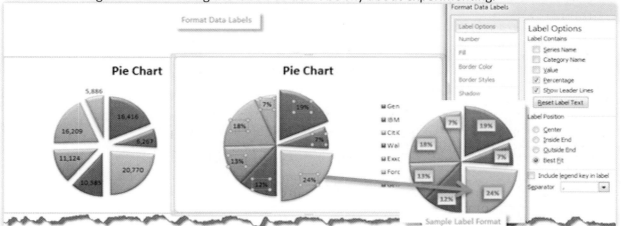

Figure 329

  - ▪ **Format Data Series** – Pie charts are notorious when it comes to the default chart aligning the Data Labels where they're not crowded into each other, as seen in this next example. In the past you were generally required to move and place most of the label elements by hand in order to space them properly. But now you can use the Series Options' **Angle of first slice** slider to move the labels into a better position. You'll still probably need to make some manual adjustments, but it beats having to do it all yourself, and that's one of the points of this lesson: given how time consuming charts can be, any amount of time you can save helps you become more efficient. Even if it's just a small aspect of chart design, every little bit can add up.

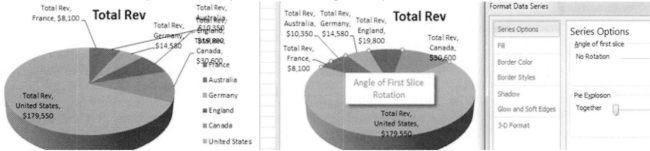

Figure 330

○ Here's an example of a finished Pie chart

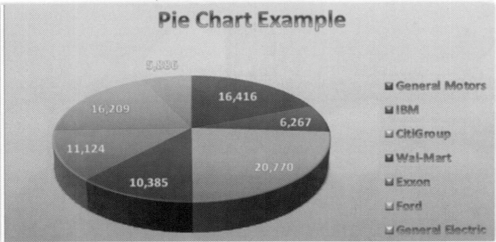

Figure 331

○ Now that you know how to add the Data Labels and adjust the Data Series we'll be discussing the final formatting elements in more detail. Particularly, formatting the rest of the chart elements so that everything comes together.

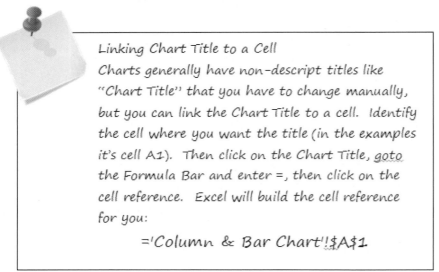

Linking Chart Title to a Cell

Charts generally have non-descript titles like "Chart Title" that you have to change manually, but you can link the Chart Title to a cell. Identify the cell where you want the title (in the examples it's cell A1). Then click on the Chart Title, goto the Formula Bar and enter =, then click on the cell reference. Excel will build the cell reference for you:

='Column & Bar Chart'!$A$1

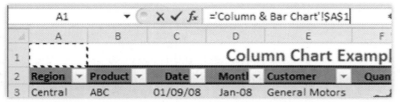

Don't ever change Chart Titles again!

Figure 332

- ***Area Charts*** – These allow you to compare like data over a given timeline. They generally obscure more information than they show, and should only be used if there are enough differences between the data sets to differentiate them well. You might need to select a few different styles in order to get all of your data points to display. The example below shows the corporate data set we used in the Column chart example. As you can see it's not the kind of data that's a good fit for an Area chart as unrelated data is plotted on the same line. A better data set would be the Product A, B & C data, as seen in the next example.

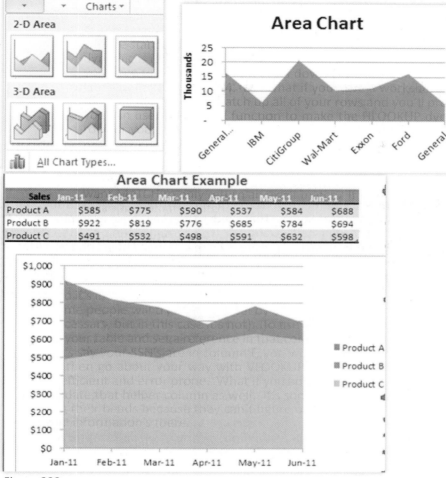

Figure 333

- But what's wrong with this example? Right, there should be three data points, but you only see two! Unfortunately, Product A's data is hidden behind B & C. The best way to solve that is either to convert the chart to a Stacked Area or 3D Area chart, then adjust the Fill's Transparency level, as seen in the next example.

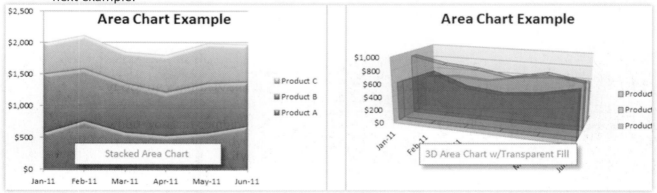

Figure 334

- ○ The Stacked area chart shows each data set in relation to the total of the three, while the 3D chart shows each data set as its own independent measure. To change the style you choose from *Chart Tools, Design, Styles*. To adjust the transparency of the individual products, right-click on the one you want to change and choose *Format Data Series, Fill*. You can adjust transparency and color at the bottom.

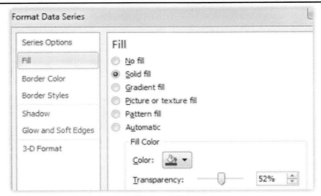

Figure 335

- ◦ Once you've adjusted the chart's primary elements you can continue with the final formatting steps, which would be applying Shape and WordArt Styles. That's where you see these examples go from a white background and default font to "finished" examples. You certainly don't need to take the additional step to modify those elements, in fact, there are probably as many times that you'll leave a chart rather non-descript (other than the data displayed) as you will take the additional steps to fully format one. An example might be a chart that's bound for the company stock prospectus vs. the annual report. They can be exactly the same charts, but the first layout dictates a very Spartan approach, while the next needs some of that Marketing department flair. Again, there are so many possible formatting options available here that you just need to experiment on your own.

Figure 336

- ◦ As you can see in the final examples, the 3D Area charts are a bit more of a challenge to format, and it is difficult to make the smaller values in the back stand out clearly even with transparency. You may well spend more time trying to get an Area chart to look right than it's worth. They can also be difficult for users to fully comprehend unless the data set is completely straightforward. If you find yourself with data that is even in the least bit ambiguous, then an Area chart probably isn't the right chart choice.

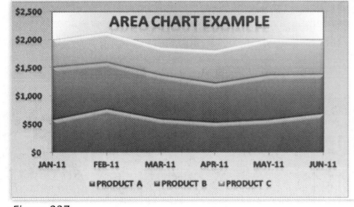
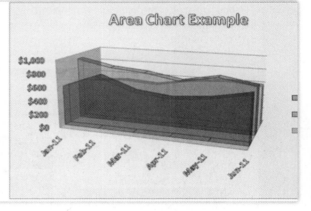

Figure 337

- **Scatter Charts** – Scatter charts are a lot like line charts, except where Line charts are good for comparing data sets over a given time period, Scatter charts are good for comparing pairs of data against each other. Scatter charts can also plot two series of data as one. Where a line chart's Horizontal (X) axis must either be text or a date, a Scatter chart can plot a numeric value on the Horizontal axis. This means that you can plot two numeric values against each other.

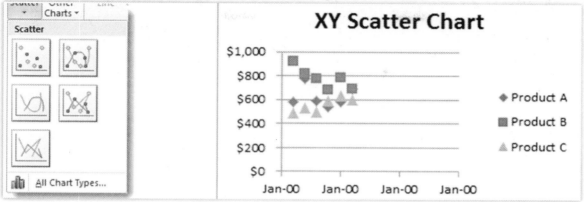

Figure 338

- ○ An example of this would be daily temperature and precipitation over a given period. Here's an example of both and you'll see why line charts aren't always a great choice when it comes to strictly numerical data.

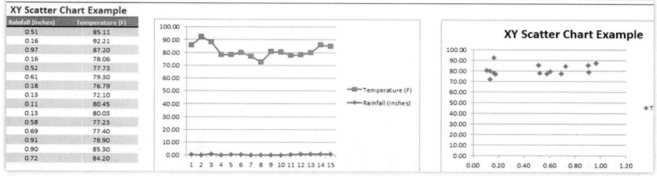

Figure 339

- ○ As you can see, the Rainfall plot is nearly meaningless in comparison to the Temperatures, while the Scatter chart ties them together with intersecting values. You might have noticed by now that we've been progressing through the most to least popular of the charts.

- ○ **Data Point Types** - As with Line charts you have the ability to use a Line, Markers or both to plot your data. You would choose the Marker option if you have quite a few data points and the addition of lines might make it hard to read. This is especially true with Scatter charts as line might wrap all over the place when following the data points, which isn't so much of a problem with Line charts since the data is plotted along consistent intervals. Here's an example of the earlier Scatter chart with lines added.

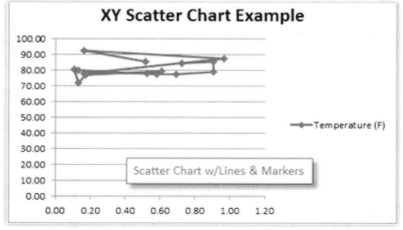

Figure 340

    o   Scatter charts can also take a bit of getting used to for the un-initiated, so unless you're in an engineering or statistical environment where people would be used to seeing them, they're probably best left alone. Here's an example of a formatted Scatter chart.

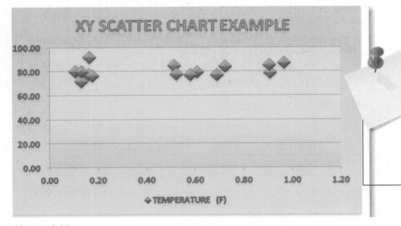

Figure 341

Using a Default Chart & Templates

If you've followed along with either the companion workbook or on your own, you've no doubt seen that charts can be complicated to set up, especially if you're not used to doing it. What stops most people from either using charts or using them efficiently is getting bogged down in constantly recreating them. Imagine a report with 10—15 charts and you have to create them each by hand. Even if it only takes you 5-10 minutes per chart that's a good chunk of your morning gone (5-10 minutes to create a chart is a perfectly reasonable time frame by the way). Now that you know exactly what kind of chart you'd use in any situation, and you've set up the perfect chart types, styles and formats for your needs, it's time to show you how to use it over and over again. Now don't think that this is going to be a panacea for never having to put any effort into charts again, because there will always be a certain degree of personalization involved, just as there are with your workbooks. But what this will do is help you eliminate the redundant work, which is often the most time consuming.

- **Default Chart** – The default chart type for Excel is the Column chart. If you primarily use a different type of chart, like Line or Pie, you can change the default chart to that type, so that every new chart you create will be the type that you determine. When you have your primary chart created, just select it and then goto **Insert, Chart, Launch the Chart Dialog** and select "**Set as Default Chart**". You can also do it from the Chart Tools ribbon **Design, Change Chart Type**. Unfortunately, this isn't as useful as it might sound, as it only sets the default chart type and nothing more. To reuse an entire chart style, you need to create a chart template. The Default chart option will only apply when you use the ALT+F1 or F11 shortcuts for creating charts. If you go through the Ribbon and select a particular chart type to insert, the default chart won't override your selection.

- **Chart Template** – This feature can be incredibly useful, especially if you create a lot of charts. This is actually very much like workbook templates that you create, except you can use multiple chart templates in one workbook. To start first create your first chart (or just open the workbook with the chart(s) in it). Assuming that your chart(s) are formatted the way that you want, and then activate the chart and goto **Chart Tools, Design, Type, Save As Template**. You'll immediately be presented with a Save Chart Template dialog, which will prompt you for a Chart name. Enter something descriptive and Save it.

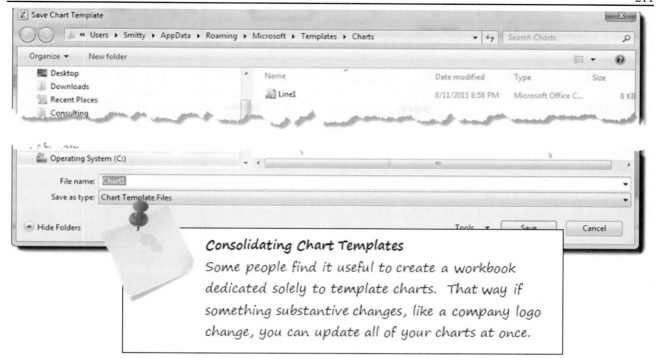

Figure 342

○ In the future if you
   ever want to apply that
   chart style to any chart,
   simply select the chart
   in question, goto Chart
   Tools, Design, Type,
   Change Chart Type,
   Templates, Select the
   template that you want

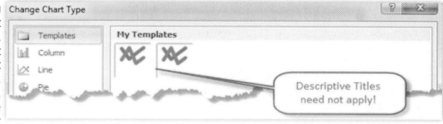

to apply. Note that the descriptive name you entered when you saved the template makes no
difference here, as all the Template manager will show you is a thumbnail indicating the chart type.
If you have multiple charts that are the same type, you might have to pick and choose before you
get the right one.

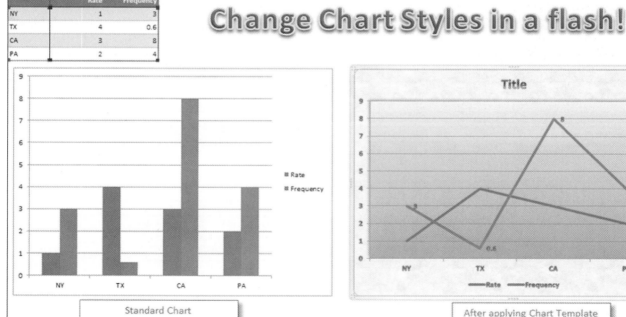

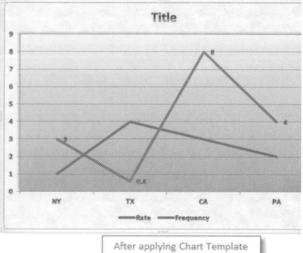

Figure 343 Standard chart vs chart template

Sparklines

While Sparklines aren't technically a part of Charts, they fit a remarkably similar need, so this is as good a place as any to discuss them. As previously introduced, Sparklines allow you to insert mini charts in a cell that represents the data you've selected (it doesn't have to be adjacent to the data, but it's a generally a good idea, so that you maintain a visual reference to it). Sparklines are a great adjunct to your data, but unlike charts that can be stand-alone and don't necessarily need the supporting data to be relevant, Sparklines actually seem to be more relevant when they're displayed in conjunction with their data. The amazing thing about Sparklines is how truly easy they are to use. Frankly, they're a lot easier to set up than Charts, so don't be surprised if you find yourself using these quite a bit. They are also a great substitute for situations where a chart might not be appropriate due to size limitations.

- You can insert a Sparkline several ways, by selecting the data range, or the Sparkline destination, then the Sparkline type (you can choose from Line, Column or Win/Loss). Note that Sparklines can only be placed in a single cell per data range, they can't span multiple rows or columns, but you can select multiple rows or columns when you're setting up your Sparklines. As soon as you select the Sparkline type the Range/Location dialog will appear to verify your selections. Or you can simply select the Sparkline type and use the dialog range selections to do the rest. It's just a matter of choice and what you prefer.

Figure 344 select the data range or Sparkline destination

- In this example we selected a three-row range to apply Sparklines. Even though the Sparklines that will be inserted represent their respective rows, you don't have to select and apply one row/range at a time, which is a real time saver. Once you confirm your selections Excel will place the Sparkline(s) on your sheet, and the Sparkline Design Tools Ribbon tab will be activated.
- Here you can edit the Data points, change the Sparkline type, Show certain data points, as well as select a Style for the Sparkline. Once again, you have too many options to detail here, but feel free to experiment with the examples in the Lesson 9 workbook, or create your own.

Figure 345

- Here are several different examples of Sparklines and the variations that you can create. Note the addition of Up/Down-High/Low indicators in other colors.

Sales	Jan-11	Feb-11	Mar-11	Apr-11	May-11	Jun-11	Jul-11	Aug-11	Sep-11	Oct-11	Nov-11	Dec-11	Line	Column	Win/Loss
Product A	$585	$775	$590	$537	$584	$688	$793	$1,888	$1,650	$2,702	$1,210	$922			
Product B	$922	$819	$776	$685	$784	$694	$776	$758	$1,104	$2,053	$2,502	$2,734			
Product C	$491	$532	$498	$591	$632	$598	$868	$1,765	$269	$921	$160	$1,160			
Sales	Jan-11	Feb-11	Mar-11	Apr-11	May-11	Jun-11	Jul-11	Aug-11	Sep-11	Oct-11	Nov-11	Dec-11	Line	Column	Win/Loss
Product A	$585	$775	$590	$537	$584	$688	$97	$2,428	$250	$2,392	$1,727	$278			
Product B	$922	$819	$776	$685	$784	$694	$175	$1,955	$1,837	$1,101	$1,574	$2,388			
Product C	$491	$532	$498	$591	$632	$598	$2,009	$1,061	$387	$1,866	$123	$1,676			
Sales	Jan-11	Feb-11	Mar-11	Apr-11	May-11	Jun-11	Jul-11	Aug-11	Sep-11	Oct-11	Nov-11	Dec-11	Line	Column	Win/Loss
Product A	$585	$775	$590	$537	$584	$688	$104	$1,406	$1,919	$2,654	$959	$643			
Product B	$922	$819	$776	$685	$784	$694	$1,584	$222	$684	$271	$283	$2,176			
Product C	$491	$532	$498	$591	$632	$598	$2,256	$2,529	$683	$77	$2,643	$2,447			

Figure 346

Quickly Hide Chart Data

If your data includes information that you don't want charted you can select just the range you want charted. Or you can select the entire data range and simply hide rows and columns you don't want charted, as hidden rows/columns won't plot on a chart.

Charting Errata

Here are a few chart Tips & Tricks that might come in handy at some point in time, although they don't necessarily fall into the realm of your everyday charting activities.

- **Display Hidden Data** – Right-click on the chart's plot area and choose the Select Data Option, then Hidden and Empty Cells.

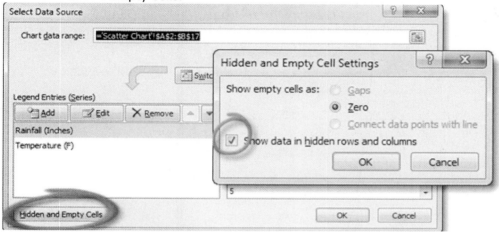

Figure 347

- **Interactive Charts** – As mentioned earlier, a Chart's default nature is to ignore hidden rows and columns, although as you just saw you can force charts to display hidden data.
  - Keeping in mind that hidden data won't plot, we can use AutoFilter to create interactivity with charts by selectively choosing which data to show vs. hide. This can give your users a lot of flexibility and let them review certain scenarios even if you're not there. This is a great tool for interactive reporting tools like Dashboards where you might want to give your users flexibility, and you don't want to prepare 27 different scenarios. In this first example, there's far too much data for the chart to be meaningful; it's just too cluttered.

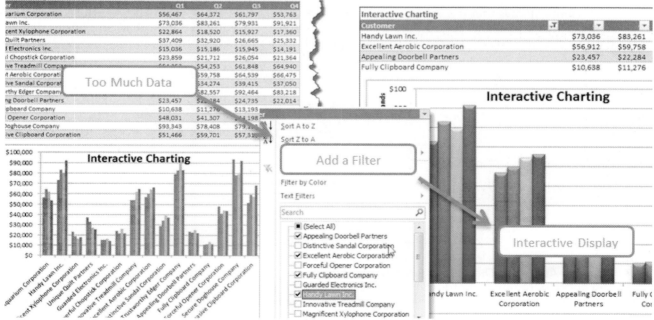

Figure 348

- ◦ By adding a Filter to the data you give the user the ability to pare down the field and create their own meaningful charts, while allowing them to make the data comparisons that they want, meaning that you don't have to do it. When the user applies the filter, only the visible filtered data will plot.

- **What to do about 0 Values?** You will often run into situations where your data isn't complete and your chart flat lines when it hits it. This is often seen when plotting a timeline series, like weeks or months, when you have year-to-date information, but no data for the portion of the period that hasn't yet occurred. In this case you need to tell Excel to ignore the missing data, which you can do via formula, specifically NA(). In the following example you'll see some linked data that goes to zero because you can only have data for periods that have actually occurred. So we need to tell Excel to ignore the missing data.

Jan-11	Feb-11	Mar-11	Apr-11	May-11	Jun-11	Jul-11	Aug-11	Jan-11	Feb-11	Mar-11	Apr-11	May-11	Jun-11	Jul-11
$1,873	$2,317	$1,956	$1,436	$1,848	$2,251	$2,578	$0	$1,873	$2,317	$1,956	$1,436	$1,848	$2,251	$2,578
$1,256	$1,538	$1,358	$2,362	$2,967	$1,794	$2,084	$0	$1,256	$1,538	$1,358	$2,362	$2,967	$1,794	$2,084
$937	$1,244	$1,139	$2,336	$1,897	$2,051	$1,987	$0	$937	$1,244	$1,139	$2,336	$1,897	$2,051	$1,987

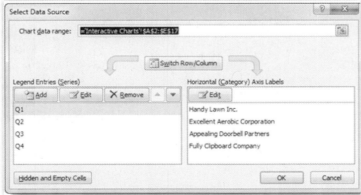

Figure 349

Using Linked Data for Charts

Many times your chart data may exist on separate sheets. Oftentimes you want to create consolidated data ranges by linking your chart data on a single chart sheet, as in the previous example. It can greatly simplify your charting endeavors and won't add much overhead to the workbook.

- ◦ The formula is a simple one and it's similar to testing for a DIV/0 error: *=IF(B9,B9,NA()),* which essentially says that if a value exists for B9, then return B9's value, otherwise return #N/A. Since N/A won't plot, this solves the flat line data problem. If you have data that isn't linked, but is manually entered then you can simply replace missing values with =NA().

Figure 350

- **Quickly Adjusting Chart Data Ranges** – So far you've seen that you don't necessarily need to select an entire data range in order to have Excel chart it. If an entire data range is to be charted then all you need to do is have the active cell somewhere within the data range and Excel will automatically include the entire range. You've also seen what can happen if the data range has areas that you don't want to chart, in which case you need to select the chart range for Excel. But what if you want to adjust the plot range after the chart's been created? It's a lot easier than you might think. You don't need to go into the chart data source manager. Remember, that as with functions and formulas, Excel will highlight the chart's data ranges for you when you select the chart plot area, so you need look no farther than the range highlights in the data itself. Going back to the interactive charting example, you can just drag the area selections to the range that you want, either expanding or decreasing the plot data range.

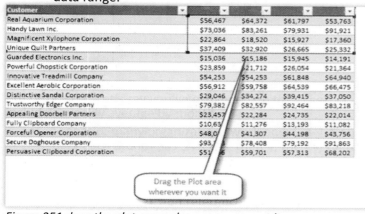
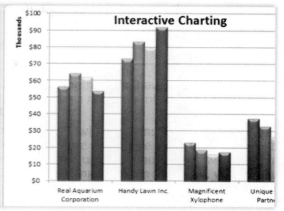

Figure 351 drag the plot area wherever you want it

- **Magnitude Charts** – There are often occasions where you need to chart two disparate data types, like Company Profit in dollars and percentages. If you recall the Line vs. Scatter chart examples, you saw that data points that are vastly different can cause graphing problems as one data series will be meaningful, while the other will be not much more than a flat line at the bottom of the chart range. You could try to build two individual charts and put them side-by-side, but a lot gets lost in the comparison that way. Fortunately, there is a trick to plotting disparate data points in the same chart. First you plot your data points just as you would normally which gives you a chart like this, and if you look very closely you'll see the percentage values just barely visible along the bottom of the X (Horizontal) axis. Not very useful is it?

	Revenue	GP%
Jan	14,715	48%
Feb	10,144	48%
Mar	11,697	48%
Apr	13,794	49%
May	14,546	47%
Jun	10,899	47%
Jul	13,491	49%
Aug	14,765	49%
Sep	12,979	46%
Oct	19,130	49%
Nov	22,079	44%
Dec	36,788	42%

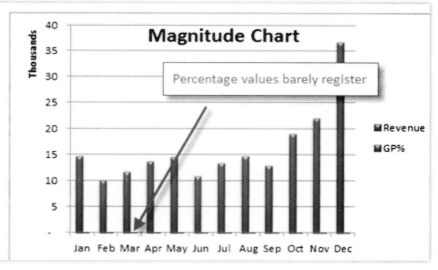

Figure 352

- Fear not, the fix is mere mouse clicks away! Select the chart (any part of it), then got Chart Tools, Layout, Current Selection, Find "Series GP%" in the list and select it, and you'll see the Percentage data selected along the X axis.

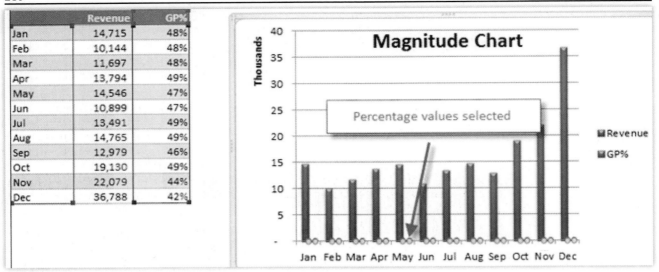

	Revenue	GP%
Jan	14,715	48%
Feb	10,144	48%
Mar	11,697	48%
Apr	13,794	49%
May	14,546	47%
Jun	10,899	47%
Jul	13,491	49%
Aug	14,765	49%
Sep	12,979	46%
Oct	19,130	49%
Nov	22,079	44%
Dec	36,788	42%

Figure 353

- ○ Then select Format Selection and you'll be presented with the Format Data Series dialog. Select the Secondary Axis option and you'll immediately see that the Percent values have been plotted on the same scale as your dollar values. Unfortunately, that view is about as useful as not seeing the values plotted, since they obscure the dollar values.

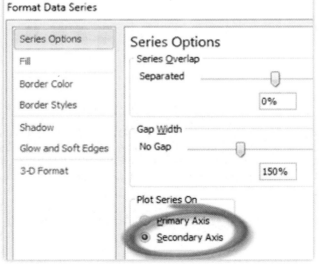

Magnitude Chart		
	Revenue	GP%
Jan	14,715	48%
Feb	10,144	48%
Mar	11,697	48%
Apr	13,794	49%
May	14,546	47%
Jun	10,899	47%
Jul	13,491	49%
Aug	14,765	49%
Sep	12,979	46%
Oct	19,130	49%
Nov	22,079	44%
Dec	36,788	42%

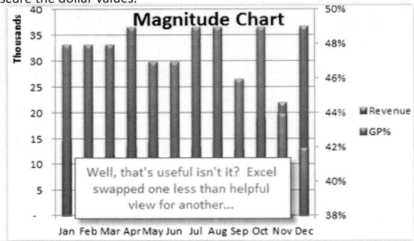

Figure 354

- ○ Right about now you're probably thinking that was a monumental waste of time, but you're almost there. Close the Data Series dialog, then go back to ***Chart Tools, Design, Change Chart Type*** and select **Line Chart**. Your chart is immediately transformed into multiple charts layered on top of each other, and your Percentage labels are displayed on a secondary Y (Vertical) axis! Who needs a Marketing department when you can do it yourself?

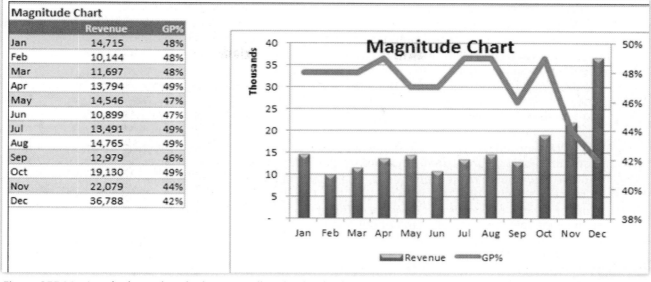

Figure 355 Moving the legend to the bottom will make the display a bit more relative

- **Charting Non-Contiguous Ranges** - As the following example will demonstrate, Chart elements don't need to be contiguous in order to work, as only the Header row and data specific to the Central region has been selected. Be aware that if you decide to use complex ranges like this Excel will not readily expose your data range by highlighting it like it would with a standard data range. To view a complex data range you actually need to select the chart, then in Chart Tools, select Design, Select Data Source. At that point, Excel will show your data range bordered by the "dancing ants", as well as displaying the Select Data Source Dialog, where the data range will be highlighted in the Chart Data range box. Don't worry too much about charting complex ranges for now

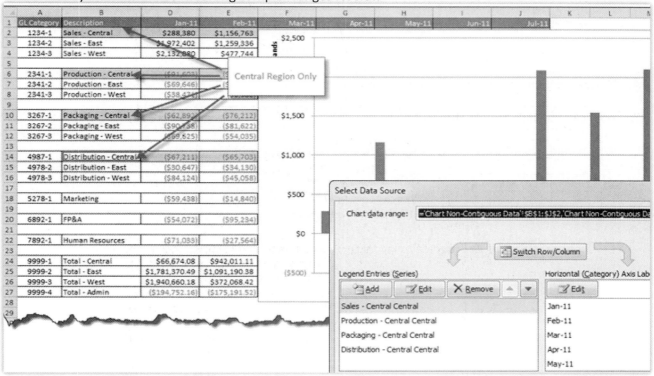

Figure 356

Unit Summary: Lesson 9 - Charts

- In this lesson you learned about the various types of Charts you can have in Excel.
- You learned that charts work best when the data is laid out in a cohesive Row/Column format, which is directly tied to good spreadsheet design, so the concepts reinforce each other.
- You saw ways to quickly draw charts either embedded in a worksheet or as an independent Chart Sheet with a single keystroke sequence.
- We discussed the core chart types, how to create each and what types of data are best for each chart type.
- We also went over some charting tips and tricks that should help you overcome obstacles that you might encounter as you start to further explore what you can do with charts.
- You were exposed to the multitude of ways that you can format charts be it changing styles to adding customized backgrounds and even WordArt elements.
- You also saw how to reuse your favorite chart designs over and over again, instead of creating charts from scratch each time!
- Most of all, this lesson should have encouraged you to not settle for the plain old boring charts that so many people feel compelled to not only create but share (giving charts a bad name). Hopefully you learned that most people create those charts because 1) they don't know any better and 2) up until now, charts took far too long to create.

Review Questions – Lesson 9 - Charts

1. Name 4 of the 6 primary Chart types.
    a. _____
    b. _____
    c. _____
    d. _____
2. Under what circumstances would you use each of the above charts?
    a. _____
    b. _____
    c. _____
    d. _____
3. What's the difference between the Horizontal (X) axis and the Vertical (Y) Axis?
    a. _____
4. Why would you include a Data Table in a chart?
    a. _____
5. How can you link a Chart Title to a cell?
    a. _____
6. Why would you adjust a Chart's Display Units? How do you do it?
    a. _____
    b. _____

Lesson Assignment – Lesson 9 - Charts

Your assignment is work with all of the Charts included in the companion workbook. Once you're comfortable with each one of them start creating your own data sets and applying the charting techniques that you've learned in the lesson.

Acknowledgments:

- Jon Peltier, www.peltiertech.com – John is a Microsoft Excel MVP, and is widely recognized as the best charting guru on the planet. His website is full of advanced Charting techniques and tutorials.

Lesson 9 Notes

Lesson 10 – Excel Tables & Sub-Totals

In the last lesson we explored Excel's fantastic charting capabilities, demonstrating how easy it is to create world-class charts in no time at all. As you learned, Charts can be one of the most time consuming elements of working with Excel, but they don't need to be. In fact, a general misunderstanding of Excel's charting prowess is generally what leads many people to either shy away from creating charts or just creating ugly charts quickly. And there is good reason for doing so, if a chart takes 10 minutes to create and you have to build many of them you'd probably try to get it done as quickly as possible, not bothering to go take those extra few steps needed to make them look nice. Fortunately, by setting up chart templates, you learned how to skip right past the hassle of recreating charts over and over again, instead relying on a few nice ones that you can depend upon.

Excel Tables are a similar tool in that they have been designed to help you work with data sets in a streamlined fashion. As you've seen in these lessons when you create a dataset you often want to take advantage of Excel's amazing capabilities as an analysis tool, by adding totals, averages, etc. Normally this means creating individual formulas and copying them across the relevant ranges. When you do this it's entirely up to you to tell Excel how big that range is and what you want to do with it. Tables put some of this burden on Excel's plate, because a Table will recognize all of the contiguous data in a Table as related information. Tables allow you quickly apply any of the extensive Table formats from the Table Styles gallery. In addition, Tables add functionality called Structured References, which is completely alien to the Function and Formula concepts you've learned so far. Structured Reference methods do to tables what the AutoSum wizard can do to simple ranges, and we will devote a good portion of this lesson to understanding them. Before moving forward though, there is a distinction between an Excel Table, which is the tool we'll be discussing in this lesson, and a table of data in Excel, which is the data we'll be converting to an Excel Table. A table of data in Excel represents your raw data that is structured in a Row/Column format. Both are tangible entities, but where one is your physical data, the other is a tool for manipulating that data. Neither should be confused for an Excel Data Table, which is an analytical tool found on the Data menu in the What-If Analysis group.

Do tables do anything for you that you can't do by yourself in Excel? Yes and no. Yes, because Tables incorporate a lot of features that you simply couldn't add as fast by yourself. Granted you could probably write your own custom VBA code to replicate a table (and until now that's what many people did to achieve the same thing), but why bother if it's provided for you? On the other hand, you can technically do everything that a Table can do, but you have to do it manually. For instance you can apply the fancy table formatting that you can get from a table, but it's going to take a lot more than 2 mouse clicks. Take the following example of unformatted data. It's not very appealing, and is about as generic a display of data as you can possibly get. Finance and Accounting types love this kind of data display, but the rest of the working world probably feels a bit differently. After all if you have to look at the data, shouldn't it at least be nice to look at it?

Sub-Totals - The primary thing that Tables can't do for you is incorporate Sub-Totals, and it is a big thing, which is why it's included in this lesson. Sub-Totals allow you to break your data down into chunks and summarize it along the way. Let's say you have a table of data that's broken down by Region, Product, Date, etc. Sub-Totals let you change it from just data to summarized data without you having to lift a finger toward the Formula menu. Sub-Totals also let you use several different functions for summarizing your data: Sum, Count, Average, Max, Min, Product, Count Numbers, and Deviations & Variances.

In the following example you'll see some table data that has had a layer of sub-totals applied to both the Region as well as the Product type. This is the same data that we'll be using in the Lesson 10 companion workbook.

Pivot Tables – Excel Tables are excellent candidates for creating Pivot Tables, which we'll discuss in depth in the next lesson. Pivot Tables give you the ability to add the Sub-Totals that you can't add in Tables.

	Region	Product	Date	Month	Customer	Quantity	Revenue	COGS	Profit
2	Central	ABC	01/09/08	Jan-08	General Motors	800	16,416	6,776	9,640
3	Central	ABC	01/12/08	Jan-08	IBM	300	6,267	2,541	3,726
4	Central	ABC	01/25/08	Jan-08	CitiGroup	1000	20,770	8,470	12,300
5	Central	ABC	02/08/08	Feb-08	CitiGroup	100	1,817	847	970
6	Central	ABC	02/09/08	Feb-08	General Motors	300	5,157	2,541	2,616
7	Central	ABC	02/19/08	Feb-08	Wal-Mart	500	10,385	4,235	
8	Central	ABC	02/20/08	Feb-08	Exxon	600	11,124		
9	Central	ABC	02/27/08	Feb-08	Ford	900			8,586
10	Central	ABC	03/18/08	Mar-08	Wal-Mart	800		776	9,920
11	Central	ABC	03/22/08	Mar-08	Wal-Mart			2,541	2,814
12	Central	ABC	03/23/08	Mar-08	Wal-Mart		3,756	1,694	2,062
13	Central	ABC	03/27/08	Mar-08		300	5,358	2,541	2,817
14	Central	ABC	04/06/08	Apr-08		300	5,886	2,541	3,345
15	Central	ABC	04/13/08			400	8,016	3,388	4,628
16	Central	ABC			Ford	200	3,802	1,694	2,108
17	Central			May-08	Exxon	500	8,785	4,235	4,550
18	Central		05/23/08	May-08	General Motors	600	11,700	5,082	6,618
19	Central		05/31/08	May-08	General Motors	700	13,986	5,929	8,057

Unformatted Table Data

	A Region	B Product	C Date	D Month	E Customer	F Quantity	G Revenue	H COGS	I Profit
50	Central	ABC	03/25/09	Mar-09	General Motors	700	11,858	5,929	5,929
51	Central	ABC	04/25/09	Apr-09	Ford	400	7,852	3,388	4,464
52	Central	ABC	04/26/09	Apr-09	Wal-Mart	600	12,360	5,082	7,278
53	Central	ABC	05/05/09	May-09	Wal-Mart	1000	18,290	8,470	9,820
54	Central	ABC	07/10/09	Jul-09	Wal-Mart	900	17,883	7,623	10,260
55		ABC Total					538,062	238,007	300,055
93	Central	DEF	07/07/09	Jul-09	General Motors	500		4,920	7,350
94	Central	DEF	07/15/09	Jul-09	Ford			7,872	9,544
95	Central	DEF	07/26/09	Jul-09	Wal-Mart			4,132	1,968	2,164
96	Central	DEF	07/29/09	Jul-09	Verizon	300	6,159	2,952	3,207
97		DEF Total					531,010	236,160	294,850
145		XYZ Total					587,562	260,610	326,952
205		ABC Total					584,251	256,641	327,610
260		DEF Total					631,700	279,456	352,244
308		XYZ Total					693,290	310,688	382,602

Sub-Totaled Data

Figure 357

- As you can see, Sub-Totaling not only does a fantastic job of almost instantaneously adding Sub-Totals, it also groups each sub-totaled section, so you can expand or collapse the data as you see fit.
- Before continuing perhaps we should lay out the Pros and Cons of Tables to let you decide for yourself it they're a worthwhile tool. We'll point this out because Tables introduce some foreign elements that can confound even the most seasoned Excel users.

Pros & Cons of Excel Tables	
Pros	**Cons**

• Instant Table Formatting
  o Header Row
  o Banded Rows/Columns
• Automatic Data Filter & Sorting
  o Multiple Filters on one sheet
• Multiple Tables on one sheet
• Related Data is grouped
• Dedicated Table Functions (Structured References)
  o Calculated Rows/Columns
  o Automatically updating references
• Auto-Expanding Ranges
• Data Validation Features
• Print Settings
	• Confusing Table Functions (Structured References)
	• No function variation in ranges
	• Data Separation
	• Can't use Table format without Table features unless you convert the table back to a range
	• Inserting & Deleting Rows/Columns isn't as straightforward as with non-Table data

One-Click Tables!
*Just hit CTRL+L or CTRL+T to instantly create an **unformatted** table.*

- By the looks of it, the Pros outweigh the Cons. If you haven't used Tables in Excel before, then you have no reason not to do so. Frankly, the people who dislike tables the most are the ones who have been using Excel for years and are used to doing things by themselves. A lot of those people would switch if they knew how easy they are to use. Does this mean that Tables are the right choice for all data situations? Of course not, in fact you'll find plenty of scenarios where they do nothing more than get in the way. But when they do come in useful, they can be worth their weight in gold, especially with regards to how much time they can save (and by now you should recognize that saving time is a fundamental tenet of this course)! If you recall the use that Data Filter can have when working with charts, then you can imagine how easy it might be for a user to work with a nicely formatted Excel Table while interacting with charts for different data perspectives.

- What type of data is an ideal candidate for a Table? Any data that is cohesive and formatted following the Rows/Columns methodology you've learned so far will work for a table. Unlike charts Tables don't require you to have numeric data, although they certainly can. Data that has poor or no structure won't do you any good as a Table, but for that matter, it probably won't be much use to you in Excel either. Ideally your data would be contiguous, but tables don't require it. The Table's Structured References will ignore the gaps in your data. This is nice in relation to functions/formulas that can potentially hiccup on gaps in data, especially if you think they're including the external ranges, but they're not. From a formula auditing perspective this can be very reassuring. However, you do need to know that if you try to use the Table Wizard to create your tables it will not include non-contiguous ranges. If you want them included you'll need to select the entire range by hand.

Convert Data to a Table

To get started you need to convert your data to a Table, but it's remarkably easy. In fact the most difficult part of creating a table is deciding on which format to choose! With the active cell somewhere in your table data range, simply goto *Home, Format as Table,* select the Table style that you want and you have a fully formatted table in two mouse clicks.

- *Table Formatting* – This is probably the most used feature of Tables, so much so that many people will never step beyond this feature. And if this is all you need then there is no reason to go any farther. For many people it's simply an added bonus that Excel Tables also include automatic Data Filtering.

	A	B	C	D	E	F	G	H
1	Region	Product	Date	Month	Customer	Quan	Reven	CO
2	Central	ABC	01/09/08	Jan-08	General Motors	800	16,416	6,776
3	Central	ABC	01/12/08	Jan-08	IBM	300	6,267	2,541
4	Central	ABC	01/25/08	Jan-08	CitiGroup	1000	20,770	8,470
5	Central	ABC	02/08/08	Feb-08	CitiGroup	100	1,817	847
6	Central	ABC	02/09/08	Feb-08	General Motors	300	5,157	2,541
7	Central	ABC	02/19/08	Feb-08	Wal-Mart	500	10,385	4,239
8	Central	ABC	02/20/08	Feb-08	Exxon	600	11,124	5,082
9	Central	ABC	02/27/08	Feb-08	Ford	900	16,209	7,621
10	Central	ABC	03/18/08	Mar-08		800	16,696	6,776
11	Central	ABC	03/22/08			300	5,355	2,541
12	Central	ABC	03/23/08	Mar-08	Wal-Mart	200	3,756	1,694
13	Central							2,541
14	Central		04/06/08	Apr-08	General Electric	300	5,886	2,541
15	Central	ABC	04/13/08	Apr-08	CitiGroup	400	8,016	3,388
16	Central	ABC	04/30/08	Apr-08	Ford	200	3,802	1,694
17	Central	ABC	05/10/08	May-08	Exxon	500	8,785	4,239
18	Central	ABC	05/23/08	May-08	General Motors	600	11,700	5,082
19	Central	ABC	05/31/08	May-08	General Motors	700	13,986	5,925
20	Central	ABC	06/13/08	Jun-08	General Electric	700	12,838	5,925
21	Central	ABC	06/25/08	Jun-08	Exxon	700	13,734	5,925
22	Central	ABC	07/30/08	Jul-08	Wal-Mart	300	5,508	2,541

A 2-Click Table!
How long would that take by hand?

Figure 358

- If this is the first time you've seen a table up close and personal, then the formatting should stick out like a sore thumb. As mentioned, this is the sole reason that many people will apply table formatting and never take a step beyond this point. To apply that formatting by hand would take the average user upwards of 5 minutes or more. That alone is enough of a reason to use them. But in case you're curious about what else you can do with tables, we'll continue exploring them next.

Removing Tables
With the active cell anywhere in the table range, goto *Table Tools→Design→Convert to Range*. This will remove all Table features (including AutoFilter), but retain the formatting. If all you want is the formatting, then this is a great way to go about it.

- The most recognizable element of Excel Tables (next to the obvious formatting) is the Auto-Filter functionality. We've already discussed the power that Auto-Filter gives you, but we'll review it briefly just to refresh your memory. One of the primary reasons to go over this is to show you how you can get data sub-totaled in your Tables, albeit for individual data sets, as opposed to Sub-Totaling an entire table of data. In this example our Table1 data has been filtered by the Central Region, Product ABC, for 2009 only. Note that there are totals at the bottom, which were applied from **Table Tools, Table Style Options, Total Row**, then selecting SUM for each of the three revenue columns (Revenue, COGS and Profit). Remember, you can quickly see which columns in a table have been Filtered by looking for the ActiveFilter symbol in the Filter drop-downs.

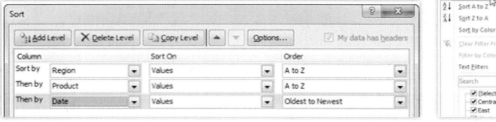

	Region	Product	Date	Month	Customer	Quan	Rever	CC	Pr
43	Central	ABC	01/04/09	Jan-09	IBM	400	$6,860	$3,388	$3,472
44	Central	ABC	01/13/09	Jan-09	AT&T	100	$1,740	$847	$893
45	Central	ABC	01/26/09	Jan-09	General Electric	500	$10,445	$4,235	$6,210
46	Central	ABC	02/04/09	Feb-09	Exxon	700	$13,314	$5,929	$7,385
47	Central	ABC	02/08/09	Feb-09	Wal-Mart	400	$7,180	$3,388	$3,792
48	Central	ABC	02/16/09	Feb-09	Verizon	600	$11,922	$5,082	$6,840
49	Central	ABC	03/05/09	Mar-09	Ford	200	$4,010	$1,694	$2,316
50	Central	ABC	03/25/09	Mar-09	General Motors	700	$11,858	$5,929	$5,929
51	Central	ABC			Ford	400	$7,852	$3,388	$4,464
52	Central	ABC			Wal-Mart	600	$12,360	$5,082	$7,278
53	Central	ABC	05/05/09	May-09	Wal-Mart	1000	$18,290	$8,470	$9,820
54	Central	ABC	07/10/09	Jul-09	Wal-Mart	900	$17,883	$7,623	$10,260
409	Total						$123,714	$55,055	$68,659

Figure 359

- **Total Row** – The example shows a Total Row, although it is technically a Sub-Totaled row. A side-effect (feature?) of Auto-Filter is that it will only apply functions to visible rows, so the rows that have been hidden are excluded from our current totals. If you were to change the filtered criteria, the totals would only apply to the new view. If you look closely at the example you'll see that there is a Sub-Total function instead of a regular SUM function: **=SUBTOTAL(109,[Revenue])**. If this table had not had filters applied* then the function would look like this: **=SUM([Revenue])**. We'll get more into the details behind Sub-Total and Structured References a bit later, but what you see here is a mix of both (note the named reference to [Revenue] as opposed to a range reference like **=SUM(A1:A10)** – when you see that you know you're dealing with Structured References). Remember that in order for filtered data to perform the way that you expect, your data needs to be sorted first, otherwise filtering can exclude some results. Fortunately, Auto-Filter contains Sorting functionality, so you don't need to leave the comforts of the Auto-Filter dialog to apply different sort criteria. You can apply multiple sort criteria by selecting the columns and sorting them in the order that you choose. You can also invoke the Sort Wizard if you want to add all of your criteria at once. However, in both cases the Sort-by-Color options will not work in Excel Tables, as the formatted table row color won't be recognized.

Figure 360

    * When is Filtered Data really filtered?

    Just because a table of data has Auto-Filter applied doesn't mean that you have to apply any of the individual filter criteria, in which case it's just a table with some drop-down selections in the header row.

- **Table Tools** – Once you've created your table Excel exposes a new Ribbon group for you called "Table Tools". It's like any of the other additional Ribbon elements you've seen so far and it deals strictly with Table elements.

- **Properties** – This is a very straightforward group in that you only have 2 options: Table Name and Re-size Table.

  ○ **Table Name** – By default each new Table that you create will be named sequentially with a non-descript "Tablexx" name. If you want something more descriptive please feel free to change it here. Note that the naming conventions for Tables are the same as with Named Ranges, so "Expense Tracking" wouldn't work, but "Expense_ Tracking" (note the underscore) would, and if you enter an invalid name Excel will be sure to tell you. In fact, Table names get stored in the Named Range Manager, so you can't have duplicate names. The Table 1 example in the companion workbook has been named "Table_1_Example". Naming tables can come in very handy if you find yourself creating a lot of them, because it's a lot easier to remember what each one does if it has a descriptive name. Although we won't cover it in this course, naming your tables also helps if you decide to interact with them in VBA at some point.

Figure 361

  ○ **Resize Table** – This is a feature that will probably see very little use, as Excel Tables will automatically expand the Table range if you add data in any contiguous Row or Column. You will use it however, if you decide to add data that is not contiguous. The following examples will show what happens if you add contiguous data vs. non-contiguous data.

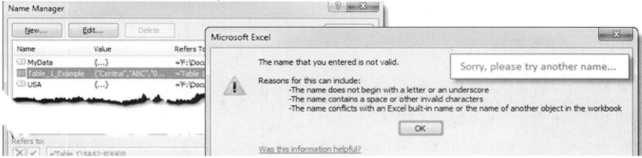

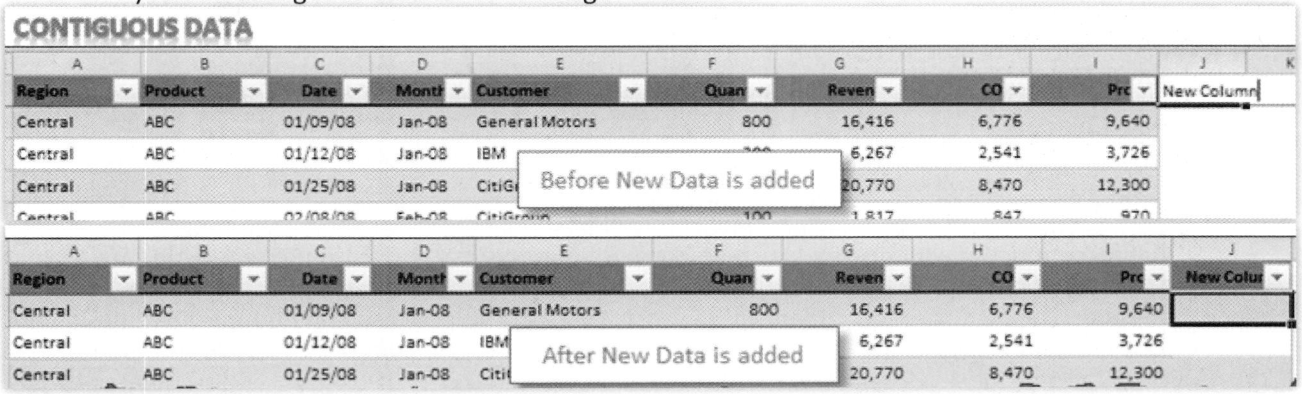

Figure 362

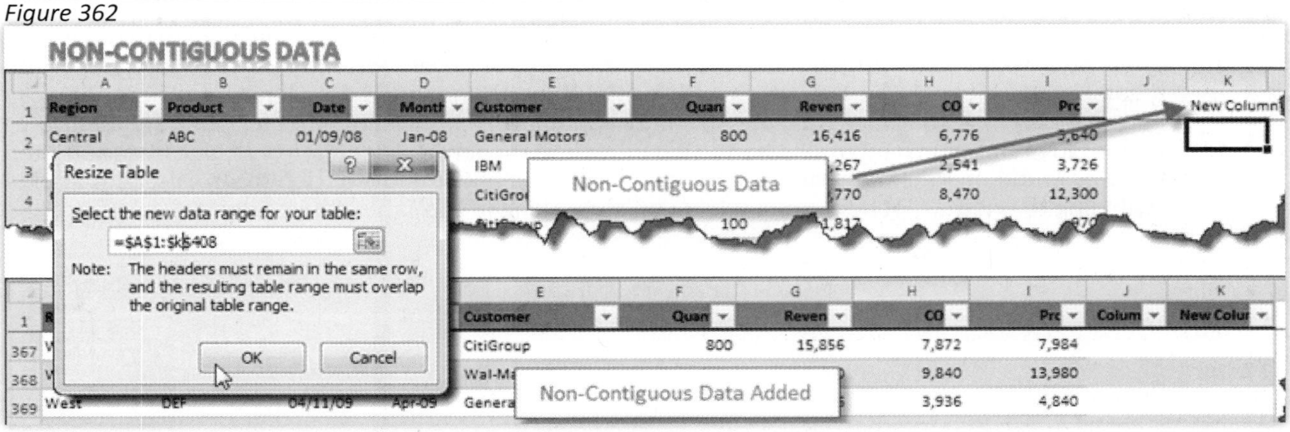

Figure 363

- As you can see in the non-contiguous data example, Excel added the new column, but it was also forced to add a column in between to bridge the gap between the existing table and the new data. Adding a non-contiguous row would be the same, except if you already have a Total row in place, in which case you have one of two options:

1. Remove the Total row by unchecking it from **Table Tools, Table Style Options, Total Row**
2. Select the Total row and insert a new row(s) with **ALT+I+R** (or any other long way to do it)
   - ○ **Sticking Point** – If you have totals in the rightmost column of the table the table will automatically expand if you enter new data in the next column, but it won't move the totals that you already have in place. In this case you're better off inserting a new column immediately before the totals with **ALT+I+C**. Perhaps in the future Microsoft will change this and have that new column automatically inserted inside of the existing totals, but for now you're well off knowing how this particular aspect of Tables behaves. As with anything else in Excel you'll get the hang of it with some experimentation.

Figure 364

- ○ **Undoing Added Data** – If you accidentally add either an extra row or column to a Table, you might notice that Excel presents you with a Smart Tag near the insertion point. This gives you the ability to undo the addition (you could also use CTRL+Z), and it gives you the option to turn of the Expanding Table behavior if you find it irritating.

- ○ **Manually Resizing Tables** – If you noticed the bottom of the Table you've probably seen the resizing handle in the lower right-hand corner. With it you can expand a table to the side or down, but not both at the same time.

- ○ **Tab your way to a New Row** – If you're in the last row and last column of a Table, you can also create a new row simply by hitting the Tab key. This will also work if you already have a Totals row, which is a bonus.

- **Tools** – There are three options in the Tools menu.
  - ○ **Summarize with PivotTable** – This is one of the most powerful side-features of Tables, in fact the entire next lesson is devoted to PivotTables, so we're not going to discuss it here. Suffice it to say, when Excel creates a Table it also takes internal stock of your data and its structure and sets it up for seamless transition as a PivotTable. Earlier in the lesson we discussed how Excel Tables don't support Sub-Totals. PivotTables are the solution to that issue and they are as powerful an analysis tool as you can possibly imagine. PivotTables make doing in Excel what could only be done with database functionality previously. If you analyze a great deal of data, the Excel Tables are a great start, and a fantastic lead into PivotTables.
  - ○ **Remove Duplicates** – This is another fantastic tool. In the past if you had duplicate data in your Excel table, you had to go through some fairly laborious steps to identify and/or remove it, many of which involved VBA code (some of it graciously provided by Microsoft because they knew this was one of Excel's weaknesses). You could also use Conditional Formatting to identify the duplicates (and you still can) or fairly complex formulas, but that also meant finding a mechanism to delete the duplicates once you identified them. More often than not it was faster to take that data, put it into a database to cleanse the duplicates and then pull the re-mediated data back into Excel. You can imagine how long that took, but the alternative in many cases was to manually identify duplicates and remove them by hand (talk about a gigantic time vacuum!) The Remove Duplicates tool is the same as found on the Data Ribbon, it's just included as a native Table option to save you the time of switching to another Ribbon group while you're working in the Table environment.

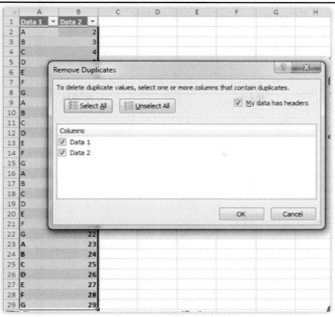

Figure 365

- Unfortunately, the table data we're using for examples isn't a good candidate for removing duplicates because it's transactional data and each row is a unique record, so we're going to use a very simple dataset instead.

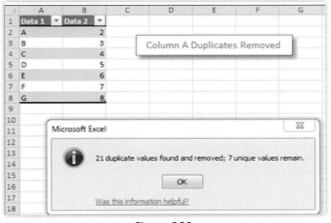

Figure 366

- In the example given, if you were to proceed with both Data points selected for elimination you'll get a message that Excel can't find any duplicates. Even though you can obviously see duplicates in column A, when you compare them in conjunction with column B's values you end up with unique data. So we're going to go back and only select the Data 1 criteria and see what happens. As you can see, Excel got rid of the Column A duplicates. An added bonus is that the list wasn't sorted when we started!

○ **Convert to Range** – If you love Table formatting, but not the added functionality that they bring you then you'll spend a lot of time here. This simply lets you remove the Table elements from your data, but retain the Table formatting. The giveaway for determining data that is an Excel Table vs. data that is formatted as a table is the lack of the Auto-Filter drop-downs.

- If you happened to have totals in your duplicate data set, then you'll see the function be converted from a Structured Reference back to a normal Excel function, although it does retain the Sub-Total functionality.

=SUBTOTAL(109,[Data 2]) vs. *=SUBTOTAL(109,Duplicates!$B$2:$B$8)*

- ***External Table Data*** – This allows you to export your Table data to outside applications, most notably SharePoint and Visio.
  - ○ **SharePoint** - If you're not in a corporate setting it's unlikely that you'll deal with SharePoint, because as we've already discussed it is prohibitively expensive for small businesses. If you do deal with SharePoint then you'll need to know the server URL for where to publish the table, as well as having the proper network access to be able to do so. If you have that information then the Wizard can walk you through it with relative ease. If you don't then you'll probably want someone from your SharePoint services/IT department to do it for you.
  - ○ **Visio** – This is another application that very few users outside of a corporate setting will likely have installed, but if you do bravo! It's an excellent application. Visio is a very complex application, but it is also remarkably easy to use without having to delve into its complexities. Simply put Visio gives you the ability to draw all kinds of diagrams, like flow & process charts, organizational charts, floor plans, network maps, database designs, etc. If you can think of data that you have that could benefit from a diagram standpoint, then you'd do well to explore Visio. When you combine Visio with Excel Tables you have a very powerful descriptive diagramming tool. Here's an example of our Excel table data output to Visio in the form of an org chart with Region and Product selected as the primary data points.

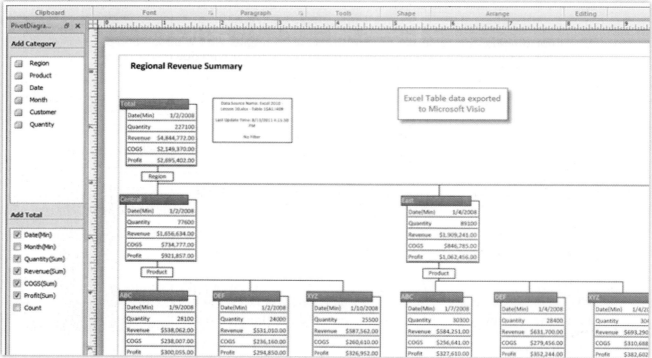

Figure 367

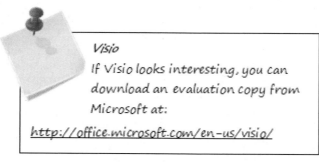

Visio
If Visio looks interesting, you can download an evaluation copy from Microsoft at:
http://office.microsoft.com/en-us/visio/

  - ○ You can add any of your Table categories (Columns), as well as any Totals that you might want. One interesting feature about the totals is that they are added to the diagram in the order that they're selected, not the order of appearance in the list (on the lower-left side of the Visio pane). Another nice feature is that once the data is exported to Visio it remains linked to your Excel Table data, so you can make changes there and have it refresh in your Visio diagram.

- ***Table Style Options*** – These options let you refine the Table Style you selected when you first converted your table data to an Excel Table, and with the exception of the Total Row, the rest of the options are purely personal preference. There is no performance loss/gain by choosing one option over another. In most cases you will at the very least have a Header Row. Here's an example with Rows unbanded and all the Column options selected so you have a better idea.

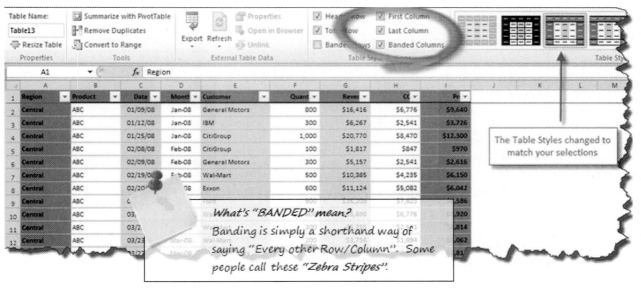

Figure 368

  - But you can overdo it, so you'll generally only want to choose Rows or Columns, but not both.

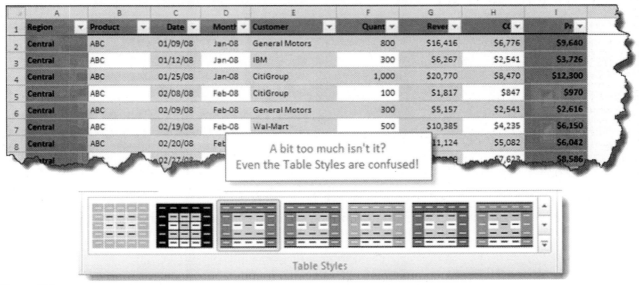

Figure 369

- ○ **Table Styles** – This allows you to apply the color theme of your choice, whether you choose to format the table when you convert your data, or if you'd rather insert an unformatted table and format it later. You can choose from Light, Medium or Dark, and all of your style colors are dependent on your Default Theme (**Page Layout, Themes**). The default is the Office Theme, but you can definitely go with some unusual colors if you've changed Themes, or created your own (although the ubiquitous high-school classroom vomit green might be a choice to reconsider).

	A	B	C	D	E	F	G	H
	Region ▼	Product ▼	Date ▼	Month ▼	Customer ▼	Quant ▼	Rever ▼	CC ▼
1
2	Central	ABC	01/09/08	Jan-08	General Motors	800	$16,416	$6,776
3	Central	ABC	01/12/08	Jan-08	IBM	300	$6,267	$2,541
4	Central	ABC	01/25/08	Jan-08	CitiGroup	1,000	$20,770	$8,470
5	Central	ABC	02/08/08	Feb-08	CitiGroup	100	$1,817	$847
6	Central	ABC	02/09/08	Feb-08	General Motors	300	$5,157	$2,541
7	Central	ABC	02/19/08	Feb-08	Wal-Mart	500	$10,385	$4,235
8	Central	ABC	02/20/08	Feb-08	Exxon	600	$11,124	$5,082
9	Central	ABC	02/27/08	Feb-08	Ford	900	$16,209	$7,623
10	Central	ABC	03/18/08	*So much for the conservative approach...*		6,696	$6,776
11	Central	ABC	03/22/08			5,355	$2,541

Figure 370

- ○ **Conditional Formatting** – Tables work very nicely with Conditional Formatting and its new Data Bars, Color Scales and Icon Sets. Microsoft added something to Tables that's incredibly useful called "Persistent Formatting", which means that if you apply formatting to an Excel Table and then add another row, Excel will automatically extend the formatting (both conditional formatting and the table formatting) to the new row. When you start working with Excel you'll see how much this simplifies things the first time you add a row to some non-table formatted data and have to apply the formatting to the new row by hand. Is that feature going to make you substantially more productive in Excel? No, but it will certainly have incremental benefits.

	Region ▼	Product ▼	Date ▼	Month ▼	Customer ▼	Quant ▼	Rever ▼	CC ▼	Pr
1	**Conditional Formatting - Data Bars**								
2
3	Central	ABC	01/09/08	Jan-08	General Motors	800	$16,416	$6,776	$9,6
4	Central	ABC	01/12/08	Jan-08	IBM	300	$6,267	$2,541	$3,7
5	Central	ABC	01/25/08	Jan-08	CitiGroup	1,000	$20,770	$8,470	$12,3(
6	Central	ABC	02/08/08	Feb-08	CitiGroup	100	$1,817	$847	$9
7	Central	ABC	02/09/08	Feb-08	General Motors	300	$5,157	$2,541	$2,6
8	Central	ABC	02/19/08	Feb-08	Wal-Mart	500	$10,385	$4,235	$6,1
9	Central	ABC	02/20/08	Feb-08	Exxon	600	$11,124	$5,082	$6,0
10	Central	ABC	02/27/08	Feb-08	Ford	900	$16,209	$7,623	$8,5

Figure 371

- **Structured References** – When Microsoft created the new Table format they also created a new function language that's similar to the function syntax you've seen so far, but it is less like native functions that use range references (=SUM(A1:A10)), as opposed to using Named Ranges in formulas. Let's say you create a data range like the one you see in the next example, then name that range "My-NewDataRange", and try to sum that new range. The result is what you would expect.

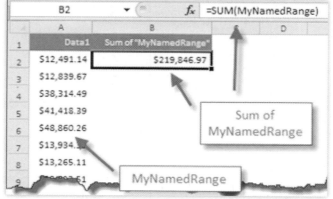

Figure 372

- ○ **Calculated Columns** - Structured References in Excel Tables are remarkably similar to using Named Ranges. As you can see in the following examples we've added **Calculated Columns** for Price, Price/ Piece & Cost/Piece formulas, as well as totals at the bottom.

	A	B	C	D	E	F	G	H	I	J	C
1	Region	Product	Date	Month	Customer	Quant	Rever	C(	Pr	Price/Pie	C(
2	Central	ABC	01/09/08	Jan-08	General Motors	800	$16,416	$6,776	$9,640	$20.52	
3	Central	ABC	01/12/08	Jan-08	IBM	300	$6,267	$2,541	$3,726	$20.89	
4	Central	ABC	01/25/08	Jan-08	CitiGroup	1,000	$20,770	$8,470	$12,300	$20.77	
5	Central	ABC	02/08/08	Feb-08	CitiGroup	100	$1,817	$847	$970	$18.17	
6	Central	ABC	02/09/08	Feb-08	General Motors	300	$5,157	$2,541	$2,616	$17.19	

Figure 373

- ▪ The formulas are as follows:
  - - Price – *=[@Revenue]-[@COGS]*
  - - Price/Piece – *=[@Revenue]/[@Quantity]*
  - - Cost/Piece - *=[@COGS]/[@Quantity]*
- ▪ As you can see, the Structured References use the Table Headers as the formula arguments as opposed to cell references. Had this example not been formatted as a table, the Price formula would have been =G2-H2. The interesting thing about the Structured References is that Excel knows where each formula is, so that it automatically updates the cell references internally without needing to display physical changes with then, like =G3-H3, =G4-H4, and so on. These are examples of Unqualified References, since Excel knows that you're referring to the current table.
- ▪ When you enter a Structured Reference in a column, Excel will automatically fill the formula in the entire contiguous range of table data, so you don't need to copy/paste like you would need to with a standard formula.

	A	B	C	D	E	F	G	H	I	J	K
1	Region	Product	Date	Month	Customer	Quant	Rever	C(	Pr	Price/Pi	Cost/Pi
402	West	XYZ	03/15/09	Mar-09	Bank of America	400	$9,240	$4,088	$5,152	$23.10	$10.22
403	West	XYZ	03/21/09	Mar-09	Verizon	400	$8,732	$4,088	$4,644	$21.83	$10.22
404	West	XYZ	04/23/09	Apr-09	Merck	800	$17,728	$8,176	$9,552	$22.16	$10.22
405	West	XYZ	05/01/09	May-09	AT&T	1,000	$25,310	$10,220	$15,090	$25.31	$10.22
406	West	XYZ	05/20/09	May-09	CitiGroup	600	$14,634	$6,132	$8,502	$24.39	$10.22
407	West	XYZ	05/23/09	May-09	Exxon	200	$4,388	$2,044	$2,344	$21.94	$10.22
408	West	XYZ	07/20/09	Jul-09	Kroger	1,000	$22,840	$10,220	$12,620	$22.84	$10.22
409	Total					629	$102,872	$44,968	$57,904	$23.08	$10.22

Figure 374

- ○ **Table Total Row** – We've already discussed this briefly, but Tables also give you the ability to add a Totals row with multiple Functions (the same as with Sub-Totals that were mentioned earlier). In the Structured References example we've added a Total row with Averages for the Quantity, Price/ Piece and Cost/Piece columns, and Sums for Revenue, COGS & Profit.
  - ▪ Here are the formulas for each column. Note that they all take the Sub-Total function arguments, which we'll discuss in more detail when we review Sub-Totals (101 – Average/109 – Sum).
    - - Quantity - *=SUBTOTAL(101,[Quantity])*
    - - Revenue - *=SUBTOTAL(109,[Revenue])*
    - - COGS - *=SUBTOTAL(109,[COGS])*
    - - Profit - *=SUBTOTAL(109,[Profit])*
    - - Price/Piece - *=SUBTOTAL(101,[Price/Piece])*
    - - Cost/Piece - *=SUBTOTAL(101,[Cost/Piece])*
  - ▪ External References to Table ranges – You use formulas to refer to table ranges, although the result is somewhat broader then the internal table calculations, as Excel needs to identify the table by name. In this case we created a formula for Revenue - COGS = Profit. The result is the same as the $57,904 Profit figure that was calculated in the Totals row in the above example, but the syntax has been expanded.
    - - Revenue – COGS , *=Table_StructuredRefs[[#Totals],[Revenue]]-Table_StructuredRefs[[#Totals],[COGS]]*
    - - Where **Table_StructuredRefs** is the table name, **[#Totals]** is called a "Special Item Specifier, and refers to the Totals Row, **[Revenue]** & **[COGS]** are called "Column Specifiers" and refer to the specific table columns as identified by the column headers. This is an example of a Fully Qualified Reference, which is necessary to let Excel know explicitly which table you're referring to.
  - ▪ If the COGS was a negative number you could use this formula instead:

-    SUM(Revenue:COGS) , *=SUM(Table_StructuredRefs[[#Totals],[Revenue]:[COGS]])*
  - In this case the syntax is somewhat shorter, because Excel knows that the arguments within the Sum function refer to contiguous columns in the table vs. the two distinct arguments in the previous formula. Again, you have a Table name, Special Item Specifier and Column Specifiers.
- ***Scrolling without Freezing Panes!*** When you scroll through a large data table in Excel you need to use View, Windows, Freeze Panes otherwise your header row will get lost and you might not know which column is which. With Tables, Microsoft took care of this in a way that you couldn't do programmatically even if you wanted to: they replace the worksheet headers (the A, B, and C) with your Table's column headers! This incredibly useful if you have multiple tables on a sheet, because it means that you won't lose track of whichever table you're in at the moment. You simply couldn't recreate that behavior in Excel because you can only Freeze Panes once. So if you had another non-Table data series underneath a first, then your second series would inherit the frozen headers from the first data set. For sake of argument, consider the following example.

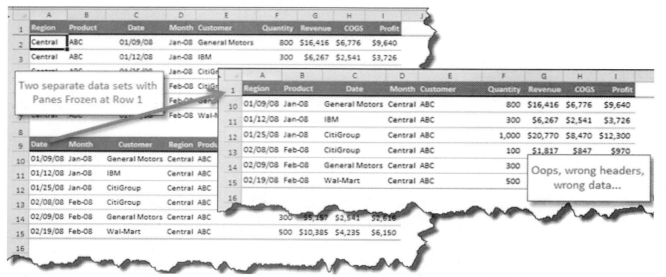

Figure 375

- If both of those data sets had been converted to Excel Tables you wouldn't have that problem.

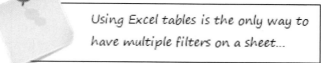

Figure 376

- If you only had a single table, then using Freeze Panes will override the column header replacement functionality.

> *Using Excel tables is the only way to have multiple filters on a sheet...*

- **_Excel Table Errata_**
  - ○ ALT+E+D+R will delete a table row, but ALT+E+D+C won't, unless you're in the Table's Header Row. You can right-click anywhere in a Table and select the Delete Table Rows/Columns option.
  - ○ You can also use the Insert/Delete functions from the Home tab.
  - ○ Referring to Tables in External Workbooks – Unfortunately, if you want to refer to a table in another workbook, Excel requires you to have that workbook open, otherwise you will get a #REF! error.

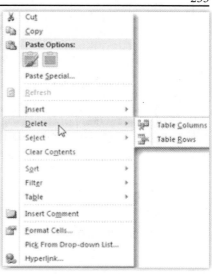

- **_Sub-Totals_**

Sub-Totals are a fantastic tool for summarizing your data without having to resort to lengthy formulas. Microsoft built in a very robust series of Sub-Total functionality to do it for you. In addition you can use what's called nested Sub-Totals in which you can sub-total one series of data and then add additional layers. We'll go back to the companion workbook and use the example that you saw in the beginning of the lesson to detail Sub-Totals and how to use them.

  - ○ The first rule of thumb with Sub-Totals is that your data needs to be sorted in the order that you want to Sub-Total. If your data isn't ordered correctly, you will experience some unexpected results. This is generally easy to fix with smaller data sets, but if you have a large data set, you might not realize that the Sub-Totals are incorrect, or at the very least you'll have a hard time spotting the anomalies that were created.
  - ○ The good news is that applying Sub-Totals is incredibly easy. Once you've sorted your data goto **_Data, Subtotals_** and you'll see the following dialog.

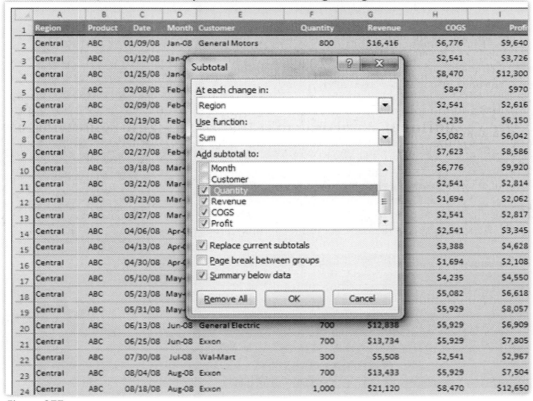

Figure 377

- Starting from the top down, select the Sub-Total criteria, in this case is by Region, which means that we want Excel to treat each Region differently. Next is the function to use, which will be SUM (your options are the same as with the Excel Table Total Rows), then check the columns you want to include in your Sub-Total. As soon as you apply the Sub-Totals you'll see that Excel has grouped your data into three distinct views.

Figure 378

- The first group is the Grand Total, the second is by the Change In criteria (Region in this case), and third is a completely expanded view. The third tier view is the default when you first apply Sub-Totals.

	A	B	C	D	E		G	H	I
E427	fx				Grand Total View				
1	Region	Product	Date	Month	Customer		Quantity	Revenue	COGS	Profit
412	Grand Total						227,100	$4,844,772	$2,149,370	$2,695,402

	A	B	C	D			G	H	I
A143	fx	Central Tota			Change In View (Region)				
1	Region	Product	Date	Month	Customer		Quantity	Revenue	COGS	Profit
143	Central Total						77,600	$1,656,634	$734,777	$921,857
304	East Total						89,100	$1,909,241	$846,785	$1,062,456
411	West Total						60,400	$1,278,897	$567,808	$711,089
412	Grand Total						227,100	$4,844,772	$2,149,370	$2,695,402

Figure 379

- Each of the Plus/Minus signs beneath the grouping options will allow you to expand or collapse each view independently of the others.
- **Adding Layers of Sub-Totals** – Very few people know that you can have more than one level of Sub-Totals, when in fact you can have about as many as you want, although you will probably never need more than just a few. There is a specific procedure to follow when doing this though. First is to apply the primary Sub-Total, and then apply the sub groups in descending order of importance, so if you wanted to Sub-Total by Region, Product and Month you need to apply the Sub-Totals in that order. Otherwise you won't end up with the results that you expected. The key to applying secondary Sub-Totals is the "Replace current subtotals" check box in the Sub-Total dialog. In this example we'll apply another layer of Sub-Totals on the Product category.
- As soon as your secondary Sub-Totals have been applied you will see another item added to the Sub-Totals grouping in the upper left-hand corner.

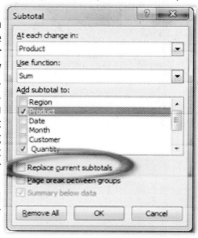

G310   ▼   *fx*   =SUBTOTAL(9,G147:G308)

		Region	Product	Date	Month	Customer	Quantity	Revenue	COGS	Profit
+	55	ABC Total					28,100	$538,062	$238,007	$300,055
+	97	DEF Total					24,000	$531,010	$236,160	$294,850
+	145	XYZ Total					25,500	$587,562	$260,610	$326,952
−	146	Central Total					77,600	$1,656,634	$734,777	$921,857
+	206	ABC Total					30,300	$584,251	$256,641	$327,610
+	261	DEF Total					28,400	$631,700	$279,456	$352,244
+	309	XYZ Total					30,400	$693,290	$310,688	$382,602
−	310	East Total					89,100	$1,909,241	$846,785	$1,062,456
+	355	ABC Total					24,800	$471,301	$210,056	$261,245
+	384	DEF Total					16,000	$349,082	$157,440	$191,642
+	419	XYZ Total					19,600	$458,514	$200,312	$258,202
−	420	West Total					60,400	$1,278,897	$567,808	$711,089
	421	Grand Total								
	422	Grand Total					227,100	$4,844,772	$2,149,370	$2,695,402

Figure 380

- ◦ If you look at each formula the Sub-Total has applied you'll see a similar syntax to the Sub-Totals that were applied in the Excel Table's Total Row.

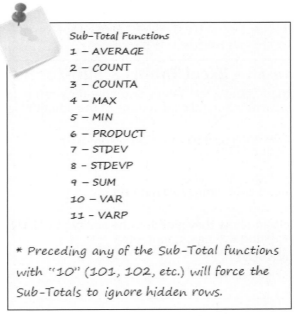

Sub-Total Functions
1 – AVERAGE
2 – COUNT
3 – COUNTA
4 – MAX
5 – MIN
6 – PRODUCT
7 – STDEV
8 – STDEVP
9 – SUM
10 – VAR
11 – VARP

* Preceding any of the Sub-Total functions with "10" (101, 102, etc.) will force the Sub-Totals to ignore hidden rows.

- ◦ **Mixing Functions in Sub-Totals** – Unfortunately, when you apply Sub-Totals you only have the option of selecting one function at a time, so you can't ask Excel to apply and Average and a Sum for the same criteria. But if you have the Sub-Total functions at the right, you can manually swap them out. In this case we probably don't want a Sum of Quantity, but an Average, so you could use Find & Replace (Ctrl+H) to change the function.
- ◦ If you have data that's been converted to an Excel table you'll first need to convert it back to a range before you can apply Sub-Totals. However, Sub-Totaling adds rows, so if you had banded rows in your Table format the banding will not stay consistent. If you want to maintain the table format and also have Sub-Total functionality you would need to use a Pivot Table instead, which we'll discuss in the next lesson.

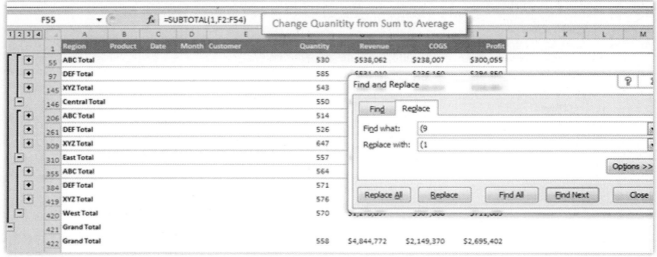

Figure 381

Find & Replace Tip

Why the "(9" instead of just "9"? Many times when you use Find & Replace you need to create a unique string so that you don't unintentionally replace something else. E.G. If there was a 9 in the formula ranges, then just using 9 and 1 would alter the ranges as well. Very often little changes like those are hard to spot until it's too late!

Unit Summary: Lesson 10 – Excel Tables & Sub-Totals

- In this lesson you learned about Excel Tables and how they can help you if you just want to quickly format your data, or go farther and take advantage of the additional tools that they offer:
  - AutoFilter
  - Integrated Sorting (including Sort by Color & Custom List)
  - Structured References
  - Total Row
  - Automatically Add Rows & Columns to a data set
  - Remove Duplicates
- We discussed Sub-Totals and how they give you the ability to quickly summarize multiple data points with different functions (Sum, Average, Count, etc.)

Review Questions – Lesson

1. Name two reasons for using Excel tables.
   - a. _____
   - b. _____
2. If you want to Sub-Total an Excel table what tool would you use (hint – Lesson 11).
   - a. _____
3. If you create an Excel Table, but only want the Table Formatting what do you do?
   - a. _____
4. How can you resize an Excel Table?
   - a. _____
   - b. _____
5. What's the difference between 109 and 9 in a Sub-Total function?
   - a. _____
6. What are Zebra Stripes?
   - a. _____
7. What's Structured Referencing?
   - a. _____

Lesson Assignment – Lesson 10 – Excel Tables & Sub-Totals

- Your assignment is to explore the Excel Tables and Sub-Totals in the Lesson 10 companion workbook.
- Take some of your own data and apply different Table styles to it.
- Experiment with Structured References
- Apply Totals to a Table structure
- Apply Sub-Totals to the same data and take note of which method would be beneficial in different situations.

Lesson 10 Notes

Lesson 11 – Pivot Tables

In the last lesson we talked about Excel Tables and Sub-Totals, both of which are amazing tools. As you've seen throughout this course, Excel is packed with useful tools and neither of those are any exception. It's just too bad that Excel Tables and Sub-Totals won't play nice with each other, so you have the option of using one or the other, but not both. The folks over at Microsoft have a solution called Pivot Tables that expose functionality that would normally only be available to those with database access. In fact, for years Pivot Tables have been considered a game changer from the Excel data analysis point of view; they let you take data and combine what you can do with Excel Tables with formatting, structured references and combine them with the power of Sub-Totals, as well as advanced Charting capabilities with Pivot Charts, which are fantastic because as you saw in our dynamic charting example using AutoFilter, as you manipulate data in a Pivot Table any Pivot Charts that you have associated with the Pivot Table will dynamically refresh. As an added bonus, in Excel 2010 Microsoft included something called Slicers, which are an absolutely fabulous way to slice and dice your data in ways that were previously impossible. Frankly, it's amazing that Excel can do so many powerful things, and Pivot Tables are the pinnacle of what you can do natively in Excel without having to turn to a database programmer. If you haven't heard of Pivot Tables outside of this course, there's ample reason: they're misunderstood and scare a lot of people, primarily because what they can do so easily just seems downright unnatural and difficult, but we're going to use this lesson to show you how incredibly easy they are to use. Another added bonus to Pivot Tables is they allow you to create complex data scenarios without having to recreate a lot of formulas; imagine a complex data analysis scenario taking minutes instead of hours!

- **What can Pivot Tables do?** Let's take a quick look at the corporate sales information example we've used throughout the course. Whether we look at the raw data, or the Table based version, it's still in a flat-file format that is so familiar in Excel. To refresh your memory, flat-file data is simply data that's arranged in a row/column format with each row ideally representing an individual record. While flat-file data should generally have some type of unique identifier, like a record number, as our data example shows it's not necessary.

Unique Record Identifiers in Flat-File Data

Our data examples don't have unique record identifiers for simplicity's sake, but it is certainly preferable. Think of our data as a second-level roll-up of information, so instead of showing 10,000 rows of data, we're only showing 400+. Pivot Tables take your data to the next level.

	A	B	C	D	E	F	G	H	I
1	Region	Product	Date	Month	Customer	Quant	Reve	C	Pr
2	Central	ABC	01/09/08	Jan-08	General Motors	800	$16,416	$6,776	$9,640
3	Central	ABC	01/12/08	Jan-08	IBM	300	$6,267	$2,541	$3,726
4	Central	ABC	01/25/08	Jan-08	CitiGroup	1,000	$20,770	$8,470	$12,300
5	Central	ABC	02/08/08				$1,817	$847	$970
6	Central	ABC	02/09/08		Flat File data format - It doesn't matter if		$5,157	$2,541	$2,616
7	Central	ABC	02/19/08		it's raw data or an Excel Table...		10,385	$4,235	$6,150
8	Central	ABC	02/20/08	Feb-08	Exxon	600	$11,124	$5,082	$6,042
9	Central	ABC	02/27/08	Feb-08	Ford	900	$16,209	$7,623	$8,586
10	Central	ABC	03/18/08	Mar-08	Wal-Mart	800	$16,696	$6,776	$9,920

Figure 382

- Remember what you can do with Sub-Totals? Well, if Sub-Totals just don't do it for you, then Pivot Tables will! Pivot Tables are so powerful that once you get used to using them you'll wonder how you ever did without them. One of the reasons that people may be afraid of Pivot Tables is the misperception that if something goes wrong you've just screwed up your data. Fortunately, nothing could be farther from the truth, because when you create a Pivot Table, Excel takes a snapshot of your data and recreates it, so your original data doesn't get altered in any way whatsoever. Another nice thing about this is that you won't find an Excel workbook blow up in size when you create multiple Pivot Tables, because the data isn't being recreated.

- There are a few ground rules for Pivot Tables, but they're pretty much the same as the spreadsheet design rules you've learned so far:
  - ◦ Your data should have unique column headers
  - ◦ There should be no gaps in your data, so no missing rows or columns
  - ◦ Don't mix data types, e.g. don't mix currency values in the same column that you have dates
- Creating the Pivot Table itself is remarkably easy. Moving forward with our Excel Table data, goto **Insert, Pivot Table**. You can work alongside this example in the Lesson 11 companion workbook, where you'll find data and Pivot Table & Pivot Chart examples.

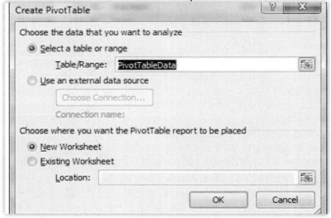

Figure 383

- The Pivot Table Wizard will automatically recognize the dynamic Excel Table range for you. You also have the choice of using external data which comes in handy if you're creating an interactive workbook for users, but don't necessarily want to include all of your data (remember, Pivot Tables only use a snapshot of your data, leaving it intact). Finally you can choose to place the Pivot Table in the same worksheet as your data or in a new worksheet. If you have multiple tables it's generally easier to keep your Pivot Tables separate from your data (it also keeps your data and users separated). You don't need to use an Excel Table for Pivot Table data though, as any Excel data range will work provided it meets the Pivot Table report criteria, you'll just need to select the range if you decide to go that way.
- As soon as the Pivot Table Wizard does its thing you'll see a new worksheet with the PivotTable Tools Ribbon activated. On the left will be a Pivot Table dialog box, while the right holds the Pivot Table Field List.

Figure 384 Pivot table ribbon elements

- This is where people tend to get confused, because Excel didn't actually create a Pivot Table for you; it merely analyzed your data and loaded it and your headers into the Pivot Cache, waiting for you to pull everything together. But the great thing about this is that it's a copy of your data, so you can do whatever you want without fear of harming your data.
- The first thing to do is determine which fields you want in your Pivot Table, so you simply check each one. As you do you'll see the Pivot Table dialog converted to a Pivot Table and the data elements that you check will be automatically added. As you'll see, the initial result isn't all that glamorous.

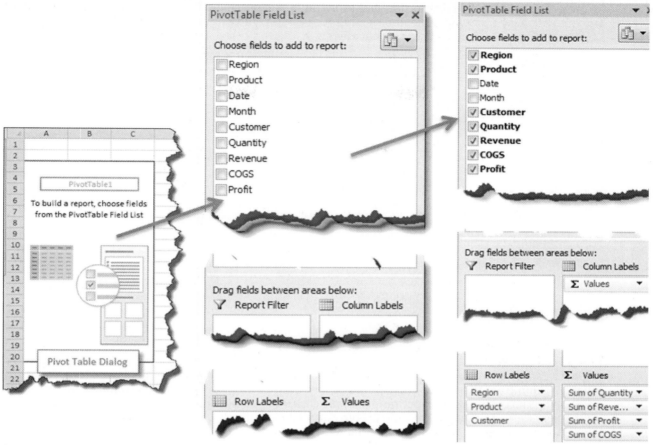

Figure 385

- Excel will automatically detect your numeric data and place it in the Values section, and it will also determine the Row labels for you. This is not always 100% accurate, because Excel is simply doing its best to interpret your data, but it won't necessarily get it right. That's one reason that the Pivot Table interface is so easy to manipulate and allows you to quickly move your data around until it displays the way that you want. The flip side to that is it adds to the misperception that Pivot Tables are hard to use because they do require a bit of work on your part; similar to what you need to do to get your Excel Charts the way that you want them. If you walk away from this lesson with just one thought about Pivot Tables you'll be in good shape: even a poorly constructed Pivot Table can literally save you hours vs. trying to do the same thing manually, and they are a lot more flexible.

- Once you've gotten to this point with your Pivot Table it's time to dive into making it do what you really want. Most of this is going to involve a certain degree of experimentation and even the most seasoned Pivot Table users will go through a certain degree of adjustment before each Pivot Table does what they want. Can that be somewhat time consuming? Sure, but it's a lot faster than the alternative.

- Here's the initial Pivot Table once you've made the selections displayed in the previous example.

	A	B	C	D	E
1					
2					
3	Row Labels ▼	Sum of Quantity	Sum of Revenue	Sum of COGS	Sum of Profit
4	⊟ Central	77600	1656634	734777	921857
5	⊟ ABC	28100	538062	238007	300055
6	⊟ Jan-08	2100	43453	17787	25666
7	CitiGroup	1000	20770	8470	12300
8	General Motors	800	16416	6776	9640
9	IBM	300	6267	2541	3726
10	⊟ Feb-08	2400	44692	20328	24364
11	CitiGroup	100	1817	847	970
12	Exxon	600	11124	5082	6042
13	Ford	900	16209	7623	8586
14	General Motors	300	5157	2541	2616
15	Wal-Mart	500	10385	4235	6150
16	⊟ Mar-08	1600	31165	13552	17613
17	General Motors	300	5358	2541	2817
18	Wal-Mart	1300	25807	11011	14706

Figure 386

- It's about as plain and boring as it gets, but if you look closely you'll see that Excel has manipulated the data in a way that would be very difficult for you to try to recreate manually. Take a look at how Region, Product, Date and Customer have been stacked in comparison to our Excel Table data. You might also notice that Excel has added an Auto-Filter to the Row Labels, which will let you narrow the field list or chose from various sorting options.

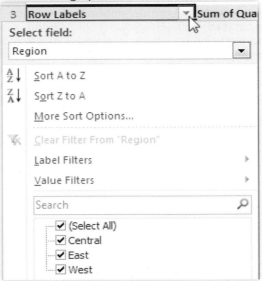

- **Pivot Table Field List** - The first thing you should do is give the Pivot Table Field List a workout and see how easy it is to add or remove elements. If you want to remove entire fields from the Table just uncheck them from the list, or you can drag them from pane to pane. You'll also find that each Field List item has its own Auto-Filter criteria. Simply click on the label and you'll see a drop-down indicator on the very right. Clicking it will expose your Auto-Filter options, which will let you narrow down your Pivot Table criteria and apply custom sorts.
  - **Report Filter** – This lets you narrow down your view by removing certain elements from the Pivot Table itself and moving it up above. In this example we'll move the Region out of the Pivot Table and use it as a Report Filter (all you need to do is drag it from the Row Labels group up into the Report Filter group).

	A	B	C	D	E
1	Region	(All)			
2					
3	Row Labels	Sum of Quantity	Sum of Revenue	Sum of COGS	Sum of Profit
4	⊟ABC	83,200	$1,593,614	$704,704	$888,910
5	⊟Jan-08	7,600	$148,976	$64,372	$84,604
6	CitiGroup	1,600	$32,398	$13,552	$18,846
7	General Motors			23,716	$31,388
8	IBM			11,011	$15,990
9	Merck	200	$3,552	$1,694	$1,858
10	SBC Communications	800	$14,440	$6,776	$7,664

Pivot Table Filter added for Region

Figure 387

- The Regions have now been moved out of the Pivot Table and into their own Auto-Filter group. Depending on the level of detail that you want you may decide not to use Report Filters in certain circumstances, because it does create a cumulative effect. So if you were to use the Filter option to select all of the Regions, all of your Product data would be summarized, not broken out into their representative Regional groups like you saw in the first Pivot Table example. Again, it comes down to you and what you want your data to say. The wonderful thing about Pivot Tables is that they are so incredibly flexible you can change that back in a few seconds if it doesn't give the detail that you're expecting. Many times you'll see this feature used to filter out date ranges. You can also use multiple Report Filters as you'll see in this example, which has filtered the date range down to 2009 transactions only.

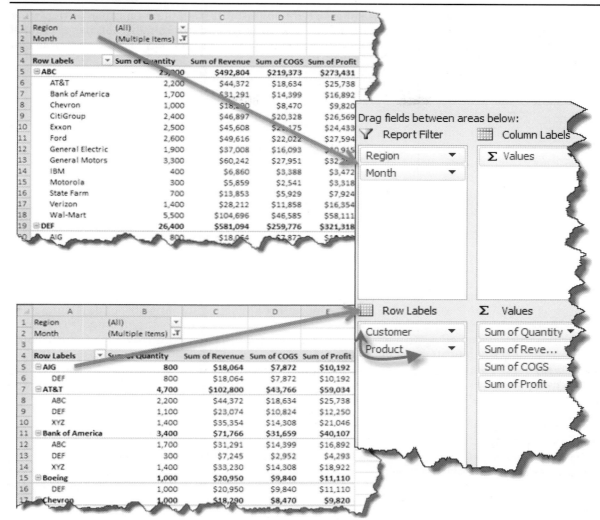

Figure 388

- **Column & Row Labels** – These determine in which position your data will be presented, whether laterally or vertically. When you experiment with these a bit you'll find that you can create some very interesting scenarios. Some might be useful, while others will be decidedly not so, and you'll probably reverse them almost immediately. You'll find that some data should just be presented in certain ways, but that is one of the Pivot Table's learning curves, and there's no escaping it. Fortunately, unlike a report you spend untold hours working on, a Pivot Table view can be changed almost effortlessly!

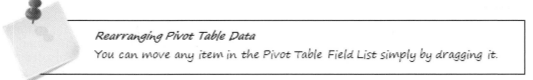

Rearranging Pivot Table Data

You can move any item in the Pivot Table Field List simply by dragging it.

- ○ Here's an example with our Column and Row labels swapped.

	A	B	C	D	E	F	G	H	I	J	K	L	M	N	O	P
1	Region	(All)														
2	Month	(Multiple Items)														
3																
4		Column Labels														
5		ABC													ABC Total	DEF
6	Values	AT&T	Bank of America	Chevron	CitiGroup	Exxon	Ford	General Electric	General Motors	IBM	Motorola	State Farm	Verizon	Wal-Mart		AIG	AT
7	Sum of Quantity	2,200	1,700	1,000	2,400	2,500	2,600	1,900	3,300	400	300	700	1,400	5,500	25,900	800	
8	Sum of Revenue	$44,372	$31,291	$18,290	$46,897	$45,608	$49,616	$37,008	$60,242	$6,860	$5,859	$13,853	$28,212	$104,696	$492,804	$18,064	$2
9	Sum of COGS	$18,634	$14,399	$8,470	$20,328	$21,175	$22,022	$16,093	$27,951	$3,388	$2,541	$5,929	$11,858	$46,585	$219,373	$7,872	$1

Figure 389

- ▪ As you can see it's probably not the most useful view around, but the nice thing is that it's entirely up to you. Just be aware that Excel will allow you to create Pivot Tables that make absolutely no sense to any one, maybe even you.
- ○ **Values** – As you saw, when you checked your numeric data in the Field list Excel automatically evaluated that data and placed it into the Values pane. By default Excel will apply a Sum to the

Value field, but you can change the calculation type simply by clicking the drop-down arrow to the right of each category and choosing the **Value Field Settings** option. You also see the additional Move options, which are just another way to move elements. It's probably faster to just drag and drop items instead of going through this menu.

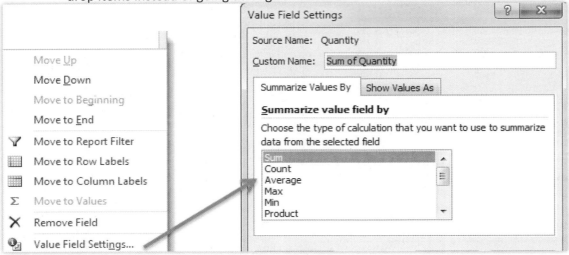

Figure 390

- In this case we're going to change the Quantity from a Sum to an Average, which you'll immediately see reflected in your data.
- As you look in the menu, you also see the additional Move options, which are just another way to move elements. It's probably faster to just drag and drop items instead of going through this menu, unless you're already here.

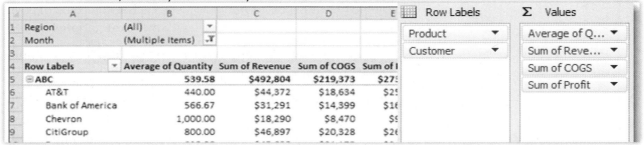

Figure 391

○ **Field Names** - You can change the Field Name if you want, but you can't use any of the names that are already in your Pivot Table 2data. So if you were to try to name the Quantity field "Quantity" Excel will tell you that name already exists. You can use an underscore or a leading/trailing space though.

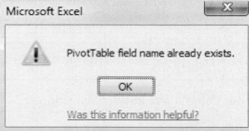

Figure 392

- **Value Field Settings** – This brings us to the second tab of the Field Settings, which holds the **Show Values As** options. This is where you can use field settings to create different data views, like % of Grand Total or even drill down as far as Percent of a particular customer. You have multiple options:
  - % of Grand Total
  - % of Column Total
  - % of Row Total
  - % of

- % of Parent Row Total
- % of Parent Column Total
- % of Parent Total
- Difference From
- % Difference From
- Running Total In
- % Running Total In
- Rank Smallest to Largest
- Rank Largest to Smallest
- Index

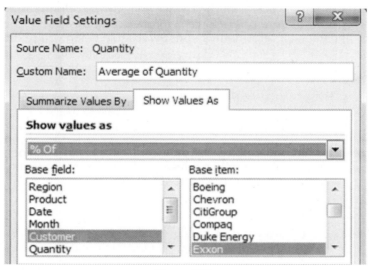

Figure 393

- The **Number Format** option will launch the Format Cells dialog (Ctrl+1), and will allow you to format your Pivot Table data. It's generally advisable to format your data and the rest of the report once you have the Pivot Table arranged the way that you want it, otherwise you might find yourself making multiple changes as you adjust the Pivot Table to display the data you want.

- **Pivot Table Ribbon Items – Options Group**
  - **Pivot Table** – Here you can name your Pivot Table and move into some more detailed options. You would probably come here once you've gotten your Pivot Table set up the way you want with regards to how the data is summarized. Under options you'll see three distinct choices. First is **Options** which we'll discuss in detail next.
    - **Show Report Filter Pages** – This creates individual worksheets for any filters that you might have in place. In the companion workbook you'll see that two views were created, first for our report Regions, second for 2009.
    - **Generate GetPivotData** - allows you to interact with your Pivot Table data via the GetPivotData function. If you exit the Pivot Table by clicking on any cell outside of the Pivot Table range, then use = and link back to any cell in the Pivot Table you'll see a GetPivotData function created for you.

	A	B	C	D	E	F	G	H	I	J	K	L
1	Region	(All)										
2	Month	(Multiple Items)										
3												
4	Row Labels	Average of Quantity	Sum of Revenue	Sum of COGS	Sum of Profit							
5	ABC	539.58	$492,804	$219,373	$273,431							
6	AT&T	440.00	$44,372	$18,634	$25,738							
7	Bank of America	566.67	$31,291	$14,399	$16,892		=GETPIVOTDATA("Sum of Profit",$A$4,"Product","ABC","Customer","Bank of						
8	Chevron	1,000.00	$18,290	$8,470	$9,820							
9	CitiGroup	800.00	$46,897	$20,328	$26,569							

Figure 394

- In this case the result is $16,892, representing the intersection of the Sum of Profit column, where Product = ABC, and Customer = Bank of America. If you uncheck the Generate GetPivotData option you'll get direct cell references, so the above example would revert to =E7. GetPivotData is an important function if you plan on referencing a Pivot Table and then manipulating it. If you had straight cell references you could end up with erroneous results depending on the changes you made in the Pivot Table, but your GetPivotData functions will continue to refer to the same information even if you change the Pivot Table. The only catch is that the referenced Pivot Table data needs to remain visible. If you're just starting out with Pivot Tables then this one can be surprising, somewhat like Structured References in Excel Tables and odds are slim that you'll use it, but it's best that you're at least familiar with it.

- **Options** – This is an Excel 2003 dialog, but it's still enormously handy. Within it you'll find six individual tabs. Most of the options are relatively straightforward, and there are just too many to go into individually, so you should experiment with them yourself, but we'll discuss the things that you probably want to leave alone. Remember, you can't screw up your original data by doing anything when you manipulate a Pivot Table!

- **Layout & Format** – Definitely play with the Layout and Format options, but you shouldn't touch the *Autofit column widths on update* or *Preserve cell formatting on update* check boxes. If you do un-check those you'll find yourself reformatting your Pivot Table when you're done <u>refreshing</u> it.

> *What's Refreshing Mean?*
>
> *OK, your Pivot Table data isn't actually linked to your Pivot Table, it's just a snapshot, so if you change something in your raw data you need to go back to your Pivot Table and tell it to capture the new information. Fortunately, it's no harder than going to PivotTable Tools→ Options→Data→Refresh.*

- ○ **Totals & Filters** – This lets you detail how you want to display or edit Totals and/or any filters that you might have applied. If you've taken advantage of Custom Lists from earlier on in the course then don't turn the Sorting Custom Lists options off.

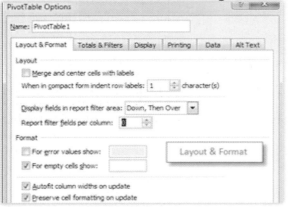
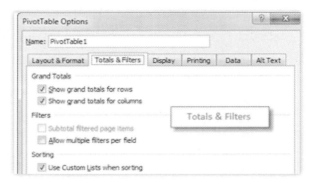

Figure 395

- ○ **Display** – The primary option here is the Classic Pivot Table view option, which reverts back to some of the detail available in earlier Excel versions, in which you dragged data points on to the physical Pivot Table itself instead of in the Field List. You can also choose to sort the Field List in alphabetical order.

- ○ **Printing** – This is straightforward and simply gives you the options of displaying the Grouping buttons and Labels when you print your Pivot Table.

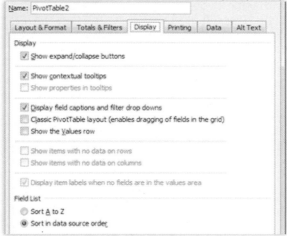

Figure 396

- ○ **Data** – You have several options here that are important especially if you plan on distributing your Pivot Tables.

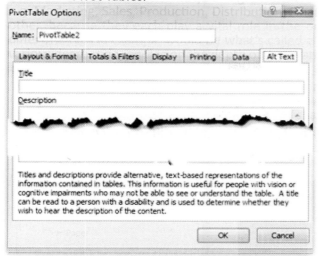

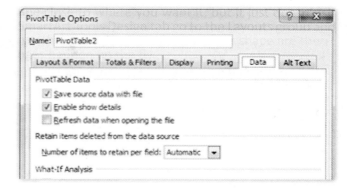

Figure 397

- ▪ **Save Source data with file** – If you want your users to be able to manipulate the Pivot Table, then you'll want to leave this option checked. Otherwise you risk them not having a data connection and the Pivot Table can fail under certain circumstances. If you only want them to have a snapshot or if you have an unusually large dataset that can be challenging to distribute then uncheck it.

- ▪ **Enable show details** – This allows you to drill down into the data that supports the Pivot Table. If you double click on a primary field in the table itself you'll get a dialog that asks which field list item you would like to explore deeper.

- ▪ **Drill-Down Capability** - If you double-click on a Pivot Table data item Excel will automatically create a new Auto-Filtered worksheet with that just item's underlying details. Drill-down functionality is a fantastic tool, but there may well be times that you don't want to share the underlying Pivot Table data with end-users. Unchecking the Show Details option will prevent you from doing this and Excel will give you a nasty message if you double-click on a Pivot Table detail.

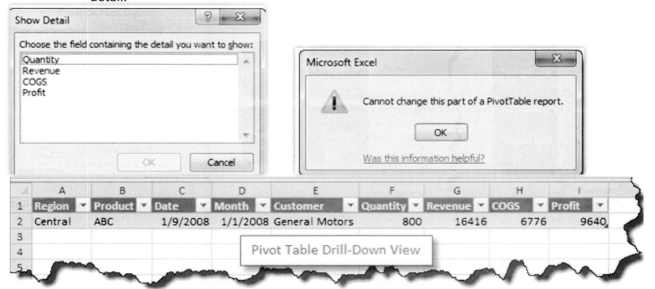

Figure 398

- ▪ **Refresh data when opening file** – If you link your Pivot Table to an external data source you might want to enable this option. Although if your data rarely refreshes or it takes a long time to refresh you'll probably want to opt for manually refreshing your dataset. You'll also want to be mindful of this option if you share your Pivot Table workbook with users who might not have access to your data source, in which case they'll receive error messages when trying to open the workbook.

- **Alt Text –** This is dedicated for people with disabilities who may choose to use Excel's Text-to-Speech options. It's not likely that you'll need to enable this feature.
- **Active Field** - This will show you which field item is active at any given time.

  - **Field Settings –** Depending on whether you're in a category or value field you'll get one of two different detail dialogs.
  - **Field Dialog –** This contains two tabs for the selected Field item.
  ○ **Subtotals & Filters –** You can select from Automatic Sub-Totals, None or Custom. You can also choose to add a new manual Auto-Filter. In the following example CitiGroup has had a Count applied to it and you'll see that the Filter indicates that it contains one record.

Figure 399

  ○ **Layout & Print –** This simply defines your Pivot Table print options.
    - **Value Dialog –** If you select a value item you will see a different dialog that lets you change how your numeric items will be displayed. These are the same options that you have if you click on any of the Value items in the Pivot Table Field List and select the Value Field Settings.

  - **Expand/Collapse Field –** These options will only be enabled if you're in a Field item area. It allows you to Expand or Collapse an entire Field items group as opposed to clicking the Expand/Collapse buttons in the Pivot Table itself.
  ○ **Group –** This allows you to add Groups within Groups. As you start defining deeper levels of details in your Pivot Table experimentation you might find this handy to isolate certain data. Depending on the Field List item you select you'll have different options. To the right you'll see the dialog for grouping a Date field, while the Pivot Table example shows a grouping on the Customer Field List item.

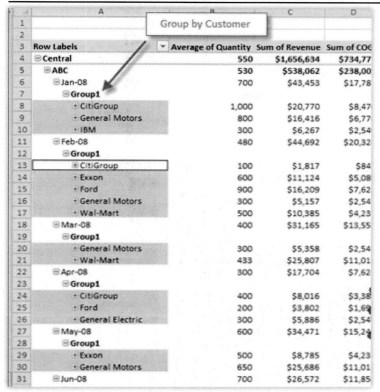

Figure 400

- ○ **Sort & Filter** – The Sort options should be easy enough to understand, but **Slicers** on the other hand represent a whole new level of detail options. Slicers are a tool that Microsoft created that allows you to set up a Pivot Table so that even the least experienced user can manipulate your Pivot Table data with ease. Think of Slivers as individual sort items that quickly display your Field List items in a handy dialog that's easy for just about anyone to understand. If you plan on sharing your Pivot Table data with people then you'll find Slicers to be an invaluable to. When you first select the Slicers option you'll receive a dialog that lists your Field List items. A Slicer will be created for each item that you check from the list. In the following example we'll create Slicers for Region, Product and Customer. Note that Excel will create your Slicers and lump them on top of each other in the middle of the worksheet. It's up to you to move them around where you want them.

    - ▪ **Slicer Tools** - You'll also notice that as soon as you create Slicers that a new Ribbon group called Slicer Tools has been created. This allows you to format your Slicers, name them, move or size them in relation to the rest of the worksheet objects, etc. As you apply Slicers you'll see the Filter icon in the upper right-hand corner of each Slicer change, and you'll see each Slicer selection highlighted.

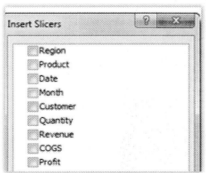

Figure 401

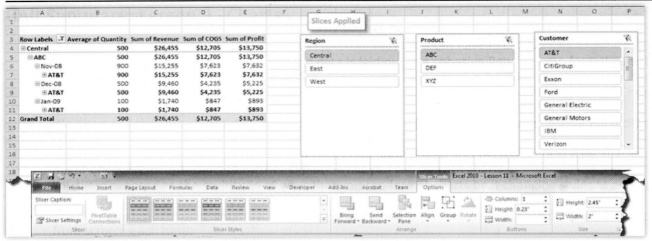

Figure 402 slicers applied

- ◦ **Data** – These options allow you to Refresh or change your data source. You probably won't change data sources too often, but you will likely find yourself Refreshing it. This is where you come if you decided not to let your data refresh when you open the workbook. Remember if you have a large dataset you might want to be prepared when you do this, as Excel will be tied up until the data has refreshed.

- ◦ **Actions** – This is another straightforward series of options.

  - ▪ **Clear** – This will reset your Pivot Table to where you started, leaving you with a clean slate and a Field List ready for you to start selecting items. If you activate this by accident CTRL+Z will restore your Pivot Table to its previous state.

  - ▪ **Select** – This allows you to select various items on the Pivot Table itself, be it Labels, Values, both, or even the entire Pivot Table itself. The **Enable Selection** option allows you to manually select Pivot Table groups by clicking on them. Selection comes in handy if you want to apply Groupings from the Group options. In the Group by Selection example you saw what selected items looks like.

- ◦ **Calculations** – The Summarize Values By and Show Values As options are the same as you would find in the Value Field Settings. This is just another place to expose that functionality for you.

- ◦ **Fields, Items & Sets** – These are where you can start getting creative with your data and generate calculations that you might not have been able to do in your data. The data examples we're using came out of an Excel Table that had already been calculated, but there will be times that you won't have that luxury. Retrieving data from an external source like a database is a perfect example. In many cases you'll only be retrieving transactional (raw) data and might not be able to calculate things like our Net Profit category. But with Calculated Fields you can quickly perform calculations, in many times faster than if you were to try to create a formula to do it.

  - ▪ **Calculated Field** - Here is an example of recreating the Profit category. When you look back at the example in the companion workbook you'll see that Excel didn't actually create a formula within the Pivot Table for you it just applied the calculation. If you were to refresh your data the Calculated Field would automatically update itself with the rest of the Pivot Table items.

Figure 403

- **Calculated Item** – This lets you combine two or more fields and create a new one, like the total of the Central & West regions.
- **Solve Order** – If you have created Calculated Items this will show you the order in which those items are being calculated.
- **List Formulas** – This will create a summary report displaying all of the Calculated Fields that you have in your Pivot Table. Here you'll see our Net Profit calculation.

	A	B	C	D	E	F	G	H	I
1	*Calculated Field*								
2	Solve Order	Field	Formula						
3		1	Net Profit	=Revenue -COGS					
4									
5	*Calculated Item*								
6	Solve Order	Item	Formula						
7									
8									
9	*Note:*		When a cell is updated by more than one formula,						
10			the value is set by the formula with the last solve order.						
11									
12			To change the solve order for multiple calculated items or fields,						
13			on the Options tab, in the Calculations group, click Fields, Items, & Sets, and then click Solve Order.						

Figure 404

- ○ **Tools** – This list some additional tools that you can use with your Pivot Tables. For this course we'll only be reviewing Pivot Charts, as OLAP Tools and What-If Analysis deal with external data sources, and could have an entire lesson devoted to them.
- ○ **Pivot Charts** – These allow you to create charts based off of your Pivot Table data. As you'll see in the following example, Pivot Charts are as easy to create as a regular Excel chart. However, you'll generally want to collapse your data down to the smallest group as too much visible data can be more than difficult to read. Fortunately, the tools that you have to Expand/Collapse Pivot Tables are incredibly useful for that, especially as only visible data will plot in Excel charts.

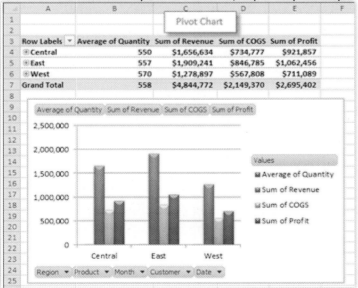

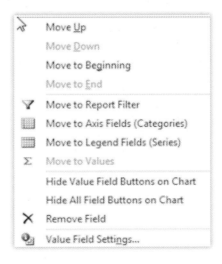

Figure 405

- Unlike Excel charts you'll see that your Pivot Chart contains all of the Pivot Table Field & Value List items and you can interactively filter each of those items. The Value List items are at the top of the chart, while the Field List items are at the bottom. Both series of items can be manipulated by right-clicking any one of them. This is another one of those areas that just has too many potential variables to discuss here, but you should certainly experiment with your charting options in the companion workbook.

- ○ **Show** – This merely exposes the Pivot Table features that you can view. To start you'll probably want to leave them all visible. When you distribute your Pivot Table you might want to hide the Field List though, just to keep your users from easily changing your Pivot Table.

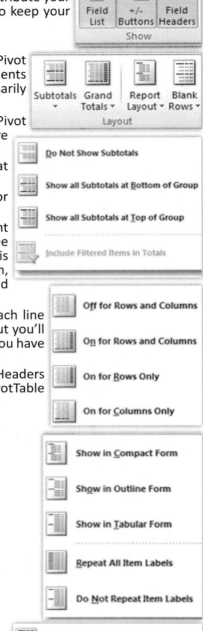

- • **Pivot Table Ribbon Items – Design Group**

You'll most likely come to the Design Group after you've completed your Pivot Table. As mentioned earlier in the Lesson, you can make so many adjustments to a Pivot Table when you're initially constructing it that you won't necessarily want to apply design elements until you're done.

- ○ **Layout** – Layout options let you define how you want your Pivot Table data to be displayed. These are more personal than they are functional and they won't alter your Pivot Table data in any way.
- ○ **Subtotals** – Here you can opt to turn off Subtotals or show them at the top or bottom of each data series.
- ○ **Grand Totals** – You can opt to toggle Grand Totals for Rows and or Columns.
- ○ **Report Layout** – Here you define the display structure you want for your Pivot Table. In the companion workbook you'll see examples of each. You have your choice of Compact, which is good for data with a lot of Field Items, Outline and Tabular form, both of which can get a bit unwieldy if you have a lot of Field Items.
- ○ **Blank Rows** – This just lets you insert a blank row between each line item. If you have a lot of data it might make it easier to read, but you'll want to be careful when you print as it can create extra pages if you have lot of rows to begin with.
- ○ **PivotTable Style Options** – Here you have the option to toggle Headers and Banding. While you can change these without applying a PivotTable Style, they generally work better in conjunction with them.
  - ▪ **Row & Column Headers/Banded Rows & Columns**

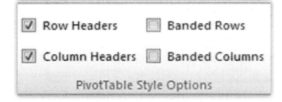

Pivot Table Styles – This is nearly identical to your Excel Table styles in that it's a pre-defined set of Gallery styles that you can select for your Pivot Table. The nice thing is that if you add or remove items from your Pivot Table the applied style will automatically adjust with the changes. This holds true when you apply filters or add calculated fields. If you find that the Pivot Table Style gallery isn't extensive enough for you, you can create your own.

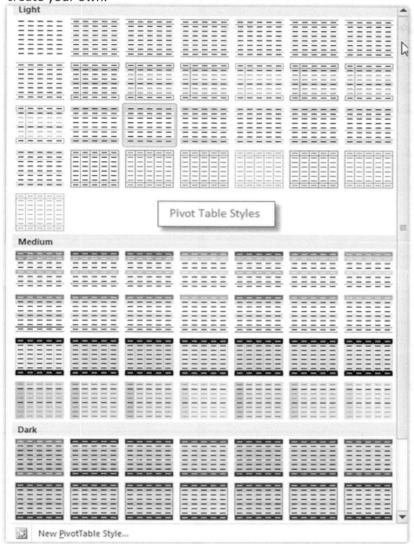

Figure 406

Power Pivot

While not covered in this course, if you find that you like Pivot Tables, you'll have to explore Power Pivot, Microsoft's newest FREE game changer: www.powerpivot.com

Unit Summary: Lesson 11 – Pivot Tables

- In this lesson you learned about what Excel Pivot Tables, which let you manipulate your flat-file data in ways previously only achievable with a database application. We showed by example how Pivot Tables should be embraced by anyone who needs to analyze their data, and how easy they are to use.
- You learned that Pivot Tables do not physically alter your data in any way, but only take a snapshot of it. A benefit of this is that your Excel workbooks won't blow up in size if you create multiple Pivot Tables based on the same data since it's not recreating it.

- You saw how easy it is to add or remove items from Pivot Tables by either clicking items in the Field List or dragging and dropping them.
- We explored the different ways to create different valuations with a click of a button, for instance changing a Sum to an Average.
- We discussed how to create Calculated Fields if your base Pivot Table data doesn't already have them.
- We showed you how to add and format Slicers to make data analysis a snap for you and your users.
- We look at adding Pivot Charts to your data and how a Pivot Table's filtering and grouping functionality can help you expand and contract your Chart data.
- Finally we reviewed your Pivot Table options when it comes to Sub and Grand Totals, as well as formatting with Pivot Table Styles.

Review Questions – Lesson

1. What can a Pivot Table do for you & why might you want to use one?
   a. _____
   b. _____
2. Should Pivot Tables be scary? If Yes, why? If No why? (Prepare to answer each argument with yourself)
   a. _____
3. Can you combine Excel Tables and Sub-Totaled Data?
   a. _____
4. If you haven't calculated column differences in an Excel Table or Dataset, can you do it with a Pivot Table?
   a. _____
5. How can you add a Pivot Table Report Filter?
   a. _____
6. What steps should you take with a Pivot Table before adding a Pivot Chart?
   a. _____
   b. _____
   c. _____
7. How many Chart styles can you use with Pivot Tables?
   a. _____
   b. _____
   c. _____
   d. _____

Lesson Assignment – Lesson 11 – Pivot Tables

- Your assignment is to review the Pivot Table companion workbook and explore all of the different tables that you see.
- You're encouraged to not only work with the example data, but bring in some of your own and see what you can do. The comfort factor with Pivot Tables will come with working with them, not by avoiding them.
- See what kind of data manipulation you can arrange with Pivot Tables.

Lesson 11 Notes

Lesson 12 – External Data Sources & Mail Merge

In the last two lessons you learned about using Excel Tables and Pivot Tables. Both of which are excellent ways for organizing and analyzing your data without having to create a lot of formulas or complicated scenarios yourself. Instead you let Excel do the heavy lifting for you. Now that your data is prepared you most likely need to share it at some point in time. Throughout the course of day to day operations in any small business there is a need to communicate with customers. Many times this is as simple as a phone call, but there may often be times that you need to communicate some form of data with them. This can start with a welcome letter, introduction to your business, Thank You's, invoices, etc. How often do you prepare this correspondence by hand, writing one letter or e-mail after another? Fortunately, there's an easier way and it involves sharing your data between Excel and Microsoft Word. This lesson is going to focus using Word to create a customer letter which you'll print and mail (although you can also choose to e-mail Mail Merge documents too), and having Excel populate that with all of your relevant customer information. As for your data, while you may well have your customer data in Excel, but in this case we're going to go on the assumption that you have it elsewhere, so another part of the lesson is going to concentrate on bringing customer information into Excel from an External Data Source, in this case, Microsoft Access.

As we discussed in the Pivot Table lesson there are often occasions in which you need to query an external data source in order to retrieve smaller data sets into Excel for analysis purposes. An example would be a transactional database in which an order entry system keeps track of customer purchases. In this case we're going to retrieve information from a database for a given time-period, perform some data analysis on it, and send our customers a quarterly purchase recap. The data source for the Lesson will be Microsoft's Northwind Database, which is included with each version of Microsoft Access. But just because we're going to use Access, doesn't mean that you can't query other data sources; you can pull data from other databases, text files, websites, etc. Once we pull the data into Excel we're going to set up a Pivot Table to summarize the data and then create a Word document that we'll populate with the Excel data. You don't necessarily need to use Excel as a data source for Word either, but we're going to approach this lesson from the standpoint of needing to perform analysis on our external data before we can use it in Word. Provided that your data is structured properly you could certainly pull directly from it without having to use Excel (but since this is an Excel course, we can't really leave it out can we?)

External Data Sources

The first thing to learn is how to get your data into Excel. As mentioned, we're going to use an Access database for this lesson, by linking to a pre-existing Access database table, but the methods will be very similar for other sources. This is simply going to give you an idea of the process that's involved.

- **Get External Data** – Anytime you want to pull data into Excel from another source you start on the Data tab. Fortunately, because Access is part of the Microsoft Office Suite of applications, they have made Access a default option, and it plays remarkably well with Access, as does Word.

Figure 407

- As soon as you click on the "From Access" option, Excel will open up a **Select Data Source** dialog, which is very much like a **File Open** dialog, where you'll see that we'll browse to the Northwind 2007 database. If you wanted to use a different data source you could either choose "All Files" from the Files of Type drop-down (which isn't labeled, but it's indicated in the example), or select one of the other options from the Data tab.

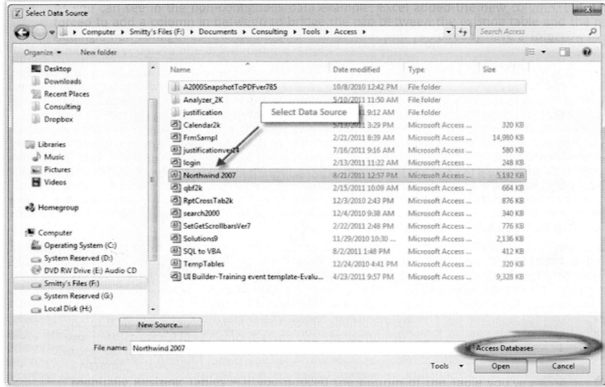

Figure 408

- ◦ Once you choose your data source Excel will load another dialog asking you specifics about the data connection, where you'll see ***Provider***, ***Connection***, ***Advanced*** and ***All*** tabs. Fortunately, Excel will do the bulk of the work for you here (especially with Access), so you generally don't need to argue with the dialog and make any changes.

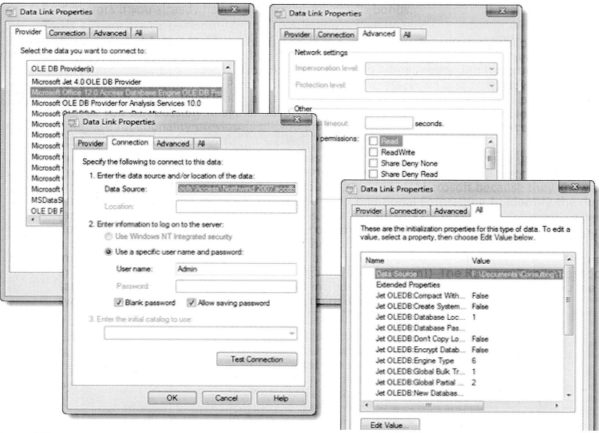

Figure 409

○   As soon as you confirm that dialog you'll get another one. Generally the only information you'll need to provide here is a password to the external data source if you have one. As soon as you do that you'll be prompted to select a table from the data source. Note that you're not limited to **Tables**, but **Queries** as well. In case you're wondering, in this case Excel is calling Queries "VIEW"s.

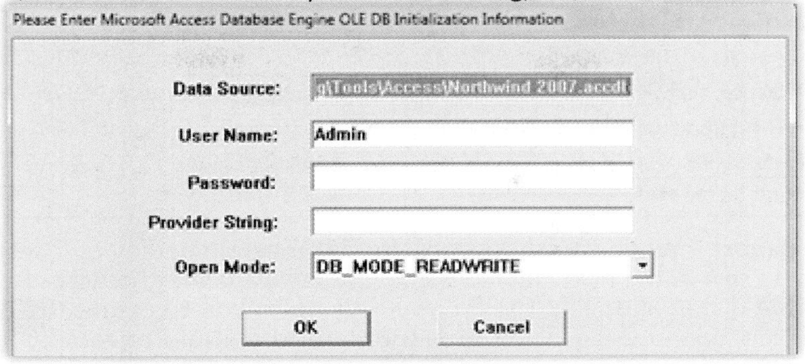

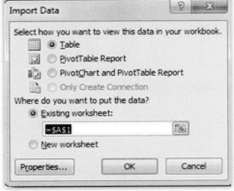

Figure 410

○   For this lesson we're going to select the Invoice Summary table which was created for this lesson (a copy of the database is provided along with the Excel companion workbook).

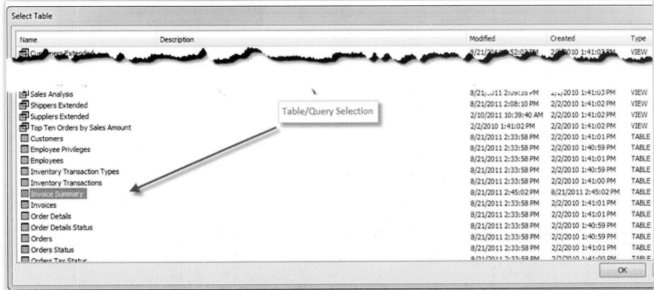

Figure 411

○   Next Excel will ask you how you want the data returned to your workbook. For example purposes we'll import the data as both a Table and a Pivot Table, examples of which you'll see next.

Figure 412

○   The first thing you'll notice about the Access query imported as raw data is that Excel automatically creates the data as an Excel Table. If your query is set up in such a fashion that it needs no further manipulation then you wouldn't need to go the Pivot Table route. In this case we want to summarize some of our order data so we are going that extra step. Note that when it comes to merging the data in Word, it doesn't care how many data fields you have; you only merge the ones that you want.

Database FAQ

Table – Where your database information is stored. It's set up like an Excel Table, with Rows & Columns. Ideally each row represents a transaction (Databases are much pickier about this than Excel).

Queries – This is how you interact with Tables and pull data out of them. You can combine the data from multiple tables provided each table has a linked reference, like a Customer or Order Number.

- **Pivot Table Report** – When you choose this format Excel isn't going to create a Pivot Table for you. Instead, as you saw in the Pivot Table lesson, Excel will analyze the Access query data and prepare the Pivot Table dialog and Field List for you. It's up to you to create the Pivot Table from there, which you'll see next where we've summarized our order information by First Quarter sales only and used the Tabular Form layout.

	A	B	C	D	E	F	G	H	I	J	K
1	Order ID	Last Name	First Name	Job Title	Ship Name	Ship Address	Ship City	Ship	Ship Z	Ship	Cust
2	30	Toh	Karen	Purchasing Manager	Karen Toh	789 27th Street	Las Vegas	NV	99999	USA	27
3	30	Toh	Karen	Purchasing Manager	Karen Toh	789 27th Street	Las Vegas	NV	99999	USA	27
4	31	Lee	Christina	Purchasing Manager	Chri	Street	New York	NY	99999	USA	4
5	31	Lee	Christina	Purchasing Manager	Chri	Street	New York	NY	99999	USA	4
6	31	Lee	Christina	Purchasing Manager	Chri	Street	New York	NY	99999	USA	4
7	32	Edwards	John	Purchasing Manager	John	th Street	Las Vegas	NV	99999	USA	12
8	32	Edwards	John	Purchasing Manager	John Edwards	123 12th Street	Las Vegas	NV	99999	USA	12
9	33	Andersen	Elizabeth	Purchasing Representative	Elizabeth Andersen	123 8th Street	Portland	OR	99999	USA	8

Access Table Raw Data Import (as an Excel Table)

Figure 413

- There is only one problem to using a Pivot Table as a Mail Merge source and that's the blank rows that Excel inserts above the Pivot Table. Word won't read the blank rows, so when your data comes over it won't have any row headers, just ambiguous field labels like F3, F4, etc., but there are workarounds that are important to know, so we're going to go that route. You could also just take the Pivot Table data only and copy it into another worksheet. The next step is to move onto Word to create the Mail Merge document and get it ready to receive your Excel data.

	A	B	C	D	E	F	G	H	I
	Order Date	(Multiple Items)							
	Customer Name	Ship Name	First Name	Last Name	Job Title	Ship Address	Ship City	Ship Sta	Ship ZIP/Po	Sum of
	Company A	Anna Bedecs	Anna	Bedecs	Owner	123 1st Street	Seattle	WA	99999	
	Company AA	Karen Toh	Karen	Toh	Purchasing Manager	789 27th Street	Las Vegas	NV	99999	
	Company BB	Amritansh Raghav	Amritansh	Raghav	Purchasing Manager	789 28th Street	Memphis	TN	99999	
	Company C	Thomas Axen	Thomas	Axen	Purchasing Representative	123 3rd Street	Los Angelas	CA	99999	
	Company CC	Soo Jung Lee	Soo Jung	Lee	Purchasing Manager	789 29th Street	Denver	CO	99999	
	Company D	Christina Lee	Christina	Lee	Purch	23 4th Street	New York	NY	99999	
	Company F	Francisco Pérez-Olae	Francisco	Pérez-Olaeta	Purch	23 6th Street	Milwaukee	WI	99999	
	Company G	Ming-Yang Xie	Ming-Yang	Xie	Own	23 7th Street	Boise	ID	99999	
	Company H	Elizabeth Andersen	Elizabeth	Andersen	Purch	23 8th Street	Portland	OR	99999	
	Company J	Roland Wacker	Roland	Wacker	Purchasing Manager	123 10th Street	Chicago	IL	99999	

Access Table Raw Data Import (as a Pivot Table)

	A	B	C	D	E	F	G	H	I
	Customer Name	Ship Name	First Name	Last Name	Job Title	Ship Address	Ship City	Ship State/Province	Ship ZIP/Postal Code	Sum of E
	Company A	Anna Bedecs	Anna	Bedecs	Owner	123 1st Street	Seattle	WA	99999	
	Company AA	Karen Toh	Karen	Toh	Purchasing Manager	789 27th Street	Las Vegas	NV	99999	
	Company BB	Amritansh Raghav	Amritansh	Raghav	Purchasing Manager	789 28th Street	Memphis	TN	99999	
	Company C	Thomas Axen	Thomas	Axen	Purchasing Representative	123 3rd Street	Los Angelas	CA	99999	
	Company CC	Soo Jung Lee	Soo Jung	Lee	Purchasing Mana			CO	99999	
	Company D	Christina Lee	Christina	Lee	Purchasing Mana	k		NY	99999	
	Company F	Francisco Pérez-Olaeta	Francisco	Pérez-Olaeta	Purchasing Manager	123 6th Street	Milwaukee	WI	99999	
	Company G	Ming-Yang Xie	Ming-Yang	Xie	Owner	123 7th Street	Boise	ID	99999	
	Company H	Elizabeth Andersen	Elizabeth	Andersen	Purchasing Representative	123 8th Street	Portland	OR	99999	
	Company J	Roland Wacker	Roland	Wacker	Purchasing Manager	123 10th Street	Chicago	IL	99999	
	Company K	Peter Krschne	Peter	Krschne	Purchasing Manager	123 13th Street	Miami	FL	99999	

Pivot Table copied to a new worksheet

Figure 414

Create your Word Document

Before you can create a Mail Merge you have to have a Word document to populate with your customer information. In this case we'll be using the *"Notice of Valued Customer Status"* letter from the Office Online Template Gallery. You can access it through Word via **File, New, Letters, Business Letters, Billing and Order Letters**, but you can certainly choose any template or letter of your own. The first things you'll see are the form fields that the template designers added for you. Note that these aren't Mail Merge fields, but form fields that we're going to replace.

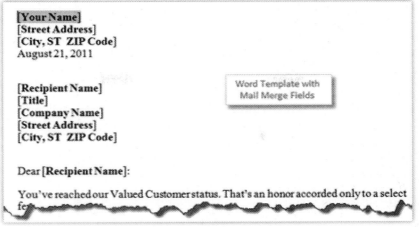

[Your Name]
[Street Address]
[City, ST ZIP Code]
August 21, 2011

[Recipient Name]
[Title]
[Company Name]
[Street Address]
[City, ST ZIP Code]

Dear [Recipient Name]:

You've reached our Valued Customer status. That's an honor accorded only to a select fe

Figure 415

Mail Merge – Step 1 - Next we're going to walk through how to link to your Excel data and bring those data fields into Word. When you're in Word, goto the Mailings tab and select Start Mail Merge, where you'll see the following dialog. The easiest selection will be the "Step by Step Mail Merge Wizard", which will immediately open a new pane on the right side of your screen. Select "Letters" then move onto "Starting Document" at the bottom of the pane.

- **Mail Merge – Step 2** – Since you've already opened the Word template there's no need to do anything other than allowing Word to proceed with the "Use Current Document" option.

- **Mail Merge – Step 3** – The next step is to select your Word document's recipients, which is where you get Excel involved. Since we already have a data source, you'll want to choose the Browse option for the "Use an existing list option". As soon as you do you'll be presented with a Select Data Source dialog almost identical to the one you saw when you pulled in the Access data.

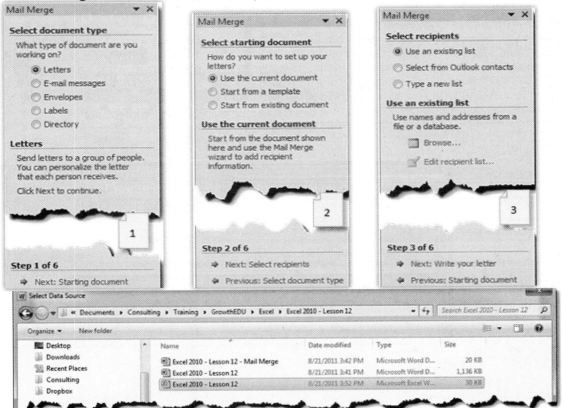

Figure 416

- Once you've selected the data source you're going to get another series of dialogs in which you'll iden-tify the worksheet and the data that you want Word to use.
- Now Word is going to analyze your Excel data and return another dialog for you. This one might seem a bit more complicated, but we'll walk through each step of the way. You're going to see two almost identical dialog examples here; the first is what you would see if you had proceeded with copying the Pivot Table data to a new worksheet. The second is the Mail Merge proceeding with our Pivot Table data. As mentioned, there is a process to fix the fact that Excel adds rows that Word can't read, and it's important to know them, especially if you find yourself in a situation where you're pulling information from a database that has less than friendly field names. The process we'll walk through is called field mapping and it's integral to being able to successfully perform Mail Merges.

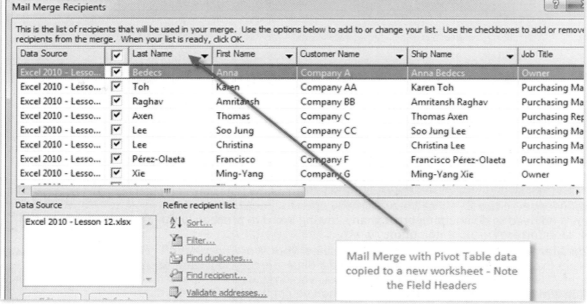

Figure 417

- ***Mail Merge Recipients Overview*** - The first thing you'll see is the top row with the Merge Field Names. Next you'll see that the first row is blank; that's because Excel adds a blank row when it cre-ates a Pivot Table and Word is seeing that row as the header row. You can go ahead and uncheck it otherwise you'll create a blank document for that row/record. The blank row is what's causing Word to use the F3, F4, F5 designations for your column headers, but we'll change that in a minute. You can also uncheck the second row which is the header row from the Pivot Table, since we're going to manually adjust the column values anyway, otherwise you'll create a document for the header row as well. Next you'll see the data source listed on the left hand side of the dialog. Since it's at the bottom of the dialog in its own pane anyway, you can just minimize that part so you can see more of the fields.

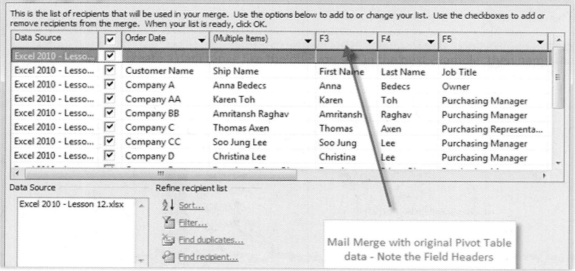

Figure 418

- **Refine Recipient List** – Since we already use a Pivot Table to narrow down our recipient list you don't need to worry about these options unless you want to explore them on your own. You should note the Validate address option though. This will take you to a Microsoft website that offers Address Verification Services through companies like Stamps.com. If you aren't sure that your customer addresses are correct you can use this option, otherwise proceed without it. One advantage to Address Verification is that it will append Zip+4's, although it would probably be better to update the original data source as opposed to the Mail Merge list.

- **Mail Merge Step 4 – Write your letter** – You'll see that you have several options here. We're going to manually replace our template merge fields with ours, so we're going to skip the Address block, Greeting line and Electronic postage options but we will walk through them. These options assume that you haven't already written your letter, so Word's giving you the opportunity to do so now.

  - **Address Block** – This allows you to insert a pre-formatted Address Block that Word will populate with your data instead of you having to input the various mergefields (recipient name, address, city, etc.). It comes with its own dialog that analyzes your data and gives you an example of how it will output.

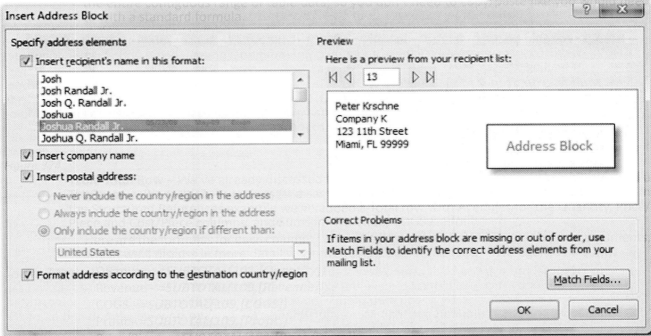

Figure 419

○   ***Greeting Line*** – Our letter already has a greeting line, but this is another way to automate one. Of note here is that Word gives you alternatives for invalid recipient names, like if a name is missing in your data. However, as we'll discuss shortly regarding Data Integrity, this should not come as a surprise, and if it does then you might have bigger issues to worry about. This option should be a last resort, not a catch all.

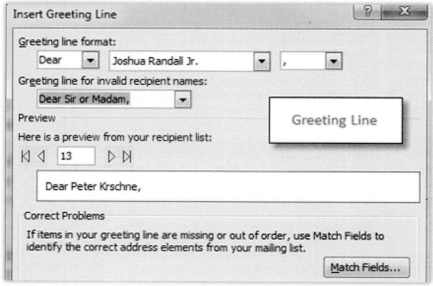

Figure 420

○   ***Electronic Postage*** – Similar to your Address Verification options from Step 3, if you have an electronic postage service you can configure it here. Otherwise you'll be prompted to goto Microsoft.com where they'll make some recommendations for you. If you find yourself doing a lot of mailing, these can be invaluable tools.

•   ***Mail Merge Step 4 (cont.) - More Items*** – The next thing we need to do is give Word the proper data for the document. You could leave the F3, F4, F5, etc. column headers, but then you'd have to remember which one corresponds to which data value. It's much easier to use Word's Field Mapping Wizard to do the work for us. So now it's time to move on to Step 4 in the Mail Merge process.

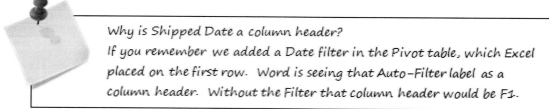

•   In this case you want to select the "More items" option, which will launch a new dialog. When you get to this point it will be helpful to have the Excel workbook open so you can make sure that you can reference the fields directly as you map them. You select the "Match Fields" option and you can start mapping the data fields to your Mail Merge document. You can see how we've matched all of the available data fields to Words' pre-defined fields. Simply select the Word field you want to match and select the appropriate Excel data field from the drop-down on the right of the Match Fields dialog. Note that Word's Company field has been mapped to our Order Date field because of the Pivot Table filter we discussed earlier. That's OK since we won't be using the first rows of the Pivot Table data, which don't contain relevant records. If you were using the non-Pivot Table data you wouldn't need to worry about this. If you'll be using the same Mail Merge data again, you should check the "Remember this matching..." option at the bottom of the Merge Fields dialog.

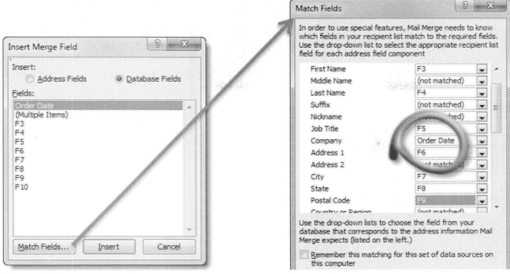

Figure 421

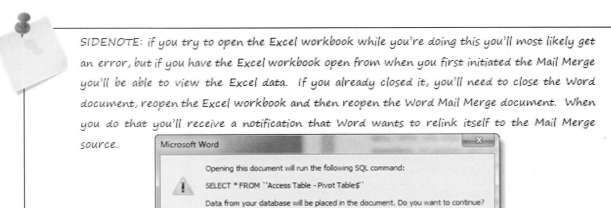

SIDENOTE: if you try to open the Excel workbook while you're doing this you'll most likely get an error, but if you have the Excel workbook open from when you first initiated the Mail Merge you'll be able to view the Excel data. If you already closed it, you'll need to close the Word document, reopen the Excel workbook and then reopen the Word Mail Merge document. When you do that you'll receive a notification that Word wants to relink itself to the Mail Merge source.

- Now it's time to start inserting the mapped fields into your Word document, so you simply start clicking away on the fields that you want added. Since we mapped the merge fields to our data you can switch to the "Address Fields" option in the **Insert Merge Field** dialog, and you'll see the same Word categories you saw when you matched the fields. Don't worry about the merge field placement for now, because we need to manipulate that in a bit. Merge Fields are noted by the **<<Merge Field>>** tags before and after the field name. You can separate merge fields with punctuation as you'll see in the final letter example.

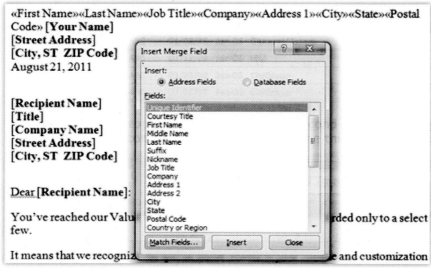

Figure 422

- You'll first need to switch back to the Database Fields option in order to add the Ship Name (Full Name) and Extended Price fields (F2 & F10 respectively), since Word didn't have matching categories for those fields. However, in this case the F2 – Ship Name field will actually be labeled "Multiple Items", since it's a Filter indicator in the Pivot Table, just like "Order Date".

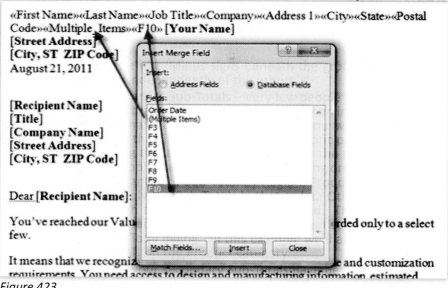

Figure 423

- Now we'll close the Insert Merge Field dialog and start making changes to our Word document, by moving the merge fields where we want them, and also deleting the place-holding fields that Microsoft put in for you when they created the template. Anytime you want to reuse one of the merge fields you can simply copy and paste it. In the following example you'll see the completed customer letter with the merge fields highlighted for clarity (they won't be highlighted in your completed document).

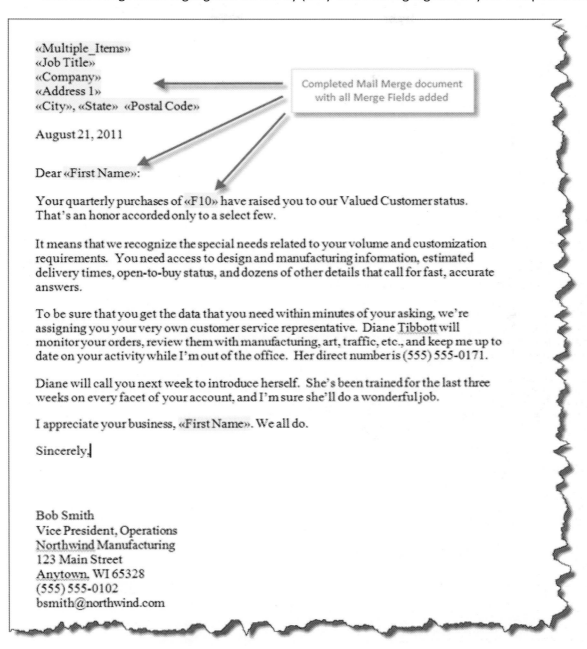

«Multiple_Items»
«Job Title»
«Company»
«Address 1»
«City», «State» «Postal Code»

Completed Mail Merge document with all Merge Fields added

August 21, 2011

Dear «First Name»:

Your quarterly purchases of «F10» have raised you to our Valued Customer status. That's an honor accorded only to a select few.

It means that we recognize the special needs related to your volume and customization requirements. You need access to design and manufacturing information, estimated delivery times, open-to-buy status, and dozens of other details that call for fast, accurate answers.

To be sure that you get the data that you need within minutes of your asking, we're assigning you your very own customer service representative. Diane Tibbott will monitor your orders, review them with manufacturing, art, traffic, etc., and keep me up to date on your activity while I'm out of the office. Her direct number is (555) 555-0171.

Diane will call you next week to introduce herself. She's been trained for the last three weeks on every facet of your account, and I'm sure she'll do a wonderful job.

I appreciate your business, «First Name». We all do.

Sincerely,

Bob Smith
Vice President, Operations
Northwind Manufacturing
123 Main Street
Anytown, WI 65328
(555) 555-0102
bsmith@northwind.com

Figure 424

- **Mail Merge Step 5 – Preview your letters -** At this time you can make changes to the document like adding your signature, company logo, etc. For our purposes we'll take it that the document is ready to go and proceed with the next step, which is to preview the letter with the actual Excel data merged into the document, so start clicking through the Recipients by clicking the >> button. You'll immediately see that it's not quite right!

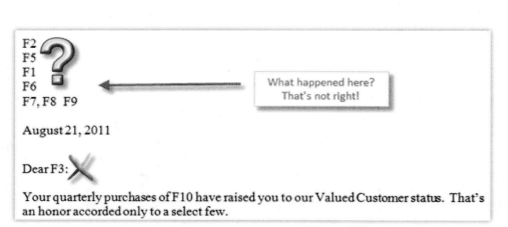

Figure 425

- I don't know that F3 will be pleased being referred to this way! So why did this happen? Remember the unnecessary data from the Pivot Table? We never told Word not to exclude it when we set up the linked data. Fortunately, Word lets you do that here, instead of taking quite a few steps backwards. Believe me, more than a few letters like this have been sent out to a fulfillment house and been processed, costing you money, so it's always a good idea to preview your mailing. Every time. This leads us to a discussion of data integrity, which is paramount for any business' communications with customers.

Data Integrity
– It seems fairly logical to assume that you need to have accurate customer mailing/ shipping information, but for whatever reason many companies stop there and don't give a second thought to things like customer names. If you want to impress your customers, it's not just the quality of the services that you provide, but the quality of communications as well. Here are some all too common examples of data that has been entered into a company system differently.

	A	B	C	D	E	F	G	H	I
1	Company Name	Contact First	Contact Last	Contact Full Name	Address	City	ST	Zip	
2	XYZ, Inc.	Bob		Smith, Bob	123 Main	Minneapulis	MN	55326	
3	ABC ENTERPRISES	Jones	FRED	Ferd Jones	456 Dumbar Av.	san antonio	tx	76269	
4	Custom Krafts	Smith	Tom	Tom Smith	789 Curry St	San Diego	CA	95636	
5	POWER SUPPLY	N/A	THOMPSON	THOMPSON/SHIPPING	986 READY LANE	KANSAS CTY	KS	45693	
6	ELECTRICO	AL	BELL	ALBERT BELL (THIS GUYS A JERK)	429 SPECIALTY LANE	FULLERTON	CA	95698	
7									
8									

Poorly managed data - It happens more than you think!

Figure 426

- How do you think Mr. Thompson will feel receiving a personalized letter to "Dear N/A:"? And you'll probably get a nasty call from Mr. Bell. Before you start laughing, this kind of data is all over the place. When business competition is so fierce, many people overlook something that is so seemingly simple, but it happens all the time. Before you start a Mail Merge, or any mass customer communication for that matter, please check your data source. The litmus test is would you want to receive a letter from your business? If not, then you've got some work to do. Fortunately, that's why we spent some time earlier in the course detailing how to address certain data issues, like Parsing and Concatenating data if your current data isn't flexible enough to personalize your communication. The use of the PROPER function is also a big one because many database systems convert all entries to UPPERCASE, or many data-entry types simply prefer to enter everything that way, since you can type faster if you never have to shift cases. You need to be able to catch things like this before you create your first letter. If you go to the effort to create a beautifully worded letter and skip these bits, not even Shakespeare's words could make up for failing to properly communicate.

- *Continuing Step 5 – Preview your Letters -* Now that the importance of Data Integrity has been addressed and you know how to fix it, we can continue with previewing your letters. The first thing we need to do is get rid of the erroneous records that Word brought in from our Pivot Table. All you need to do is click the "Exclude this recipient" and Word will ignore it. Once you've gone through your data then you can proceed to the next step. Normally all you'll need to do is first verify your data's accuracy in Excel, then eliminate the ghost records created between Word and the Pivot Table and proceed, although it's generally a good idea to review the first ten or so letters just to make sure that they do what you want with different data. Here's what you should see once you get past the erroneous merge records.

Anna Bedecs
Owner
Company A
123 1st Street
Seattle, WA 99999

Where's the Currency Formatting?

August 21, 2011

Dear Anna:

Your quarterly purchase of 1674.75 have raised you to our Valued Customer status.
That's an honor accorded only to a select few.

Figure 427

- ◦ *Field Switches* – Did you notice that Word brought over the straight value data, and not the formatting, even though it was formatted in Excel? To fix this you need to use something called Field Switches, which allow you to apply the formatting directly in Word. Before you think "hey, I could just add a $ before the merge field and be done with it", you could, but what about the comma to separate hundreds and thousands? Field Switches will take this into account. The first thing is to hit ALT+F9 to toggle the MERGEFIELD view. It will look like a lot of gibberish, but once you take a closer look at it you'll see a definite logic there.

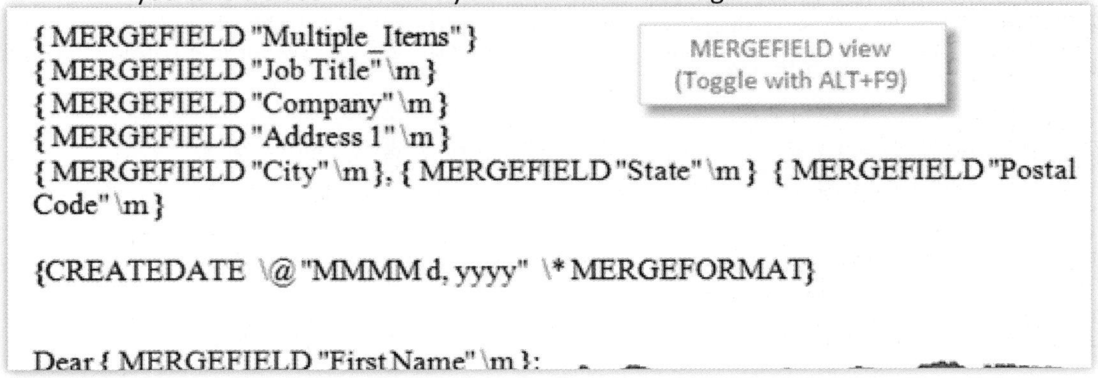

{ MERGEFIELD "Multiple_Items" }
{ MERGEFIELD "Job Title" \m }
{ MERGEFIELD "Company" \m }
{ MERGEFIELD "Address 1" \m }
{ MERGEFIELD "City" \m }, { MERGEFIELD "State" \m } { MERGEFIELD "Postal Code" \m }

{CREATEDATE \@ "MMMM d, yyyy" * MERGEFORMAT}

Dear { MERGEFIELD "FirstName" \m }:

MERGEFIELD view
(Toggle with ALT+F9)

Figure 428

- ◦ Something that might be interested is that you can see where Word created its own Mergefield for the date, which was inserted through *Insert, Text, Date & Time*, so this is Word's internal structure and Microsoft gives you the ability to change it. If you were to change the "MMMM d, yyyy" format you would see the change as soon as you toggle the Mergefield view (Alt+F9) back off. IF you recall in our earlier discussion about using the TEXT function in Excel to convert numeric entries, field switches are very similar, and you can use them to format Dates, Phone Numbers, Zip Codes, Social Security numbers, etc., some of which are detailed below.
  - Currency - {MERGEFIELD number \# $####,0.0}

- Phone Number - {MERGEFIELD phone \# ###'-'###'-'####}
- Date-Time - {MERGEFIELD date \@ "MMMM d, yyyy"}
  - Now that you see what the Currency Mergefield looks like we'll go ahead and make that change in the Word document, which you'll see here.
  - If you toggle Mergefield view again, you'll now see the new formatting applied.

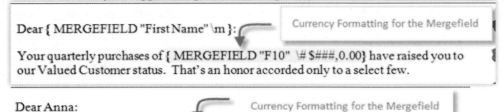

Dear { MERGEFIELD "First Name" \m }:   Currency Formatting for the Mergefield

Your quarterly purchases of { MERGEFIELD "F10" \# $###,0.00} have raised you to our Valued Customer status. That's an honor accorded only to a select few.

Dear Anna: Currency Formatting for the Mergefield

Your quarterly purchases of $1,674.75 have raised you to our Valued Customer status. That's an honor accorded only to a select few.

Figure 429

- **Mail Merge Step 6 – Complete the Merge -** Now that's done, and you can finish previewing your letters. But wait, there's one more thing you can do! You can actually edit individual letters depending on any special notes you might want to make to certain customers. As you've seen Mail Merge allows you to personalize what's normally called "Form Letters". You can take it a step farther with custom messages, like "Bob, thanks for the interest in our new widget. I sent some samples out to you this morning." or "Betty, it was so nice to see you at the convention last week!"
  - **Edit Individual Letters** – There is a justifiable argument that if you're going to take the time to edit individual letters through Word that you might as well do it by hand, but there is a certain caveat. If you are creating Mail Merge Letters, then it's quite possible that you'll create Mail Merge Envelopes as well. If you pull a letter out of the stack in order to personalize it, then you need to make sure that you put the letter back in exactly the right order otherwise you risk sending the wrong personalized letter to the wrong recipient(s). Talk about embarrassing, and it does happen!
    - If you decide on individual personalization, just follow the Wizard, indicating if you want to personalize all of your letters, the current letter, or a range. Word will open your selection(s) in a new document, where you can make your changes and then print. Note that this will disconnect you from your Excel data source, and the comments about Letters and Envelopes still applies.

Figure 430

Avoid Mis-ordering Mail Merge Letters & Envelopes!
One solution is to use Window envelopes. All you need to do is make sure that the address information lines up correctly on the page when it's printed and then folded. It takes some experimentation, but it can save a lot of headaches. The downside is that it does lack the personalization of a printed envelope.

- **_Ready to Print!_** – After all that you're finally ready to print your letters. You can print to a local printer, PDF, or other source. If you choose that route, then you can follow the dialogs, although many times you'll choose to send the entire print, fold, and stuff and mail job out to a mail house that specializes that. If you choose to do that you must also include the Excel data source, otherwise all the mail house will have is your letter with a bunch of dead links. This has caused more than one mailing to go out late. Most mail houses will have the most up-to-date software versions, but you should always check beforehand. If added a company logo or special fonts, you will also need to make sure that you include those.

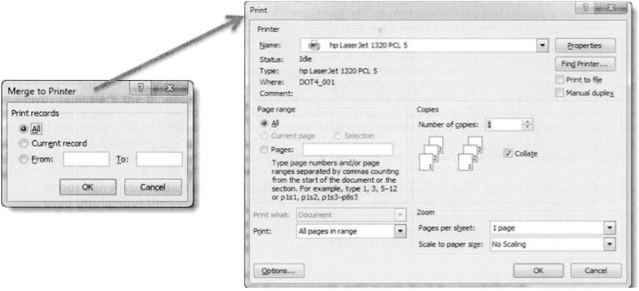

Figure 431

Finally, you should be aware that you are by no means limited to creating customer correspondence with Mail Merge. You can use any list-based data in Mail Merge, like nametags for an event, recipes, asset tags for corporate equipment, etc. And you're not limited to creating letters; you can also create E-Mails, Envelopes, Labels and Directories.

Unit Summary: Lesson 12 – External Data Sources & Mail Merge

- In this lesson you learned How to retrieve data in Excel from other data sources. While we certainly couldn't cover every external data application you got a good idea of where you can look and how to do it. Once you get the hang of it it's remarkably uncomplicated, provided the data source is readily accessible. Note that not all Internet data is formatted to be readily retrieved.

- We moved onto importing external data directly into Excel, where it will be converted to an Excel Table, or choosing to import it as a Pivot Table in the case that your external data doesn't meet your needs and requires further manipulation.

- Next we walked through the six steps to creating a Mail Merge document in Microsoft Word, beginning with choosing a template from the Word Template Gallery, actually linking the document to our Excel data, then adjusting it based on the way that Word reads the Excel data since Pivot Table and Excel Table based data will be read differently.

- We reinforced some of the Data integrity issues that we've discussed throughout the course and showed some examples of data gone bad and the responses you might expect to get from customers if they saw it (especially if it was addressed to them!)

- Finally we looked at MERGEFIELDS to format Excel data that had reverted to its lowest numeric values when Word merged it into your document.

Review Questions – Lesson 12 – External Data Sources & Mail Merge

1. What are some of the external data sources that you can use to pull data into Excel?
   a. _____
   b. _____
   c. _____
   d. _____
2. What options do you have when returning external data to Excel?
   a. _____
   b. _____
3. What does Mail Merge let you do?
   a. _____
4. Is a Mail Merge limited to letters that you print?
   a. _____
5. When creating a Mail Merge document do you have to use a Template document?
   a. _____
6. Why is important to make sure that your customer data is verified before creating a Mail Merge?
   a. _____
7. What are some other Mail Merge uses outside of Customer Communication?
   a. _____

Lesson Assignment – Lesson 12 – External Data Sources & Mail Merge

- Your assignment is to review the Excel workbook and Word documents provided with this lesson. Walk through the Mail Merge steps to become familiar with them.
- Create some Excel data of your own and explore the different types of merges you can create, be it E-mails, Envelopes, Labels or a Directory.
- Finally, if you have Access work on retrieving data in Excel from the Northwind 2007 sample database. If you don't have Access, then try to retrieve some data from any available source, whether it's a company data warehouse, or even the Internet.

Lesson 12 Notes

esources

I learned a lot about Excel simply by using it, but there are times when you just don't know how to do something. In many cases you can look at Excel's "helpfile", but what happens a lot of times is that you just don't know what you're looking for or how to ask for it. Here are some resources that I use regularly, and highly recommend:

MrExcel Message Board (www.mrexcel.com/forum) – This is without a doubt the world's #1 resource for real-time Excel questions and answers. With over 200,000 registered members you can ask any kind of Excel question and literally have an answer in just a few minutes, free of charge, day or night. But there is a rule of thumb: the less clear your question, the less clear the response you'll get, so try to be a specific as possible when asking a question. Even if you don't know what it is specifically you're looking for in Excel terminology, if you spell it out someone will be able to figure it out.

Microsoft Template Gallery (http://office.microsoft.com/en-us/templates/) – Sometimes when you need to design a new spreadsheet you need ideas. Look no further than the template gallery, which is stocked with example files for Excel and the other Office applications (Word, PowerPoint, Access, etc). Microsoft has invested a lot of resources into developing these templates, and they're free.

Microsoft Knowledge Base (http://support.microsoft.com) – This is a great place to look when the helpfile just doesn't cut it. Note that the MSKB articles can be very detailed and technical, and while Microsoft has done a great job of enlisting MVP's to write about real-world use, many of the articles are difficult to absorb.

Chip Pearson (www.cpearson.com) – For detailed Excel discussion ranging from formulas to VBA and programming, Excel MVP, Chip Pearson has a wealth of articles and downloads for you.

Ron De Bruin (www.rondebruin.nl) – If you've ever thought about automatically sending your Excel documents via Outlook, then Excel MVP Ron De Bruin has you covered.

VBA Express (www.vbaexpress.com) – This free message board, managed by Excel MVP Jacob Hildebrand, is specifically dedicated to all things VBA.

Sample Files for this text can be found at: http://www.mrexcel.com/busbasics2010/bb2010sampledata/

About the Author

Chris "Smitty" Smith currently lives in Fort Worth, Texas with his wife, Cyndi and daughter, Campbell after relocating from the San Francisco Bay area. He graduated from Texas Christian University's Ranch Management Program, and spent time working as a Cow Boss/Ranch Manager/Ranch Hand on ranches in the Western US and Australia before settling down and moving to the corporate world, where he spent 15 years working in California in Marketing and Sales Management for a Fortune 500 organization. He has spent the past several years as a Business Consultant/Trainer developing and teaching Microsoft Office based business solutions.

He has worked on projects and facilitated Excel training for organizations like Apple, Verizon, Ralph Lauren, US Treasury Department, Yum! Brands (Pizza Hut, KFC, Taco Bell), Fred Pryor, Charles Drew Medical University, etc.

Smitty has been recognized by Microsoft as an Excel MVP since 2007 for his outstanding technical contributions to the worldwide community.

Index

TODAY 140

Today's date

  function 131

Top 10%

  highlighting 158

Trace formulas 96

Trademark 88

Translation settings 43

Transpose 50

Trendlines 202

Trust center 39

Turn sideways 50

U

Used

  range 2

Uses of Excel 2

V

Validation 101, 123

Values, paste as 120

Vertical text 55

Views 108

VLOOKUP 141

W

Watch cells 188

Web

  save to 23

WEEKDAY 140

What-if tools 102, 136

Window size 7

Word 260

  embedding 86

WordArt 77, 85, 183, 185

Word document 19

Worksheets

  changing many at once 126

  copying 62

  # in new workbook 26

  moving 62

  navigation 7

  renaming 62

  tab color 63, 157

  vs. spreadsheets 1

Wrap text 54

X

XY charts 209

Y

YEAR 140

Z

Zero

  show or hide 34

Zipcode format 54

Zoom 109

Also from Holy Macro! Books

http://www.mrexcel.com/store/

For the Excel Beginner

Don't Fear The Spreadsheet

Slaying Excel Dragons

For the Excel Guru

Excel Outside The Box

Excel Gurus Gone Wild